GLIMPSES OF INDIAN CULTURE

GLIMPSES OF INDIAN CULTURE

(History, Religion & Culture)

MOHAN LAL VIDYARTHI

SHARADA

Sharada Publishing House
Delhi-110 035
2003

First Published : 2003

ISBN : 81-85616-85-X

Published by :
SHARADA PUBLISHING HOUSE
(Publishers on India's Past and Present)
40, Anand Nagar, Inder Lok,
Delhi-110 035
Ph. : 3657538

Laser Typesetting by :
Creative Graphics
Ph. 2195643

Printed at :
Santosh Offset, Delhi

CONTENTS

IV
MODERN AGE

FOREWORD

"Signs of the times point unmistakably to an eventual blossoming of a composite world culture in which all the strains of the cultures evolved hitherto will combine to form an orchestral whole. And if we would have an adequate idea of the lines on which the future of humanity is likely to be shaped in its cultural aspect, it is necessary that we study the various cultures that have been so far thrown upon the banks of time by the stream of history. The book "Glimpses of Indian Culture" is a helpful contribution to the subject.

India's culture is easily one of the oldest of cultures on earth and significantly the only one of its antiquity to be yet alive, not merely alive, but self-rejuvenating, growing and vigorous. Its story of more than five millenniums from the early dawning of prehistoric ages to the present day has been narrated by Prof. Vidyarthi as comprehensively as it was possible to do so in four hundred pages... the special feature of this work lies in that the author has taken the vision and exposition of Indian Culture by Sri Aurobindo as his basis and presented the thesis in this new light. A book like Prof. Vidyarthi's is invaluable in as much as it helps us to look at our cultural heritage with this fresh eye or at any rate prepares us to do so.

"...The Indian Renaissance is arising... the recovery of the old spiritual knowledge and experience in all its splendour, depth and fullness is its first and most essential task...(to quote Sri Aurobindo)"

"Spirituality is indeed the master-key of the Indian Minds"

(Late) Sri M.P. Pandit

Ex-Secretary, Sri Aurobindo Ashram, Pondicherry

The author says "this book is bound to appeal to those who look forward to see India as a leader of the forces striving for world unity with a spiritual background.

PREFACE

The Author takes this opportunity to re-emphasise his thesis as presented in his book that India's salvation lies in a vigorous pursuit of Integral spirituality. But spirituality is not an antithesis of matter, rather spirituality embraces matter also. Today we have a civilizational crisis, consumerism has run riot and materialism is now failing to deliver the goods.

Future progress must come from within When the Soul in man begins to take the lead, we would have begun the process of transformation of man. For this transformation to begin, clues can be found in the Indian Culture based on spirituality or Hindu Dharma. A resuscitated Hindu Dharma will provide an inspiration and incentive to the world, it is hoped.

Finally, the author acknowledges his deep gratitude and indebtedness to Sri Aurobindo and the Mother of Sri Aurobindo Ashram for the ideas propounded in this works on Indian Culture.

MOHAN LAL VIDYARTHI
(Ph. D.) Ex. Principal, D.S.N.P.G. College

INTRODUCTION

In the present works we make a panoramic survey of India's culture down the ages. We emphasise that essentially our culture reveals deep and diverse experiments with spiritual truth. The soul of India lies in the universal and creative spirituality of the Vedas, the Upanishads and the Gita. The world is the rhythmic manifestation of the Spirit, Nature and life are making progressive efforts to incarnate the Spirit in Matter. Such was the message of the ancient Indian culture. To quote in support from the ancient scriptures :

"Threefold are those supreme births of this divine force that is in the world, they are true. He moves there wide-overt within the Infinite and shines pure, luminous and fulfilling .... That which is immortal in mortals and possessed of the truth, is a god and established inwardly as an energy working out in our divine powers... Became high, uplifted, O Strength, pierce all veils, manifest in us the things of the Godhead".[1]

"The soul seated on the same tree of Nature is absorbed and deluded and has sorrow because it is not the Lords, but when it sees and is in union with that other self and greatness of it which is the Lord, then sorrow passes away from it."[2]

"Rare is the great of soul to whom all is the Divine Being."[3]

"All things are self-determining of the Divine knowledge."[4]

"Thus the realisation of the Divine was made central in life and the inspiring fount of all activities."

But spirituality did not stand for negation of the good in materialism. For four thousand years atleast India has been giving to the world, republics, empires, philosophies, sciences, creeds, arts, literatures, monuments, communities, laws, codes, industries, commerce, cultural missions abroad, yogas and religions. In each of these she issued forth in myriad forms.

She expanded too outside her borders, crossing the seven seas, brimming over to Judea, Egypt and Rome and overflowing into Java, Sumatra, Indo-China and Ceylon, her religions flowed into China, Japan, Korea, Tibet, Ceylon, Nepal and Burma. Her philosophies supplied elements to Neo-platonism. Thus, India showed that spirituality also flourished when the race had lived most richly and thought most profoundly.

In the Middle Ages also we maintained progress, at least in the externalities of life. In the realm of the spirit, however, there was an ebb-movement with the exception of the blossoming of the Bhakti movement. The decline of our culture led to the dark age in the eighteenth century and India was conquered by the British, albeit through our own weakness and by our own soldiers. The causes of this cultural decline were fundamentally threefold. There was, firstly, the failure of the fount of vital energy consequent on the studied 'denial of the ascetic', his systematic refusal to look at the world and appreciate its multi-coloured magnificence. This other-worldly outlook, looking at life as an illusion, permeated the thoughts and activities of the masses also leading to poverty and indigence.

Secondly, there was a failure of the fount of intellectual energy and a consequent torpor in the realm of the scientific, the critical and the intuitive mind. Finally, spirituality was mistaken for religiosity, traditionalism and ritualism. The best minds failed to assert themselves and lead the masses. Devotion and quiescence became the essence of religion or spirituality.

The West came, broke the spell and gave us the necessary shock which made us realise the nature of our stygian darkness. We woke up. Our intellect and critical impulse revived; our life was to be no longer sicklied over with the pale hue of illusion and our spirit revived to face the novel conditions and ideals in no spirit of revivalism but in an urgent quest for assimilation and adaptation. Still lack of freedom arrested the proper evolution of our culture in the modern age. Consequently today even after the dawn of freedom, confusion, strains and stresses—the legacy of the past—are still with us. There are those who stand for secularism, an ideal which alone is not sufficient to inspire the masses or enthuse in them the necessary urge for a supreme creative effort. They are opposed by the so-called protagonists of Indian culture, whose opposition to the Hindu code is symptomatic of their narrow vision and lop-sided mentality.

What is the way out? It is suggested by Sri Aurobindo that we must recover the old spiritual knowledge and experience in all its splendour, depth and fullness. We must allow this awakened spirituality to flow into new forms of philosophy, literature, art, science and critical knowledge.

We must in our own original way deal with modern problems in the light of Indian thought and endeavour to formulate a greater synthesis of a spiritualised society. To do this we have firstly to realise that mind and its pet child science are not alone sufficient to cure the world of its evils. Our ancient knowledge long ago painted out that mind is an instrument of ignorance and all mental principles tend to be lopsided. There can be no harmonious adjustments of all conflicting claims on the mental plane. Whatever progress man could attain through mind, he has attained. We now see how all present progress is matched by a greater recoil or reaction in the opposite direction so that wars and crises have become endemic in mankind. Our second task is to develop a new consciousness. Evolution must take a new leap. Progress can only come from within. "Mind is the highest term yet reached in the evolution, but it is not the highest of which evolution is capable. There is above it a supermind or eternal truth-consciousness which is in its nature the self aware and self-determining light and power of a Divine knowledge .... It is only by the descent of this supermind that the perfection dreamed of by all that is highest in humanity can come".[5]

Socialists or Communists see in such an answer no solution to our economic problems. We do not ignore the urgent necessity of solving the economic crisis. But even the economic problem can be perfectly solved only when man is no longer a prey to passions and instincts. After the analysis of Freud or Jung and after the 'rape of the masses' by the dictators it should be obvious that man is the central problem today. With his perfection only can there be perfection in the outer world. A profound psychological revolution is the first task of mankind today.

This conviction of a spiritual revolution is growing in the West also. Men like Aldous Huxley, Gerald Heard, Christopher Isherwood and John Van Druten recognise that man's real nature is divine and the aim of human life is to realise this divine nature. Science has failed to solve our problems. As Aldous Huxley observes, "We are living now, not in the delicious intoxication induced by the early successes of science, but in a rather grisly morning-after, when it has become apparent that what triumphant science has done hitherto is to improve the means for achieving unimproved or actually deteriorated ends".

Time is, therefore, ripe for a new psychological discipline, for an integral yoga which will endow us with a new truth—consciousness. We see all over the world small groups of seekers attempting to blaze a new trail and bring out a new light which gives to the old truths fresh aspects and therefore novel potentialities of creation and evolution. These groups of aspirants after achieving integral perfection will become lighthouses and exemplars to the rest of the world which will then realise that life is indeed a common enterprise, a kind of partnership concern, of man and God, the finite and the Infinite, who are bound together in a sort of creative comradeship.

This view is corroborated by two perceptive western thinkers, namely — Dr. T. Capra and Dr. P.A. Sorokin, Says Dr. Capra, "What we need then, is a new "Paradigm", a new vision of, reality .... The eastern mystics have a dynamic view modern physics is holistic and ecological. It emphasises the fundamental inter-relatedness and inter-dependence of all phenomena .... Such a view comes very close to the views of mystics of all ages and traditions, and in particular to the views of the spiritual traditions of India.[6]

Again Sorokin says in his book "Reconstruction of Humanity", "If we desire to foster altruism and to suppress egoism, to do away with or reduce inter-personal and inter-growth conflicts, the main properties of our materialistic or sensate culture must be eliminated. The major premise of sensate culture must be replaced by the broader, deeper, richer and more valid premise that the true reality and value is an infinite manifold possessing not only sensory but also super sensory (spiritual) and super rational aspects, all harmoniously reflecting its infinity".

India's cultural history imparts us a message of cultural synthesis, spiritual dynamism and reconciliation of life impulses with the spirit and once again India is called upon to lead the world towards a new synthesis of the East and the West. Such a lead is to be given not in a spirit of chauvinism but in a spirit of humility which is not to be confused with self-depreciation. This duty is India's for her history alone reveals that India has been consistently, comprehensively and constantly a laboratory for spiritual experiments.

"India has the key to the knowledge and conscious application of the ideal; what was dark to her before in its application, she can now, with a new light, illumine; what was wrong and wry in her old methods she can now rectify; the fences which she created to protect the outer growth of the spiritual ideal and which afterwards become barriers to it's expansion and farther application, she can now break down and give her spirit a freer field and an ampler light: she can, if she will, give a new and decisive turn to the problems over which all mankind is labouring and stumbling, for the clue to their solutions is there in her ancient knowledge. Whether she will rise or not to the height of her opportunity in the renaissance which is coming upon her, is the question of her destiny".[7]

REFERENCES

1. 'Vamadeva - Rig Veda,' IV, I, 7; IV. 2 I; IV, 4, 5 Translated by Sri Aurobindo.
2. 'Swetaswatara Upanishad,' IV. 7. Translated by Sri Aurobindo.
3. 'Gita', VII, 19. Translated by Sri Aurobindo.
4. "Vishnu Purana,' II. 12. 39. Translated by Sri Aurobindo.
5. 'Among the Great,' By Dilip Kumar Roy, p. 367.
6. 'The New Vision of Reality,' by Dr. T. Capra, Bhartiya Vidya Bhavan, Bombay.
7. 'The Renaissance in India' by Sri Aurobindo, p. 90.

SIGNIFICANCE OF CULTURE

(Indian Culture Defined)

THE WORD CULTURE is one of the terms that have suffered the most ups-and-downs in all languages, in a universal masquerade of misunderstanding. Clarity is, therefore, essential so far as the connotation of the term 'Culture' is concerned. In this connection attention may be drawn to the content of culture as decided by the members of the Indian Congress for Cultural Freedom Meeting in Bombay in March, 1951. According to them, culture serves the following purposes :

1. Culture has both an individual and a social content Individual culture is an attitude to life on the part of a human being who seeks awareness of himself and of the world. Social culture results from the integration of the culture of the members of a community and of the social relationship emerging in the geographical environment and historical tradition which define the community. Neither individual nor social culture can be complete unless it rests on the underlying unity of mankind.
2. Culture can only flourish, find its 'best' expression, and be secure in a free society. A society is free in which the integrity of the individual is recognised and respected as a primary ethical value, with all the guarantees of social justice, including equality of opportunity which this principle implies. All spiritual pursuits and attainments arising from culture are rooted in this fundamental principle.
3. While culture has a universal basis, its expression is as

particular and varied as the communities themselves. This variety is inherent in the creative genius of peoples and enriches the content of human experience on which universal culture is based.

4. The best expression of a free culture presupposes an attempt to widen, deepen and perfect the individual's awareness of himself and of the world. In modern times civilisation has been mostly governed by an undue emphasis on externalities and a tendency towards standardisation of human life.

This description of culture brings out succinctly the main aspects of culture. Culture has an individual and a social aspect; it is universal and also national; and finally it implies the full development of personality. According to Malinowski in the Encyclopaedia of Social Sciences, culture comprises inherited artifices, goods, technical processes, ideas, habits and values. In other words, culture has a material content and also consists of a body of intellectual knowledge, of the system of moral, spiritual and economic values, of social organisation and of language. Culture, therefore, is an all-embracing word which includes all significant aspects of man's life beginning from philosophy and religion and ending with social institutions and manners.

Further, culture is never static. It is always dynamic and assimilates or should assimilate the best in every epoch or age. We have endeavoured in our book to maintain an integral outlook and discuss all these aspects of culture. It should, however, be emphasised that in culture, stress should not merely be laid on the externalities of life. Rather the emphasis should be on the inward development of man and as man becomes inwardly perfect, a spiritual being, his external outlook will also tend towards perfection.

Connected with the question of culture is the value and importance of Indian Contribution in this sphere. What do we understand by the Indian Culture ? There are various and varied ideas that pass through our minds when we reflect on this question. To some of us philosophical and spiritual beliefs are the basis of the Indian Culture. Others feel that our dreams and ideals as embodied in our best architecture, the sculpture and paintings reflect Indian Culture. Others again would point to various symbolic representations of thought-forms like the concept of Natraj or to the Indian music with its varied Ragas and Raginies as the essence of our culture. We would do well to discover same common thread running through all these forms wherein the Indian mind and spirit demonstrate themselves.

That common thread has been India's belief in spirituality. In the words of Sri Aurobindo, India's constant effort has been to find a basis of living in the higher spiritual truth and to live from the spirit outwards as the old Vedic seers would put it, our divine foundation is above with its rays reaching downward, out through our inner being. It should, however, be pointed out that spirituality does not mean religiosity or discarding of all interest in the so-called worldly life. An integral conception of spirituality stands for a synthesis of the best in Eastern philosophy, life and spirituality. We seek indeed a larger and completer affirmation. 'We perceive that in the Indian ascetic life the great Vedantic formula, 'one without a second', has not been read sufficiently in the light of that other formula equally imperative, All this is the Brahman'.[1]

These days the sociological or the materialistic conception of culture is in great vogue.We would do, therefore, well, to understand why an economic conception cannot be the be-all and the end-all of culture. The economic aspect is only one of the aspects of man's life. In essence, it is an aspect which emphasises desire and possession as the goal of life. Just as the physical barbarian, so to say, makes the excellence of the body and the development of physical force, health and prowess his standard and aim, so the economic barbarian makes the satisfaction of wants and desires his standard and aim.

The accumulation of wealth and more wealth, the adding of possessions to possessions, opulence, show, pleasure, a cumbrous inartistic luxury, a plethora of conveniences, life devoid of beauty and nobility, religion vulgarised or coldly formalised, politics and government turned into a trade and a profession, enjoyment itself made a business, this is commercialism.[2] The result of such a conception need totalitarianism. As in Germany, we were confronted with a black-out of culture. But culture will triumph even in such an atmosphere. Its vitality springs, not from any particular man of genius, but from the uninterrupted flow of generations of men across the centuries. It is historic continuity that gives man's brief passage on this earth a resonance transcending the limits of his mortal life. Culture, which is an ethereal message of the spirit, floats above the most violent upheavals, or remains hidden in the shadow for generations, patiently awaiting the opportunity of claiming its right to life.

The Indian culture, therefore, seeks a wider harmony reconciling spirit with matter, preserving the truths of material-science and its real utility but at the same time keeping intact the spirit as the key-stone of the arch of our culture.

We may also discuss here the influence of geographical and racial factors on the Indian culture, for culture is Pre-eminently a product of the interaction of environment and man. Before, however, we attempt this task some description of India's geography is called for.

Geographical Factor

The name India has been given to different regions in different periods. In its original Persian sense it meant the Sindhu river, what the Greeks called the Indos, and so, by derivation, all the land lying beyond the Indus, both the Northern plains and the Deccan. We may take India as that portion of Asia comprised between the 37th and 38th degrees of latitude north and 67th and 98th degrees of longitude east having an area of about 1,900,000 square miles (not excluding Pakistan).

The most ancient part of this vast country is the Deccan which was an island when Hindustan (the Northern India) was still under the sea. The land of Gondwana', as Pre-historians call it, was itself the result of the dislocation of an Austral continent, which may have been extended from Australia to South Africa and which has left remnants in Ceylon, the Andamans and the Malay Peninsula. A volcanic upheaval, which submerged very ancient lands, gave the Deccan the peninsular shape, while in the north Cretaceous sea-bottoms not only appeared above the water but rose to heights nearly double those of the highest peaks of Europe (thus arose the Himalayas from the sea). By that tipping of the scales, India, hitherto, part of the Austral Continent became an integral part of the Northern Hemisphere.

The Himalayas, 'the Dwelling of the Snows', bounds India on the north, in a crescent tilted from north-west to south-east. India is thus closed on the north of its great river basins and on the east of Bengal. In the west, the right bank of the Indus is dominated by the highlands of Afghanistan and Baluchistan; but here access is given to the Indian plain by passes famous in history.

The rest of the country is surrounded by the sea. Southwards it grows very much narrow. The Deccan, properly so called, steps at the Nilgiri Hills, east of Calicut, but is continued in a subsidiary massif which forms Cape Camorin. On the north it begins on the southern slope of the contrary valleys of the Indus and the Narbada, its last spur to the north-east being the Rajmahal hills, round which the Ganges flows before spreading out into a delta. Along the sides of the plateau run two ranges of Ghats, the Western and the Eastern Ghats. Along the northern edge of the Deccan are the Vindhya Mountains, which extend from the northern slope of the valley of the Narbada to the plains of the Ganges. The Arravallis, in the west, are the highest part of this terrace which falls gently eastwards.

As for the rivers, not only have the rivers of the Deccan broken the line of the Eastern Ghats into sections but the Himalayas itself is pierced by the Indus and its tributary the Sutluj and by the Ghagra and Brahmaputra, which flow into the Ganges or Ganga. The two great rivers of Hindustan are marked by a kind of reverse symmetry. The five rivers of the upper basin of the Indus, form what is like a delta upside down, traversed by rich valleys, while the lower course of the river is between two torrid deserts. The Ganges runs through fertile land all the way, collecting the streams of the whole southern slope of the Himalaya, but divides its waters in a delta in which the lux-uriance of life baffles the foreigners.

Two chief factors govern the hydrography of India — the inexhaustible reserve of ice and snow stored in the Himalayan heights, and the wind which in summer and again in autumn blows from south to north across the Bay of Bengal. This latter is the monsoon, which bears torrential rain. The rains are heaviest in Bengal and tend to decrease as one goes up the river Ganges. Between the Ganges and the Indus irrigation becomes scantier, and a vast desert extends to the Arabian sea. The result of the uneven fall of the rains is that the fertile land is very unequally distributed. The valleys of the Punjab are productive, but the basin of lower Indus is only saved from sterility by artificial irrigation. Beyond the Thar, great Desert of Rajputana, the alluvium of the Baroda District, between Ahmedabad and Surat, is remarkably fertile. The valley of the Narbada, the plateau of Kathiawar and the Carnatic plain, from Madras to Tuticorin are also fertile. In fertile districts which have not been cleared jungle reigns, for example, the Tarai of Bengal.

In shape India is an irregular quadrilateral. Ancient geographers referred to it as being constituted with four-fold conformation, Chatur Sanisthitam, the Himalayas, the ocean and the hills in the west and the East form the sides of this quadrilateral. In ancient literature we have reference to a five-fold division of India. In the centre of the Indo-Gangetic plain was the Madhya-Desa stretching from the river Saraswati (now disappeared) to Allahabad and Banaras, to the Rajmahal Hills. The western part of this area was known as the Brahmarshi-desa, and the entire region was roughly equivalent to Arya Varta as described in the Grammar of Patanjali .... To the north of the Madhya-Desa lay Uttarapatha or Udichya (North-West India), to its west Aparata or Pratichya (Western India), to its south Dakshinapatha or the Deccan, and to the east Purva Desa or Prachya, the Prasi of Alexander's historians ....[3] The whole country was called Bharata-Varsha or the land of Bharata, a King famous in Puranic tradition. It has also been called Jambudvipa, a term better reserved to that part of Asia, outside China, throughout which the prowess of the great imperial family of the Mauryas made itself felt.

In many ways this geography of India has affected the course of her history and culture. For instance, the spirit of tolerance has been nurtured and fostered both directly and indirectly by India's geography. Directly the vastness of the land and its climate have influenced the Indian mind. The great variety in landscape, climate and conditions of life prepared in the mind a readiness to accept differences. Besides, the vast spaces offered room for slow infiltration by newcomers and allowed each locality, unhampered scope of development along its Own lines. Indian climate generally makes for lassitude and languor. History glides along in leisured dignity. This fosters toleration and easy acceptance of differences.

Again here geographical isolation and natural frontiers have given her sense of unity. A compact territorial unit, her internal cohesion is matched by her sharp differentiation from all external lands. Nature has generously placed within her boundaries almost all the resources that man needs for a civilised and creative life. One might go so far as to say that Indian geography compelled unity out of her history, physical features so sharply mark off India from the rest of Asia that attempts either to divide the country or to expand it beyond its natural frontiers have invariably failed.[4] Thus geography has compelled the Indian rulers to seek unity, as witness the attempts of Chandragupta, Asoka, Chandragupta Vikramaditya, Mohammed Tughluq, Alauddin, Akbar, Aurangzeb and the British.

Again, the fertility of the land and its agricultural economy for thousands of years explain, partly atleast, the depth and tenacity of her culture. Common economic organisation has led to the development of common characteristics and a common outlook. The vagaries of monsoon have bred, it is said, fatalism in India. Difficulties of communications have prevented administrative unity, thus the geography of India explains the fundamental basis of Indian culture, unity amidst diversity. It has also been said that the vast landscape of India, the clear sky and the starry firmament have bred a philosophical outlook and started the query for the knowledge of the heavens beyond.

We discover at the same time in the Indians a genuine love of the soil and its physical features, its fauna and flora, its rivers, mountains and valleys, its teeming life and ceaseless activity—such as expressed in the Nadi-Sukta of the Rig-Veda and the Prithvi-Sukta of the Atharva-Veda. This level of the soil has depened and expanded till the conception of the country as sanctified land emerged in the Puranas and the Epics. It roused a geographical consciousness, so to speak, a realisation of the territorial basis of the life of society. This idea of patrie is to be found in other countries also but here we add to this idea of holy land and blend with it a sense of special virtue in its very soil. The religious culture is rooted to the soil. The limits of Brahmavarta, Madhya-desh and Aryavart are precisely defined by Manu and the twice-born-castes are enjoined to live within these boundaries. Thus our geography and culture are intimately related. We develop the conception of motherland expressing it by the name Bharatvarsha for the whole country. It was regarded as the Karmabhumi, the land with which all the efforts and activities of the Indians must be specially connected. In Vishnu Puran we can study the implications of the geographical influences on Indian culture.

We must, however, be cautious in attributing most of the facts of Indian history to the influence of her geography. Starting from Hippocrates in Greece who in On Airs, Waters and Places, attributed loftiness, bravery and gentleness to the people of the hilly countries and a masterful and intractable nature to the peaple of the dry lands, a long line of geographers have unduly emphasized the role of geography. In the words of Lucien Febvre Man exists first, the geographer should say. His habits his special character, his way of life are not a necessary consequence of the fact that he is placed in this or that environment. These are not the product, to use that bold formula, of the environment. Man carries them with him, he transports them with him. They are the consequences of his own nature. We must not say blindly that such and such region necessarily constrains its inhabitants to adopt such and such a way of life, but rather that under the powerful action of organised and systematised habits gradually deepening their roots, and thus imposing themselves with greater and greater strength on successive generations, stamping their mark on minds and giving a definite trend to all progressive forces, the aspect of a country may be completely transformed.[5] In the antinomy between man and the environment, the former plays the bigger part.

Racial Factors

We have now seen how India' geography has influenced her culture. As for the racial factor, that too, has been responsible for the shape the Indian culture has assumed through the course of centuries. The fundamental thing about culture is its intimate association with historic development. Indian history explains why the mosaic of our culture is so rich and multi-coloured. Races after races have poured into India, lent their original contribution to our culture and have been assimilated in the Indian milieu.[5]

India has been called a museum of races. A classification of Indian races has been made by B.S. Guha, Former Director of the Anthropological Survey of India. He classifies the races as follows :

(l) The Negrito, (2) the Proto-Austroloid, (3) The Mongoloid consisting of (i) Plaeo Mongoloids of two types, (a) Long headed, (b) Broad headed, (ii) Tibeto-Mongoloids, (4) The Mediterranean, comprising (i) Palaeo-Mediterranean, (ii) Mediterranean, (iii) The so-called oriental type, (5) The Western Brachycephals, consisting of (i) The Alpinoid, (ii) The Dinaric and (iii) The Armenoid, (6) The Nordic.

Of the above races the Negrito is all but extinct. A small group survives in the Andamans and among the aboriginals of Cochin and Travancore Hills, Assam and the Rajmahal Hill tribes in Eastern Bihar. The Negrito strain is indicated by the shape of the skull and grizzly hair. The Proto-Austroloids survive in good many aboriginal people of present-day and some of them can also be traced in the lower castes of the Indian people. The Austroloids have steep forehead, snub nose with wide nostrils, retreating chin and thick set body. The Mongoloid group are found in Assam, Chittagong Hills and Bhutan. The Mediterranean people are in Kannada, Tamil, Malayalam, Punjab, Gangetic Valley, Sind, Rajputana and other places. The Mongoloids have long head, flat nose, high cheek-bones and oblique slit-eyes. The Brachycephals are well marked in Bengal, Orissa, Kathiawar, Coorg, Gujarat, along the western coast of India except Malabar, along the Himalayas and parts of Bihar and eastern U.P. They are short-headed. The Nordics who gave to India its Aryan speech, organisation, imagination, adaptability and basis of Indian culture are strong in North-West Frontier, Punjab, Rajputana, Kashmir, Upper Ganges valley and in Maharashtra among the Chitpawan Brahmans. They are tall, fair skinned, with eyes light brown or black.

This classification is not, however, watertight and there is considerable overlapping. Characteristics in many cases are toned down by economic conditions, environments, group-life and so on. As a result of common life in India these races have been modified in either characteristics and evolution of a common Indian type and culture has been the result. We may now discuss some of the contributions made by those races to the Indian culture.

So far as the Negritos are concerned, it is probable that the cult of the ficus tree, associated with fertility and with the souls of the dead and some ideas about the path of the dead to paradise may have been derived from them. The Proto-Austroloids are supposed to have given us the custom of disposal of the dead by exposure, communal houses, head-hunting, canoe cult, introduction of canoe and cocoanut, pottery, use of the blowing gun, ideas of totemism and religion, terrace cultivation of rice and some fruits and vegetables. They may have also given us some words for fruits and animals. Thus, it would appear that some of the fundamental features of Indian culture have been derived from them. Again, some notions of future life, some forms of rituals and the habit of counting on the basis of twenty may have come from them. It is said that the Austric temperament is marked by superstitions, cheerfulness, love of music and gaiety, submissiveness, hard work, respect for Convention and belief in the soul. These people have survived in the Munda and Santhals, etc., who have dark skin and snub nose. They have also affected the Aryan speech in many ways.

The Mediterranean people represented chiefly by the Dravidians who are long-headed, have been responsible for the city culture. They have also led India in the matter of international trade. Their language now forms a solid block in the Deccan and South India. It is said that in Baluchistan the 'Brahui' speech is Dravidian and some traces of their languages can also be found in North Indian languages. It is surmised that the people of Harappa and Mohenjo-Daro were Dravidians. The Dravidians have contributed the cult of Shiva, the worship of Mother Goddess or Shakti and also the institution of 'Yoga'. They have also given us various symbols associated with these gods and goddesses, e.g., the lion and the bull. Many features of our temple architecture have been of the Dravidian origin. They were also acquainted with the working of metals. It is also said that the Tantric tradition is derived from the Dravidians. Further, the Pooja (religious worship) rites like the offering of flowers, leaves, fruits and water, etc., are pre-Aryan. We may, therefore, say that so far as the Hindu culture is concerned much of its basis is a contribution from the Dravidians. Further, the acceptance of the pre-Aryan ritual meant also the acceptance of the conception of the Divinity and of the mythological figures of the gods and goddesses which were current among the Dravidians. Among the articles of food, the Dravidians have, it is said, given us wheat, rice, milk, pulses, vegetables, cotton dress, dwellings, counting on the basis of eight, customs like the familiarity of the wife with her brother-in-law and respect for the brother-in-law elder to her husband, many wedding customs, phonetic sounds and many myths in the Puranas. The Dravidians have adopted Sanskrit and in common with the Aryans their Varna-System. The Muslims have also influenced our culture. We discuss in a separate chapter of this book their contribution in this domain. So far as Mongoloids are concerned their influence has been local.

We thus see that both geography and the racial factor have considerably influenced our culture. The influence of the Aryans is too patent to be missed. They have given us through their philosophical, religious and spiritual ideas the original and fundamental basis of Indian culture. In our own days we are witnessing the beginning of a fresh synthesis; the East and the West have met on our soil and out of their meeting we are likely to have another fusion of cultures and this may well provide a basis for the world-culture of tomorrow.

Distinguishing Features of our Culture

Our culture is distinguished by its possession of a number

of important characteristics or qualities. In the first place, our culture is characterised by tolerance. All sorts of races and creeds have found their habitation in India but they have not been persecuted as in the case of the medieval Europe. Together with toleration, we have balance or equipoise also as a marked characteristic of our culture not only in life as a whole but also in the correlation of its various parts and in embodying in them an ever developing whole in keeping with our conception of God who is not only absolute but also infinite. Again our culture is characterised by harmony or rhythm, what the Vedas called 'Rita'. Things happen not fortuitously or accidentally, but according to certain order and in a certain continuity. This is specified, for instance, in the law of Karma and the transmigration of souls. Another quality of our culture has been ceaseless search after truth which has been characterised by the word Abhaya, by fearlessness, a spirit of adventure and as we know very few items of speculation in whatever fields of life have escaped the investigation and analysis of the Indian thinker. Therefore, when we think of a cultured Indian we should at the same time remember that he should be the embodiment of these values.

Fundamental Unity

India presents a land of great contrasts and of bewildering variety. But we should not run away with the impression that there is no unity in our culture, that it is a plethora of conflicting beliefs and ideas, multiplicity of forms and formulas, presenting a great variety of languages, manners, dress and food, among other things. Deep down fundamentally and essentially India has always possessed great unity and continuity of culture.

In the first place, India had found unity in religion and spirituality. All her art forms expressed the same truth. In the words of Annie Besant, 'Indian Art is a Blossom of the Tree of Divine Wisdom, full of suggestions, from worlds Invisible, striving to express the subtle'. This feeling of unity was reinforced by the geographical unity of the country. We had grasped the notion of a common motherland. The song Bandematram is symptomatic of this sentiment. The Puranas spoke of Bharatvarsha 'the country living north of the ocean and south of the snowy mountains, marked by seven main chains of mountains .....where dwelt the descendants of the Bharatas, with the Kiratas (Barbarians) living to its East, the Yavanas (Greeks) to its west, and its own population consisting of the Brahmans, Kshatriyas, Vaishyas and Sudras'. The name Bharatvarsha has a historic significance indicating the country of the Bharatas, of Indo-Aryan culture of which the Bharatas were the chief bearers.

'The Hindus in one of their common prayers recall and worship the image of the mother country as the land of seven sacred rivers, the Ganga, Yamuna, Godavari, Saraswati, Narbada, Sindhu and Kaveri, which between them cover its entire area. Another prayer calls up its image as the land of seven sacred cities : Ayodhya, Mathura, Maya (modern Hardwar), Kashi, Kanchi, Avantika (Ujjain), Dvaravati (Dwarka) representing important regions of India'.[6]

The Hindu custom of religious pilgrimages betokened the same consciousness of a common homeland, for these pilgrimages covered the whole length and breadth of India. It is undeniably a most powerful factor for developing the geographical sense in the people, which enables them to think and feel that India is not a mere congeries of geographical fragments but a single though immense organism filled with the tide of and pulsating life from end to end,[7] observes Radha Kumud Mookerjee. The same spirit impelled Sankara to establish his four Mathas (monasteries) at the four extreme points of the country, viz., Jyotir Matha in the North (near Badri-Kedar on the Himalayas), Sarada Matha at Dwarka in the West, Goverdhana Matha at Puri in the East, and Sringeri Matha in Mysore. Sectarianism is thus an aid to nationalism in Indian culture. In our religious literature also, for instance in the Bhagvata Purana or Manu Smriti, passages are found describing Bharatvarsha in patriotic fervour, the land made by the gods, ending in such utterances as 'Mother and mother-country are greater than Heaven'.

Janani Janmabhumischa Svargadapi gariyasi

We had thus elevated patriotism into a religion. In the

words of Sri Aurobindo, the feeling of almost physical delight in the touch of the mother-soil, of the winds that blow from the Indian sea, of the rivers that stream from Indian hills, in the hearing of Indian speech, music, poetry, in the familiar sights, songs, habits, dress, manners of Indian life, this is the physical root of the love. It is through this appreciation of the romance that India outwardly is that we begin to feel within us a kind of inner relationship not only with her material embodiment but also with her soul; and as this feeling deepens, the mere external fact vanishes, and there emerges before our mind's eye, no less vividly, an idea, a dynamic concept, of which the land becomes a symbol, an image, an object, as it were, of our love and veneration'.[8]

Thus the fundamental unity of India was rooted in the psychology of the Indians. Politically also, the attempts at empire-building embracing the whole of India indicate the trend towards unity. The Vedic words like Samrat, Asvamedha and Digvijaya confirm this. So far as races are concerned it has been said that India has stamped them with a common seal and has wrought a out recognisable type amid a great profusion of species. It has also been pointed out that there is an underlying uniformity of life from the Himalayas to the Cape Camorin, the existence of a general Indian character, a general Indian personality which one cannot resolve into its component elements. The various provinces have shared in each other's past. For instance, a Bengali feels pride in the Rajput history.

Culturally, therefare, there is a complex harmony of composites. We find certain common ideas practised by the Indians from times immemorial, viz., a sense of unity of all life through its being an expression of the unseen reality, a desire for synthesis, recognition of sorrows, of life leading to a sincere attempt to go to the root causes of these with a view to remove them from the life of the individual and the community, a desire to attain to the unseen reality as the solution of all evil and suffering, mystic realisation by discipline, faith and devotion, a sense of the sacredness of life, charity and tolerance. Tagore speaks that 'the realisation of unity in diversity, the establishment of a synthesis amidst variety that is the inherent, the Sanatan-dharma of India'.

The Western people have not been able to discern this cultural unity and have been more impressed with the differences in rituals and social practices in India. For them, the following observatian of Sri Aurobindo should prove very opposite. To the Indian mind, dogma is the least important part of religion, and the religious spirit matters, not the dogma, but to the Western mind a fixed intellectual belief is the most important part of a cult, its core of meaning, the thing that distinguishes it. That notion is a consequence of the Western idea that intellectual truth is the highest verity. The Indian religious thinker believes on the contrary that all the highest eternal varieties are truths of the spirit, intellectual truth turned towards the infinite must not be one but many sided, the most varying intellectual beliefs may be equally true because they mirror different facets, forms, however separated by intellectual distances, so many side-entrances which admit us into the precincts of the eternal verity'.[9] Therefore, in our spiritual culture is grounded the fundamental unity of India.

We have discussed the nature and significance of the Indian culture. There is, however, one moot point. Can we formulate or discover any principle or principles which have been the guiding factors in the evolution of the Indian culture? Are there any principles that can explain the various cultural phenomena appearing in the various stages of the Indian culture?

Many thinkers have attempted to explain historic facts and forces by reference to one principle or motive force. Among these the most famous in our own day has been the materialistic interpretation of Karl Marx. But the cardinal defect in such an interpretation is two-fold. In the first place this analysis concentrates attention on the external data, laws, institutions, rights, customs, economic factors and developments while the deeper psychological elements so important in the activities of a mental, emotional, ideative being like man are neglected. This hypnotising credulousness and belief in the all sufficiency of matter to explain mind and soul is not the right attitude. Secondly, this economic emphasis ignores the fact that man is a bundle of personalities and his physical life is only one element in the integral human existence. A full and materially prosperous life is desirable for men living in society, but on condition that it is also a true and beautiful life. Neither the life nor the body exist for their own sake, but as instruments to subserve a higher purpose, a supreme good which is more mental, ethical and spiritual rather than physical.

We cannot, therefore, accept only one principle as the guiding factor behind the various stages of the Indian culture. We can only say that a certain tendency or principle dominated a particular stage of Culture and that there were other overlapping factors or principles which were also operating though not with the same force as the main principle concerned. Before we point out the main principles of our cultural evolution, we must demarcate the various stages of our cultural history.

The first important landmark, the basis of our culture is the Vedic age including in the term the periods of the Upanishads, Ramayana and Mahabharata. Then we have the classical stage beginning with Buddhism and ending with Harsha. After this, we have the medieval age beginning with the Rajput culture and ending with the Indo-Muslim contacts, then follows the modern age, the impact of the West on the Indian culture and the beginning of the Indian Renaissance.

Taking our cue from Sri Aurobindo, we may throw certain broad hints about the main principles guiding the various stages of the Indian culture. These principles, psychological in character, are symbolical, typal, conventional, individualist and subjective. The symbolical was operating during the Vedic period, the typal in the age of Dharma, the conventional in the medieval period, the individualist in the modern and the subjective principle has just begun in the most recent epoch.

In the early stages of the Indian culture, we can see a symbolic mentality pervading thought, customs and institutions. This symbolic mentality is associated with imaginatively religious feelings. The symbol is representative of something occult, mysterious, divine or unfathomable. In his various customs, institutions and phases of life man finds symbols to express what he knows or guesses of mystic influences that are behind his life and can change it. We take some concrete instances.

The religious institution of sacrifice colours the whole

Vedic society in its various activities. We are apt to take it as a physical or traditional performance because we have lost the symbolic mentality. However, during the Vedic age sacrifice was a symbol, an offering to the gods. The Vedic idea of sacrifice with the soul of man as the enjoyer of its fruits points to the path that leads to self conquest. Of all his gains and works, of all that he himself is and has, man must make an offering to the powers of God-head, the powers of consciousness, the gods, who recognise in the soul of man their brother and ally and desire to help and increase him by themselves increasing in him so as to exalt and enrich his world with their strength and beauty. Again, the Indian ideal of the relation between man and woman was governed by the symbolism of the relation between Purush and Prakriti, the male and female divine principles in the universe, Or the Som-Ras was not so much a drink as a symbol of divine bliss. From this symbolic attitude came the tendency to make everything in the society a sacrament, religious and sacrosanct but not in any narraw sense. The spiritual idea governed all, but the social forms were lax, free and capable of infinite development because God could not be cribbed cabined or confined in one particular mould or groove. Similarly in the Upanishads, in the Epics and the Gita this symbolic mentality persists but at the same time we witness the beginning of another stage. The religious and the spiritual are supplemented and even superseded by the psychological and the ethical as signals of the emergence of the typal stage.

In the typal stage, religion becames a mystic sanction for the ethical motive and discipline, Dharma, and it also moves towards the stage where asceticism and other worldly turn of mind are commended, e.g., in Buddhism where desire is to be suppressed completely and an ascetic attitude towards life is to be encouraged. Also in this stage we have the aims which man has to progressively realise, viz., Kama, Artha, Dharma and Moksha (desire, self interest, religion, salvation). Desire and self-interest stand for egoism and it was recognised that man must live-out fully his ego-life so that it may be fully satisfied and also its disadvantages may be appreciated. We were warned, however, not to set too great a premium upon self will, passion and self interest. Another power it was said, claims man, over-topping desire and self interest and self will, the power of the Dharma. The ideal of Dharma inspired the ethical and social life of the Classical stage. But this Dharma was not a procrustean bed. The man of knowledge, the man of power, the productive and acquisitive man, the scholar, the priest, the fighter, the worker and the craftsman—all had their own law of being, Dharma. Each had his type of nature and there must be a rule for the perfection of that type or each his function and there must be a canon, an idea of that function. The honour of each type consisted in the proper performance of the functions suited to its nature, Guna. There was, however, to be a harmony of this complexity of Artha, Kama and Dharma. This harmony was to be realised through a higher principle. Human life was to be exalted beyond its self into something spiritual and divine. Not a noble but ever death-bound manhood, but immortality, freedom, divinity are the highest heights of man's perfection. This was the significance of the ideal of Moksha, liberation. But we find that in the Classical stage also there is a fading away of these ideals of life and Dharma. They become more a convention than a reality of life.

Thus we arrive at the medieval stage of society when Conventions, forms, externalities and rules become more important, the spirit fades away. The 'priest' and the 'pundit' masquerade under the name of 'Brahman', the feudal baron under the name of 'Kshatriya' the trader and the money-getter under the name of 'Vaishya' and the economic serf under the name of 'Shudra'. Society becomes rigid, religion is stereotyped, education is bound by traditions and man is shackled by the forms he has himself created. There were noble efforts to stem the tide. Religious reformers like Shankaracharya, Ramanuj, Kabir, Nanak and Chaitanya tried to recall man to his worthier ideals and aims but their efforts failed in the long run. The iron grip of conventionalism fell on the new movements and annexed the names of its founders. Thus, the medieval period in India ended in darkness and weakness.

When the old truths are lost, when the conventional age

results in corruption, anarchy and failure, a revolt rears its head. This is the revolt of reason, the dawning of the age of individualism as a protest against the conventional social tyranny. It was first in Europe that reason as the spearhead of individualism made its appearance and carried all before it. United with science and therefore with a materialistic view of life it dethroned conventionalised religion from the seat of power. It came to India also in the wake of Western capitalism and imperialism.

The individualistic age has been a revolt of reason in its beginning and a triumphal progress of physical science is its culmination. Its dawn is always a questioning and a denial. So in India also the modern age dawned with the denial of the practices of life common to the Indians of the early nineteenth century. But this denial was marked by such a great extremism that it bred a reaction in India and many religious reformers and thinkers arose to question the efficacy of materialism alone to fulfil the law of man's life.

We are, therefore, now reaching a stage in our cultural evolution when the age of reason and science may well be supplemented by, or rather sublimated into, the subjective age. The subjective age stands for freedam and initiative so far as the individual is concerned. It also marks the beginning of an age of spiritualism and has been the result of the exaggerations in the claims of science and reason. The advent of this age is due, in the first place, to the fact that rationalistic attitude and physical science have over-reached themselves and must be over taken by a mounting flood of psychological and psychic knowledge. Secondly, novel ideas like Bergson's intuition, Nietzsche's will-to-live, and German meta-physical tendencies are challenging the claims of reason to answer all our doubts and demands. Thirdly, the awakened East is veering anew towards subjectivism and practical spirituality. Reason and its ally science have failed to solve all our problems. The West is groping for the light. The East must show the way. The ideas of a subjective age can be discerned to a certain extent in the new theories of education. Formerly, education was merely a mechanical, forcing of the child's nature into arbitrary grooves of training and knowledge. But new education must be a bringing out of the child's own intellectual and moral capacities to their highest possible value and must be based on the psychology of the child-nature. Eventually it will be realised that man should also be left to bring out the best in himself, that he should be provided an environment which may help him to find his deeper self, the real psychic entity within.

Indian cultural evolution, therefore, can be best understood in psychological terms. Beginning with the symbolic age, passing through the typal, the conventional age and the age of reason, we seem to have arrived at the subjective age. It is hoped that an Indian cultural revolution in the near future will lead to the dawn of a spiritual age when man will have transcended himself through self realisation, by becoming one with the Universe and with God.

REFERENCES

1. Shri Aurobindo, *Life Divine*, Vol. 1, p. 30.
2. Shri Aurobindo, *The Human Cycle*, p. 95.
3. R.C. Majumdar et.al, *An Advanced History of India*, pp. 4-5.
4. Humayun Kabir, *Our Heritage*, p.9.
5. Lucien Febvre, *A Geographical Introduction to History*, p. 368.
6. Radha Kumud Mookerji, *Hindu Civilization*, p. 57.
7. Radha Kumud Mookerji, *Fundamental Unit of India.*
8. S.K. Mitra, *The Vision of India*, p. 45. p. 39.
9. *The Arya*, Vol. VI, No. 1, p.26

2

ANCIENT CULTURE

BEFORE WE DEAL with the cultural evolution of ancient India, some description of chronology and politics of the period is called for. The period begins with the culture of Harappa and Mohenjo-Daro. Its chronology is not yet certain but it may be said on the basis of various authoritative pronouncements that this civilisation may be assigned a date between 3250 B.C. to 2750 B.C. So far as its politics are concerned, we are yet waiting for the proper deciphering of the script of the period to say anything about the matter.

As for the Vedic culture, the period of the Vedas and the Upanishads, here also various surmises have been made and we may roughly put the dates of the period between 2500 B.C. to 1500 B.C. Politically the Vedic period witnessed the rise of tribal chieftainship and democratic assemblies but so far evidence does not suggest the institution of kingship based on territorial sovereignty. It is only later during the age of the Upanishads that we have the birth of territorial sovereignty and the conception of Bharatvarsha. According to the Puranas during this period two chief dynasties originated, viz., the Manava Dynasty and the Ail Dynasty ruled over by Ikshvaku and Puruva respectively. Later on, in the Ikshvaku dynasty we have the famous kings, Mandhata, Harishchandra, Dashratha and Ram.

The Ail Dynasty later split up into a number of branches like those of the Yadavas and the Puru whose people were called the Yadavas and the Pauravas respectively. Among the Yadavas we have the famous king Krishna and the Pauravas gave us Bharat with whose name is associated the name of our own country Bharatvarsha. The Paurava dynasty again split up and one of its branches was Kuru, the people being called Kauravas who are famous in the Mahabharata. Thus, we find that during the period of the epics India was divided into a number of kingdoms. Territorial sovereignty had come into existence and attempts were made to weld the whole country politically into one unit under one sovereign or samrat, the conception of Chakravarti had come into existence. Notable attempts in this direction were those made by Bharat, Shri Ramchandra and Yudhistira. As for the dates, we may say on the basis of the study of the Puranas that roughly the age of Bharat would be somewhere about 2250 B.C., Ramchandra 1900 B.C., and of Mahabharat 1500 B.C. and so also of the Gita.

During the period of the rise of Buddhism and Jainism (600-400 B.C.) Northern India is said to have been parcelled out among Sixteen states, ruled over by Mahajanpad or kings. These were 'Anga', 'Kuru', 'Panchal', 'Matsya', 'Sursen', 'Ashmak', 'Avanti', 'Gandhar', and 'Kamboj'. Some of these states were ruled by kings and some by assemblies, which periodically elected a chief, who was given the courtesy title of Raja. Some of these states were a form of confederation with a common government for two or more states, joining the confederation. 'Anga' and 'Magadh' were mainly in what is the present Bihar, Kashi near the present Banaras, Kaushal in the eastern part of Uttar Pradesh, Mull and Vrijji were also in the eastern U.P. and there were the two peoples 'Videha' and 'Lichhavi' the latter have given to us Mahavir, the propounder of Jainism. Vatsa was towards the west of Kashi and Chedi in modern Bundelkhand. The capital of Vatsa was the famous city Kaushombi. Kurus and Panchals were in the western U.P. and the Punjab. Avanti was in Central India with Ujjain as its capital. Gandhar was towards the extreme end of the Punjab with Taxila, a famous University town, as its capital. Kamboja was in what is the modern Pamir and Badakshan. Besides these Kingdoms or states there were smaller chieftainships or governments based on class rule like that of the 'Sakyas' in the north of Kaushal. In the south there were the Andhras and the

Tamilians. During this period there was a contest for supremacy between these kingdoms and eventually Magadh came out triumphant under Ajatashatru (552 B.C.). These were the main political divisions of India during the rise of Buddhism and Jainism.

After this we have the dawn of the Classical age and the chronological uncertainty disappears to a certain extent. Politically Magadh continues to be the centre of attraction and therein we have first the dynasty of the Nandas and then of the Mauryas. During the rule of the Nandas, the attack of Alexander over the Punjab follows in the year 320 B.C. The Maurya dynasty under Chandragupta began in the year 322 B.C. and ended in 185 B.C. Its famaus kings were Chandragupta Maurya (322-298 or 302 B.C.) and Ashoka (273-232 B.C.). Under this dynasty once again the political unity of India is restored. As a result of this political unity both political and cultural consciousness of the people reached a very high watermark and both in the sphere of administration and of culture great experiments and innovations were made so that the period can very well be compared with any in the modern age.

After the break up of the Mauryan Empire India once again is broken up into a number of independent kingdoms and in Magadh we have the Sunya and the Kanva dynasties from 185 B.C. to 225 A.D. At the same time there is an incursion into India of foreign races like those of the Sakas, Greek,(the Bactrians and the Parthians) and the Kushans, a branch of the Yueh-Chis. At the same time in south and central India we witness the rise of Satvahans one of whose kings was the famaus Vikramaditya who is said to have signally defeated the Sakas. Among the kings of foreign extraction the most famous was Kaniska who ruled about 120 or 78 A.D. Under him once again a large part of Northern India was politically united and a great cultural upsurge was witnessed in the country. After him we have once again various dynastic struggles notably between the Sakas and the Satvahans.

Sometime afterwards we witness the rise of a fresh empire under the Guptas from 319 or 320 A.D., with Patliputra as their capital. The Gupta period marks the golden age of Indian culture in the Classical period. The most famous kings of the dynasty were Samudragupta (340-380 A.D.) and Chandragupta II (380-415 A.D.). These kings restored the political unity of India and, by their patronage of the Indian culture, raised it to its greatest heights. After Chandragupta II the attacks of another foreign race, the Huns began and the Gupta Empire began to shrink, though it continued to exist down till 528 A.D. In other parts of India many dynasties arose among whom the most famous were the Chalukyas.

At the same time in the North we have the rise of the Thaneswar dynasty under Prabhakar Vardhan. Under king Harsha of this dynasty Northern India is once again united. Harsha ruled from 606 to 647 A.D. Culturally, this is the culmination of the classical age. And thus we come to an end of the ancient period whose cultural progress we trace in the pages that follow.

3

THE INDUS CIVILISATION

THE EARLIEST STORY of India's past is revealed by the recent discoveries made by the Indian and Western archaeologists in the Punjab and Sind, the region watered by the Indus, hence the name given to these cultures as the Indus valley civilisation. The remains of this civilisation have so far been discovered at Harappa in the Montgomery district of the West Punjab, at Mohenjo-Daro (city of the dead), about twenty-five miles south of Larkana, in middle Sind. Other allied sites have been discovered belonging to the same period, for example, Nal in Baluchistan, Amri, Jhukar, Lohumjo-daro and Chanhu-daro, in Sind and Kotla on an ancient caravan road strung with a number of pre-historic settlements running from the North-west India and Baluchistan by way of the Mahran coast and Iran to Mesopotamia.

The credit of realising the pre-historic nature of the site at Mohenjo-Daro must be given to an Indian, R.D. Banerji, who discovered the remains in 1922. His reports encouraged Sir John Marshall, the Director of the department of Archaeology in India, to probe further. Since then a group of archaeologists, British, Americans and others, have been busy discovering the remains at various places in Western India. In fact, Sir John Marshall is confident that this culture spread to, even if settlements were not actually made, in the Ganges Valley. As Professor Childe has pointed out, this civilisation must have embraced an area very much larger than either Egypt or Sumer. The objects found in Harappa are practically identical with those found in Mohenjo-Daro.

Age

The age of the Indus civilisation is not absolutely certain but it has been inferred from certain general resemblances between it and the other early civilisation of known dates, for instance, the early civilisations in Mesopotamia, Western Persia, Egypt and Seistan. Certain specific resemblances are also disclosed in a variety of objects recovered from these places, which can only be explained as the outcome of active intercourse between these regions at the close of the fourth millennium B.C. The most important of these Objects are Five seals bearing the unmistakable 'Indus' pattern (the script and humped bull) discovered in Mesopotamia. Two of these seals are assigned to an age before 2800 B.C. Dr. R.K. Mookerji in his book Hindu Civilisation, assigns this civilisation to a date between C. 3250-2750 B.C. Dr. E. Mackay has also discussed the question of chronology. According to him the cylindrical seal discovered in Tell Asmar near Baghdad resembles the seals found in the upper levels of Mohenjo-Daro and is certainly of Indian workmanship. The Asmar site has been given C 2400 B.C. as the date. It is interesting to note that on the seal are found Indian animals like the elephant, rhinoceros and gharial (fish eating crocodile) and the carving is also Indian.

Besides seals, knobbed pottery of Indian origin has also been discovered at this site. A framed Greek cross resembling that of a seal in Mohenjo-Daro has also been found in Northeast Greece. Beads in Egypt have been found resembling those in the Indus Valley remains. Hence, Dr. Mackay believes that the early Mohenjo-Daro culture might be placed at about C. 2500 B.C. The Harappa civilisation being older must be assigned a prior date. Hence, the estimate of Dr. R.K. Mookerji is probably correct.

Mohenjo-Daro seems to have been a smaller city than Harappa, but even so, it occupies nearly a square mile of ground. It may have been larger for its outskirts are buried beneath the silt deposited by the river Indus. The bed of the Indus river has risen some twenty feet or more in the course of the ages and it is, therefore, almost impossible to explore the earliest levels of the civilisation.

Mohenjo-Daro consists of one very large mound with smaller mounds to the north and east. These mounds are of a light red tint. The cities were built of burnt brick. As for the people who built these cities no definite answer can be given about their identity. Their language has also not been deciphered.

Language

There are various guesses of course. The script on the seals, it is said, is pictographic bearing a close resemblance to the Erato-Elamite script in Babylonia. Father Heras, S.J., regards it as Proto-Dravidian. The writing is made up of syllabic signs, with ideograms and perhaps determinative. A group of Indian writers (Barna, 'The Indus script and the Tantric code') would see in the animals on the Harappa seals symbols for phonetic values, a kind of writing used in the Tantric books. There are found 396 signs of the script, accompanied by inscriptions on seals, sealings, pottery, copper tablets and even bangles. The direction of the writing is generally from right to left.

The People

Who were the people inhabiting these cities ? The human remains found at Mohenjo-Daro have been assigned to four racial stocks, namely, the Proto-Austroloid (now represented by the Kols etc.), the Mediterranean (modern long-headed Hindustani), the Mongolians and the Alpinians (represented by the Gujaratis, Marathas and the Bengalis). All this suggests that the people were cosmopolitan hailing from various parts of Asia. It is also suggested that they were either Dravidians or allied to them. The remains suggest that the people were highly civilised, superior in culture to that of Elam or Sumer in Western Asia. They were probably using bark, cotton fabric, leather or palm leaves as writing materials. The peaple must have lived for a considerable period in India by the time when we first know them. Not only do their exceptionally well-built cities but also their religion (animal and phallus worship) show that they were not from the contemporary civilisations in Western Asia. The people were, at first, assumed to be peace-loving as not much evidence was found of the burning of the cities on account of wars, but now fortifications have been found. Evidence suggests that the cities declined on account of change in the course of the river Indus. They were probably flooded by the river. Temples have not been found in these places.

Architecture and Masonary

From their foundation the cities appear to have been laid out in accordance with some pre-arranged scheme. For example, at Mohenjo-Daro the streets run in straight lines and are crossed by others at right angles. This shows planning and existence of some authority to control the development of the city and to avoid tortuous alleys. Town-planning was also accompanied with strict enforcement of building regulations as greatest care was taken to prevent any structure encroaching upon the streets. The people must have been extremely prosperous, judging from the excellent masonry and carefully built houses. Due regard was paid to sanitation and hygiene. For instance, the streets were all aligned from east to west or from north to south as a north or south wind sweeping down a broad thoroughfare, would suck the stagnant air out of the smaller streets and lanes running at right angles, thus amply ventilating them. Streets are wide, the most important thoroughfare being thirty-three feet wide. The buildings made of burnt bricks are generally plain devoid of decoration. The windows were non-existent and the entrances were placed in narrow by-ways. The police system is suggested by the evidence at these cities with the area divided into wards for protection. There were two or more stories in the buildings. The pottery jars were used as cupboards and probably there were wooden shelves also. Beds, stools and boxes were also in use. There were small kitchens though most of the cooking was done in the courtyards.

Sanitation and cleanliness are evidenced by the use of bathrooms and proper drainage system found in all buildings. The spill-way of many of the channels used for drainage were stepped at varying angles so that the water pouring down should not splash the passer-by in the street. Every street had its brick-lined drainage channel and so had even quite small lanes and into these ran smaller tributary drains from the houses on either side. The waste water and sewage from the various houses were usually not permitted to flow into the main street drains direct but first passed into a sump or cess-pit in which the solid matter was deposited. When the sump was three quarters full, the water flowed into the larger drains, and by this method overflowing was prevented. Large brick culverts were constructed on the outskirts of the city to carry away storm water. All these are proof of the excellent sanitary engineering and high degree of civilisation developed by the people. Wells show that excellent water-supply was maintained. The buildings show the existence of wealthy administrative and merchant class, a larger class of artisans and possibly slaves.

One of the most interesting buildings is the great public bath, constructed entirely of burnt brick and measuring thirty-nine feet three inches in length and twenty-three feet two inches in width. This bath can be entered at either end by means of a staircase with treads a little over nine inches wide and eight inches high. Immediately below the foot of each stairway is a broad platform sixteen inches high and thirty-nine inches wide, which extends the width of the bath. A paved walk surrounded the top of the bath. The openings in the wall gave access to a cloistered walk continuing right round the bath and outside the cloister there is a series of rooms of various sizes. A vertical mainhole at the western end made it possible to inspect and clear the passage.

The water passed out thence through a culvert. There is also a large well in a room to the east of the bath accessible to the main street outside also. An annex to the great bath suggests arrangements for hot air bathing with a hypocaust system of heating. North of the Great Bath is a group of bath-rooms with stair cases for upper storey. No door exactly faces another, this device made it impossible for anyone to peep into the priests with their cells on the upper storey. Bathing was probably an essential ritual of these people.

Buildings in many street corners suggest hotels or eating houses where merchants and others would have met to arrange business deals and to combine gossip with eating and drinking. Stone was used in frontier towns.

Religion

Evidence of religion is found not in any documents but in the seals, images and other materials unearthed there. The only stone image yet discovered is a white steatite head and bust. This figure is clothed in a robe which is carried over the left shoulder and under the right arm, and on which is carved in relief the trefoil pattern that is obviously a sacred symbol. The figure has a short beard and shaven upper lip. The hair, practically cropped, is parted in the middle and secured by a fillet tied round the head with two long ends hanging down behind. Signs show that a necklace was also worn. The half shut eyes suggest Yogic contemplation. Numerous pottery figurines suggest worship of the female deities probably representing the Mother-Goddess worshipped in the Near and Middle East also in ancient times. Clay figures wear the horns of a goat or bull suggesting that animal worship was also common. Fusion of two or more deities is also suggested. The seal, amulets and talismans of stone and pottery provide the largest contribution to our store of knowledge concerning the religious beliefs of the Harappan people. The most interesting image is that of a deity, nude with horns and three faces, seated on a stool with heels closely pressed together suggesting some ritualistic posture. A number of animals deer, antelope, rhinoceros, elephant, tiger and buffalo, surround him. Large number of bangles adorn either arm and a headdress rises from his head between horns resembling those of a bull or buffalo. Sir John Marshall regards it as Shiva in his aspect of Pasupati, Lord of the Beasts. No less than three seals bearing a representation of this deity have been unearthed.

Another interesting seal-amulet shows a horned goddess in the midst of a pipal or sacred fig tree before which another horned deity is kneeling and doing obeisance. A row of female spirits or deities occupies the whole of the lower register of the seal-amulet, each figure wearing a spring on the head, a long pigtail behind, but no horns. These figures recall the goddess Sitla and her six sisters. Stone objects found also suggest that veneration was paid to phallic symbols. Tigers with a goddess seated on them have also been found on seals. Carved figure of a snake has also been discovered. Dove was also looked upon as a sacred bird. Demons or semi-gods are suggested from figures fighting with animals. Sun was regarded as one of the greatest gods. Depositing of votive-figures of animals and human beings in shrines seems to have the aim of ensuring the favourable attention of the God or Goddess. People believed in magic and superstitions also and wore amulets for some protection, etc. A bronze figure of a dancing-girl has also been found suggesting ritual dancing in the temples. Excavations also suggest burial as one of the ways of disposing of the dead, though generally people cremated the dead.

Thus, all available evidence suggests that many of the features of modern Indian cults are derived from very ancient sources. In the Indus civilisation we find worship of the Sakti, Shiva and his consort, worship of the animals like the tiger, the bull, the goat and the snake and also the worship of trees like the Pipal and the Neem. But one kind of worship namely of the horned deity was original to these people and the same is true of the man-bull. These occur, however, in the contemporary Sumerian civilisation. It is also suggested that four-armed deities anticipate Gods like Brahma and Vishnu, while the standing deities suggest Jain Yogis in the posture of yoga known as Kayatsarga. If so, Jainism and Shaivism must be ranked as two of the oldest religions and may bridge the gulf between the Indus and subsequent Indian civilisations.

Dress and Ornaments

The dress on the clay figurines may be taken as the normal attire of the female population. These figures are bare to the waist and wear only a very scanty skirt. The skirt is held by a girdle that seems to be made either of beads or of bands of woven material secured in front by a brooch or fastening of some kind. One figure wears a cloak wrapped about the upper part of the body. There are also head-dresses probably made of stiffened cotton cloth. A very curious tight collar which gives an appearance of greater length to the neck is worn by a few of the figurines. It is difficult to know what dress was worn by men.

The male figures are generally nude. Probably a robe with

or without embroidery was worn over the left shoulder and under the right arm. The figure of a man on a sherd found at Harappa might be wearing breeches or, alternatively, a close-clinging dhoti. No footwear is to be found. Cotton was used but no proof is available of the use of linen and wool.

The people seem to have been fond of jewellery and hair-dressing. Various types of jewellery have been unearthed, both of stones and of gold and silver, etc. Men had varied styles of hair-dressing, for example, one wears his hair parted in the middle and the short locks at the back of the head are kept tidy by a woven fillet. Some statues show it closely gathered up in a bun with hair first plaited. Others show hair coiled in a ring on the top of the head and in similar rings concealing the ears. Curling hairs are also found. Beards were also trimmed in various fashions.

The metal ornaments were made of gold, electrum, silver, copper and bronze. Stones used were like lapis lazuli, turquoise, jadeite, carnelian besides riband-jasper, agate, onyx, amazonstone, heliotrope, plasma, tachylite, chalcedony, nephefine sodalite, shell, pottery, faience, vitreous paste, quartz, breceia, serpentine and haematite. The ornaments are girdles, necklaces, bracelets, pectorals, beads, canes, ear-rings, nose rings, finger-rings, anklets, bangles, hair-pins and bracelets.

Customs and Amusements

Combs were also used. Buttons are comman, mirrors were used, as also rouge and some black substance for the eyes. Some paints were used and powder also to whiten the face. Minute razors were also employed by both the sexes for depilatory purposes. Not only the people loved fashion and jewellery, but evidence is also forthcoming of their love of children as innumerble toys have come to light, such as miniature household articles, clay whistles, marbles, gamesmen, animals with wagging heads, two-wheeled carts drawn by humped oxen, dice and musical instruments. They also indulged in gambling. A game was played resembling the ancient Egyptian game of Sent. This was the board game in which men were moved on the boards and dice was used. The board probably consisted of twenty-six compartments, arranged with twelve in three rows at one end, twelve in two rows at the other, and two between. Games were also played with pebbles or beans. Dancing was also popular. Among musical instruments have been found the drum, tambourine, castanets, harps and lyres. The peaple were flesh eaters, fond of hunting and fishing. Boar was also hunted. Possibly gamecock fighting was a sport. Partridge was also trained to fight, it is assumed. To eat their food people probably sat on mats round their dishes. Chairs and tables have also been identified. Spoons and cups have also been discovered.

The country was supplied with fruits also. Colonel Sewell has suggested that powdered horns were used for medicinal purposes. Silajit, a specific for various diseases of spleen, liver and stomach, has also been found. In short, the people were well advanced from the points of view of manners, customs and amusements.

Art and Crafts

The people of the Indus Valley had a large variety of pottery, both decorated and plain. Practically all the ornamented wares are coated with opaque, red slip, upon which various designs and motifs are painted with a thick black pigment. The most popular design is composed of a series of intersecting circles. Figures of trees, animals and birds also occur. There is nothing primitive about the pottery for the shapes are varied and the technique advanced.

Pottery was used as jars, cess-pits, for storage purposes of various kinds, for drinking and keeping ornaments. In fact the utilitarian aspect, the dominant feature of their architecture is also evidenced in their pottery. Clay was used for the pottery. Pottery, drain pipes, wheels, spindle whorls, bracelets and images have also been found. Copper was variously used and hence this civilisation has also been called Chalcolithic preceding the Iron Age. No worked stone tools or implements have been found beyond simple ribbon flakes of flint and some ploughshares. The drill has also been discovered. The steatite statue is a creditable piece of sculpture.

The seal-amulets are, however, the most successful artistic achievement of the inhabitants of the Indus Valley. These amulets made of steatite range in size from half an inch to just over two and a half inches square. There are two main types, the first, square with a carved animal and an inscription, the second, rectangular with an inscription only. Animals are beautifully portrayed and various scenes are beautifully depicted. Human and animal figures are executed with skill. Use of glaze has also been found, objects of extraordinary fine workmanship made in faience and vitreous paste have been unearthed, among them two monkeys are very remarkable. Ivory has been also found used in vases. Gold needles have been discovered, probably employed in embroidery. Very few agricultural implements have survived. Cherts, flakes, blades are some of these.

Agriculture must have been one of the chief industries for many large cities had to be supplied with food. Cotton, wheat, barley, melons and dates were cultivated. Boat-building was also one of the crafts. The country seems to have depended upon flood for irrigation. Copper, bronze and nickel were mixed together for making tools and utensils. Iron has not been found. Tin was also used. Among the tools and weapons mention may be made of blade-axes, adzes, swords, spear-blades, daggers, arrow-heads, chisels, and fish-hooks. Stone mace-head and saddle querus have also been found. Utensils discovered so far are dishes, palettes, spoons, etc. besides, weights, measures, pedestals, candle-stick and shells.

Such was the civilisation of the Indus valley as gleaned from the remains so far discovered. This study raises several interesting problems that have still to be answered by the historians.

For instance, nothing is absolutely certain about the origin of civilisation. It is said that the development of this civilisation was part of a larger movement which manifested itself in the growth of similar early civilisation, in the Chalcolithic Age along the broad Afrasian belt upto Western Persia and Mesopotamia, as the offspring of the great rivers, the Nile in Egypt, the Euphrates and Tigris in Mesopotamia, the Karun and the Karkheh in Western Persia and the Helmand in Seistan. The common features of these civilisations are the art of spinning and weaving, painted pottery and in some places use of pictographic scripts. The specifically Indian features are the use of cotton, higher standard of life and culture as seen in proper sanitatian, hygiene, commodious houses, baths and high level of achievement in art more specially in the faience models and engravings. Religion also is of an advanced character and resembles our own in many ways. According to Radha Kumud Mookerji, the Indus Valley civilisation is not closely connected with, nor has barrowed much from the Mesopotamian civilisation and he quotes the opinion of Beck in support of his views. He also says, 'opinion is gaining ground that the Indus civilisation was the earliest civilisation in the world'.

There is also the question of linkage with the Aryan civilisation. Most of the European scholars prefer to treat this civilisation as very distinct from the Aryan civilisation. They also date it before the Rig-Vedic civilisation and do not find a trace of it in our literature.

According to Professor Radha Kumud Mookerji the references in the Rig-Veda about the non-Aryans may be taken to be for the Indus Valley. He quotes the inscription of Hittite capital of the fifteenth century B.C., as establishing the fact that the Aryan civilisation must have originated earlier to have its culture migrate from India to Mesopotamia. The oldness of the Sanskrit language as compared to the Brahmi script which is derived from the Indus Script is a further proof of the prior origin of the Rig-Vedic civilisation. The Rig-Veda also mentions significant characteristics of non-Aryan culture recalling and resembling those of the Indus. Thus, the non-Aryan is described as speaking a strange language, not following Vedic rituals, Gods, devotions, sacrifices but following his own system. It was said that he was a phalus worshipper.

Also, according to Dr. Mookerji there is nothing in this description which goes against its identification with the Indus culture. As regards the material aspects of non-Aryan civilisation, the Rig-Veda refers to towns and forts, broad and wide, full of kine, of 100 pillars built of stone, to autumnal forts as refuge against inundation's and to 100 cities in a non-Aryan Kingdom. Even Indra is designated as Purandara 'Sacker of cities'. The Rig-Veda also refers to a mercantile people calling them Panis. Some racial characteristics of the non-Aryans mentioned in the Rig-Veda are found in the skulls discovered in these cities. Horses were not domesticated by the Indus people but most of their animals are known to the people of the Rig-Veda. So also about the ornaments, jewels and metals which as found in these places were known to the Aryans. The Rig-Veda knows of some kinds of armour not known to the people of the Indus Valley. Cotton was well known to the Vedic people.

Thus the Rig-Veda shows wide acquaintance with the non-Aryan world, its conditions of life and culture. Hence some historians opine that the Rig-Vedic civilisation was at least contemporary with the Indus civilisation if not prior and preceding it. Research is still necessary to establish the racial origin of these people and their relationship with the Rig-Vedic civilisation. It cannot be just now accepted that the Aryan civilisation is the sole foundation of all subsequent civilisations in India. There are striking differences between the two, for instance, the absence of iron and horse in the Indus Valley civilisation, the Vedic People being more rural, the Indus Valley people being more urban and mercantile, the Aryans more developed religiously than the Indus people.

4

THE VEDIC CULTURE

NO CONTEMPORARY ARYAN monuments, no historical records have survived to make the Aryan habitation in India tangible to us. Inspite of this, a vast archaic literature has been handed down, which faithfully preserves the ideas and ideals of those far-of-times. That vast literature is the Aryan legacy to India. That literature depicts the varied ideals and practices of the Aryans and show how deep-rooted our culture has been and how continuous, for our ideals down to this day have continued to be broad based on the Aryan cultural heritage so wonderfully preserved.

European scholars have been trying to prove that the Aryans came to India from outside and their guesses have extended to all sorts of places like Scandinavia, Austria, Czechoslovakia, Russia, Turkey, Central Asia and Armenia. But any of these places cannot yet be said to be really the homeland of the Aryans. We are still in the realm of speculation and are likely to remain so.

As for the chronology of the Aryan civilisation in India, we have one discovery in Asia Minor which establishes the hoary antiquity of the Vedic culture. An archaeological signpost has been discovered near Ankara, the present Turkish capital. The little village of Bohgazkeui marks the site of the one time capital of the powerful Hattite Kingdom which came into prominence in the twentieth century B.C.

Here two Hittite inscriptions record a victory of the Hittite over their southern neighbours the Mitanis, and mention a royal marriage to cement the peace treaty between the two nations. Five Aryan deities are invoked as witnesses of contract. They are: Indra, Varuna, Mitra and the Asvins under the name of Nasatya. Since this victory is definitely known to have taken place about 1400 BC it is clear that the Aryan gods were being worshipped in Asia Minor at that date. This fact can either mean that the Aryans were on their trek of India from some upland in the north or the Indo-Aryan culture had already expanded from India as far as Asia Minor. Either way it is obvious that the Aryan civilisation takes no back us remote ages.

This earliest period is the most brilliant and creative in the world of the spirit. Indeed whatever efforts in the same sphere India made in the subsequent epochs have, all of them, been inspired by the truths that had come to the intuitive vision of her early seers. The wisdom of these seers finds embodiment in the Vedas, the main records of the Aryans or Aryas. (The term Árya which seems originally to have meant merely 'Kinsman', was understood in later times to imply nobility or respectability of birth, as contrasted with Anarya 'ignoble').

Nature of the Vedas

What is the Veda ? No logically correct definition can be given. Veda means firstly knowledge (from the root Vid 'to know'); secondly, the term denotes works containing the knowledge, the most sacred knowledge whose authority is not to be questioned and are the last tribunal in matters of dispute, whether in religion, or philosophy, or social customs. To Some, Veda also means revelations made to our seers by the Supreme.

Generally speaking, Sanskrit literature may be classed under two broad division : Vedic literature, and post-Vedic literature. To the latter belong the codes of law by Manu and others, the epics, classical literature, philosophical works, commentaries and manuals. Vedic literature, may be divided into three : the Mantra (the Samhita), the Brahmans and the Sutras.

A distinction is also made between Sruti and Smriti. Mantras and Brahmans are called Srutis, while the Sutras are called Smriti's. The Sruti is what is heard. It is revealed scripture, not composed by any human authors. The Smriti's are the traditional works of human origin, based on the Srutis.

To the first or Samhita period belong the four Samhitas or the four Vedas, The Rig-Veda, the Sama-Veda, the Yajur-Veda and the Atharva-Veda. Of these the Rig-Veda is the oldest and most important. It is said originally there were only three Vedas, the Trayi, the Atharva was added later to the triad.

The Rig-Veda is a compilation composed of several books. It is said that the different hymns ((Mantras) were composed long before they were brought together and arranged systematically. There are two ways of dividing the content of the Rig-Veda, one into ashtaks, adhyayas and vargas, and the other into mandals, anuvaks and suktas. The Rig-Veda is divided into eight ashtaks, each ashtak consists of eight adhyayas and these into several vargas. A varga is usually made up of five riks or verses, sometimes more, sometimes less. Or it is divided into ten mandals. Each mandal contains five or more anuvaks and each anuvak contains a number of suktas (hymns) and each sukta is made up of a number of verses. Every sukta has a rishi, a deity and a metre. The mandals are each ascribed to a rishi or one family or rishis (seers). Thus, the rishi of the third mandal is Vishwamitra.

The Sam-Veda has many verses taken from the Rig-Veda. The Sama-Veda consists of two parts, the first part consists of six lessons, each of which contains ten decades of stanzas except the last. The second also consists of several sections. The hymns are also set to music and are called gans. The Yajur-Veda is solely meant for purposes of the sacrificial ritual. It is twofold, shukla (white or pure) and krishna (dark or hidden). Perhaps shukla means that this part is pure, free from the mixture of the Brahmans as opposed to the krishna Yajur-Veda which is a mixture.

The shukla part is divided into forty adhyayas each of which is again divided into short sections. The krishna part is divided into seven ashtaks or kandas containing from five to eight lectures, which are sub-divided into anuvaks.

The Atharva-Veda is divided into twenty kandas, each kanda is divided into several anuvaks, and anuvak contains a number of sutras. The Atharva-Veda gives us an insight into the habits and customs of the masses in general and also contains magical formulas and charms.

Vedic Literature

To the Vedas are attached Brahmans. The Brahmans are liturgical in character. All the trifling details of the sacrificial ceremonial are minutely treated and fantastic etymologies of words are given. So Brahmans are explanations of the Vedic mantras. They are prose works while the Vedas are poetic works. They are called Brahmans probably because they are written for the priest, by the priest and as works relating to Brahman. Several Brahmans have as their concluding portions, the Aryankas and the Upanishads.

The Aryankas and Upanishads are distinct categories of Vedic literature. The Aryankas are so-called perhaps because they were works to be read in the forest in contra-distinction to the regular Brahmans which were to be read in the village.

The Aryankas contain explanations of the rituals embodied in Brahmans and also allegorical speculations thereon.

The Upanishads are philosophical works. They are also called the Vedanta perhaps because they form the closing part of the Vedic Canon or because they contain the highest and ultimate goal of the Vedas as they deal with questions of salvation and supreme bliss. The word Upanishad originally meant a 'sitting, confidential secret sitting' and then a 'secret teaching, secret doctrine'. There are ten principal or major Upanishads known as Brihadranyaka, Aittareya, Chhandogya, Taittirya, Isa, Kena, Katha, Prasna, Mundaka and Mandukya.

'What is this world?' 'Who am I?' 'What becomes of me after death?' such questions are asked and boldly answered in these Upanishads.

The Sutra works form the connecting link between the Vedic and the post-Vedic literatures. The style of these works is very peculiar and stands unrivalled in the history of all the literatures of the world. A Sutra means an aphorism, a sentence highly artificial, enigmatic and as brief as possible. The Sutras were invented so that it may become easier to memorise the vast Vedic literature. The most important Sutras are the six

Vedangas known as pronunciation, metre, grammar, astronomy, etymology and ceremonial. Thus, the Sutras explain the pronunciation, grammar, metre, etymology and rituals of the Vedas. There are also the Grihyasutras and Samyachariksutras. The first deals with ceremonies performed by the married householders and the second deals with rules to be observed by the rising generation regulating the various relations of everyday life.

Content of the Vedas

The study of the Vedas is essential to the Indian student of the present day for many reasons. Firstly, it is the sole means of knowing the history of the early Aryans. In the Vedas we are face to face with our ancestors, we see how they lived, how they spoke, how they thought and what their ideals were. Secondly, the Indian mind is the same in many respects, whether in Vedic Age or in the present day. If it be asked what that unifying principle is which runs through all the several aspects of Indian life and temperament, we reply, it is the influence of the Veda and the Vedic Age, which has permeated all strata of Indians and which is seen in every little act of ours. Whether it be religion, or philosophy, or morals, literature or social habits, we detect its influence everywhere. Our religious ceremonies are based on those of the Vedas. Our books quote the authority of the Vedas for their basis and authenticity.

Thirdly, it is essential for a student of the world history to study the Vedas. To quote Max Muller, 'In the history of the world the Veda fills a gap which no literary work in any other language could fill. It carries us back to times of which we have no records anywhere and gives us the very words of a generation of men of whom otherwise we could form but the vaguest estimate'. Fourthly, the study of the Vedas has given us the science of language or Philology. 'No single circumstance more powerfully aided the onward movement (of study of languages) than the introduction of the Western scholars to Sanskrit, the ancient and sacred dialect of India. Its exceeding age, its remarkable conservation of primitive material and forms, its unequalled transparency of structure give it an indisputable right to the first place among the tongues of the

Indo-European family. Upon their comparison, already fruitfully begun, it cast a new and welcome light, displaying clearly their hitherto obscure relations, rectifying their doubtful etymologies, illustrating the laws of research which must be followed in their study, and in that of all other languages,'* 'The Devanagri alphabet is a splendid monument of phonological accuracy'. says Sayce in The Science of Language. For all these reasons the study of the Vedas is essential for the understanding of the basis of our culture.

In the Vedas we come across the outpourings of a young, adventurous and joyous race that gloried in strength and splendour and was not afflicted with pessimism or the malaise of a sophisticated era. The gods are greeted like parents and frank requests are addressed :

'O' Gods, 'May we hear with our ears words that are auspicious O Gods, worthy of our offerings, may we see with our eyes sights that are auspicious, with firm limbs and bodies, and singing your praises, may we attain the God given length of life'. There is also in the Vedas, daring spirit of enquiry. In the Rig-Veda occur these remarkable lines :

'He whose shadow is immortality as well as death, that unknown divinity, who is the supreme let us worship'.

Thus, the Vedas reveal an advanced civilisation and culture. For our purposes we may study them under the heads of social and economic institutions, education, religion and philosophy.

Social and Economic Conditions

Rig-Vedic society was well-organised. The unit of life was the family based on the headship of the male that is the patriarchal type of family. Indiscriminate marriages were tabooed. Sexual morality was very high. Child marriage was unknown. There was dowry system but the girls and wives were respected and occupied an honoured place in the household. The wife participated in religious functions and there are references even of a widow-remarriage when the husband had died without an issue. The right of property was

* Whitney, *Language and its study*, p. 4.

VEDIC LITERATURE

Vedas	Schools	Samhitas	Brahmans	Aranyakas	Upanisads	Kalpa Sutras
Rig Veda	Attareytns	Riksamhita	Aitareya	Aitareya	Aitareya	Asvalayana
	Kaushitakins		Kaushitaki	Kaushitaki	Kaushitaki	Sankhayana
Yajur Veda	Kathakas	Kathaka		Taittiriya	Taittiriya	Kathaka-Grihya
	Taittriyas	Taittiriya	Kathaka		Mahanarayana	Baudhayana
	Maitrayaniyas				Svetasvatara	Apastamba
	Kapishtalakathas	Maitrayani	Taittiriya			Hiranyakesi
	Madhyandinas	Kapishtala		Vajasaneyi	Brihadaranyaka	Manava
	Kanvas	Madh.Vajasaneyi	Satapatha	Vajasaneyi	Brihadaranyaka	Manava
		Kanviya Vaj		Kanviya	Isa	Eatyayana
Sama Veda	Tandins	Kauthuma-	Tandya			Latyayana
	Talvakaras	Ranayaniya	Shadvimsa		Chhandogya	Gobhila
		Jaiminiya	Jaiminiya	Nil		Khadira
			Talavakara			Samavidhana
						Brahamana
					Kena	Jaiminiya
Atharva Veda	Atharvanas				Mundaka	Kausika
		Nil	Nil	Nil	Prasna	Vitana-Srauta
					Mandukya	

known. The inheritance went to the male child unless the daughter was the only issue.

Economic life centered round the cattle. In the work of ploughing and that of drawing carts, bulls and oxen were used. Horses pulled the chariots and were also employed in racing. Other domesticated animals were sheep, goats, asses and dogs. The cattle grazed on pastures under a herdsman called gopala. Thus great importance was attached to agriculture. For irrigation purposes there were the wells with water drawn out by means of a bucket tied to leather strings pulled round a stone-pulley. The water, then was led into broad channels for irrigation. Wealth was counted in cattle, in heroes, in horses and in 'good sons'.

Hunting was also common both for livelihood and for sport. In the handicrafts, carpentry was foremost. The carpenter made the implements for war, for agriculture and for sport.

Then there was the worker in metal, and other materials, making vessels, fashioning ornaments, designing articles of leather and weaving cloths.

As far trade and money, we find the Vanik, the trader in the Vedas. Barter system was in vogue. Contracts and haggling were known. Indebtedness was also there. There are also references to sea-borne trade. As for the dress it consisted of an under-garment (nivi), a garment, and an over-garment called adhivasa. It was generally woven of sheep's wool. Embroidered garments were also used. Ornaments were in use like necklaces, ear-rings, bracelets, anklets, jewels and garlands. The hair was combed and oiled and plaited, specially by women. Beard and shaving are also mentioned.

Milk and its products were the most important articles of food. There is a mention of 'mess of grain cooked with milk' and of a kind of cheese. Cake of rice or barley was eaten mixed with ghee. Meat was also used in the sacrifice, animals like sheep and goats were killed. The cow was not to be killed. Liquor was not to be taken. It is not clear what Soma-Rasa meant though it is thought that it is a symbol of bliss that comes from contact with Divinity.

Among the sports and amusements there were the chariot-racing, horse-racing, dicing, dancing and music. Dancing was indulged in by both the sexes. There were musical instruments like the drum (dundubhi), lute (karkari), harp (vina) and the flute (nadi). There was monarchy but people's assemblies were also there, called the sabha and the samiti. We have also references to system of Justice and to the wards for defence and conquests.

Learning and Education

The Vedic civilisation was based on plain living and high thinking. Life was simple but the thoughts touched the highest peaks yet reached by man's imagination.

Students were taught at the home of teacher where he taught the particular sacred texts for which he was responsible. The texts were, in the first instance, learnt by rote, enunciation and pronunciation being particularly taken care of. In education emphasis was laid on Tapas, practice of austerities for the sake of self realisation. Thus were produced the Muni (of divine afflatus), the Vipra (the inspired singer) or Manishi (comprehending all knowledge) concentration and intuition led to profound enlightenment.

Philosophy and Religion

In religion we have worship of the Supreme and also of the various deities, both males and females as expressions of different aspects of the Supreme. We come across gods like Dyaus (sky), Prithivi (earth), Varuna (the sky-god proper), Indra (the God of rains), the Sun worshipped in five forms, namely, Surya, Savitri, Mitra, Pushan and Vishnu, Savitri representing the quickening power of the Sun, Mitra associated with Varuna, Pushan symbolising the power of the Sun in its effects on vegetable life and Vishnu representing the swift moving Sun. Other gods were the Rudra (storm god), the two Asvins (morning and evening star), the Maruts (attendants of Rudra), Vayu (wind), Vata (the wind gods), Ushas (the goddess of dawn), Agni (god of fire), Soma (daughter of immortality) and Parjanya (the god of rain, waters and rivers).

The European scholars see in these gods the Aryan worship of phenomena of nature. It is however, more pertinent to think of them as symbols of powers or various expressions of one God.

The Rig-Vedic religion consisted principally in worship being offered to the gods whose favours or boons are solicited by the performance of prescribed sacrifices. Many ceremonies and rituals had developed and necessarily therefore, arose a class of priests. There was also the worship of Sakti (power), the germ of Tantric system in the Rig-Veda.

In Philosophy, the Aryans reached a stage which is yet to be surpassed. In their intuitive Imaginings, in their visions and thoughts they discovered the supreme reality and showed a breadth of vision, a spirit of toleration and fearlessness unmatched in the history of speculation. Their spirit of adventure knew no bounds. The Vedas reveal the visible universe being unfolded from a finer invisible form, to which it is destined again to go back— thus giving us the theories of evolution and involution, the universe coming out and going back in an endless procession of revolving cycles. In the tenth mandala of the Rig-Veda we have the solemn searching of the soul, seekings of answers to profound questions about the origin and nature of universe, the mysteries of life and death, the relation of human beings to the Eternal.

One hymn names the Universal Being as Purusha and to this may be traced the conception of the many armed, many-eyed gods represented in the Hindu art. We have sentences like, 'Then there was neither death nor deathlessness. Nor was there the knowledge of the distinction between night and day. That One, the source of light, existed without the motion of life. It existed, united as one with its power. Other than it, there was nothing'.*

Interpretation of the Vedas

The various hymns of the Vedas have been variously interpreted. There is the literal interpretation of Yaska and Sayana who studied the language and grammar and emphasised the theological point of view. The Vedas mainly

* Nasadiya Sukta of the *Rig-Veda.*

dealt with ritual, detailing religious ceremonies woven round gods and sacrifice (Yajna). Taking their cue from them, we have the European interpreters a long line of them, specially, the Germans like Rosen, Rath, Weber, Maxmuller, Ludwig, Grassmann, Pischel and Geldner, Oldenberg, besides the English scholars like Wilkins, Colebrooke and Muir. In fact, it would not be wrong to say that the Europeans discovered the Vedas to the modern Indians. The European scholars adopt mainly the literal interpretation and have described the Vedic religion as nature worship, found the origin of the caste system, discovered the affinities of the Indians with the Persians, Greeks and Romans, painted the mutual relations of Brahmans and Kshatriyas and depicted Indian Mythology, society and life from their study of the Vedas. This literal interpretation has given to us the Karma-kanda theory emphasised by the Mimamsakas, according to which the main purpose of the Vedas is to denote some Karma or rite and, therefore, all those portions which do not explicitly speak of rituals should be considered as redundant or figurative.

Then there is the Jnanakanda school according to which the Vedas deal principally 'with the knowledge of the transcendental reality, the really real the realisation of which alone can dispel the ignorance that leads man to bondage and misery'. Attempts have been made to combine the two interpretations and especially to see a esoteric significance in the Vedic hymns. The hymns embody a hidden meaning which only the seers and the yogis are qualified in discovering. Rishi Dayanand of Arya Samaj laid emphasis on such a view and in our own day this view finds expression in the writings of Sri Aurobindo. He observes in The Human Cycle 'if we look at the beginning of Indian society, the far-off Vedic age which we no longer understand, for we have lost that mentality, we see that everything is symbolic. The religious institution of sacrifice governs the whole society and all its hours and moments, and the ritual of the sacrifice is at every turn and in every detail, mystically symbolic. The theory that there was nothing in the sacrifice except a propitiation of Nature gods for the gaining of worldly prosperity and of paradise, is a misunderstanding by a later humanity which had already become profoundly affected by an intellectual and practical bent of mind, practical even in its religion and even in its own mysticism and symbolism, and, therefore, could no longer enter into the ancient spirit ..'....

Take the hymn of the Rig-Veda which is supposed to be a marriage hymn for the union of a human couple and was certainly used as such in the later Vedic ages. Yet the whole sense of the hymn turns about the successive marriages of the Sun, with different gods and the human marriage is quite a subordinate matter overshadowed and governed entirely by the divine and mystic figure and is spoken of in the terms of that figure .... or let us take .... the Vedic institution of the four fold order, Chaturvarna.... This appears in the Purusha-Sukta of the Veḍa where the four orders are described as having sprung from the body of the creative Deity, from his head, arms, thighs and feet. To us this is merely a poetical image and its sense is that the Brahmans were the men of knowledge, the Kshatriyas the men of power, the Vaishyas the producer and support of society, the Shudras its servants. As if that were all ... to us poetry is a revel of intellect and fancy .... the nautch-girl of the mind but to the men of old the poet was a revealer of hidden truths... The image was to these seers a relative symbol of the unrevealed... To them this symbol of the Creator's body was more than an image, it expressed a divine reality. Human Society was for them an attempt to express in life the cosmic Purusha who has expressed himself otherwise in the material and the supra-physical universe.*

Vedas as the basis of our Culture and Philosophy

According to P.M. Oursel, H.W. Grabawska and P. Stern, Joint authors of Ancient India and Indian Civilisation, 'In the magic of the Atharva Veda and the verses of the Rig-Veda we have the whole of the origins of the Aryan religion of India. All that Brahmanism afterwards claimed to be was the inheritance of the Vedic tradition, certainly it was the exploitation of it'.**

---

* Sri Aurobindo, *Human Cycle*, pp. 4-7.

** P.M. Oursel *et.al.*, Ancient India and Indian Civilization, pp. 129-30.

To quote Swami Sharvananda in the Cultural Heritage of India, 'A Hindu is taught by tradition and belief to trace the original source of his cultural life to the dim pre-historic past of the Vedic Age. The Vedas are held to be divine truths revealed from time to time to the rishis in their supra-normal consciousness'.* He further writes to say that all subsequent developments in Indian thought whether in the realms of religion, philosophy, ritualistic practices, civic conducts, social relations, the Itihas, law and arts are to be traced to the Vedas. The whole life of a Hindu from the conception upto the last rites on the funeral pyre has to be sanctified by the recitation of Vedic mantras.

The philosophy of the Vedas was very synthetical and all-embracing. In the words of Sri Aurobindo, 'The One existence to whom sages gave different names of the Veda, the one without a second of the Upanishads, is the fundamental seeing of Indian spirituality this is the first idea of the religious mind of India'.

'The second idea is the manifold way of man's approach to the Eternal and Infinite. All cosmic powers and manifestations are of the one and behind the working of Nature are to be seen and adored powers, names, personalities which are the god heads of the One God head .'..... 'He creates and is Brahma, preserves and is Vishnu, destroys or takes to himself and is Rudra or Shiva'. 'But also there is a third idea of strongest consequence, that only through aspects of the universal spirit and all inner and outer nature can the Divine be approached, but each individual object and being is in its spiritual being ultimately one with the one divine Existence. In each individual man is the divinity, Narayana; all corporate or collective being is a form of the divine Narayana. God is in ourselves and in ourselves we have to find him'. 'To see the supreme altogether and in all. ways and grow to be at one with him, that is the eternal religion, *esha dharmah Sanatanah*'.* The Vedas have given us the living words that still form the basis of our culture *Satyam Jnanam Anantam Brahma* : Brahma is truth, Brahma is wisdom, Brahma is infinite.

* Cultural Heritage of India, Vol. I, p. 1.

In all departments of life, whether religion, philosophy, politics, language or education, they have left abiding monuments, specifically, the Aryan Heritage contains the following features : In the first place this heritage has given us the rich ideas associated with the concept of spirituality. Their conception of spirituality has been positive and integral.* Their was not creed of world shunning philosophers. They visioned God in all, animate or inanimate. They emphasised physical, vital, mental and material perfection because in these also we had to manifest the best, the divine, in us. They exhorted us to transcend our outer, ignorant personality, to find the base of action in the soul or spirit and to attune ourselves to Divinity, to God who was omnipresent.

Secondly, this richer spirituality urged them to seek perfection in all arts, specially to systematise all branches of science and arts so that their inner and outer harmony may be fully brought out. Because of this urge for balance, order and harmony their literary and artistic creations give us a synthetical outlook, refreshing approach and a constructive imagination which has nothing of ludicrousness, exaggeration and sensuousness. Thirdly, they have given us the Varnashrama Dharma, what is now known as the caste system. The economic basis of this system is too obvious to need discussion but it must be emphasised that it had a spiritual basis also to which we have made a reference in the foregoing pages. Again, the social system was not based on any narrow ideology. All castes had their honorable place in society. Women also occupied a distinguished place not only in the family but also in the public, freely participating in ceremonial functions and public debates.

Fourthly, the spiritual motive was continuously stressed and from the very commencement of life, people were initiated into the religious spirit which was then predominating. Hence, education was imparted in Ashrams where love, duty and instruction were so dovetailed into each other that an integrated personality emerged. The Gurus also provided guidance to the kings in their problems both of life and of administration.

---

* Sri Aurobindo, 'Defence of Indian Culture', *The Arya*, Vol. VI, Chapter VII.

Fifthly, the Aryans have left for us a wonderful literature which has not been fully understood even by now so that commentaries and explanations are galore and continue to be out down to this day. From this copious literature we have got the ideas which form the warp and woof of our culture.

Sixthly, the Aryans have left psychological discoveries so rich in their contents that in comparison the modern systems of psycho-analysis pale into insignificance. They discovered that behind the outward physical vital, and mental sheaths, there were the subtle physical, vital and mental sheaths. Behind all these there was the soul or the spirit and even in this region before we could reach Divinity we had a number of planes like the (Anand) 'bliss Purusha and the Vijnana (super-mental) Purusha or planes of consciousness'. There was concealed behind the Vedic hymns even richer psychological analysis.

Thus, the Aryan culture was very dynamic and profound. The Aryans went all out, as it were, to plumb all mysteries, nothing could escape their intuitive vision Matter, life, mind and world were analysed, dissected and studied. We boast of our scientific technique but the Aryans, even in the absence of such scientific apparatus, went for daring adventures in all realms. They gave us the Sanskrit language which is regarded as the most perfect and scientific language in the world and has formed the basis of the science of philology. Today once again we need their intuitive insight to solve our problems.

The culture thus revealed shows how much our Indian civilisation is indebted to the Aryans for the bases of our life and thought. The Aryan legacy is thus variegated and multiform. It has given us the norms of arts and philosophy. It has permeated our thoughts and habits and has been so infused in us, become so instinctive, so to say, that we have to make an effort to reanalyse the sources of our life and speculations in the realms of philosophy.

5

POST-VEDIC AND EPIC CULTURE

BY THE TERM later Vedic or post-Vedic civilisation we mean the civilisation or culture revealed in the Vedic works like the Brahmans, the Aranyakas, the Upanishads and the Sutras, while the epic civilisation refers to the culture as gleaned from the Ramayana and the Mahabharata.

In the period of the Rig-Veda, the centre of civilisation was shifting from the west, the land of the famous five rivers in Punjab, to the east, the land between the Sarasvati and the Drishadvati, the home of the Bharatas. By the end of the epic period this civilisation encompasses the whole land of India. Let us first take the post-Vedic culture.

Social System and Economic Life

This period saw the development of the full-fledged caste system due to differentiation of occupations growing in number and variety with the progress of settled life and due also to contact with aborigines raising questions of purity of blood and the colour bar. We may here appropriately discuss the origin and trace the development of the caste system.

The caste system is said to be derived from the Vedic institution of the four-fold order, Chaturvarna. It is said that the institution of the four orders was the result of an economic evolution complicated by political causes. This is a plausible and superficial explanation of the origin of the caste system. The Aryans always looked at the spiritual and psychological aspects of social ideas and institutions.

To the Aryans the symbol of the creation of the four varnas from Brahma's body expressed a divine reality. Human society was for them an attempt to express in life the Cosmic Purusha who has expressed himself otherwise in the material and the supra-physical universe.

From this symbolic attitude came the tendency to make everything in society a sacrament, religious and sacrosanct, but as yet with a large and vigorous freedom in all its forms. Thus, we have first the symbolic idea of the four orders, expressing the Divine as knowledge in man, the Divine as power, the Divine as production, enjoyment, and mutuality, the Divine as service, obedience and work. These divisions answer to four cosmic principles, the wisdom that conceives the order and principle of things, the Power that sanctions, upholds and enforces it, the Harmony that creates the arrangement of its parts, the work that carries out what the rest direct. Next, out of this idea there developed a firm but not yet rigid social order based primarily upon temperament and psychic type (Guna) with a corresponding ethical discipline and secondarily upon the social and economic functions (Karma). But the function was determined by its suitability to the type and its helpfulness to the discipline; it was not the primary and the sole factor. Thus, the primary idea behind the four Varnas is spiritual and religious, the ethical, economic, physical and psychological aspects are secondary.

In the age of the Sutras this primary idea is over-shadowed by the psychological and ethical ideas. Religion becomes a mystic sanction for the ethical motive and discipline, Dharma, becomes its chief social utility. The idea of the direct expression of the Divine Being or Cosmic Principle in man ceases to dominate and in the end disappears even from the theory of life. In this stage we have the idea of social honour; the honour of the Brahman resides in purity, in piety, in a high reverence for the things of the mind and spirit, the honour of the Kshatriya resides in courage, chivalry, strength and nobility of character; the honour of the Vaishya maintains itself by rectitude of dealing, mercantile fidelity, sound production and philanthropy; the honour of the Shudra lies in giving obedience, in subordination, faithful service and a disinterested attachment. But even these ideas remain as ideal and live more in tradition than as a reality of life.

Gradually the emphasis is shifted from the inner to outer or external aspects, the body becomes more important than the person. Thus in the evolution of caste, the outward supports of the ethical four-fold order, birth, economic function, religious, ritual and sacrament, family customs, each began to exaggerate— enormously its proportions and its importance in the scheme. Faculty and capacity (swabhava) gave place to birth as the determinant of the caste of a person, the son of a Brahman, for example, came always to be regarded as Brahman; birth and profession became the double bond and this became hereditary.

Finally, even the economic basis began to disintegrate : birth, family, customs and remnants, deformations, new accrètions of fanciful religious sign and ritual became the riveting links of the system of caste in the iron age of the old society. After the epic period the priest and the Pundit masquerade under the name of the Brahman, the aristocrat and feudal baron under the name of the Kshatriya, the trader and moneygetter under the name of Vaishya, the half fed labourer and economic serf under the name of Shudra. Later on with the break up of the old system, there remains only a name, a shell, a sham and today it must either be dissolved in the crucible of an individualist period of society or else fatally affect with weakness and falsehood the system of life that clings to it.

Thus, the caste system began and developed. Freedom gave place to rigidity, exclusiveness was embraced in preference to catholicity, rules and Conventions were formulated to keep the castes cabined and confined in their particular moulds. In the post-Vedic period we gradually find intermarriages being restricted, change over from one Varna to another becoming rarer and the predominance of the two Varnas becoming established.

In the economic sphere we find a continuous growth and progress. Agriculture and pastoral pursuits recorded great development. For instance, the plough became large and heavy enough to require a team of twenty-four oxen to drag it. Many kinds of grain were grown such as rice, barley, beans and sesamum.

New occupations sprang up and striking developments occurred in the realm of industry. New occupations like fishing, fire-ranging, cloth-washing, butchering, making of jewels and cutting of hair are mentioned in the books.

Architectural skill is indicated in the construction of the Fire-altar with 10,600 bricks and shaped like a large bird with outspread wings. Women also figured in industry. Metal-industry was much advanced.

The Sutras show even a greater social development than the Vedic period but at the same time a rigidity, happily missed in the earlier period. Let us take some notice of the two classes of Sutras, namely, the Grihya Sutras and Dharma Sutras. The Grihya Sutras deal mainly with family, the home life and domestic ceremonies of the individual. They present the whole duty of man as a householder from boyhood to burial, indicating the ceremony marking every important phase of his life. There are ceremonies prescribed before birth, at birth, at the naming of the new born child, at his first feeding with solid food, when his hair is cut, at his initiation into studentship and at his return home from his preception to enter upon the householder's life by marriage.

Eight kinds of marriage are distinguished, viz., (1) Brahma, (2) Prajapatya, (3) Arsha, (4) Daiva, (5) Gandharva, (6) Asura, (7) Rakshasa, (B) Paisacha.

The first four are regarded as lawful and the last two are disapproved. In Brahma marriage, the bride is offered out of free will in Prajapatya, the offer of marriage comes from the wooer in Arsha, the bride's father receives a pair of kine as presents in Daiva, the bridegroom is a sacrificial priest, the Gandharva is love-marriage; in Asura marriage dowry system prevails and is open only to the Vaishyas and Shudras; Rakshasa marriage is effected by abduction with force and fighting and in Paisacha there is secret abduction. Every householder is to perform daily Pancha Mahayajnas, the five great sacrifices : (1) to Brahman in the form of study and teaching, (2) to the ancestors by tarpana (offering of food and water), (3) to the gods by the sacrifice of burnt oblations, (4) to the Bhutas by the offering of the bali, and (5) to the fellow-men by the entertainment of guests. There were also periodical sacrifices. The social system rested on Varnasrama dharma based on caste and Ashrama.

The caste system had become rigid as already described. The rules of Ashrama were also very important. These Ashramas were the four stages through which an individual must pass, viz., these of the Brahmachari or initiated student, the house holder or married state, the recluse (Vanaprastha) and the hermit (the Sanyasi). The Dharma Sutras are a record of social customs and usages and the civil and criminal law was based on them. The customs and usages were not uniform all over India. There was a great difference between the North and the South.

For instance the North would not sanction the Southern custom of marrying the daughter of a maternal uncle or of a paternal aunt while the South abhorred the customs of the North like the trade in arms, dealing in wood and going to sea.

Laws

The source of law was not the sovereign but the Vedas and other scriptures. There was also respect for group and regional laws and conventions. The communities were to legislate for themselves. Trade guilds and corporations enjoyed autonomy. In the civil law there was discussion about taxes and inheritance. In criminal law, the chief crimes treated were assault, adultery and theft. Women were not independent either in respect of sacrifice or of inheritance. The sutras have no liking for town life.

Education and Learning

The period was the golden age of literature no doubt, the outcome of schools remarkable for the efficacy and fruitfulness of their method of teaching. The student was initiated by the ceremony of Upanayana by which he entered a new life, described as a second birth, whence he becomes a dvija, twice-born. In the new life of a Brahmachari the student follows the maxim of simple living and high thinking. His is a strictly regulated life. The aims of learning are faith, retention of knowledge, progeny, wealth, longevity and immortality, thus comprehending both secular and spiritual aims.

The essence of the system was that the student had to take up residence in the home of his teacher. There his main duties were to beg for his teacher, to look after the sacrificial fires and tend the house and also his cattle. Sleeping in day time was forbidden. Begging produced humility, tending fires led to the kindling of the spirit in him, and tending cattle would give the pupil wholesome exercise in open air, training in dairy, farming and other accomplishments. The teacher then initiated him into the various aspects of knowledge.

Besides the domestic schools, there were specialised agencies and discussions in the houses and among the members of the family. There were the wandering scholars, Charakas, who spread education in the country. For advanced studies there were Parishads. Education was also advanced by learned conferences convoked by kings. We have in the Upanishads a reference to a conference called by King Janaka in which Yajnavalkya was the leading figure.

Women freely participated in these conferences. Women like Gargi addressed a congress of philosophers. In the Rig-Veda we have women as composers of hymns. The Kshatriyas also encouraged learning and were in many cases the intellectual leaders of the age.

Education aimed at the highest knowledge, the knowledge of the Atman (soul) or the absolute or self realization. This may be illustrated by the story of Nachiketas in the Katha Upanishad.

Nachiketas was a Brahmin lad who was taught by Yama, the lord of death. The father of Nachiketas performed a great sacrifice, promising to give away, in charity all his possessions. But what he gave-away were his old barren cows and other useless things. Nachiketas, turning to his father, asked, To whom wilt thou give me ?' Angrily came the answer. I shall give thee unto death'. The words once uttered, could not be unsaid and Nachiketas set out for the abode of death. Yama was away and Nachiketas had to wait without getting the usual hospitality. Yama returned and offered three boons as amends.

Nachiketas first asked for his father's forgiveness. Second, he asked instruction in the great fire sacrifice. Finally, he asked,

'There is that doubt when a man is dead, some saying, he is, others, he is not. This I should like to know, taught by thee'. Yama in vain tried to divert him from such a question offering instead great wealth and many sons, etc., Nachiketas replying said, 'These things last till tomorrow, or Death. Even the whole life is short. Keep thou thy horses, keep dance and song for thyself. No man can be made happy by wealth'. Yama was pleased and proceeded to tell the boy about the nature of Brahman–the unborn, eternal, everlasting. Thus did Nachiketas join the wise who, knowing the 'self' as unchanging among changing things do not grieve any more.

Religion and Philosophy

There was a great growth of ceremonial religion and consequently the growth of priesthood. There is, however, no mention of idol-worship. There is only the building of the altar for sacrifice and for the sacred fire. Modern Hindu Gods begin to emerge like Shiva and Vishnu. The Aitareya Upanishad brings up Bhutapati, representing the dread forms of the gods.

The period, however, was most remarkable for the development of philosophy as expressed in the Upanishads. The ten major Upanishads have already been mentioned. Besides them, the Muktika Upanishad gives a further list of about 100 Upanishads.

The Upanishads develop the ideal that are in germs in the Samhitas (the Vedas) and in so doing refine them and make them plain to the reasoning minds of men. The central theme of the Upanishads is to seek unity in the midst of diversity. 'What is that by knowing which everything in this universe is known ?' The answered is found in the conception of God or Brahman as the ultimate cause of the universe. The Atman is co-existing with God. 'The intelligent one is never born nor dies ... it is birthless, eternal, undecayed and ancient'. Soul, Nature and God form the three principal themes of the Upanishads.

In addition to the body, there is a soul distinct from all the organs, from the mind, from the vital force (prana). It is indestructible. After death it goes to different worlds, high and low, according to its past work and knowledge, and may return to this world. We cannot discover the Atman so long as we are in the state of ignorance. When we are no longer prey to our senses, when by self control and restraint we have purified ourselves, then by Concentration and meditation we may realize the Atman which is identical with God. Nature also, like the soul, is held to be without beginning for we cannot trace its exact origin. The Universe proceeded from the Immutable, the Brahman. 'From the Atman identical with Brahman, the ether was produced, from the ether air, from air fire, from fire water, from water earth'. These elements have other properties and all combine in different proportions to produce all bodies and also minds.

God or Brahman of the Upanishad is both personal and impersonal (Sāguna and Nirguna). In the former aspect, 'He is the Lord of all, Omniscient, the internal Ruler, He is the cause of all'. Brahman is the ruler of the universe. He projects it, maintains it and dissolves it at the end. He is termed Ishvara who comprehends all bodies and all minds. In his impersonal aspect, He is devoid of all attributes. He is the eternal witness, He is Satchidanand, absolute bliss. The impersonal God can only be indicated by the negation of all attributes neti, neti and so on.

The dominating characteristic of the Upanishads is the dependence on truth. 'Truth wins ever, not falsehood. With truth is paved the road to the Divine'. The Upanishads have deeply impressed even the Western philosophers. Schopenhauer said 'They are the products of the highest wisdom .... the study of the Upanishads has been the solace of my life, it will be the solace of my death'.

The Upanishads also show that acquisition of wealth and worldly goods was not incompatible with the growth of spirituality in the person concerned. Thus, the people had discovered true harmony. Harmony among parts of nature is emphasised in the Upanishads as a basic necessity in life. But the base of this harmony was the spirit, the highest truth of man. The Upanishads did not deny life but held that the world is a manifestation of the Eternal, of Brahman and all here is Brahman. The statement of the Chhandogya Upanishad *Tatvamasi* (That thou art) and the realisation embodied in the Brihadaranyaka Upanishad *Aham Brahmasmi* (I am Brahman) taken together with other injections embody the humility of the seeker. They also affirm the unity of the human spirit. The mind must perceive that there can be no separateness in the world. Another saying is also apposite :

> 'The supreme spirit is not reached by the weakling nor is it attained by extravagances nor by purposeless or undirected asceticism'.

Upanishads, therefore, are a fitting culmination of the Post-Vedic culture and make explicit what was implicit in the Vedas.

THE AGE OF THE EPICS

The culture depicted in the Ramayana and the Mahabharata belongs to the Epic Age.

India had epic legends even at an early age but it did not produce an epic poem. The Rig-Veda has its akhyans, stories, there are itihas (iti ha asa, i.e. it was so') or legends in the Brahmans, there is a whole literature of Puranas, tales of 'Old days'.

There are few people so fond of listening to the story-teller as Indians were. We have our class of bards, Sutas and Kusilavas, Kathaks and other popular story-reciters. Indian working men wearied with the toil of the day, are capable of spending the whole night seated in a circle round the fire listening attentively to a drama of three thousand years ago.

What has become our national epic is a collection of songs composed in different ages by many authors and refashioned by many editors, but gathered round a nucleus of ancient heroic legend.

The Mahabharata

Mahabharata, the 'Great Epic of the War of the Descendants of Bharata', consists of a central theme, on to which a multitude of subsidiary stories are grafted to illustrate the central theme. The main theme is as follows : Pandu, King of Hastinapur, died prematurely, and his elder brother, Dhritarashtra, who, being blind, had had to cede throne to him, returned to power. His sons, the Kauravas, were reared along with the Pandavas, the sons of Pandu. Discord soon sprang up between the cousins. The excellence of the five Pandavas excited the jealousy of

Duryodhan, the eldest Kaurava and caused them to be driven to the forests. In the forest the brothers moved towards Panchala whose king had to give his daughter Draupadi in marriage and she became the wife of all the Pandavas. The Pandavas go back to part of their inheritance and settled in Indraprastha (Delhi).

Again, Duryodhana enticed Yudhishthira to play at dice and by trickery caused him to lose his Kingdom, his-brothers, his own person, and their wife were cruelly insulted. With the aid of their uncle, the Pandavas escaped and went into exile. At the end of the period of exile they asked for their portion once more, and when their enemies refused it, war began. The Pandavas were helped by Sri Krishna, famous as an Avatara (incarnation of God) who gave a discourse to Arjun, famous as the Gita. In the war the Pandavas emerged victorious. The Kauravas were killed almost to the last man. Dhritarashtra retired to the forests. The Pandavas returned to Hastinapur and ended their days with various fortunes.

The Mahabharata is full of stories and took centuries to be fully edited. The same conclusion is obvious from a study of its poetical structure. The chief epic metre is the Sloka, a stanza of two lines, based on the old anushtubh, which consisted of four hemistichs of eight syllables each, with two iambic at the end of each line. But one finds other metres, all of Vedic origin. There are passages in prose also. The language also fluctuates between that of the Vedas and that of the poetry of the Classical Age (200 B.C. to 400 A.D.).

The Mahabharata is the biggest of the world's epics, said to consist of 1,00,000 slokas or verses. Its heroes find prominent mention in the Indian literature of all ages from the fifth century B.C. onward. Its tales have spread to all parts of the world. It constitutes a veritable treasure-house of Indian lore, both secular and religious, and gives, as does no other single work, an insight into the innermost depths of the soul of the people. It is great as a collection of stories, great as a Kavya or epic-poem describing in magnificent language, the various emotions and events, great as sastra or manual of law and morality, great as a record of social and political philosophy and great as a sacred treatise showing the way to salvation. 'This is the holy mystery,' declares the Santi Parva of the great epic, 'There is nothing nobler than humanity'. The poem is said to have been composed by the great sage Krishna Dvaipayana Vyasa. When the epic began, the centre of civilisation was in the valleys of the Ganga and the Yamuna, where rose flourishing Kingdoms of the Kurus, the Panchalas, the Salvas, the Matsyas and the confederacy of the Yadavas of Mathura. By the end of the epic the Aryan civilisation had extended over the whole of the vast sub-continent named after the illustrious Bharata.

Social and Economic Life

The caste system had become rigid though not so watertight as later. Besides the four varnas there were mixed castes. The fact that Dronacharya refused to teach Ekalavya, a Shudra, shows the rigidity of the caste system. There are, however, passages declaring that there is no distinction of caste. In the Vanaparva qualities of the four varnas are described, for example, the Brahman is one who forsakes wrath and infatuation, speaks the truth, pleases his elders, never injures another, has his sense under control, is virtuous, devoted to studies, teachers and others.

Women were accorded a place of honour. It is said three things do not become impure, 'women, gems and water'. The tales of Savitri, Sakuntala, Damayanti and Tapti illustrate the nobility found in women. Epic heroines received a liberal education in their father's houses and developed into well-taught and clever disputants. Women could choose their own husbands and move out in the public.

Economically also the age registered a great progress. Contacts were widened and trade became India-wide. If legends are to be believed Indians went even across the seas and conquered what is now known as America. Many people have traced close resemblance between the old American Maya civilisation and the ancient Indian civilisation. Besides trade, industries, arts and crafts also flourished and town life came into prominence. People were, on the whole, happy and prosperous.

Philosophy and Religion

In religion we find in greater prominence the worship of

the trinity, Brahma, Vishnu and Shiva, specially the last two. Worship of Krishna and Ram had also come in vogue. The Vedic-gods had become less prominent though we have references to Kuber, Varuna, Prana and Indra. Ritualism or worship of externals in religion had become all important. Taboos of all sorts were coming into existence.

But whether in religion or in philosophy the background continues to be the Vedic Age. Great changes in details, however, continued to take place. New divinities like Skanda and Visakha were introduced. Deification of heroes went apace. The whole cosmos was conceived as a perpetual process of creation and destruction filling eternity with and everlasting rhythm, and the entire scheme is placed under the law of 'Karma' which provides that every individual shall reap the fruits of deeds performed in previous lives. This law can be modified by the grace of the lord if the requisite devotion is forthcoming on the part of the devotee. Thus, the bhakti form of religion was coming into prominence. Bhaktas or devotees have rival gods to love, and divisions appear among them. Separatism was sought to be checked by showing Vishnu and Shiva identical.

The unity of Brahman taught by the Upanishads is re-emphasised and the concept of Trimurti is enunciated. Self restraint, renunciation and vigilance lead one to Brahman, death comes from infatuation and immortality is acquired by truth.

The Ramayana

The Ramayana is an older work though it has also suffered from interpolations. It is a single work, harmoniously constructed and written in a language which bears witness to a high literary and aesthetic culture. Valmiki, the great rishi was its author. The poem is divided into seven books of which the first and the last were composed later on. The story briefly is that pursued by the Jealousy of his stepmother, Ram, eldest son of Dasaratha, king of Ayodhya is exiled for 14 years to the forests and is accompanied by his wife and one brother Lakshman. His wife Sita is carried off by force by Ravana, the king of the Rakshasas (demons), who takes her in a flying chariot to the island of Lanka. Ram starts in pursuit and is aided by the tribe of monkeys whose leaders were Sugriva and Hanuman, Ravana refused to parley with Ram and surrender Sita. War ensues in which Ravana and his tribe are killed almost to a man and Ram returns to Ayodhya having thus rescued Sita.

Social and Economic Conditions

The Ramayana gives a many-sided picture of a perfect life. The Kingdom attained a high level of prosperity. People had a plentiful supply of the good things of life, of horses and cattle and corn and wealth. The various orders of society discharged their proper responsibilities. Agriculturists and traders received special attention. The capital was well-kept, roads spacious, well laid out and regularly watered. Merchants came from various countries. Militarily the state was thoroughly equipped. People were freely and regularly consulted by the powers that be.

Education was so organised that each section of the society knew not merely the details of fulfilling its own special function but also the relative place of its contribution in the general scheme. The royal patronage was extended to all centres of learning.

Every sacrifice was an occasion for making all sections of society meet together, dedicate their skill to the success of the function and receive adequate presents. It was more or less a 'world's fair' or a 'Parliament of religions', of ancient days. The sovereign gave his all in these sacrifices.

Women were considered to be the equals of men in the sense that whatever the husband did for the acquisition of merit or spiritual evolution was to be fully shared in by the wife, who was usually to sit by his side during the ceremonies. Marriage was considered to be a sacred trust.

Religion and Philosophy

As in the Mahabharata so here also we get the same worship, same symbolism and Ritualism. Gods and goddesses like Vishnu, Shiva, Lakshmi and Parvati receive reverence and veneration from their numberless devotees. Bhakti is again emphasised. A moral tone is adopted. Ramayana presents a complete picture of the working of the Indian mind, and it has in turn been responsible for the normal Indian attitude towards life's problems. It may, however, be re-emphasised that the philosophy is as old as the Vedas only the colouring or expressions change. A few sentences are cited.

'O King, common indeed are persons who always speak that which is pleasing but rare indeed is he who will speak that which is not pleasing but good, and rare too is he who will hear it'.

'O noble one, hope is indeed mighty. There is no power mightier than hope. To one possessed of hope there is nothing unattainable in this world'.

To this day the Ramayana, translated into the living languages of modern India, is the favourite book of the Hindus and Rama is the favourite hero. Temples are dedicated to him. The stories of Ramayana have formed the themes of many Indian books of note. In the Northern India the Ramayana by Tulsidas is the standard work and in it we find the essence of wisdom enshrined in the Vedas, Upanishads and the Puranas.

The age of these two grand epics is the age of Dharma. All the human activities depicted therein were inspired by the ancient ideals, although a tendency towards external formation and construction is visible. In this age of Dharma man was a full-fledged mental being—his intellect was keen and capacious and masterful. Great emphasis was laid on the development of morality and virtues. The ethical side of man's nature is given great importance and its fulfilment is sought through the sincere performance of the duties formulated by the ancients. We have an age of heroic action and of an early and finely moral civilisation. But a tendency was visible in which man becomes a prisoner of principles and creeds and sought to clamp the same captivity upon life's free and fluid movements. Nevertheless the Aryan heritage was still finding expression in the Epics.

6

JAINISM AND BUDDHISM

BOTH JAINISM AND Buddhism are regarded as heterodox systems of religion and philosophy, greatly diverging from the main streams of Hindu culture and religion. This view held by many European scholars has been challenged by the Indian school of historians.

In the first place, the Hindu culture has never been a 'closed system'. We have the profound saying that truth is one though sages call it by various names and, therefore, Hindu philosophy has encouraged many branched thoughts and has never cribbed, confined or cabined human imagination and speculation. The fact that 'Mahavira' and 'Buddha' were incorporated in the Hindu pantheon of gods speaks eloquently of the truth of the above proposition.

Secondly, these religions are to be viewed as the off shoots of indigenous culture, of Brahmanism or Vedism. They take their stand on certain aspects of the pre-existing system, which they select and emphasise to the exclusion of other aspects.

Both emphasise asceticism specially in their initial stages of foundation and in this respect they propound nothing new except possibly the phraseology. In the Vedas we have references to the rishi or seer who practised asceticism to gain the real knowledge. The Aranyakas are themselves the products of hermitages, of the forests whether the Upanishads recommend retirement as essential for those who seek the highest knowledge, the knowledge of the Atman. The Smritis emphasise Sannyas as the last phase of a man's life. There are also references about the wandering saints or Yogis. These ascetics organised their own individual schools or orders and as early as the time of Panini (about sixth century B.C.) we know of what were then called the Bhikshu Sutras, the codes of discipline governing the life of these wandering monks and mendicants. Buddha's injunctions to the Bhikshus are to be found here anticipated, for example, his rules about the Bhikshu stationing himself in a fixed retreat during the rains and that the Bhikshu must not store up articles of consumption nor kill life or even seeds.

Again, the precepts of morality advocated by these schools are to be found in the Upanishads. Similarly, the spirit of enquiry and intellectual discussion and debates encouraged by these two schools were nothing new to the post-Vedic times. In the Upanishads we have famous discussion like those initiated by Raja Janaka in which even women participated. Further, contemporary with these two schools there were hundreds of ascetic orders wherein we can find the gems of philosophy and practices of Buddhism and Jainism. There was also the materialistic or atheistic school of Charvak anticipating the doctrines of these two religions in many respects. Ahimsa or respect for life of all kinds was not foreign to the Hindus.

Neither Buddha nor Mahavira claimed to have founded a new religion. Fundamentally in the Vedic philosophy and practice freedom has often warred with ritualism and the cramping effects of creeds and traditionalism. When, therefore, the true seeker found that religion (in the fifth and sixth centuries B.C.) was compromising with life, subjecting its high spirit to the satisfaction of the latter's unspiritual demands and was thereby deteriorating into soulless forms of mere externalia and priestly obscurantism, it was but natural that he should think of nothing else but an ascetic withdrawal from life in order to be able to live the life of freedom, to live in the spirit, in the pure truth of religion. Buddhism and Jainism, therefore, represent an important phase in the spiritual life of India and are not to be regarded as heterodox.

JAINISM

Chronologically Jainism preceded Buddhism. There is a belief that Jainism was founded by Mahavira but the Jains do not give credence to this assumption. According to Appaswami Chakravarti, Jainism is probably as old as the Vedas. In the Rig-Vedic mantras we have clear references to Rishabha and Arishtanemi, two of the Jain Tirthankaras, the former being the founder of Jain dharma of the present age. He also mentions that the story of Rishabha occurs in Vishnupurana and Bhagvatpurana wherein he figures as an avatara (incarnation) of Narayana in an age prior to that of the ten avatars of Vishnu. In the Mahabharata there is a reference to Neminatha who is recognised as the twenty-second Tirthankara by the Jains. Parsvanath, the last but one Tirthankara, is a historical personage anti-dating Mahavira by above 250 years, according to Jain tradition.

Mahavira was the twenty-fourth or the last great Tirthankara (literally meaning ford makers), also called Jinas 'Conqueror' from which Jainism is derived, Parsvanath is said to have founded the order of the Nirgranthas (those without ties) to which the parents of Mahavira were strongly attracted. According to this school one must observe four vows—not to kill (ahimsa), to speak truth (sunrita), not to steal (asteya), and to be chaste (brahmacharya). This pure life is possible because our acts are the result of moral autonomy.

Life of Mahavira

Mahavira, variously known as the Nirgrantha, Jina and Sramana, was born in 599 B.C., according to the Jain tradition. Radha Kumud Mookerjee places his death in the year 546 B.C., and as he lived for seventy-two years his birth date would be 618 B.C. The Cambridge History of India places his death in the year 467 B.C. Mahavira was named Vardhamana and belonged to the Jnatrikas clan of Kundapura near Vaisali, north of Patna. His father Siddhartha bearing the courtesy title of Raja, had married Trisala, the sister of the Raja of the Lichchhavis.

From his early childhood he had a reflective mind. After

undergoing all the education and training usual for princes of the time he realised the transitory nature of the world and became an ascetic at the age of thirty. He practised hard penances and meditations for twelve years in the course of which he had to bear many persecutions at the hands of the ignorant people till, at last, he attained enlightenment.

Thus, in the 13th year he reached Nirvana and became an Arhat, a Jina, and a Kevalin, an omniscient. He then took to a life of wandering and preaching. In his wanderings also he had to suffer much from crawling insects, from bad people, from the attacks of the village-guards and lance-bearers, from domestic temptations, from women and even from other wanderers.

In his wanderings he met Gosala and they lived together for six years. Then they differed and became critics of each other. Gosala then founded Ajvika sect. Thus, already in his life Jainism had begun to split. Mahavira had got powerful royal patronage which caused the spread of his doctrines. Kings and princes like Bimbisara, Ajatasatru and the then Lichchhavi king Chetaka supported him. His influence thus penetrated into distant kingdoms allied to the princes mentioned above. He also got support from the republican governments of the age.

He had a number of great disciples known as the Ganadharas or Apostles of the Jain church, 11 in number, besides other notable disciples.

Mahavira's Teachings

The Jain philosophy might be summed up in one sentence. The living and the non-living, by coming into contact with each other, forge certain energies which bring about birth, death and various experiences of life; this process could be stopped, and the energies already forged destroyed, by a course of discipline leading to salvation. This means seven things. 'Firstly, that there is something called the living; secondly, that there is something called the non-living; thirdly, that the two come into contact with each other; fourthly, that the contact leads to the production of some energies; fifthly, that the process of contact could be stopped; sixthly, that the existing energies could also be exhausted; and lastly, that salvation could be achieved. These seven propositions are called the seven tattvas or realities by the Jain'.*

From the above it is clear that actions should be annihilated or destroyed. One living in a household can do so gradually according to the Jain if he first avoids evil Karmas and gradually ceases from Karma. To equip himself for such a task, the person should observe the five rules or vows of morality, namely, ahimsa, satya, asteya (not to commit theft), brahmacharya and aparigraha (set limit to property). There are also minor vows of morality, for example, a householder should each day feed out of what is cooked for himself such holy persons as may turn up at his house at the proper time. The whole course of conduct is finally divided into stages so that ultimately salvation may be achieved. The line that distinguishes the monk from the layman is the complete abandonment of all worldly possessions and ceasing to dwell under a roof which may be called his own. The monk should walk only by day taking care that he kills no being. In his talks he must not indulge in censure of others or self praise or talk about women. He must so train himself as not to be affected or moved by the objects of the senses. His should withdraw his senses from all objects and with meditation, concentration and reading of the life of Arhats and Siddhas prepare himself for salvation. Salvation, therefore, depends upon right belief, right knowledge and right action which are known as Ratnatraya, the three Jewels.

In this book we have tried to show the deep connection and relationship of our culture with the Vedic traditions. Jainism is no exception to this. Avoidance of evil action and performance of good ones are enjoined in the Upanishads. For example, 'By good action one becomes good and by bad action bad'. Again, the five major vows mentioned above and the emphasis on austerities can he found in the 'Yoga'. 'Yoga supplied the whole of India with the example of a practical method, and the heterodox sects of the sixth century in particular with the prototype of an obstinate will aiming at the liberation of the mind'.

* Hiralal Jain, *Cultural Heritage of India,* vol. I.

After the death of Mahavira schisms began to appear in Jainism. During the Mauryan period especially the cleavage widened and the two sects became rivals, known as the Digambars and the Svetambars, the 'sky clad', that is naked and those wearing clothes 'white-clothed'. During this time some Jains also migrated to the South. Besides these two major sects there are minor ones also.

Jain Canon

(a) The Jain literature written in Ardhamagadhi (an ancient dialect of India) and in Sanskrit or Sauraseni (a dialect of Mathura) may be divided according to the two main schools of Svetambars and Digambars.

The canon of the Svetambars comprises 11 sections (anga), 12 sub-sections (upanga), 10 collections of miscellanies (painna, prakirna), six books of statutes (chhedasutra), four fundamental books (Mulasutra), some unattached texts. The angas contain subjects dealing, for example, with monastic conduct, distinction between true and false faith, edifying stories, problems and solutions.

The Upangas deal with geography, knowledge of the sun and moon, description of the underworld and sermons of Mahavira etc. The Painnas deal with matters of discipline, human physiology, rules of morality, classification of gods and astrology among other subjects.

The Chhedasutras deal with disciplinary rules and conduct. The Mulasutras refer to ballads and parables etc., relating to monastic life, observances obligatory to monks, maxims of monastic life and morality.

The Svetambars reject the Angas and instead have the three treatises, the Dhavala, the Jayadhavala and Mahadhavala, all in verse and not yet published. The sect has also four Vedas written in Sanskrit or Sauraseni.

The Jainas have also handed dawn a great mass of non-canonical literature, dealing with dogma, the sciences and history or legend, besides epics, stories, and works on poetry.

Influence of Jainism

The Jain community as a whole now number about a million

and a half in India. All through the centuries the Jain contribution to art and literature in India was distinctive. They lend their own styles of painting and sculpture to the Indian arts, for instance heavy out-lines and bold, brilliant colours in painting, colossal free-standing statues and giant bas-reliefs of their saints in sculpture. There is the stone image of Gautama seventy feet high. The medieval Jain temples are amazingly beautiful. On out of the way mountain tops, the Jains, built veritable temple cities. Girnar and Palitana (the later has 883 temples) in Gujarat, white marble temples at Mount Abu in Rajputana are some of the famous examples of the aesthetic sense developed by the Jains, as for example in Mount Abu.

BUDDHISM

Lord Buddha was the founder of Buddhism though traditions and legends speak of a long line of great ones, 24 other Buddhas preceding him. Each made, a great resolve to become perfectly enlightened, and then, as a Bodhisattva (one destined to become a Buddha) strove through countless lives to do good and to acquire the Buddha qualities. Similarly, Lord Buddha had evolved from lower to higher forms of life, had been successively rat, fish, lizard, frog, snake, peacock, wood-pecker, jackal, deer, elephant, lion, tiger, potter, smith, gambler, thief, king, ascetic and Brahman.

He was born in Lumbini garden (now in Nepal) in the country of Kapilvastu. His father, named, Suddhodana was of the Gautama family of the Sakyas and Maya was the name of his mother. Prior to his birth, it is said, she had dreamt that a six-tusked white elephant had entered her womb. His father was not a king in the modern sense of the word but only one of the chiefs of the Sakas who were living under a republican form of government. According to the Ceylonese tradition he was born in 523 BC and lived for eighty years. His mother died a week after his birth and he was brought up by the step-mother and aunt of his mother. He was called Siddhartha.

He is known by various other names like Sakyamuni, Sarvarthasiddha, Gautama Buddha and Tathagat. He was brought up in luxury and married to Yasodhara (the name given in the Northern Buddhist texts). He had one son by her. Various sights like those of 'old age, sickness, death, sorrow and impurity' had profoundly grieved him and when a son was born he left the house the very night at the age of twenty-nine.

He first took to various teachers for finding out the secret of life and the path to salvation. When unsuccessful in his quest he took to a course of very severe austerities and reduced himself to a mere skeleton. But this also did not satisfy him. He had been joined by five other persons who now deserted him thinking that he was deviating from the right path.

After six years of penances he began again to wander and reached the Nairanjana river. It is said that in Buddha-Gaya he attained enlightenment under a fig (Peepal) tree or Bodhi-tree as it is now known.

He then began his wanderings and preaching. The first sermon was preached in the Deer Park near Banaras where Sarnath has now grown. His first pupils were the five Brahmans who had been with him in his penances. He continued to preach and convert others and also gained much royal patronage. He died in Kusinara at the age of eighty.

Teachings of Buddha

A monk should avoid the two extremes conjoined with (1) Self torture and (2) Passions. He should follow the middle path by first grasping the four truths (1) The truth of pain manifest in birth, old age, sickness, death, sorrow, lamentation, dejection and despair; (2) the truth of the cause of pain, viz., craving for existence, passion, pleasure, leading to rebirth; (3) the truth of cessation of pain by ceasing of craving, by renunciation and (4) the truth of the way that leads to the cessation of pain, viz., the Middle Path (or the Eight-fold Path), consisting of right views, intention, speech, action, livelihood, effort, mindfulness and concentration.

It was the living of the holy life that was the centre of his teachings. The three hindrances to enlightenment were lust, greed and delusion. He taught the people to recognise the nine fetters of the mind, covetousness, ill-will, anger, deceitfulness, jealousy, obstinacy, arrogance, vainglory and heedlessness. He laid stress on kindness (or ahinsa) to all, including animals.

The Buddhist faith consists in recognising the excellence of three Jewels, Buddha, his law and the community (Samgha).

The laity are asked not to kill, not to steal, not to lie, not to get drunk and not to fornicate. The clergy must abstain from all sexual intercourse and posses nothing, save yellow dress, rice bowl, a razor, a needle and a strainer to prevent him from killing little beasts by swallowing them when he drinks. The monks live in Viharas where there are gradations, the neophyte (Bhikshu) going through training before he is admitted as a full-fledged Bhikshu. Buddhism is also indebted to Hinduism as obtaining in the Upanishads for many of its ideas. The theories of Karma, Sanskar and Transmigration are there in the Upanishads. There are many resemblances between the Sankhya philosophy and the Buddhist philosophy. 'The rapid success of the Jains and Buddhists is to some extent explained by the likeness of the morals and opinions which they professed to those of two types of men which were very active on the fringes of Brahmanism from the earliest historical the Yogins and the Sophists'.*

Like Jainism, Buddhism also split into sects a reference to which will be made later in this book.

Jainism was confined to the bounds of India and the Jains are to be chiefly found in Central India, Gujarat and Rajputana. Buddhism however, spread to all parts of Asia, specially the South-East Asia. Both Jainism and Buddhism have grown a vast literature.

The causes of the phenomenal expansion of Buddhism are :

(1) Buddhism steered clear of all ritualism that has so obscured the purity of Hindu doctrines in the sixth century B.C. and applied rational methods to the problem of life.

(2) Buddhism had a comprehensive moral code easily understood and free from mysticism.

---

* P.M. Oursel and others, Ancient India and Indian Civilisation, p. 142.

(3) Buddhism appealed to the masses in their own vernacular and avoided Sanskrit.

(4) The patronage extended by royal personages specially Ashoka and Kanishka.

(5) The cult of service and self sacrifice, the exhortation to love all beings also played their part in the success of Buddhism.

(6) Above all, the institution of Sangha, the Church, with its votaries, their discipline and example, was instrumental in spreading the doctrines.

The Buddhist Canon

The whole corpus, the Tripitaka or Threefold Basket, is divided into three sections. They are printed either in Pali or Sanskrit, Tibetan or Chinese. The sections are Vinaya (discipline), Sutras, stories and Abhidharma, the metaphysics :

(1) Vinaya contains explanations of the Sutras, sections on the daily life of monks and nuns and other relevant topics.

(2) Sutras contain among other subjects homilies, Dhammapada (as famous as the Gita for its moral maxims), spiritual aspirations, Jatakas (stories of previous births of Buddha), and legends of 24 Buddhas prior to Sakyamuni.

(3) Abhidharma deals with philosophical theories for example about individuality, factors conditioning psychical phenomena and a manual of controversy for the use of monks. Besides these there is a great mass of non-canonical literature like the *Milinda-Panha* or questions of King Menander, Kathas, Singalese Chronicles- *Dipavamsa* and *Mahavamsa* - and many other works.

Influence of Buddhism

Unlike Jainism Buddhism became an exportable article and attracted people in all parts of the world, specially in South-East Asia. Ruins in central Asia recently discovered have brought to light Buddhist monasteries which were engulfed later on by the Gobi desert. Western scholars have also been attracted by Buddhism which according to some people supplied many of the principles of Christianity. The notable Western writers are Sylvain Levi, Edouard Chavarnes, Minaer and Scherbatski in Russia, Italian Tucci besides the famous scholars Rhys Davis and Oldenberg.

In India Buddhism influenced our religion also. Its emphasis on Ahimsa became part of Hinduism and Buddha was accepted as an incarnation of God. Mahayana Buddhism familiarised us with idol worship.

The Buddhist Samgha

Many western writers have sarcastically noted the absence of democratic institutions in India. Recent researches have proved the hollowness of this theory. Right from the Vedas to the Buddhist literature we have evidence of governments democratically governed. The Saṁgha or religious order established by Buddha gives us instance of practices associated with democratic form of government.

Buddha never claimed to be the head of the Church and refused to nominate his successors even among his famous disciples like Sariputta and Moggallana.

A sramana (monk) joining the order was free to choose his acharya (Guru - master).

The monk who recited the rules of the Sangha (the book of Patimokkha) was for the time being the chief of the Sangha and was called Sainghatthera or Sainghaparinayaka.

The chief must be a true Brahmacharin and well-versed in philosophy and rules of Buddhism. When the assembly of the monks met in the hall the seats were arranged in the order of seniority by a special officer.

For different purposes of Sangha different quorums were fixed, of 4, 5, 10, 20 or more persons. There was a whip for completing the quorum called Ganapuraka.

Rules of business were fixed and resolutions were to be moved in the form of a motion. Formal presentations and proclamations were necessary. The motions received from one to three readings. The resolutions passed were called Sangha-Karma, an Act of the Sangha.

There were devices for bringing about agreements in disputes. For instance, the dispute might be referred to the larger assembly or the leaders might be asked to refer it to their parties; besides, time limit was also fixed, or a sub-committee was appointed to negotiate and bring about an agreement. When disputes could not be settled by these methods, they were referred to the whole Sangha where majority opinion prevailed. A polling officer was appointed by a special resolution of the Sangha. A vote was called significantly Chhanda which means freedom. Voting slips were made of wood of different colours to represent different opinions. There were securities or clerks to record the proceedings of the meetings. Referendum was also accepted for instance in Jataka no. 1 a king was said to have been elected by votes of the entire city.

It is not accidental that two important religious movements, in many-ways remarkably alike, should spring at the same time and in almost the same locality. The spirit of the new age initiated by the Upanishads was one of free enquiry, opposed to rituals and sacrifices. It expressed itself in an intellectual rebellion against the Brahmans and their claim to act as sole interpreters between gods and men. It was also a reaction against the cruelty of animal slaughter, on a vast scale, involved in the sacrifices. Further in the areas where the two prophets preached a democratic atmosphere had prevailed, republican forms of government had been set up and these republics helped the movements immensely. There are many resemblances between Jainism and Buddhism besides the above.

Both are typically Indian, their roots buried deep in the past of traditional Indo-Aryan thought. The ideals preached had their foundation in the Upanishads. Both accepted the current concept of rebirth and Karma and also the prevailing ideal of asceticism to a large extent. Both emphasised that an active life based on morality will lead to salvation, Nirvana or Moksha which is nothing more than the state or condition of freedom resulting from spiritual enlightenment and understanding of truth.

It is not right to say that these religions condemned belief in God. Rather, they did not worry about such questions and kept their ears more to the ground. But they were not far away from the main streams of Indian religion and spirituality. It may be that they emphasised one aspect of Hinduism more to the exclusion or ignoring of the other aspects but love for a partial truth is a common human failing, even of the prophets.

7

THE SMRITIS, THE PURANAS AND THE GITA

The SMRITIS LAY down rules and laws that have from times immemorial governed Hindu society. At one time they covered the whole of India. They are part of the main streams of Indian culture that have flowed from the Vedic sources. The Smritis embody Sanatana Dharma which may change according to the spirit of the times provided its unity or individuality, its foundation in the Vedas are not affected. The smritis were finally edited in the Gupta period but their basic ideas are older. There are many Smritis but the most famous is the Manu Smriti, traditionally ascribed to Manu, the great law giver. The Smritis are not mere law-books. They cover all significant details of the Hindu life both in its individual and social aspects.

Manusmriti

It is the standard work an Hindu law and social institutions. The name Manu is of great antiquity, mentioned as a Vedic Rishi in the Taittiriya Samhita and also as the first progenitor of the human race and its first king. Manu Smriti is confined to the description of the Hindu customs and laws north of the Narmada. We may study the civilisation dealt with in the Manu Smriti under the headings of social customs and institutions, economic life and education.

Social Life

It was made up of the Dvijatis, the threetwice-born castes of Brahmans, Kshatriyas and Vaishyas and the Ekajatis, the Sudras. There were mixed castes also springing from adultery, marriage with ineligible women and violation of the duties of caste. Issue of non-Aryan wife married to an Aryan could be admitted into the Aryan fold if he was virtuous. Thus, the foreigners were also accommodated. Social life was governed by the regulations of castes and ashrams.

The status of a Brahmana depended upon his character and spirituality. He was known for his knowledge of the absolute, for asceticism and universal goodwill. He acted as a teacher, judge, priest and prime minister. He ceased to be a Brahmana if he violated rules regarding food, gifts, professions and occupations.

The Kshatriyas and the Vaishyas besides their common duties like study, performance of sacrifices, charity had their special functions, the one pursued a military career, the other could take to agriculture, trade, commerce or cattle-rearing.

For Sudra service was the main function. He was eligible for the sacraments but not for hearing sacred texts except their substance. But he was not denied the rites of marriage, cooking of daily food in the grihya fire and sraddha. Manu mentions even Sudra teachers and pupils. There were slaves also, seven classes of them being mentioned.

The woman was not eligible for the study of the Veda nor for the use of Mantras in performing her sacraments except marriage. She was successively under the guardianship of father, husband and son (in her old age if a widow). She could not own property except stridhana or gifts made to her. Her main work was the management of the domestic life.

Economic Life

Manu speaks of both urban and rural life, of cities (Nagara), towns (Pura) and villages (Grama). Houses were constructed of mud, brick, stone and timber. The art of building was well-developed. Temples were built in the outskirts.

Agriculture was the main occupation. The genuineness of

seeds was guaranteed by penalty. The crops grown included cotton, barley, wheat, rice, sugar-cane and vegetables. The agricultural implements included wooden plough, yokes, ropes, and leathern vessel for irrigation purpose. Cultivation was by the sudra labourer on stipulated terms. Such as half the share of the produce to the cultivator who supplied also the seeds. The royal share was one fourth, one-eighth, one-twelfth, according to rule. The livestock included buffalo, cow, sheep and goat. Dairying was another occupation.

Arts and Crafts

Artisans working in the crafts enjoyed a status higher than the sudras. Among the arts and crafts mention may be made of goldsmith (hemakara), the black-smith (karmkara), the dyer, the launderer, the oilmen, the tailors, the spinner and the weaver, the potter, the leather worker, maker of bow and arrow, the distiller and the brick-kilners.

In trade there was both money and barter economy. Prices were fixed by government in consultation with the traders. Trade routes were both by land and by water. The export trade was controlled by the government in many articles, for instance, elephants, saffron, silk, woollens, precious stones and pearls. Trade had to pay customs, excise and octroi. Money was lent on interest and on promissory notes. Debtors were protected from usury by the government.

Coins were of gold, silver and copper. Mines of gold, silver, copper, bronze, iron and lead were worked. Servants were paid daily wages. The Joint family continued to be the characteristic feature, partition in the life of the father was disapproved. The ownership of property was vested in the father but the rights of the different sons and brothers to their separate shares were recognised. What later on came to be known as the Mitakshara system of inheritance was prevailing and thus the son had a right to the ancestral property by birth, not possible under the Dayabhaga scheme of inheritance. Adoption was not much approved. Niyoga was permitted. Property of widows not having a son was liable to escheat to the crown. Daughters having brothers had no share in father's property. pre-puberty;

marriages were becoming the order of the day. Widow-marriage was becoming unpopular, Inter-caste marriage was not approved. Females of upper classes took the veils when going out. They were taught at home.

Education

Studentship began with the ceremony of Upanayana performed at the age of 8, 11, 12 for the Brahamana, Kshatriya and Vaishya pupils respectively. Students lived in the house of their teachers who prescribed a course of discipline and austerities as regards dress, food and habits, based on Brahmacharya. The aim of education was both intellectual and spiritual development. The subjects of study were (i) the three Vedas called Sruti, (ii) select Vedic hymns and verses, (iii) Atharva Veda, Brahmans, Aranyakas and Upanishads. Besides these, other studies included philosophy (Darsana), Smritis, Itihasa and Purana, Dharma Sutras and Varta or secular subjects. Students specialised as Vaidikas, Sastrins, Ritvijas and Brahmavadins.

The period of schooling varied from 9 to 36 years. A student might break off after completing his study but not fulfilling his vow or fulfilling the vow without completing his study or completing both and would be known respectively as vidya or vrata or vidyavrata-snataka. A student devoting his whole life would be called a Naishthika, the academic year was of two terms. Each term was begun and ended with formal public ceremonies. The first term began in July and closed by the end of December.

There were various holidays in the months and in the year, for example the two Pratipadas, two Asthmis, two Chaturdasis, Amavasya and Purnima in every month and the last day of each of the four seasons. Teachers were of two classes, the upadhyayas teaching as a profession and only a portion of the Veda or Vedanga and the Acharya who taught the Veda and the Upanishad free to the pupil. There were also educational experts called Adhyapanavidhijnah.

Religion and Philosophy

The Smritis give us the traditional religion of Hinduism that we have today, the various vratas (fasts), offering of prayers to the traditional gods and goddesses and the oblations to the manes. sacrifices were performed and meat-eating was not banned. Sixteen sankaras were regularly performed and the age was particular in offering 'shradha' to the ancestors not once a year but once every month.

The philosophy behind the Smritis is at least as old as the Upanishads. The Universe is one vast pulsating life. The manifestation of that life is different in different beings. Man is essentially divine and immortal. But he lives in ignorance and will learn his true nature not in one term but in several. Man is but the result of his past and present actions in all the three spheres of his existence, physical, mental and spiritual. Men are in different stages of evolution, are hence, of different types and have to perform different functions and this explains the basis of the caste system.

The study of the Smritis shows the growth of rigidity in social forms and institutions. The freedom in Dharma is being replaced by convention in religion. In short we have the dawn of the conventional age 'in India when religion is stereotyped, education and training are bound to a traditional and unchangeable form, thought is subjected to infallible authorities and a stamp of finality is cast on what is regarded as the finished life of man. In such a society the form prevails and the spirit recedes and diminishes'.

The rules and regulations regarding castes, marriages, food and women exemplify the truth of the above remarks. In the age of the Smritis social and religious life was following a track which was not absolutely on the line of the old Vedic and Upanishadic religion, philosophy and the social system.

But the best minds of the age were alive to these defects and the renaissance that followed in the Gupta Age shows that freedom and initiative were not dead. People had still the realisation of the fundamental unity of all religions and all life. Buddhism, Jainism and Hinduism lived side by side without producing religious wars and violent discords. Harmony and tolerance were still the key notes of Hindu life and philosophy. The spirit of adventure was not yet dead.

THE PURANAS

Time was when the Puranas were laughed at and looked with derision as the embodiment of superstitious beliefs, myths and incredible tales. This impression fostered by many European scholars is now giving place to a more correct appreciation of the Puranas.

The Puranas are important from the points of view of religion, history and sociology. They enable us to know the true significance of the ethos, philosophy and religion of the Vedas. It needs a sympathetic vision and imagination to understand symbolisms frequently used in the Puranas. Take for example, the story of the Avatars. The Avatars vividly symbolise the stages of evolution of the world. The first Avatar is of the world of Matsya, occupying the universe when even before the birth of reptiles, the fishes were the first evidence of life. And then we come to the period of the amphibia (Kutchha), then to the period of the half-man (Narsingh), to that of the dwarf man (Vaman) and then to the period of the primitive, the uncontrolled, the impulsive man. We may later come to the period of the man more or less perfect, until that man is equated with and vanishes into the Supreme. The whole of our philosophy is founded upon the acceptance of the theories of evolution in all departments of life and the Puranas in their theories of Avatars vividly portray this.

It is, of course, true that there are many things in the Puranas that were either of use only in the contemporary period of their origin and writing or were very mythical but that does not mean that we should condemn the Puranas wholesale.

The Puranas are attributed to Suta as the rector and to Vyasa as the author. They were written with the object of popularising the truths taught in the Vedic literature by presenting them in relation to concrete personages and to the events of their lives.

The Purana means that which lives from of old or that which is always new though it is old. There are references to the Puranas in the Dharma-Sutras, in the Mahabharata and in Kautliya's Arthasastra. They are the work of many minds of diverse times and Vyasa was probably only an editor. The Puranas generally contain five sections or features, viz., primary creation, secondary creation, genealogy of gods and Prajapatis, periods of different Manus and histories of royal dynasties. The world is created from Prakriti or primordial matter under the control of Isvara (primary creation), in the secondary creation, from Prakriti come the five subtle elements. From these there are born organs of knowledge, mind, organs of action, the five bhutas (elements) and the prana. When all these are combined the universe is born.

The Puranas then describe the evolution of human destiny in terms of the Yuga, Krita (satya), Treta, Dvapara and Kali, the first three are four times, three times and two times the duration of the Kali Yuga which will last 4,32,000 years. When the world ends, involution takes place that is all the manifestations are reabsorbed into Prakriti which goes back into Isvara who is one with the Absolute.

There are eighteen major Puranas dedicated mostly to one supreme God, Vishnu, Shiva, Brahma etc., but there is no rivalry for the Padma Purana says, 'Brahma, Vishnu and Maheshvara, though three in form, are one entity. There is no difference among the three except that of attributes'. The eighteen Puranas are Padma, Vishnu, Bhagwata, Naradiya, Garuda, Varaha, Brahma, Brahmanda, Brahma-Vaivarta, Markandeya, Bhavishya, Vamana, Siva, Linga, Skanda, Agni, Matsya and Kurma.

In twelve Puranas an account of royal dynasties in India is given. There is not, however, full agreement about names and events.

We have no archaeological or epigraphic evidence to test the histories of events prior to the period of the Mahabharata.

The Puranas refer to three great dynasties after the war, viz., the line of the Purus, the line of the Ikshvakus and the line of the Magadha kings.

Details can be gleaned from various Puranas, for example the fourth book of the Vishnu Purana deals with the genealogies of the Kings of the solar and the lunar race and brings then up to the Kali Yuga, among whom are included the Magadha and the Andhra kings.

The ethical purpose of the Puranas as given in the Vishnu Purana is : 'He who has heard of the races of the Sun and Moon, Ikshvaku, Jahnu, Mandhatri, Sagara, and Raghu, who have all perished : of Yayati, Nahusha and their posterity, who are no more of kings of great might, resistless valour and unbounded wealth, who have been overcome by the still more powerful time and are now only a tale; he will learn wisdom, and forbear to call either children, or wife, or house, or lands, or wealth, his own'.

In the differences found in the various Puranas local excellence is discernible for instance an Orissa stamp may be detected in the Brahma Purana. The geography of India given in the Puranas is very precise. India called Bharatvarsha is defined as the country that lies north of the ocean and south of the snowy mountains. It is said that much help was derived from the Puranas in tracing the source of the Nile in Egypt.

On the basis of facts from the Puranas, Pargiter has worked out the date of the Mahabharata. Taking the beginning of Chandra Gupta Maurya's reign to be 322 B.C., it has been computed that 100 years passed between him and the nine Nandas. The first Nanda Mahapadma became king in 402 B.C. by this calculation. Now between this Nanda and the Mahabharata there reigned most probably 24 Aikshakus, 27 Panchalas, 24 Kasis, 28 Haihyas, 32 Kalingas, 25 Asmakas, 26 Kurus, 28 Maithilas, 23 Surasenas and 20 Vitahotras, that is 257 Kings. If we take 18 years as the average period of each king's reign, we get the period of 468, and we add the times the kings preceding the three kings of the dynastic list aforesaid and get the years 950 BC as the date of the Bharata Battle. This date is, however, based on average calculations and can only be accepted with due caution. On the basis of facts given in the Puranas Pargiter also argues that the Aryans lived in the Doab and migrated west-ward towards the Punjab. Radha Kumud Mookerji gives the date of the Mahabharata as 1400 B.C. and places the time of Parikshit I and of Satapatha and the Aitareya

Brahman about the year 2000 BC This will push further the date of Rig-Veda and is likely to link it up with the Indus civilization.

It is thus clear that the Puranas are a vital portion of the Scriptures of the Hindus and also afford us valuable facts about our geography and history. They have largely moulded public life, belief and conduct in our land for thousands of years and they must he fully utilised by us if we are to realise the truths of the Vedas.

THE GITA

The Gita is one of the most famous books not only in the Indian literature but in the world literature as well. Probably next to the Bible it is the most translated book. In it the philosophies of the Upanishads have been synthesised. Commentators have tried to read in it their partial theories, some regard it as favouring action without the thought or wish for reward, some look at it as favouring Bhakti or the path of devotion and some regard it as approving the renunciation of the world having attained right knowledge. The Gita is in reality a synthesis of knowledge, work and faith or devotion.

Its origin is traced to the discourse of Sri Krishna on the battle-field of Kurukshetra when Arjun was moved with pity and refused to fight his relations, the Kaurvas. The discourse of Sri Krishna (incarnation of God) convinced Arjun of the folly of his action and he went into fighting with Duryodhan and his armies. The historical truth or otherwise of the battle and the discourse given therein cannot detract from the Justice of the stand taken in the Gita.

The Gita does not preach non-violence. It preaches resistance to evil, violently or non-violently as the circumstances may warrant but the fighters in the cause of truth must be free from passions, free from selfishness or egotism and have no desire to seek personal advantages from the struggle for truth and righteousness.

The doctrine of Divine Incarnation preached in the Gita is also very significant, ordinarily it is understood to mean that there is divine manifestation upon the earth whenever virtue subsides and irreligion prevails. But an incarnation is also a remainder to man that he too is divine and can transcend himself to attain the same status as that made visible by God manifested in human form.

The Gita is a gospel of Yoga. Yoga not in the sense of Hatha Yoga or that of Patanjali prescribing certain austerities and moral virtues but Yoga in the sense of union with God. This union is to be achieved by a synthesis of the three methods of Yoga viz., Karma, Jnana and Bhakti. As a corollary of this union with God is our union with our fellow beings. It behoves the spiritual man to see the same spirit or Atman in all beings and extend to them the hand of comradeship. Thus in the modern world with international war threatening chaos, the teachings of the Gita have a great part to play. True world unity can only come on a spiritual basis. Any other basis must remain an external basis and this must lead to errors because external and outward facts and motives are often misleading. Only when our souls are attuned, only when we passionately feel the sense of spiritual oneness can there be true world unity. This is one of the major teachings of the Gita.

Another major principle of the Gita is the conception of svadharma linked with the conception of Svabhava.

Svadharma means that every man has certain natural endowments and propensities to be fitlly developed and wisely directed so that he may play his part efficiently in God's universe. Every man has his own Svadharma based on his svabhava (nature) and if he follows the law of other man's nature he commits an outrage and nature will wreak revenge in such a case. A Kshatriya has fighting, defending the weak and governing the people as duties proper to his station. If he takes up the work of Brahman he does violence to his Svadharma and will develop a truncated personality. As the Gita says, 'it is better to die in one's own dharma, for the dharma of another spells death'.

So far as action is concerned Gita places greatest emphasis on disinterested service. Action should be done without attachment to the fruits thereof. Again action should lead one towards God. Further at a certain stage actions should be such as to show that man has become the instrument of God and finally God and man should became identical.

True knowledge is the knowledge of God, the knowledge of man's relations with God and the knowledge of his relation with the Universe.

Devotion is not a mere ritual to be performed sometimes in a day. It is a function coterminous with every movement of life. God becomes the only object of his love, and he abides and delights solely in Him. Such a man must be perfectly free from the slavery of senses and the desires pertaining to them. He should have no thought of his desire-self or be egotistically minded. He should work because God is also working without the works defiling Him or touching Him.

The teaching of Gita may be summarised in the words of Sri Aurobindo (Essays on the Gita-2 Vols.). 'The difficulty of human action is that the soul and nature of man seem fatally subjected to many kinds of bondage, the prison of the ignorance, the meshes of the ego, the chain of the passions, the hammering insistence of the life of the moment, an obscure and limited circle without an issue'.

The soul 'must first of all renounce this absorption, must cast from it the external solicitation of outward things'. 'It must arrive at an inner inactivity'. That is we should develop 'an understanding without attachment in all things, a soul self-conquered and empty of desire'. Secondly, we must become divine by 'putting off the lower mental, vital, physical existence'. 'And the man who has thus inwardly renounced all is described by the Gita as the true Sannyasin'. Then comes 'the extinction of ego and its demands of all sorts'.

But there should be no cessation of work, action must be done as an offering to the Divine. Finally, one develops integral knowledge, the knowledge of the Lord secret in the heart of man. God becomes the Lover and Beloved of his worship and adoration.

'All that we do is done for the sake of the Lord seated in the heart of all, for the Godhead in the individual and for the fulfillments of his will in us, for the sake of the Divine in the world, for the good of all beings, for the fulfillment of the world action and the world purpose, or in one word for the sake of the Purushottam and done really by him through his universal Shakti'.

'The Gita declares that all can if they will, even to the lowest and sinfullest among men enter into the path of this Yoga. And if there is a true self surrender and an absolute unegoistic faith in the indwelling Divinity, success is certain in this path'. 'Adore and sacrifice to Him with all you are : remember Him in every thought and feeling, every impulsion and act. Persevere until all these things are wholly his and he has taken up even in most common and outward things as in the inmost sacred chamber of your spirit his constant transmuting presence'.

8

THE CLASSICAL AGE

THE RIG-VEDIC and subsequent civilisations had laid the foundation of India's culture. The superstructure is now raised in the Mauryan and the following ages and we witness the richest flowering of the Indian genius in all the realms of art and in all the departments of life. This period may be called 'the Classical Age of India'.

One special feature to note is that Indian genius as revealed during these period is not confined to spirituality alone or revels in an ascetic withdrawal from life or is impervious to the demands of life. When all is Brahman, life too is God's, it cannot be neglected and must be given its due attention. In other words spirituality and life were reconciled and richness of thought translated itself into richness of practice.

We may first study the Mauryan culture in the realms of religion, philosophy, social life, arts and economic institutions.

For a description of the state of religion in the days of the Imperial Mauryas we have to rely on Greek and Latin authors, inscriptions and coins, the Mahabhashya of Patanjali and the testimony of later writers. The worship of the Vedic gods still lingered, for instance the raingod (zeus ombrios) worshipped then represented probably Indra or Parjanya. We have also the worship of gods who came into prominence during the Epic period, namely, Shiva, Vishnu, Brahma, Sri Krishna, Skanda and Visakha. Even Asoka paid homage to the traditions when he called himself Devanampriya, beloved of the gods.

The Vedic rite of sacrifice continued to enjoy great

popularity. The kings took a leading part in the performance of sacrifice. Private persons and institutions also participated in such ceremonies. It is said that drink was freely provided on these occasions. Asoka tried to put a stop to the practice of killing animals on these occasions while others like the Vaishnava reformers tried to rediscover the spiritual ideas behind sacrifice, ideas prominent in the Vedic period. For during the Vedic Ages sacrifice was a symbol, an offering to the gods. The Vedic idea of sacrifice with the soul of man as the enjoyer of its fruits points to the path that leads to self conquest. Of all his gains and works, of all that he himself is and has man must make an offering to the powers of the Godhead, the powers of consciousness, the gods, who recognise in the soul of man their brother and ally and desire to help and increase him by themselves increasing in him so as to exalt and enrich his world with their strength and beauty. Similarly, the Fire worshipped by the Aryans and around which the sacrifice developed, was a symbol. It signified quenchless, indomitable Seer-will, clearing through all the planes of consciousness, devouring all the desires of man, consuming all the rank weeds of his ignorance, till it lands the soul, free and immune, upon the shoreless ocean of immortality. Time, however, has left the sacrifice to us as only a meaningless ritual with all its deep Vedic significance lost.

During this period thanks to the efforts of Asoka Buddhism developed into a great world religion. It enjoyed great popularity in India also, specially in the eastern parts. The Buddhist teachings were engraved on pillars and rocks. These inscriptions are to be found in all parts of India. These edicts and inscriptions are human documents of rare charm and high moral significance. They record the virtues of the emperor - his truthfulness, kindness, personal humility, piety, tolerance and administrative capacities. And these virtues he wanted all his people to follow and develop. To quote his words :

> 'Obedience must be rendered to mother and father, likewise to elders; firmness (of compassion) must be shown towards animals; truth must be spoken; these moral virtues must be practised'.

'In the same way the pupil must show reverence to the master, and one must behave in a suitable manner towards relatives'.

It is further declared that 'happiness in this world and in the other world is difficult to secure without great love of morality, careful examination, great obedience, and great fear of sin and great energy. Towards the end of his career Asoka gives greater prominence to reflection and meditation rather than to moral regulations.

It should also be noted that Asoka was true to the traditional Indian spirit of tolerance. He was never a sectarian, a bigot trying to impose his Dharma upon the people. Other faiths also continued to develop in India, for instance, Jainism and Vaishnavism or Bhagavatism in which Vasudeva, the God of gods was paid the greatest homage.

Social Life

Varna (caste) and Ashrama (stages of social and religious discipline), the chief institutions of the Hindu life were firmly moulded during this period. Inter-caste marriages and adoption of a profession foreign to one's family traditions were frowned upon. Philosophers lived in simple style and spent their lives listening to serious discourses. There were also wandering ascetic orders. The rise of many creeds and evolution of complex rituals, the advent of the foreigners and growth of social life contributed to the rigidity of the caste system. The Kautilya Artha Shastra mentions agriculture, cattle breeding and trade as the common occupation of Vaishyas and Sudras. According to the Greek writers new groups had emerged like those of the husbandmen, herdsmen, traders, the physicians, the wood, dwellers, the hunters, the soldiers, the overseers and the councillors.

Women continued to be honoured and respected. Some of them pursued philosophy and lived a life of continence. But married women did not share with their husbands a knowledge of the sacred lore. Instances of polygamy are on record. Women also acted as body-guards and it is recorded that a woman who killed a king when drunk was rewarded by becoming the wife of his successor. Women delighted in the practice of rituals and ceremonies. Ladies are said to have ruled during the minority of kings.

Slavery was also an established institution. It is recognised by the law-book and has been referred to in the inscriptions. Asoka draws a distinction between a slave and the hired labourer and recommends kindness towards all of them. Buying and selling of women also took place.

Indians lived frugal life and observed good order. People were mild, gentle and truthful. Theft was a rare occurrence. Wine was drunk only at sacrifices. Food generally consisted of rice. Laws were simple and suits were rare. Houses and property were not meticulously guarded.

There were many festivities and merry gatherings, utsava and samaja. Gifts were given liberally by the kings on these occasions. Dancing, singing and joust of arms, were parts of the ceremonies. Fights between animals were also taking place as sports. There were chariot races with teams of oxen and horses. There were dramas also mentioned, for example, by Patanjali. Dice-play was also indulged in. A play resembling the chess-game is also mentioned. Thus, the key-note in social life was a joy for life and a joy in life. Many among the masses and the classes drank deep of the worldly enjoyments without forgetting their dues to the manes and the gods. Life was a synthetic whole in which religion and materialism were happily married.

Economic Conditions

A Science named Vartta is mentioned devoted to the study and management of the conditions of material life. Brahmanism, according to the tradition of Manu, holds that the three sciences which make up human knowledge are Vartta, Dandaniti (politics) and Trayi, the three Vedas. Kautilya says that artha is the Vritti of man, in other words, that it means the whole of human activity. The close connection of the two lies in the fact that artha raises the question of ends and Vartta that of means. Mythology also expresses this close connection by calling Manu Prithu, not only the sacrifice but also a fire-bringing Prometheus and the inventor of agriculture. Thus, India did not neglect the economic life and paid to it due homage and importance. The

Vaisyas were the aristocracy of the workers. Base and arduous tasks were left to the Shudras. Of the industries, cotton was the most important. Earlier, we have references by Herodotus of the cotton dress worn by the Indian soldiers of Xerxes. Carpets, brocades and embroideries marked an advance in manufacture. Muslin and silk were also manufactured.

Metals wrought and worked were bronze, copper, tin, lead. Gems were also prized. There was also the manufacture of chariots, arms and waggons. Woodwork was of a very high order as buildings and palaces were generally built of wood and so also stupas and boats.

Trade was also very brisk. Manufactured goods were exchanged or sold. Towns were connected by tracks, with wells at intervals. The commercial centres grew up at the more important intersection routes. We find from the Buddhist books that 'Patliputra was connected with Gandhara by an imperial highway. For caravans loaded with goods of Bactria and Kashmir, Mathura was the first large city in Madhya Desa as one came out of the Indus valley .... From Patliputra three great roads radiated to the frontiers of the Empire, the south-western by Kaushambi and Ujjayani, the northern to Nepal by Vaisali and Sravasti, and the north-western'. According to Kautilya road-making was an important duty of the king.

Much use was also made of the water ways. Indians have forgotten that our country was one of the greatest marine and colonising-powers of the past. One took ship for Ceylon not only at Tamralipti, the chief port of Bengal, but also at Banaras and Patna. Bharukachchha (Broach) was connected with Babylon and with Suvarna Bhumi (Lower Burma). Connection was also established with the Egyptians and the East Africans by the Red Sea.

Shipping also plied between China and India with many colonising and trading centres in between. There was great commercial activity between the Roman Empire and India after the Mauryan period in particular. Indian trade was connected with that of Central Asia by a mountain track which ran from Kabul to the upper valley of the Oxus, east of Balkh (Bacteria). Here it was crossed by the route which running from west to east, passed round the north of the Hindu Kush, crossed the

Pamir and the upper Tarim and went to the Chinese Turkestan and Yarkand.

By these trade routes Buddhism also travelled to various parts of Asia. The Government derived great profits and income from duties and customs on the merchandise travelling through the routes, care was taken about weights and measures and the quality of the goods produced. The trade consisted of gems, spices, silk, cotton, gold, silver, wines, choicest of ointments and even beautiful maidens and singing boys. Coinage or medium of exchange was both by gold and by silver coins. Copper coins were also there. There were trade unions or economic organisations, guilds or Sreni. This term stood now for corporate association which embraced many kinds of workers, tillers of the soil, herdsmen, sailors, artisans, traders, bankers, including experts in the Veda.

At the head of each corporation was a deacon (jetthaka), who acted as president (Pramukha) and was an important personage at the King's court. Occupations were handed down from father to son. Sometimes different guilds were federated under a common head who was their president and also treasurer (Bhandagarika). There were guilds even of robbers or Brigands. Trade had its chief called Setthi. The head of a commercial federation was called Mahasetthi, with many Anusetthis under him. Caravan traffic had also its companies under a captain called Sattha-vaha. Agricultural chief was called Bhojaka. The powers of the guild were legislative, judicial and executive. Order was maintained by rigid discipline and the king safeguarded the customs and decisions of the guilds. The guilds of craftsmen were most developed.

Agriculture was the chief occupation. The very name Arya, it is said, meant (root krish) the tillers of the soil. The chief grains were rice and barley. Other important crops were sesame, beans, maize and lentils. Wheat was at first conspicuous by its absence. The agriculturists were fairly prosperous. They were exempted from fighting and other public services. They were not molested in times of war. They paid to the government a share of the produce of the soil besides a land tribute. In times of emergency other imposts were also levied.

The people lived in villages, surrounded by a fence and a ditch. Guards kept watch at the gates and pits were dug to catch wild beasts. Kautilya mentions special officers for the inspection of cattle, pastures and forests. Distilling and salt-deposits were state monopolies. Flood, fire, locusts and famines were also taking place. For famines Kautilya mentions remedies like creation of reserves, providing work for the poor, public assistance, and calling on allies for help besides extensive irrigation.

Pundits warned the people of the coming of droughts, wet weather, diseases and also told of the coming of propitious winds. Implements of agriculture were made by the artisans.

The king was the organizer and user of all property. The flow of wealth of all kinds to the central government was simplified and stimulated by the use of money. Kautilya shows the extent to which economics contribute to politics and advises princes to have superintendents to control mines, weaving, irrigation, stock-raising and trade, all the sources of wealth. Rules for controlling all these were laid down in great details. Thus, India gave to the world the first taste of state socialism.

Arts and Crafts

Craftsmanship usually rested on hereditary skill. The Jataks mention eighteen important handicrafts like the wood-workers, the smiths, the leather-dressers and the painters. Kammara was the Indian term for smith. Vaddhaki was the term applied to all kinds of woodcraft. Boats, ships and buildings had their artisans and craft-makers. Other dignified crafts were ivory making, weaving, confectionery, jewellery, work in precious metals, pottery, making of bow and arrow, of garlands and the like.

It is only in the age of Asoka, the great Mauryan emperor, that we come across monuments of high quality in large number which enable us to form a definite idea about the nature of the Indian Art.

Asoka was also responsible for a new development in the Indian art. It was during his reign that, for the first time, stone came into wide use in India for sculpture and building purposes, previously wood being mostly used. At this place we may conveniently outline the history of the Indian art upto the Mauryan age under the headings of architecture and decoration, religious art, sculpture, painting, dancing and music.

The Theory of Indian Art

At the outset we may describe the fundamental 'Motif' of the Indian art. The Indian art differs from the European art in the sense that the former is based on the expression of the 'Spirit,' of the soul in outward form of artistic creation while the latter is true to the dictum 'Art for art's sake'. In the words of Mahatma Gandhi, 'All true art is thus an expression of the soul. All true art must help the soul to realise itself'. According to Annie Besant, 'Indian Art is a blossom of the tree of the Divine wisdom, full of suggestions from worlds invisible, striving to express the ineffable, and it can never be understood merely by the emotional and the intellectual only; in the light of the Spirit can its inner significance be glimpsed'. To quote Coomaraswamy, 'Religion and art are thus names for one and the same experience—an intuition of reality and of identity'. The artist, in his creations, mirrored nature and life but in their spiritual significance and this they could do only because a rigid discipline was imposed upon them.

According to one of our Shilpa Shastras, 'The Shilpin (artificer) should understand the Atharva Veda, the thirty-two Shilpa Shastras, and the Vedic mantras by which the deities are invoked'. 'The painter must be a good man, no sluggard nor given to anger, holy, learned self-controlled, devout and charitable—such should be his character'.

Tagore speaks of the hunger of self expression growing at the roots of our being. In more philosophical language the impulse to art is the urge in the form to reveal the indwelling spirit. All art is an expression of beauty but not of ephemeral beauty. True beauty is inward, is of the soul and only a Yogi in the artist can bring that beauty out in his creations. So, the Indian art is an intuitive and spiritual art. Its highest business is to disclose something of the self, of the Divine, of the infinite through its living finite symbols. There can be no true realisation of political unity until Indian life is again inspired by the unity of national culture. Indian art is the clearest expression of that unity, the unity in diversity, the unity founded in spirituality. Art, in this sense, is a door for thought to pass from the seen to the unseen, a source of noble dreams and inspiring visions. 'All Indian art,' says Sri Aurobindo, is a throwing out of a certain profound self vision formed by a going within to find out the secret significance of form and appearance, a discovery of the subject in one's deeper self, the giving of soul form to that vision and a remoulding of the material and natural shape to express the psychic truth of it with the greatest possible purity and power of outline and the greatest possible concentrated rhythmic unity of significance in all the parts of an indivisible artistic whole'. 'To the artist the outer is but a garment of the inner. And if he makes the garment glow and glitter, it is only to convey a bare hint, shoot a single ray of the infinite effulgence within, which is the glory of his vision'.

The Indian art, therefore, is faithful to the basis of the Indian culture, its foundations in spirituality. That is not to say that the Indian artist was blind to the perfection of technique, ignored the form for the spirit. There was technical perfection, much in Indian art was secular in character but behind all was a vision, an insight into the deeper things of life. We may now trace the outline of Indian art taking architecture in the first place.

We do not have survivals of the Vedic architecture. Probably for the Vedic cult neither permanent buildings nor representations of the gods are necessary. It is probable that the remains of the Vedic architecture perished because the material used was wood. As soon as architecture makes its appearance in India, two distinct currents are seen, one local, the other imported. The most important feature of local wooden facades is the horse-shoe-shaped projection forming a kind of canopy over a door or window, (for example, in the Sanchi Stupa). It is often the end of a vault of the same shape, supported by beams. In time the ends turn in and became ornate (the ends of the horse-shoe). As art develops, the arches of the horse-shoe become more and more numerous and smaller and smaller. Later on the arches are supported by balustrades and stepped cornices, replaced again by curved cornices (exterior of Cave 19 in Ajanta). Another important feature is the column, a simple eight-sided shaft (Cave at Bhaja). Here some trace a foreign influence. Specially, it is said, the pillars of Asoka show this influence. They are round, slender columns, without a base, with a bell-shaped Capital (according to Havell it is inherited lotus, typically Indian) surmounted by a fillet and an abacus carved with emblems (Asoka capital at Sarnath). Changes take place in the capital which becomes bulbous and later takes the form of a turban.

Another form of architecture is the Cave. It is of two varieties. The simplest type consists of a small apartment cut in the rock, square or oblong, with a flat roof, round which are the cells of the monks. In the other type the plan is long and the upper part, high and rounded, seems to have been supported by wooden arches. The front is adorned by a great horse-shoe arch (cave 26 at Ajanta).

Decoration

The earliest examples are at Bharhut (second century B.C.) consisting chiefly of heavy plants treated in high relief (lotuses and other plants with dangling garlands), often accompanied by acquatic creatures. There are animals also, often fanciful, having short curved wings and sometimes prancing with little riders on their backs. There are griffins, winged horses, lions, centaurs, serpent-tailed men, horses, etc.

The Stupa

It is a fundamentally Indian structure consisting of a hemispherical mound of masonry, set on a base and crowned by a cubical 'tee' and an umbrella. Sometimes the 'tee' is surmounted by a stepped cornice.

The Stupa was a funerary monument made to hold the ashes of Buddha which were, it is said, divided into eight parts and laid in eight Stupas. Asoka collected the ashes, divided them and built a large number of these gigantic reliquaries for them, so the function of the Stupa was extended; it served to protect the ashes of the saints also and where ashes were lacking, other relics of the Blessed one. It was also used as a memorial to mark the scene of a miracle or other great event. Stupas were of all sizes. The large ones were often surrounded by balustrades with entrance-gates to keep out malign influences and to bound the holy ground. At first the dome of the Stupa was flattened and the terrace was low. Later on both were higher. The dome assumed a bell shape (Ajanta cave 26). The Stupa structure declined in India with the decline of Buddhism. Later on the Stupas are ornamented with sculpture.

In sculpture the Asoka pillars hold the field. They were of fine-grained sandstone, varying from forty to fifty feet in height and weighing about fifty tons. They came out of the Chunar quarries, not far from Banaras. They were used for engraving the inscriptions of Asoka. They rise abruptly from the ground. The rounded tapering shaft is perfectly plain but highly polished, this glass-like lustre is retained even to this day and is the marvel of science. In the case of finely executed Lion Pillar at Sarnath, there was a further addition of a great metal wheel symbolic of the Buddhist doctrine or Law. The feat of moving these great stone pillars long distances and setting them up obviously required technical engineering skill of a high order. According to the method used by Firoz Tughlak, wrapped and in thick layers of cotton and skins, the pillar was lowered into a specially constructed wagon with 21 pairs of wheels with 200 men at each wheel. Thus 8,400 men pushed and pulled the cart from a point 150 miles away from Delhi to the Jamuna river where it was transferred to grain boats lashed together and floated down to Delhi. Here it was again put on the cart and through a complicated system of pulleys was re-erected at the capital.

Religious Art

The purely religious art at first is mostly Buddhist. It is remarkable that in the earliest art there is no representation of Buddha himself. His place is marked by an empty seat, by his footprints, by a riderless horse and his presence is indicated by an umbrella. An empty seat with a tree or an empty seat with a wheel indicates Buddha at the moment of the illumination or of the First Sermon. Birth is indicated when Maya, the mother of Buddha, is shown standing or sitting on the lotus with two elephants carved above her ritually asperse the unseen child, in accordance with the legend. The departure of Buddha leaving his family was represented by a riderless horse under an umbrella, with deities supporting its hooves.

Thus, a whole religious art became established. Buddha was also shown in his previous lives, in his various forms. It was under the influence of Buddhism that Asoka began the excavation by monk-artists of a series of cave temples in Western Ghats in what is now famous as the Ajanta Caves which will be described later on in this book.

It is quite evident from what has been said above, that Mauryan art exhibits in many respects an advanced stage of development in the evolution of the Indian art. Therefore, there must have been a long history of artistic effort behind the artists of the Mauryan epoch. How are we to explain the absence of specimen of the Indian art before C. 250 B.C. ? The reason for this paucity of architectural achievements was the perishable character of the material then used, which was earth or wood, stucco, bamboo, or timber. It was also probably due to a philosophy of life which insisted on simplicity. The Indian art originated in the religious need of constructing Yajna-Vedis and Yajna-salas, altars and halls for the performance of sacrifice. Vedic fire-altars, tombs and burial mounds have been unearthed in the South. In Rajagraha (Bihar) we have remains of houses and forts. We may also assume that specimen of earlier art may yet come to light or that they are related to the Indus art recently discovered.

Dancing and Music

Indians have been saturated with a love of dance for thousands of years and some of the old traditions have survived even now, for instance, in Malabar. All Indian dancing has been traced mythologically to Shiva who as God represents creation, preservation and destruction. These three processes are regarded as a cycle and are symbolised by a mythological dance, viz., the Tandava Nritya of Natraj, a specimen of this is to be found in Tanjore.

The first important treatise on dancing is the Natya Shastra of Bharat Muni which is supposed to have been written three hundred years before Christ. This treatise is mainly concerned with drama and describes both music and dancing as subsidiary parts of dramaturgy. Indian dancing can be divided into four schools, viz., Bharata Natyam, Katha-Kali, Manipuri and Kathak and from the emotional point of view it can be divided into two main categories, the Tandava or the vigorous dance and the Lasya, the soft one. Generally in a dance we have nine basic movements of the head, eight glances of the eye, six of the eyebrows, one of the neck and about four thousand of the hands and the feet. Every dance has an ideal side which is nothing short of divine and also a practical side which falls short of the original side. This linkage of the Indian dance to spirituality distinguishes it from the West. Their techniques are also, to a great extent, different.

The 'Bharat Natya' belongs to the South. It is a temple dance and has been performed for hundreds of years in the temples of the South. Its main theme is devotional. It is elegant, refined and consists of delicate and rather extra-ordinary movements. In recent years there has been a great revival of this school of dancing.

The 'Katha-Kali' dance (Katha - story, Kali play) is a dance-drama. It has been in vogue for thousands of years in an unbroken tradition in Kerala (Old Malabar). In 'Katha-Kali' themes of Ramayana, Mahabharata and other heroic legends are staged as well as their battle with the forces of evil. The real 'Katha-Kali' is very virile and women are not permitted to take part in it.

The 'Manipuri' is mostly to be found in Assam. It has got much in common with both 'Kath', and 'Bharat-Natyam'. It is danced mostly in rhythmic phases. The face should be immobile and movements of dance convey all that is necessary through their lyrical and rhythmic movements without the aid of facial expression. It is a form of ballet woven round legends of Krishna and Gopies and is accompanied by songs.

The 'Kathak' is popular in Northern India. It resembles 'Bharat-Natyam'. Its present form is a product of the Muslim and Hindu synthesis of culture in the medieval period. It is mainly concerned with expression of love between Radha and Krishna. It specialises in foot-work. There are folk dances also like the 'Marwari' dances, the staff dances in Mysore and 'Garba' dances in Gujarat.

Together with dancing, India has produced unique music. To the Hindu mind the arts of vocal music, instrumental music and dancing are so intimately connected with each other that the term 'Sangeet' was used by the ancient writers to include all the three together. Although strictly speaking it is applicable only to vocal music.

Like all arts the origin of music has also been traced to the 'Vedas'. The 'Vedic Index' shows a very wide variety of musical instruments like Dundhbhi, Veena and Nadi. By the time of Yajur Veda, professional musicians were also arisen. The art reached a greater perfection in the period of the Sama Veda. During this period the hymns used to be chanted and gradually they were set to tune and rhythm. This brought into existence a class of singer-priest. Appreciation of pronunciation and emphasis on particular syllables and words must have produced the essentials of melody and rhythm.

After the period of Sama-Veda, we have reference to music in the Grammar of Panini who mentions Silalin and Krisasvin as the authors of two sets of 'Sutras' on dancing. It is also said that in Rik-pratisakhya of 400 B.C. seven notes of music are mentioned. In Ramayana and Mahabharata also we have singing of ballads and other types of music. All these developments led to the formulation of the laws of music by the sage Bharat in his 'Natya-Shastra' in which he has devoted three chapters on music. But in his book there is no mention of the system of the 'Ragas' and 'Raginis' which we come across in the medieval times. Only 'Jatis' are mentioned and these are now regarded as the parent of the present 'Ragas'. But the Bharata Natya-Shastra gives us no guidance about the main features of the musical notation of the times and no connection is established between Sama music and that of the older music. Thus, we are very poorly equipped in the matter of reliable records for a faithful history of music of the early period of

Indian history. These were the developments that we can so far visualise in the history of ancient Indian dancing and music.

To conclude, the evidence supplied to us by Kautilya, Megasthenes (the Greek ambassador at the court of Chandra Gupta Maurya) and the inscriptions of Asoka give a picture of a richly cultured life lived by the Indians in the Mauryan period.

The Kushan Period

The culture as depicted in the Mauryan period continued but some foreign tribes entered into India at this stage and supplied their own elements into the fabric of the Indian culture. The Kushans specially contributed to the enrichment of Indian life and culture. We may specially note three important features of this period, namely, commercial intercourse with the West, split of Buddhism into Hinayana and Mahayana and the evolution of the Gandhara school of art.

It was during the period of Kushan rule, particularly under their greatest king Kanishka, that Indian relations actively developed with Rome, as well as with China. When Augustus proclaimed himself emperor of the Roman Empire, some of the Indian kings sent to him missions of congratulations. The historian Strabo (Rome) has left an account of one such mission, dispatched by a 'lord of six hundred kings' called Poros by some, and Pandion by others. The head of this mission carried a letter written in Greek, inviting Augustus to form an alliance with him and offering Roman citizens free passage throughout his dominions. The party first set out from Barygaza (Broach) at the mouth of the Narbada river in 25 B.C. They sailed through the Persian Gulf, travelled up the Euphrates and thus struck overland to Damascus and Antioch. It took the mission four years to reach Augustus before whom they were presented in the island of Samos. They delivered, besides a letter, a number of gifts consisting, for example, of tigers, a python, gigantic tortoises, a Himalayan pheasant and armless body who shot arrows with his toes. The tigers were the first to be ever seen in Europe.

The Kushans, in imitation of Roman gold-coins, struck in India also gold-coins of precise weight, fineness and proper value in order to promote trade with Rome. Thus coinage in India was improved as a result of foreign contacts. On one side of these coins were the portraits of the Kushan kings and an the other side were the images of foreign or Indian deities. Among the Indian ones were Siva with his bull Nandi, his son Skanda, and Buddha.

At the beginning of the second century A.D. the frontier of India and the Roman world were actually no more than six hundred miles apart. A Kushan embassy to Rome was greatly welcomed in A.D. 99. They were given senator's seats in the theatre. India was immensely rich in all those articles of luxury for which Rome developed an avid taste, namely, jewels and fine muslins, ivory and tortoise shell, indigo, drugs, cosmetics, perfumes, condiments and spices. Roman gold flowed into India in such vast quantities that emperors like Tiberius complained of the shortage of money to provide for military and administrative needs. Gold coins of Rome have been specially unearthed in the Deccan and thus testify to the brisk trade of India with Rome. Indians, in exchange, imported from the West only limited quantities of linen, coral glass, antimony, copper, tin, lead and wine, so that the balance of trade was always in Indla's favour and Rome had to settle her bills in gold.

At first the bulk of this trade passed along the overland routes criss-crossing Asia and converging from all directions in Bactria. There was of course a water route also used by the Persian, Greek, Arab and Indian ships, along the coast between India and the Persian Gulf, Aden, Mocha and Solomon's ancient port of Ezian-Geber, at the head of the Gulf of Aquba on the Red Sea. But dangers from inclement weather, rocks and pirates made it impossible to use this route frequently. We have a record of the voyage made by this route by an unknown Alexandrian captain. The record known as the Periplus Maris Erythraei, Periplus of the Erythrean Sea, describes the voyage between Egypt and India in the first century A.D., and makes mention of interesting topics such as the dangerous tides of Broach, the Indian imports of singing boys and choice girls for the royal harem and quarrels between Shaka and Pahlava princes in Saurashtra (Kathiawar). Various ports of southern India are also described.

Soon in the first century A.D., a discovery opened brisk trade between India and Alexandria (Egypt), the principal entrepot for the Indian trade with Rome. It was the discovery of trade winds or monsoon through the help of which voyages could be made safer. Alexandria was now a meeting place for the traders and adventurers, the philosophers and scholars, the saints and mystics, of three continents– Asia, Africa, Europe.

It is said that many Indian ideas were now becoming part of the Alexandrian medley of cultures. For instance, people in Alexandria knew of the works of Indian Yogis, they read about Hindu cave-temples and Buddhist monastic life. Some of the Christian orders now founded probably took some of their rites and ideas from the Buddhist religious lore, for instance, the use of the rosary, the ringing of the bells, the strict discipline of the brotherhood. Indian numerals, miscalled Arabic, were now introduced into Alexandria by the second century A.D. It was an Indian who made the greatest contribution to arithmetic, viz., the invention of the place-value system and zero. The numerals acquired a value depending on their place or position, in a series of numbers built up an the decimal plan. The same numerals in 12 or 21, for example, express different values, depending on their sequence. Thus, the civilised world owes a great debt to India for the discovery of the numerals which passed from India to Europe by way of Alexandria.

We thus find evidence of great commercial and cultural intercourse between India and the West by way of Alexandria which had now become a far-famed seat of culture and learning. Indian manufactures were finding great markets in Europe and Africa's gold was pouring into India and at the same time Indian ideas were becoming the property of the-then-known world. Thus, the myth that India lived in ancient times in isolation has been exploded and the fact established that from very early tines India has played a great civilising role in the world and for the world.

Another notable feature of this period was the great division of Buddhism into Hinayana and Mahayana.

From the first century before Christ to the second century after, the great initiative in Indian speculation was taken by Buddhism, which gives proof of a marvellous effort in philosophy. The movement was led by a comparatively new Buddhism which, about the second century after Christ, came to be distinguished from the old by the name of Mahayana, the Great Vehicle, as opposed to Hinayana, the Small Vehicle. These two forms of Buddhist thought would react. One on the other until, Buddhism being eliminated from India itself. Hinayana was confined chiefly to Ceylon and certain colonies (Siam, Burma), while Mahayana spread over Central Asia and the Far East (China, Japan, etc.). Hinayana is also sometimes called the Southern Buddhism, while Mahayana is known as the Northern Buddhism though it was first in the south of India that Mahayana had spread.

The term Hinayana was unknown to the early Buddhists. It came into use in the early Buddhist Sanskrit works. About the use of the prefix, Maha and Hina, there are various theories. It is said that Mahayana carries an adept to the highest goal, the Buddha-hood as was attained by the Lord himself while Hinayana carries the adept only to the stage of an Arhat and is meant only for persons of average intellect. Some say that Mahayanists seek their salvation only when they have helped others to attain their salvation while the Hinayanists are more concerned with their own good.

Political and social events contributed to this Change in teaching. It was not by mere chance that the north-west played a chief part in the advent of the Mahayana. We know that this was the side by which foreign elements could always enter the country easily, and there was a connection between the appearance of the new Buddhism and the assembling of a great council in Kashmir under Kanishka, Greek, Semitic, Iranian and Chinese influences created from Sind to Pamir, a peculiar environment into which would come Buddhism which had just assimilated on the upper Ganges what it could borrow from Brahmanic classicism. Thus, the two important reasons for the rise of the new Buddhism were the influence of the foreigners who came here and the reaction of Brahmanism upon Buddhism.

At the very time when Buddhism was becoming less Indian because more universal in its appeal, it was becoming more 'Hindu'. The popular religions like Shaivism and Vaishnavism were tending to creep into the dogmas of Buddha as into that of the Brahmans. Mahayana not only thus got its metaphysics or philosophy from Hinduism but also its mass of fables and superstitions. In short, Buddhism would have its Tantras and, in a fashion, its Puranas. Buddha was deified, made into God, or Avataras and ceremonies crept into the system. Buddhism now stood for a zeal for all mankind, which, by the laws of transmigration, is one with the whole world. The two chief methods employed by the new Buddhism were a certain dialectic, and a sort of concentration inspired by yoga.

The dialectic as a method of discussion is found in Milindapanha used there by Nagasena. The method was based upon dexterity in argument. Everything was interpreted in a negative fashion. Nothing existed save emptiness, characterlessness and indifference or Sunya, zero. From this it was easier to lead men away from reason to faith and make them believe in the mythology of the new Buddhism.

From Yoga they took their philosophy. The leading part played in this change over was by Ashvaghosha, a contemporary of Kanishka, a most representative figure of India. a musician, a founder of Sanskrit poetry, and a Brahman who became father of the Buddhist church. He was the author of the books, Buddha-charita and Sutralankara. In these books the themes of Mahayana have been discussed.

The cardinal principles of Mahayana are : (1) the conception of trikaya (three bodies of Buddha), (2) Dasabhumi (ten stages of sanctification), and (3) Anutpattika dharma-Kshanti (belief in the non-origination of all things).

(1) It was said that Buddha never appears in this world but sends out his images or bodies which were those of law, enjoyment and that in Nirvana.
(2) This gives us various stages of spiritual progress.
(3) This is the philosophy already referred to, that things of this world have no real origination, do not exist in reality and it is our imperfect mind which assigns reality to this great illusion.

For the masses the most interesting thing in Mahayana was the deification of Buddha and the multiplication of saviours. Besides the Adibuddha, the Primal Buddha, there were particular Buddhas such as Amitabha and Amitayus. Infinite Light and Infinite Duration and Maitreya, the Buddha of the future. These had their female counterparts also. These have their own paradise, to which their followers aspire. Devotion, therefore, became a paramount thing in the new Buddhism. The Far East took to it readily because they wanted less of asceticism (as compared to the old Buddhism) and more of faith and devotion. These Buddhas were further sub-divided. For instance, the concentration of Adibuddha produced five Buddhas of concentration (Dhyani-buddhas). Then follow Dhyani Bodhisattava and Manushi Bodhisattavas. From Mahayanism arose new vehicles, like the Vajrayana, a Buddhist Tantricism. Further, as Buddhism spread in other parts of the world it took many features of the myths and religion of those places and in this way we have a complex Buddhism with its philosophy, mythologies and ceremonies. It is also obvious from the above that Mahayana was considerably influenced by the new Hindu sects arising then in India.

It was natural that Mahayanism should evolve its own art and give India what is known as the Gandhara school of art, a mixture of the Greek and other art-influences. It has been said that until the Greek writers interpreted Buddha as a god of Olympus, he was never represented by an image. After that the Indo-Iranians working for the Kushans established the various characteristics by which the various Buddha should be recognised. Then the Chinese, Japanese, Tibetans and Khmers adapted these to their own spirit. The most astonishing transformation was that by which the Chinese turned the charitable Bodhisattava into a Madonna named Kwanyin.

The Graeco-Buddhist or Gandhara art, combining Greek methods and Indian religious subjects, developed about the middle of the first century B.C., onwards in Gandhara in the north-west of India and south-east of the present Afghanistan. The earliest figure of Buddha is a Graeco-Buddhist work. It wears the monastic dress treated as a classical drapery and has the signs of perfection of the universal lord and great religious reformer and various other marks of beauty such as the long ears and the small circle, in relief between the eye-brows. He was given wavy hair tied on the top into a bun. Later on under Indian influences (that of Mathura) the ritual bun and curls were adopted in place of the wavy hair. This art also represents the Bodhisattava as covered with jewels and wearing a moustache. By the new art Hellenistic models were transformed, a new strength and youth breathed into them.

According to John Irwin there are more traces of Roman than of Greek influences in the Gandhara school of art which died down about the third century A.D. To sum up, although Gandhara art made use of Graeco-Roman ideals in the modelling of the Buddha's head, more like an Apollo than an Indian mystic, and in certain technical details, such as the handling of the folds of the monk's robe, the original conception of the Buddha figure was basically Indian and evolved in strict accordance with the ideal description of the thirty-two auspicious signs on the Buddha's person, as given in the earliest Buddhist literature, for instance, the mark of wisdom between the eyebrows, the long ears, long arms, the eyes all but closed in inward contemplation and other gestures indicating spiritual acts like teaching and blessing. The Gandhara school also threw off a new offshoot, the Indo-Afghan art, resembling the later Gothic art of Europe and giving us a great variety of finely modelled sculptures. The Gandhara school had its influence on the art of the Far East also and later it acted and was acted upon by the Mathura school of art.

Besides the sculpture, under the Kushans, a new type of Buddhist monastic architecture came into being in the northern region Previously monastic buildings had been grouped around open-air stupas. Now they became part of small fortified cities. The monks' cells were ranged in double-storied rows round three sides of an open courtyard and faced inward so that only blank walls greeted the beholder from without. It is easy to understand why the Kushans imported foreign ideas into our art. They had come into India by way of Bactria, which at the time of their invasion had sixty large-Hellenic towns.

They had remained there and imbibed the culture of the place. Greek realism must have appealed to them. Besides Mahayana also appealed to them by its complex imagery and mythology and these influences evolved the Gandhara School of art.

Thus, almost the whole of the northern India was rapidly transformed by Kushan zeal into a second Buddhist Holy land. Mahayana gave to them Buddhist legends in plenty and numerous Stupas rose up to commemorate these legends and to enshrine supposed relics. But this culture received a rude shock at the hands of the Huns. 'With barbaric shouts and the loud trampling of horses' hoofs, the white Huns came and went by this route, like a gusty storm, rudely breaking the peace of the great monasteries and leaving death and ruin in their wake'.

The Gupta Age

We next come to the great flowering of the Indian culture and genius in the age of the Gupta's. This civilisation has been variously termed as the Periclean or Augustan Age of India. It witnessed a fresh renaissance in India. It was the golden age, a classical age when Indian culture attained greatest perfection and firm moulding. The age was essentially a synthesis between matter and spirit, life and religion, philosophy and science. In this synthesis it was true to the basic conceptions of our culture, the sources of which lay back in the Vedas. There are many hymns in the Rig and the Atharva Vedas which exhort man to be united with all, in heart, in aim and in work, to be friendly with all and to pray so that all may be friendly with him. They also give us the essential ideas of our social thinking. The keynote in all their social thinking is that man is not a machine but a god in the making born to blossom forth to the best of his potentialities and the chief function of society is to give him every facility so that he might fulfil his highest destiny both in his individual and collective life. 'The business of culture and social organisation in ancient India was to lead man, satisfy and support him in some harmony of the four aims of life is desire and enjoyment, material, economic and other aims of the mind and body, ethical conduct and right law of the individual and social life and finally spiritual liberation, Kama, Artha, Dharma, Moksha. The insistence was always there that except in rare cases the full satisfaction of the first three of these objects must precede the last, fullness of human experience and action prepare for the spiritual liberation, the debt to the family, the community and the gods could not be scamped'.

We saw life steadily and saw it whole, our other worldliness, therefore, is as great a myth as our alleged stay-at-homeness. The Gupta cultural heritage is a confirmation of the ancient Hindu synthesis of karma, jnana and bhakti—action, knowledge and devotion. It would be, however, a cardinal error to describe the Gupta Age as a break with the past or a new culture. It was more a culmination than an efflorescence of our classical culture. The contributions of previous epochs made possible the progress now achieved. We may now describe the chief features of the Gupta Age under the headings of social and economic conditions, religion and philosophy, education, literature, sciences and arts.

Social Conditions

The caste system and the four stages of life, Ashramas, continued to be the backbone of society. It was, however, still elastic to a certain extent. Marriages were usually endogamous but marriages of higher with lower castes called Anuloma marriages were not altogether absent. In such marriages bridegroom belonged to the higher caste whereas in Pratiloma marriages he belonged to a lower caste as compared with the bride. These often took place in society. Inter-racial marriages also took place thus assimilating the foreigners into our society inter-dining also continued, though in a restricted fashion. Professions also were not very rigidly determined by caste. For instance, Brahmans followed trade, architecture and service as professions. They even became kings. The Gupta emperors were Vaishyas. The Kshatriyas also followed commercial and industrial vocations. There were more sub-castes among the Vaishyas and Shudras than among the higher castes. Kayasthas frequently figure in contemporary epigraphical records, usually as professional writers. Shudras also could become traders and agriculturists like the Vaishyas. There were untouchables living outside the main settlements. They used to strike a piece of wood when entering the city so that men might know of their coming and avoid them. They used to follow hunting, fishery, scavenging and similar dispised professions.

The Brahmans received the greatest homage. Their relations with Kshatriyas were cordial. They were divided into several shakhas (classes) based upon the Vedas which they studied and our epigraphs enable us to get a fairly accurate idea of their distribution. For instance, Orissa, Telengana, Koshala and Madhya Pradesh were the stronghold of Yajurvedin Brahmans and the same was probably the case with U.P. Kathiawar was the stronghold of the Samavedins ; an Atharvedin is mentioned in Mysore, in Belgaum, at Valabhi and in the Kangra valley.

The Rigvedins figure very rarely in our records. The Kshatriyas continued to enjoy their old privileges, belonging to the status of dvijas (twice-born). So was the case with the Vaishyas who also knew their Gotras and Pravaras. The Vaishyas were famous for their charitable disposition. (The Gotra is clan with a specific name). Each Gotra has what is called a Pravara–names of rishis or seers stated to be their ancestors. A person who pays his respect to an elder announces himself in these terms. I invoke your blessing, I am the descendant of Angiras, Brihaspati and Bharadvaja of the gotra of Bharadvaja, follower of the Apastamba Sutra, of the name of N.N., venerable sir. Marriages were not permissible between families with common pravara rishis.

Slavery is mentioned in the Narada Smriti. Prisoners of war often met with this fate. Sometimes debtors unable to pay their debts had to become slaves of their creditors. Slavery, however, was not lifelong and liberty could be regained. They also received better treatment than their prototypes in the West. Freedom from slavery followed after proper ceremonies. The Joint family continued to be the basic feature of the Hindu private life. Partitions in the life-line of the father were not approved. Ownership of property was vested in the father but the rights of sons and brothers to the property are recognised. Women had no such rights unless the father had no male issue.

Adoption was not very much approved. There were differences of views with regard to the share of the widow to her husband's property. Mostly she was entitled to a maintenance. Prepuberty marriages were becoming common. Thus marriages at the early age of 12 or 13 naturally led women to having no say in the settlement of their marriage. Education of women was permissible but they could not recite the Vedic mantras. Purdah among higher castes was beginning. The life of a woman was still not unpalatable. She was the mistress of home. Sometimes widows could remarry. Satis are mentioned during the period though they were rare. Women as shown in contemporary plantings could move freely in society. We must not forget the fact that ideally woman was regarded as Shakti, the energising principle. She was both Saraswati and Kali, creator and destroyer. Mother and motherland have been regarded as worthier of adoration than heaven. Itself, according to Manu, 'Where women are honoured, the gods rejoice where they are not respected, all actions become futile'. Thus, women in the Gupta period continued to enjoy freedom, respect and honour.

Society was in a very flourishing stage. As for dress, the male population wore an upper garment and a lower dhoti though the Scythians introduced coats, overcoats and trousers, often worn by the Indian Kings. Head-dress was worn on auspicious occasions.

Women either wore a petticoat and a sari over it or a long sari served both the purposes. A bodice was used below the sari to cover the bust. The Scythians used jackets, blouses and frocks. Silken garments were worn on ceremonial occasions. Ornaments of women were very varied. A large number of them were used over the forehead. So also there were various designs in the ear-rings and necklaces. There were various types of zones (mekhalas) and a gauzy pearl ornament was used over the breasts as well as the thighs. There were also armlets, bangles, rings and anklets. The nose-ring was yet unknown. Men also were fond of wearing ornaments.

The fashion of dressing the hair was very numerous. They may well be the envy of the most fashionable woman of today.

False hair was used to give different artistic shapes. The use of paints, pastes, powders and lipsticks was not unknown.

Water clocks were used in various places and institutions. The clock consisted of a small pot, kept-floating-in a larger vessel filled with water. The pot could be filled in 24 minutes (ghatika) by water slowly coming into it through a hole made at the bottom. An attendant was necessary to empty it out and float it again the moment it was filled.

Dice and chess were the favourite indoor pastimes and hunting, ram fights, cock fights and ball games were the outdoor amusements. Fairs, shows and dramas provided a variety of entertainment.

Thus, the social conditions of the period show us a people happy, well-placed in life and fond of the good things of life. To quote Fa-Hien, the Chinese traveller, visiting India in the days of Chandra Gupta II, 'The people are numerous and happy. They have not to register their households, or attend to any magistrates and their rules. The king governs without decapitation or other corporal punishments. People of a various sects set up houses of charity where rooms, couches, beds, food and drink are supplied to travellers'.

Economic Conditions

As in the Mauryan period, India continued to make great progress in the economic sphere. Her sons went abroad and planted her culture in various countries during this period. They also acted as travelling agents, so to say, of Indian trade and commerce, taking her manufactures, exchanging them with either money or by barter. Trade and industry were organised in guilds as in the past. These guilds were also doing banking business and receiving permanent deposits guaranteeing regular payment of interest. The affairs of the guild were managed by the president and a small executive committee of four or five members.

The peace and prosperity prevailing in the age gave a great impetus to inter-provincial and inter-state trade and to cover them federations of guilds were also organised as is evident from the seals found at Basarh, the ancient Vaishali. These guilds sometimes managed the finances of temples and also offered monetary help to the government. Partnership transactions were also widely prevalent. Some guilds had their own militia to protect the person, property and merchandise of their members. The main articles of trade were probably different varieties of cloth, food grains, spices, salt, hullian and precious stones. The trade was both by land and by river. Principal towns like Broach, Ujjayini, Paithan, Vidisha, Prayaga, Benares, Gaya, Pataliputra, Vaishali, Tamralipti, Kaushambi, Mathura, Ahichchhattra and Peshawar were connected by roads. Goods were transported by carts and by pack animals. Riverine traffic was along the Ganges, the Brahmaputra, the Narmada, the Godavari, the Krishna and the Kaveri. Ships were built. Tamralipti (modern Tamluk) was the principal port in Bengal and carried on an extensive trade with China, Ceylon, Java and Sumatra. The southern ports carried on an extensive trade with Eastern Archipelago, China and Western Asia. Even Roman ships used to come to these ports for trade. The principal items of export were pearls, precious stones, cloths, perfumes, incense, spices, indigo, drugs, cocoanuts and ivory articles and the main items of imports were gold, silver, copper, tin, lead, silk, camphor, corals, dates and horses. The main items of natural wealth were rice, wheat, sugarcane, jute, oilseeds, cotton, jwar, bajra, spices, betelnuts, medicinal drugs, products of forests and mines of precious stones. Among the industries the most important was that of cloth. Then came other crafts and industries like sculpture, inlaying, ivory work, painting, smithy, ship-building, etc. It is said that the monthly cost of feeding one individual sumptuously was about Rs. 2. Living was thus very cheap in the Gupta period.

Agriculture was the main occupation of the masses. There was nothing like the modern zamindari system in Bengal or Uttar Pradesh. The tenants of a landlord not tilling the lands received as their share of working the fields 33 to 50 per cent of the gross produce. Land was regarded as a very valuable piece of property and its transfer could be effected only through the consent of the fellow villagers or the permission of the village or town council. The fallow and waste lands belonged to the state in theory. State also owned fields of cultivable land in various village, known as Rajyavastu (crown lands). These often came into the possession of the state on account of want of heirs or failure to pay the land tax. Thus generally, 'the ownership of the cultivable land vested in private individuals or families and not in the state'. The facts cited above show India economically a great and wealthy country with immense foreign trade. The economic prosperity reacted on Indian culture and gave the people time and leisure to cultivate the finer arts of life.*

Religion and Philosophy

This period witnessed the revival of Brahmanism. Hindu Society was given its popular faiths or sects. It was also provided with great philosophies, the six darshans. The new Hinduism was a fusion of the ideas and ideals drawn from the two main racial streams of India, namely, Aryan and Dravidian. The austere ideal of the impersonal God was supplemented with personal God, variously called Shiva, Vishnu, Devi or any of their multiple names. The Vedic gods receded into the realms of mythology. Idol worship with temple architecture now came into vogue. A whole paraphernalia of rites and ceremonies developed.

The Gupta Age is usually regarded as an era of Brahman revival. It would be more correct to call it a period of culmination, of florescence rather than of renaissance. The recrudence of Brahmanism in the Ganges valley is as old as the time of Pushyamitra, while in the South we have a long succession of dynasties that counted it as their proud boast to have repeatedly performed Vedic rites like the Vajapeya and the Ashvamedha. The devotional faith like those of Vishnu and Shiva were also prevailing there. Then also some of the foreign kings preceding the Guptas were adherents of two great Hindu sects, namely, Shaivas and Bhagavatas.

---

* *A New History of the Indian People*, edited by Dr. A.S. Altekar, Vol. VI, pp. 361-362.

Bhakti

The most noticeable aspect in religion was the growing importance of Bhakti (devotion) and the love of fellow beings which found expression in benevolent activities and toleration of the opinions of others. Bhakti, that is, intense devotion to God conceived of as a person, a Saviour worthy of trust and ready to shower his blessings or grace is an important element of Vaishnavism and Shaivism as expounded in the Gita and the Svetavastara Upanishad. Thus, in this period Brahmanism assumes its classical forms. In this transformation it was also influenced by Buddhism with their beliefs in transmigration, Karma and Moksha or Nirvana. Mahayana or the popular form of Buddhism had an effect, if only by contrast, on Brahmanic thought. The masses also had their beliefs and superstitions. There was also the tantric philosophy with its own form of worship. All the above influences combined to form the syncretic Hinduism we have got today as a legacy from the Gupta period. The two things characteristic of this Hinduism are the belief in a metaphysical first principle periodically becoming incarnate in Saviours of the human race (the avatars), and secondly, a pious devotion which connects the relative with the absolute not so much by knowledge as by sentiment (Bhakti).

Shaivism and Vaishnavism

The great god is Shiva, in whom his worshippers recognise a 'Lord', Ishvara. His origins are partly Vedic, for he is derived from Rudra, who slays cattle but also preserves them and partly from the Tantric forms which probably gave the erotic significance to Shiva emphasising the generative aspect of God, whom it adores in the form of the phallus (linga). Shiva is now worshipped in many forms and consequently we have many sects of Shaivites.

Another form of Shakti was symbolized in the rise of Vaishnavism with Vishnu as its main deity. In this period Vishnu-worship was further supplemented by Vasu-Deva worship or its more popular form, Krishna-worship. References to Vishnu have been traced to the Vedas and the Upanishads.

Vasu-Deva is also an old god. Panini (in the fifth century B.C.), mentions Vasudevakas and Arjunakas, sects worshipping the heroes Vasu-Deva and Arjun, celebrated in the Mahabharata. In the first years of the second century B.C. the column of Besnagar, in the south of Gwalior, was erected in honour of the same Vasu-Deva by the Greek Heliodors of Takshashila. He is also mentioned in the Chhandogya Upanishad. Now, Vasu-Deva is another name for Krishna who is mentioned by Patanjali in his Mahabhasya about the second century B.C. Vasu-Deva was also known in the Brahmana period as Narayana.

It should, however, be mentioned that in the earlier accounts nothing is said about the boyhood of Krishna. It is only now, specially in the Puranas, that a new popular Krishna appears, baby Krishna full of mischievous pranks, and Krishna, the charming youth, companion of the cowherds and milk-maids of Brindaban. This new Krishna rapidly won the hearts of millions of devotees. Again like Shaivism, Vaishnavism or Krishna-worship has split up into many sects, worship in public temples became fairly common in the Gupta period. Temples became centres of Hindu religion and culture. Their construction and decoration, their ceremonies and sermons offered scope to the sculptor, the architect, the painter, the musician, the dancer, the pauranika and the philosopher. Hindu rites and popular beliefs developed and vratas (fasts) came into existence like the vrata of Ekadshi.

Another development in Indian religion was that of Tantricism which requires some notice at this stage. People have traced Tantricism to the Vedic times and even earlier to the Indus valley civilisation. Tantric ideas, names, forms and symbols were, it is said, concrete representations of the combined monism, Unitarianism, universalism and synthetism of the Vedic scriptures. Tantricism is a remarkable flowering of the Indian spirit and another indication of the spiritual renaissance in India. During the Gupta Age, many of its scriptures including the Chandi, were written in Bengal. Tantricism sought to raise the whole man into the divine perfection as envisaged in the Vedas. Regarding life as the cosmic play of the Divine, it postulates a purpose in the play which is possible of fulfilment only in man, who alone of all creations has the unique privilege of awakening to the power of consciousness latent in him. And when that potential power (kundalini) sleeping at the base of his physical system is roused, it proceeds upwards to the centres (chakras) or planes of the forces rendering them dynamic with its own powers, so that they converge in all their new-found strength on the realisation by him of a stage in which the possesser becomes possessed by a higher consciousness. In the Tantric sadhana an absolute self-surrender to the will of Mahamaya the Shakti is imperatively necessary. The Tantras aim not only at the liberation (mukti), into the Brahman but also at a liberated enjoyment of the delight (ananda) of the universal play of the supreme Shakti; (symbolised by the five makars). The Tantrics thus delved deeper into life and tried to find its unity with the spirit. Later on they degenerated and became a theme of formulae and occult mysticism. Tantra furnished the basis for Shakti worship, God and Nature were worshipped in the female forms and were regarded as embodiment of power. We have as a result various goddesses—Ashtabhuja Devi, Durga, Kali, Chandi and others. God or impersonal Brahman thus became dynamic or active in this world through Mahashakti or mother-power which was symbolised by various goddesses mentioned above.

Philosophy

The Gupta period also developed great philosophical systems which are known to us as the six Darshans, the philosophies of Samkhya, Yoga, Nyaya, Vaisheshika, Purva Mimamsa and Vedanta.

Samkhya

Samkhya and Yoga are regarded as complementary, the one theoretical and the other practical. The philosophy of Sankhya is based upon dualism variously expressed, for instance, between Purusha and Prakriti (God and nature). Primarily, there is Purusha (God) in the Universe. From Him emanates Prakriti or Nature. Nature is analysed into three elements (guna) which are in everything unequally combined.

These elements are Sattva, Rajas and Tamas. There are further divisions, namely, those of Akasha (ether), wind, fire, water, earth, sound, contact, taste, shape and scent. There are also evolved organs of knowledge and action like hearing, touch, sight, taste, smell, voice, feet, hands and the organs of generation and evacuation. These are connected with Ahankara and Buddhi (ego and intellect). These 24 principles lie at the base of the evolution of the world.

Yoga

The Yoga-Sutras, reputedly the work of Patanjali, who may be another man than the grammarian of the second century B.C., are roughly of the fifth century of the Christian era. The Yoga philosophy has given us most profound ideas of psychology and formulated methods of attaining salvation. These are the eight stager or yogangas, namely : 1. Yama (moral virtues), 2. Niyama (observances), 3. Asana (posture), 4. Pranayama (control of breath or vital force), 5. Pratyahara (withdrawing of the senses from external objects), 6. Dharana (retention), 7. Dhyana (meditation) and 8. Samadhi (perfect concentration). By the help of these, mind is purified, enlightened and controlled. Then one understands things in true perspective. Then alone Yoga or union with God can be attempted by concentration and meditation. Patanjali also refers to self surrender to God in all respects as of great importance in making union with God possible.

Nyaya

The Vaisheshika was regarded as a complement of the Nyaya system in which it merged in the eleventh century. Nyaya philosophy gives us an art of reasoning or logic. A man who can argue rightly avoids false knowledge, vice, action, birth and pain. Thus, proper reasoning leads to salvation. Various modes of knowledge or reasoning are given in this philosophy : for example, perception (pratyaksha), and inference (Anumana), analogy (Upamana) and testimony (sabda). The system also gave us a sort of syllogism, for instance - There is fire on the mountain (pratijna-assertion), because there is smoke on the mountain (hetu - reason). Everything which contains smoke fire, for example, the hearth (undaharanam - example). But it is so here (Upanaya - application to the particular case). Therefore, it is so (nigamanam - result). These two philosophies of Vaisheshika and Nyaya are, therefore, distinguished by their realism.

Vaisheshika

This philosophy gives us an atomistic doctrine. There are four kinds of atom, those of earth being qualified by scent, those of water by cold touch, those of fire by heat and those of wind by tangibility. Further, this philosophy seeks to provide a clear-cut formula for the achievement of salvation. This sutra attributes the authorship of the Vedas to persons of superior wisdom. According to this philosophy God is the creator and controller of all things. For the sake of making the beings experience the fruits of the actions of their past lives, there arises in the mind of God a desire for creating the world over again. When this desire appears in God, it sets in motion all the potential tendencies and forces in the jivas, which, operating upon the various atoms lead to the formation of the world. According to this system when a man with due knowledge and intelligence performs righteous acts without any selfish motives, he comes to be born in a pure family. Thus circumstanced, gradually the desire for salvation arises in him and by stages he attains to it and there is no further body for him. This system also gives correct mode of forming judgements and gathering knowledge.

Purva Mimamsa

Mimamsa means the reasoning which has to be adopted in order to understand the connotation of a word or sentence. The prefix purva is added because it deals primarily with the method of reasoning regarding the rites which form the purva or earlier portion of the Vedas. Thus, the Subject-matter of this system is the study of the Vedic rites. This philosophy discusses the nature of the Vedic rites, their primary and secondary character, their priority and posteriority in the matter of performance together with their results and purposes. Thus, performance of rituals or ordained actions is necessary for salvation according to this philosophy.

Vedanta

Also called the second (Uttara) Mimamsa otherwise Vedanta (completion or end of the Vedas) is the most famous of Indian philosophies. According to Sankara, Vedanta asserts the freedom of the self from the world, it boldly denies the world calling it an Illusion, Maya, means mistaking the rope for a snake. It prescribes renunciation of the world in spirit, this renunciation to be achieved gradually and methodically as suited to the capacities of each individual. Brahman or God is the only reality. Salvation comes from inwardly realising Brahman and after a certain stage the world is shaken off. Vedanta is more idealistic than realistic emphasising knowledge rather than action, contemplation rather than rituals and ceremonies. People have variously interpreted this philosophy. The most famous interpretation is that of Badarayana in his works the Brahma Sutras. Vedanta is also known as Advaita or non-dualistic, that is, there is no double principle, God and matter are only one principle God or Brahman. We should see God in everything and become one with Him. This is a monistic philosophy. Later on it was modified by many others resulting in the philosophical schools of Ramanuja, Madhva, Nimbaraka and Vallabha. This philosophy, found also in the Upanishads, has greatly attracted the Western scholars.

Thus, in the realm of philosophy India reached the highest watermark in the Gupta period. But our philosophy was not merely barren speculation or abstruse thinking in a vacuum. It was pre-eminently evolved to achieve certain ends related to the higher life, the life of the spirit. Our philosophers were, therefore, seers, engaged in sadhana and gave us philosophy of salvation or moksha. Our philosophy was, therefore, dynamic. The acts which make a man a slave are those which he does without perfect knowledge. Those which he does with that knowledge (given by philosophies), not only do not enslave him but effect his freedom. India sought not merely deliverance, negatively, she sought to achieve liberty, positively. The lesson India has given to us is that to understand better is to free oneself.

Education

From times immemorial, education in India has been a private concern, the teacher teaching the taught at his home and being paid by the pupils with occasional grants from the state or private charitable institutions. He also supplemented his income by performing professional duties like those of the priest. Holy places and capitals of kingdoms were, therefore, the common centres of learning as offering the best chance of earning a decent income. Among the capitals, Pataliputra, Valabhi, Ujjayani and Padmavati were famous centres of learning while Ayodhya, Banaras, Mathura, Nasik and Kanchi, among the tirthas (holy places), were famous centres of education. Taxila had declined completely during this period. There were also the Agrahara villages, containing learned Brahmans who were supported by the revenues of these villages assigned to them for maintenance by the state. The teachers there often attracted students from far and wide. In South India centres of learning were known as Ghatikas, being probably in the nature of post-graduate colleges, technical education was imparted usually in the family itself, as most of the professions had become hereditary. Sometimes artisans took outside students as apprentices. Information about elementary education is meagre. It probably commenced at the age of 5 and was imparted by teachers who were called Darakacharyas.

Very often teachers of higher grade initiated their pupils in the three Rs. Lipishalas or primary schools existed in many villages. Children used to write either on wooden boards in colour or by the finger on the ground covered with sand or fine dust.

But the most famous centres of learning were the monastic colleges founded mostly by the Buddhists. These centres contributed to the building of a harmonious cultural life of the people. Their germs lay in the hermitages of well-known sages in Vedic India where students flocked from all places. In the

Mahabharata Naimishan forest is mentioned as such a centre where Shaunaka was the presiding officer or Kulapati (Chancellor). Taxila, Banaras, Ujjayani and Amaravati were other famous centres of learning before the Gupta Age. We may take Nalanda as the epitome of such centres and describe some of its features.

Nalanda was the international university attracting students from Asia and was situated in Magadha. It was the largest of its kind in the contemporary world to which scholars of different castes, creeds and races hailing from India and from countries like–China, Japan, Korea, Java, Sumatra, Tibet, Mongolia and Bokhara flocked for purposes of advanced studies. Of the 10,000 residents in the university, 8,500 were alumni and 1,500 were faculty members. There was wide catholicity of method in education and liberal character of curriculum. Through discussion and debate and conference according to the traditional Indian method it helped to unite its varied elements into a superb intellectual fellowship and the wide variety of subjects taught provided a veritable feast of reason. The curriculum included all systems of philosophies of different religions in India as well as arts and sciences. The state had given the revenues of more than hundred villages for the upkeep of the university. There were a hundred lecture halls where classes were held daily. Scholarship was measured by the number of Sutra collections a student was able to master. Time was regulated over a wide area of Northern India by the Nalanda water clock; such was its great importance.

Valabhi in Gujarat and Vikramasila in Bihar were other famous centres of learning.

'Night was to descend on all the great centres of traditional Indian learning, however, when the untutored Muslims of Central Asia poured into India with fire and sward at the beginning of the 11th century'.*

Literature

We may take up poetry, drama, narrative works and

* *The Pageant of India's History*, pp. 275-276.

religious literature as exemplifying the high literary activities of this period.

Poetry

In poetry (Kavya) the greatest poet of India lived at this period, namely, Kalidasa. His life is shrouded in mystery but it is said that he was the son of a Brahman who having lost his father early was reared by a cowherd. Coarse and uneducated, fate brought him a princess in marriage.

This put Kalidasa to great shame. He called on the goddess Kali for help, dedicating to her entirely his self and thus got the name of Kalidasa (slave of Kali). He became a learned man, elegant, cultured and aristocrat through and through. He was one of the nine gems of king Vikramaditya, the others probably being Varah-Mihira, the astronomers Brahmagupta, the mathematician, Vararuchi, the grammarian, Amarsinha, the author of a Sanskrit dictionary; Dhanvantari, the physician : Shankhu, the architect ; Kshapanaka, the astrologer and Vaitalika, the magician. Kalidasa's inspiration is lyrical but he also wrote dramas and epics. He took his subjects from the Puranas and epics, and one theme from the Veda.

His epic poems are the Kumarasambhava, the 'Birth of Kumara' and the Raghuvamsha, the 'Race of Raghu'. Kumar is another name of Skanda, the war-god. The story runs that the Gods in their unending war with the Asuras needed a leader. Only Shiva could provide such a leader. He was in meditation. His samadhi was broken by Kama, the god of love, accompanied by his wife Rati but Shiva resented this and burnt Kama-Deva with the glance of his third eye. Devas or gods interceded for Kama who was restored to life. Shiva then had a son from Uma married to him after great penances and trials. Kalidasa describes the married bliss of the two in such lively colours that European taste is sometimes embarrassed by his frankness. The Raghu-Vamsha, presents the genealogy of Ram and gives us the life of Raghu who gets a child after serving Nandini, the great cow. He gets a son Aja. From him is born Dasaratha, the father of Ram. A garland of flowers falling from the sky kills Indumati, the wife of Aja. We also find a description of a king Agnivarna who is described as being licentious and given over to the practices of Kamasutra—art of erotic love.

Kalidasa achieves lyrical perfection in the poem, Meghaduta, the messenger of cloud. The subject of the poem is married love. A Yaksha, a divine being in the service of Kubera, god of wealth, is banished by his master. He has to leave his wife. He pines for her and pours out his grief to a cloud drifting towards his home where his wife lived. His wife also passes her days in grief. It is said that Kalidasa also wrote other poems like the Ritusamhara, the descriptions of seasons, and Shringara Tilaka, collection of erotic stanzas. He is regarded as the best poet in Sanskrit. His poetry is characterised by grace, simplicity, sentiment and is decorated by striking figures of speech, specially the smiles with their beauty, variety and appropriateness. His characters are masterpieces. He is superb in describing the emotions of love and pathos. They also give us the ideas of the age. His description of nature is unrivalled. Other epic poets of the period are Bharavi and Magha, the former's Kiratarjuniya is very famous, Magha was a poet of love'. Of later age is Bhartrihari, 'the philosopher of love'. There were minor poets of middle rank like Harishena, with his panegyric of Samudra Gupta, Vasula, the court poet of Yashovarman and others like Vatsabhatti, Kubja and Saba.

Drama

In India, dramatic art had reached great perfection quite early. There was a complete theory of the drama with fixed rules and classifications. The Vedas furnish us rudimentary specimen of this art and the Krishna cult with its devotional dances and gestures provided another element in the foundation of the Indian Drama. There are several words to designate an actor like Jayajiva, Bharata, Sailusha and Kusilava. He is known also as nata literally dancer and a dramatic work is called nataka and the theatrical art is termed-natya. All these words have dance for their primary meaning and in the popular dance and the mime of the popular festivity we must seek the origin of the Indian drama. It is interesting to note that in India female parts were acted by women when in Europe only males were allowed to act on the stage.

In the first century of the Christian era probably the Bharatiya-Natya Shastra (treatise on the theatre) was written by the sage Bharat. The book is an encyclopedia of the arts of the theatre. There we get that Brahma created the theatre as the fifth Veda. The theatre should represent truth alone. Shiva teaches the actors the tandava dance while Parvati teaches the actresses the feminine lasya dance. It is remarkable that Indian dramas do not take tragic themes. That shows how in ancient India life was full of comedy or pleasure. The Natya Shastra also gives us the methods of building the theatre, of action, dancing and make-up, as also what languages to use on appropriate occasions. Theories of rasa, taste, emotion are also given, the main emotions are love, mirth, pity, fright, heroism, fear, disgust and admiration. The higher dramas are of ten kinds (rupaka) in which poetry is the chief thing. In addition, there are farces (prahasanas), fairy-play and various kinds of shows. The performance was given by day, from the morning on. The actors were required to be men of character and the religious character of the theatre appears in all the preparations.

The earliest known dramas belong to the Buddhist Sanskrit literature. Recent discoveries in Central Asia confirm this. Ashvaghosha was one of the famous Buddhist dramatists. Another famous dramatist living before Kalidasa was Bhasa. He takes his subjects from Mahabharata, from the legends of Rama and Krishna. His dramas are, for instance, Panchratra (five nights, dealing with an episode in the war of the Pandavas with Kauravas), Dutavakya (the message), Pratima-nataka (the play of the image), Abhisheka-nataka (play of the coronation) and his masterpiece Svapna-Vasa-vadatta (Vasavadatta in a dream). About 13 of his plays have come to light. He displays great skill in dramatising them. Characterisation is effective and the language and style are racy and direct. Other famous dramatists are Shudraka with his drama. Mrichchhakatika (the little clay cart) and Vishakhadatta with his play Mudrarakshasa (the seal of Rakshasa).

But the most representative dramatist of the age was Kalidasa. His first work was the Malavikagnimitra. The play is about a löve and intrigue of the king's harem. In Abhijanana Shakuntalam (the recognition of Shakuntala) Kalidasa's genius attains its highest point. The story is too well known to need narration here. The subject is taken from the Mahabharata and the Puranas. The play was first translated into English by Jones in 1789. Goethe wrote about it, 'flowers and fruit, all that delights and all that sustains, all heaven and all earth, are expressed in the name Shakuntala'. The verses are simply enchanting. His third play was Vikramorashtya (Urvasi won by heroism). No one has equalled Kalidasa in the art of calling up the most delicate shade of feeling and no one has painted nature as he has done. None has had his grace, his elegance and his noble rhythm. He is truly the Shakespeare of India. Among Kalidasa's successors the greatest was Bhavabhuti after the Gupta period. With him ends the great age of dramatic literature. Shallow plays were also produced like the bhana (a monolague) and the prahasana (a farcical comedy).

Narrative Literature

Indians have shown the greatest aptitude for this kind of literature. The earliest of such stories were the Jatakas translated now into many European languages. They were written in Pali, with over a hundred tales. They contain both tales and fables. In the latter form of tales India has led the world. The Panchatantra is the most famous of such works. It has been translated into European languages. It was part of Tantrakhyayika (collection of little tales) which is lost to us. The Panchatantra (five threads or books) was a hand-book of politics (niti-shastra), giving advice to the princes in the form of tales told by animals. The fables of Panchatantra have sunk so deep into Western and Eastern literature that only an expert can identify them. In these fables animals play the part of kings, ministers, courtiers, spies and lowly born hangers on. The presentation is witty and gives in a natural manner some lesson of practical wisdom. One of the Indian versions of these fables is the Hitopadesha written in the 14th century. Panchatantra first went to Persia in the sixth century. Then it passed into Arabia and Syria. From there the Greeks took it and later translations were made in Hebrew, Latin and Spanish. They formed the basis of Aesop's Fables. 'The Arabian Nights' also owe a debt to these collections. It is said that Chaucer's Canterbury Tales in some of their stories owe their inspiration to Panchatantra and so also Decameron of Baccaccia and La Fountain's Fables.

Among the literary stories we have Brihat-Katha (the great romance) by Gunadhya, narrating stories about king Udayana who is mentioned by Kalidasa in Meghduta; Katha-sarit-sagara (ocean of River of Tales) by Somadeva (in the 11th century in Kashmir) and Shuka-Saptati, (seventy tales of the parrot). The story of Sindbad the Sailor seems to be of Indian origin. Among the romances mention may be made of those by Bana like the Harsha-Charita and Kadambari.

Religious Literature

The age was famous for the final recensions of works like the Gita, the Puranas and the Smritis. Famous Buddhist works belonging to the Mahayana school were also written during this period, for example, Lalita-vistara (a miraculous life of Buddha), Buddha-charita by Ashvaghosha who also wrote philosophical works like the Lankara Sutta and the Mahayana Shraddhotpada. Nagarjuna, another famous Buddhist, wrote his Madhyamika, or 'middle way' defining and describing the doctrine of 'Sunyata'. In Peshawar there were the two brothers Asanga and Vasubhandhu, founders of the Yogachara of idealist school. It was in this period that the great philosophers composed the six systems of philosophies described above. Among other pieces of literature may be mentioned the Kama-sutra of Vatsyayana.

The Gupta culture presupposes an advanced stage of Indian languages with their vocabulary and grammar properly evolved and fixed. In this period Sanskrit received its classical shape. The Aryan language was Sanskrit and showed similarity to Homeric Greek, Latin and other languages of Europe. The Dravidian languages were not related to any known speech. Each of these had their literature and the Tamil language, for example, does not fall behind Sanskrit literature in richness. The language has now been permeated by the Sanskrit language.

Sanskrit has passed through three stages, old Indian,

Middle Indian and Modern Indian. Old Indian is Vedic and is so like Avesta, the sacred language of the old Iranians that if one knows Vedic one can soon understand it. Vedic is not a homogeneous language and shows signs of foreign influence.

The language gradually changed in the post-Vedic and the Sutra periods. About half way through the fifth century B.C. it was codified by the celebrated grammarian Panini. It became the Sanskrit or perfect language (Sans-krita means adorned, arranged). Sanskrit was not the language of the masses. Only the upper classes spoke it. It was learned by rote. In Sanskrit different stratas are traceable, the Panini, Epical and classical periods.

By the side of Vedic and Sanskrit, there developed popular or Prakritic languages, which reached maturity in the post epic period. We thus got-Pali, the ecclesiastical language of the Buddhists of Ceylon, Burma and Siam.

Development of Language

Besides Sanskrit, the vernaculars derived from the Vedic period also developed now. They are termed 'Prakrits' which are thus the earlier forms of Indian Vernaculars. They differed phonetically from Sanskrit owing to their avoidance of harsh combination of consonants and to their preference for final vowels. Thus, the Sanskrit 'Sutra' and 'Dharma', for example, appear in 'Prakrita', as 'Sutta' and 'Dhamma'. A form of 'Prakrita' used by the Buddhists, was that of Pali in which the edicts of Asoka were inscribed. Of other 'Prakrits' the following were important :

(1) Shauraseni, spoken round Mathura,
(2) Ardha-magadhi, spoken in Oudh and Bundelkhand,
(3) Magadhi, spoken in modern Bihar,
(4) Maharashtri, spoken in Berar.

The last stage of the 'Prakrit' was known as 'Literary Apabhranshs'. When the 'Prakrits' came to be used as literary languages, the Indian grammarian began to apply the term 'Apabhramsh' or corrupt to the true vernaculars that were the basis of the literary 'Prakrits'. Later these 'Apabhramshs' themselves came to be used for literary purposes, and the modern vernaculars are the direct descendants of these

Apabhramshs'. From the Apabhramsh of Shauraseni are derived Punjabi, Western Hindi, Rajasthani and Gujarati, from the 'Apabhramsh' of Ardhamagadhi is descended Eastern Hindi. From the 'Apabhramsh' to the east of the Indus are derived Kashmiri and Lahada and from Vrachada is derived Sindhi. Maharashtri has given us Marathi and Magadhi blossomed into Bihari, Oria and Bengali. There was also a Paishachi spoken by the lowest of the people. These were the main developments in the history of languages in the ancient period.

Art of Writing

Many people aver that the art of writing in India is not very old. But historians like Gauri Shanker Ojha have tried to prove that the art of writing was known even in the Rig-Vedic period. The traditions of both the orthodox and the heterodox sects of India points to the invention of writing to very ancient past. We have references to the art of writing in Brihaspati, in Untsang, in the Jain Samawayang Sutra and in the Chinese Buddhist Fawnshulin. The pre-Mauryan inscriptions like the Piparvaha, Vasa and Bhali inscriptions dated 487 B.C. also point to an early development in the art of writing. These epics and the 'Smritis' are full of references to the written document. Kautilya's Arthashastra also refers to the written word. The development of grammar, meters and arithmetic, presupposes the knowledge of writing. Panini refers to the terms like 'Lipi', 'Lipikar' and 'Yavanani', which means the script of the 'Yavana' and he also calls the written book 'Granth'. The Chhandogya Upanishad mentioned the term 'Akshar' and explains the mystic significance of the vowels and in other Upanishads, we have enumeration of the three genders and the description of the manner in which the word 'Om' is formed. In the Buddhist literature, especially Tripitika we have numerous passages showing acquaintance with writing and writers, for instance. 'Lekhak' and 'Lekhakaras'. Also the writing board (Phalak) as well as the wooden pen (varnak) are also mentioned. For the fourth century B.C. there is a statement of Nearches according to which the Hindus wrote letters on well-beaten cotton cloth. We have also evidence from the inscriptions about the development of scripts. The Asokan script was Brahmi, the parent of Devanagri. In the ancient period there was also the Kharoshthi script written from right to left, in the north-western parts of India. All these evidences point out to the development of the art of writing in India thousands of years back. So far as the writing material is concerned, it was generally birch-bark or palm-leaves or wooden tablets or copper plates. Paper was introduced only in the medieval age probably by the Mohammedans. According to some people the art of writing was not extensively developed because of the belief that sacred works were better preserved by memory and ear than by manuscripts. They would be profaned if revealed to all and sundry.

Sciences

In this age sciences also attained considerable perfection. Among the most prominent of the sciences were mathematics, astronomy, medicine, chemistry, physics and metallurgy. The most epoch-making achievement in the realm of arithmatic was the discovery of the decimal system of notation, based upon the principle of the place-value of the first nine numbers and the use of the zero. Geometry also attained great heights and many theorems relating to circles and triangles are mentioned. The most famous works in mathematics was that of Aryabhatta, the Aryabhattiyam written in 499 A.D. The work deals with arithmatic, geometry and algebra. At this time trigonometry was also being cultivated. In the realm of mathematics, therefore, it is clear Indians took the lead over the Greeks. Astronomy also made great progress during the age. Varahamihira and Aryabhatta were the most important astronomers. Aryabhatta pointed out that eclipses were caused by the moon coming within the earth's shadow or between the earth and the sun, he discovered that the earth rotates round its axis and utilised trigonometry in astronomy. He worked out accurate formulas to measure two consecutive days. He obtained the correct equation for the orbit of a planet. Thus, Aryabhatta was long in advance of the European astronomers. Some Greek theories of astronomy were adopted by the Hindus but in most cases their theories were the results of independent research.

Medicine

The most important works of medicine, the Charaka-Samhita by Charaka and Sushruta respectively received their final form in this period. Their conclusions are presented in the Ashtanga-Sangraha by Vagbhata I. Charaka and Sushruta placed very high ideals for a physician. He was to be a yogi, noble in character and benefactor of mankind. He was not to charge much for his medicines. He was not to distinguish between the rich and the poor. The government and the public provided for the establishment and maintenance of hospitals where men and animals both were looked after. Nagarjuna was said to have discovered the process of distillation and use of disinfectants. Indians knew of inoculation for small pox. In medicine the Hindus were most original. Indian medicine dealt with the whole area of the science. It describes the structure of the body, its organs, ligaments, muscles, vessels and tissues. Vast collections of drugs belonging to the mineral, vegetable and animal kingdoms are mentioned in the Hindu books of medicine. Much attention was devoted to hygiene, regimen of the body and diet. In surgery also the ancient Indians were great discoverers. They conducted amputations and operations as well as improved deformed ears and noses. Surgical instruments were carefully made.

Sushruta, expert on surgery, describes no fewer than 20 surgical instruments. Charaka, the great physician, says to the physicians, 'Not for money, nor for any earthly object should one treat his patients'.

Chemistry and Metallurgy

No books of this period dealing with these subjects are available. Nagarjuna is mentioned as a great chemist. The famous Iron Pillar near the Qutab Minar stands, however, as a silent witness to proclaim the striking metallurgical skill of the Hindus. This pillar has been exposed to rain and sun for the last 1500 years but has neither rusted nor corroded. Its polish still retains its brightness. The modern scientists cannot explain how this has been possible. Even the forging of such a pillar 24 feet in height, six and half a tons in weight, was an impossible feat for many centuries in Europe and in Asia. Use of mercury and iron in medicine shows that chemistry must have been greatly practised. Varahamihira was a scientist of versatile tastes. He was at home in astronomy, mathematics, astrology, metallurgy, chemistry, jewellery, botany, zoology, civil engineering, water-divining and even meteorology.

In its pride in its own creation, Science, the West is ever ready to blame India for having contributed little to this most valuable of all the conquests of man. But the above facts show that science was cultivated with enthusiasm in ancient India and many important discoveries were made which were passed on to Europe by the Greeks and the Arabs.

Arts and Crafts

The Gupta period marks the phase of classical age in the evolution of Indian arts. By the efforts of centuries, techniques of arts were perfected, definite types were evolved and ideals of beauty were formulated with precision. The art of this period is the envy and despair of the Indian artists of subsequent ages. Before describing these something may be said about the various schools of arts existing before the Gupta period, namely at Bharhut (Madhya Pradesh), Bodh Gaya, Sanchi (Madhya Pradesh), Mathura, Gandhara, Amaravati and Nagarjunakonda, the last two in the south. We have already referred to the Gandhara school. Something may be said about the three most famous schools of Sanchi, Mathura and Amaravati.

Sanchi contains now three big stupas. The one constructed by Asoka was now enlarged and four gate-ways of elaborate construction were added to the railing, one in each cardinal direction. The gate-ways illustrate the Jatakas and various episodes in the life of Buddha. The human figures are elegantly carved, great skill is shown in grouping, in expression and in decoration. There is a very great sense of beauty, rhythm and symmetry. We get a panorama of scenes of daily life and concrete illustrations of ethical virtues practised by the people.

Mathura has proved a large treasure-house of the ruins of this period. We have railings, images and statues. For the first time Buddha is represented as a human figure. The technique and vision are fundamentally Indian and not a copy of the Gandhara school. The distinct features of the images are prominent breasts, head and stylised folds. There is also a headless standing statue, probably of Kanishka. In Amaravati beautiful stupas were erected. The designs are quite original. The figures are slim with blithe features and most difficult poses and curves. The plants are very beautifully executed.

Thus, we find that the Gupta period was preceded by great advances in the realm of fine arts. The artistic activities covered the various forms of arts, like sculpture, architecture, terracotta and painting.

Sculpture

Sculpture has contributed most to the high esteem in which the Gupta art is held. The voluptuousness of the earlier art is modified by a balanced synthesis in accord with the moral sense of community. Nudity is eliminated. The inner spirit shines through the external form. This is exemplified in the Buddha images of the period, for example, the seated Buddha image from Sarnath, the standing Buddha in the Mathura museum and the colossal copper statue of Buddha now in Birmingham museum. The spiritual expression, the tranquil smile and the serene contemplative mood show us the highest triumph of Indian art in the statue at Sarnath. Buddha is given in these statues beautiful curly hair, bands of graceful ornamentation and transparent drapery. Thus, the Gupta art reveals the Indian genius in which spirituality is expressed in external forms with great grace, refinement and beauty.

The worship of Shiva and Vishnu is also reflected in the sculpture. In Mathura there is a statue of Vishnu with its face revealing celestial contentment and severe spiritual contemplating. Many legends of Vishnu and Shiva are sculptured. So also stories of Rama and Krishna are delineated with effective success in the Deogarh temple, now in Jhansi district. The Gupta sculpture is rich in charming ornamental designs. The foliated scroll is a special trait of Gupta art. Thus, Gupta sculpture had achieved great finish. It was imbued with beauty, grace, restrained elegance, dignity, tranquillity, intellectuality and spirituality.

Architecture

Temples were now being multiplied in India and great temples arose both in the south and in the north. There are many surviving temples of the period, for example, the temple at Bhitargaon (Kanpur) made of brick, the Vishnu temple, Tigawa (in Jubbulpore) and Shiva temple at Bhumara (Nagod).

The Bhitargaon temple is important as possessing the earliest true arch found in India. It is beautiful with several courses of well-preserved friezes and bricks with varied and beautiful designs. Scenes from Hindu mythology are depicted.

The stone temples are the earliest known Hindu shrines. They are, therefore, simple, small, unimposing and not made for big gatherings. Only later on we have high shikharas (pinnacles) and extensive mandapas (halls).

The cave architecture continued to be pursued diligently. Both Chaitya and Vihara caves were excavated at Ajanta. The Chaitya cave is a cave temple enshrining a Stupa or Buddha image, the vihara cave is primarily a monastery. These are among the best monuments of the age. They show beautiful pillars, great harmony of design and form and refinement of taste.

The secular buildings shown in the sculpture of the period were imposing structures several storeys high with windows, balustrades, pillars, terraces and balconies. The rich had in their houses picture-galleries (chitrashala), and concert halls (sangitashala). Comparatively, however, the period was not so rich in architecture as in sculpture and painting.

Terracotta

In this modest medium gifted clay modellers created things of real beauty and achieved a wide popular basis for their art. Clay figurines served as poor man's sculpture and contributed largely to popularise art and culture. In homes and palaces they were displayed. In the temples also bigger plaques and statues in clay were used. These were specially in demand on festive occasions. The terracottas represented gods and goddesses, male and female figures, animals and other miscellaneous objects. They combined elegance of forms with gorgeous coiffure and constitute a veritable gallery for the study of beautiful types of that age. Recently they have been recovered in Rajghat excavations and present a feast of beauty to the eye. The artist adorned what he touched.

Painting

This art reached its perfection in this period. These paintings are to be found in the Bedsa caves, in Bagh caves and specially in the Ajanta caves in Maharashtra. The paintings show that the masters were in love with nature. The flowering trees, quietly flowing streamlets and the roaming denizens of the forests are beautifully painted. According to Sir John Marshall, 'The school which those paintings represent was the source and fountain-head from which half the art of Asia drew its inspiration, and no one can study their rhythmic composition, their instinctive beauty of line, the majestic grace of their figures, and the boundless wealth of their decorative imagery without realising what a far-reaching influence they exerted on the art, not of India alone and her colonies, but of every other country to which the religion of the Buddha penetrated'. The refined art of Ajanta is clearly the culmination of hundreds of years of cultivation and practice.

'In their combination of decorative power, versatile characterisation, and dramatic expressiveness, the feeling for the characteristics of animals and birds, and above all in rhythmic quality, these paintings stand alone'. (quoted by Wilkinson in Indian Art).

To sum up, the art of the Gupta period reveals the following chief characteristics. It is marked by refinement and restraint, signs of a highly developed cultural taste, and aesthetic enjoyment. Balance, freedom and elegance are properly combined.

Secondly, there is worship of beauty but not at the cost of

good taste. Beauty was the expression of the nobility of the soul within and could not be sullied by notions or feelings of sheer sensuousness.

Thirdly, the Gupta art had great religious and spiritual appeal. The artists were shilpa-yogins, the monks who had dedicated their lives to higher things of life and gave their best by chiselling the stones.

Fourthly, there is great simplicity of style combined with felicity of expression. The technique and the subject were blended in a harmonious whole. Thus, the Gupta period gives us the Indian art at its best.

Some mention is necessary of Ajanta which typifies in more senses than one, the Gupta art. Ajanta (now in Maharashtra state) lies in that part of the mountain chains known as the Western Ghats, which marks the boundary of the Deccan table-land and separates it from that of Khandesh, along the valley of the river Tapti. The excavations of Ajanta caves were begun by the Buddhist monks a little over three centuries before the Christian era. The excavations continued for a period of about one thousand years. The caves, 29 in number, are rich with the most wonderful art-relics of India. An outstanding feature of Ajanta art is that it combines, in its variety of expression, the three vivid art forms that were cultivated in India, architecture, sculpture and painting. These in Ajanta are blended into a marvellous unity of conception. The selection of the site shows good taste. The situation is romantic and full of natural scenery. The vision of Ajanta was only possible to Indian artists who were to 'attain to the images of the gods by means of spiritual contemplation only. The spiritual vision was the best and truest standard' (Shukracharya). Thus, the soul in the artists of Ajanta, awakened to a consciousness of its own power, found its vehicle in the elegant creations of art depicted in these caves. The mural paintings are among the best of Ajanta art. They are the soul figure of which physical things are a gross representation. The famous group of the mother and child before the Buddha in cave XVII is a great example of the highest that Ajanta achieved. In it one finds intense religious feeling of adoration, the turning of the soul of humanity in love to the calm and benignant God in Buddha, the glad and child-like smile of awakening with promises of the deep spirituality to come. The artists pour out their souls in colour, articulate in line a beauty that is not of this earth, a grace that is supernatural and all this to such a high degree that even ordinary events are wrapped with mystic significance.

The sculpture is best seen in cave IX where a Nagaraja is seated with his queen. Both of them are in a mood of contemplation and are deeply absorbed in what they are hearing. The innumerable figures of the Buddha suggest the exuberance of the artist's devotion.

The Ajanta tradition furnished a basis for new creations both in India and elsewhere. For instance, the frescoes at Sigiriya in Ceylon, the paintings at Bagh in Gwalior, frescoes in the temple of Sittannavasal in Tamilnadu State, the paintings of the Rajput and Pahari schools, the art-relics of Central Asia, China, Japan, South-East Asia and Tibet show the great influence of this tradition. According to Havell these paintings constitute India's claim to the respect and gratitude of humanity.

Thus the Gupta Age, the classical age, was an age of scholars, legislators, dialecticians and philosopher. It witnessed the creative and aesthetic enthusiasm of the race pouring itself into things material, into the play of the senses, into the pride and beauty of life. Never in her history has India seen such a many sided blossoming of her force of life. Culturally, she has never been so rich, so colourfully creative. 'Here the mind of India was seeking to infuse its light of the spirit into the materialised vitality of man, and was trying to have an insight into the truth of the matter'.*

Travellers in India

Ancient India was visited by many travellers among whom the most famous are Megasthenes (who came as ambassador), Fa-Hien, Hiuen-Tsang and I-Tsing. Their accounts throw much light on the Indian culture. Much of what they wrote is already embodied in this section and here a few typical remarks are given.

---

* S.K. Mitra, *The Vision of India*, pp. 20-22.

Megasthenes

Megasthenes, a Greek ambassador from Seleukus, arrived in Pataliputra in 302 B.C. He has described the administration of Mauryan King. Chandra Gupta in great details which show it to be based on modern lines.

Megasthenes states that a strange bodyguard of armed foreign Amazons was always in attendance upon the Mauryan King and was even present in his sleeping quarters. He confused Indian gods with Greek gods, identifying Shiva with Dionysos and Krishna with Herakles. He did not know the difference between the Jain, Buddhist and other recluses. He describes a group of monks as 'living sparely, practising celibacy and abstinence from flesh-food and listening to grave discourse'. The chief subject was death, 'for this present life; they hold, is like the season passed in the womb, and death for those who have cultivated philosophy is the birth into the real, the happy life'.

He also mentions seven castes confusing them with professions, for instance, the philosopher is one such caste. He also says that, 'no Indian has ever been convicted of lying'. According to him famine has never visited India. The inhabitants have abundant means of existence and exceed in consequence the ordinary stature and are distinguished by their proud bearing. They are well skilled in the arts. He says that all Indians are free and no one is a slave. In war fields of the peasants are not ragged. There are many strange stories told by him for example, he describes the existence of golden ants.

Fa-Hien

He came from China and was in India from 405 to 411 A.D. He found Buddhism flourishing in the north and there were hundreds of Sangharamas where pilgrims were hospitably entertained for three days. At Peshawar he saw a Stupa which was the highest tower in India. In the east he found all kings professing Buddhism, patronising the learned and giving alms to the poor. People were well off without poll-tax or official restrictions. Punishments were light, truth was spoken and crimes were few and far between. He found the ruins of Asoka's magnificent palace which, according to him, in its sculptured designs was no human work. He found monasteries both of Mahayana and of Hinayana by the side of this palace. They contained about 600-700 priests from all parts of the world. Their behaviour was decorous and orderly. The Brahman teacher is called Manjusri, the Great Sramanas, all Bhikshus esteem and respect him. The towns, in Behar, were the largest in India. The people were rich and prosperous. There were hospitals of all kinds. People received all attention and free treatment there.

Hiuen Tsang or Yuan Chwang

He came in 630 A.D. and lived for 15 years. Like Fa-Hien he came to seek the true law (Buddhism). He has given a vivid account of the religious ceremonies performed by Harsh at Prayag and also of the religious conference convened by Harsh for disputation and discussion about the merits of Mahayana. The latter was attended by 20 kings besides thousands of Buddhists, Brahmans and Jains. Impressive spectacles were presented by a golden statue of the Buddha kept in a lofty tower and a gorgeous procession of elephants that escorted an image of the Sakya sage to the hall of the assembly. The gathering at Prayag included about 500,000 people from all parts of India who came to receive gifts from the king. Images of the Buddha, Adityadeva (Sun), and Isvaradeva (Shiva) were installed on successive days and alms were distributed. When the accumulation of five years was exhausted, the emperor wore a second-hand garment and paid worship to the Buddhas of the relions. According to the traveller the people were clean and wholesome in their dress and lived in a homely and frugal way. Shoes were rare. 'People stained their teeth red or black, bound their hair and pierced their ears for ornaments'. People were upright, honourable and in money matters, without craftiness. About the people of the Deccan he says, 'To their benefactors they are grateful, but to their enemies, relentless. If they are insulted they will risk their lives to avenge themselves'. Again, 'if a general loses a battle, they do not inflict punishment, but present him with woman's clothes and he is driven to seek death for himself'.

I-Tsing visited India in 685 A.D. Conditions in India had now deteriorated. He was more than once attacked by robbers in Bihar. The Buddhist monasteries were still flourishing. The kings had bestowed lands for their upkeep. His account of primary system of education as prevailing at Tamralipti is very interesting. Indian boys began their education at six, with forty-nine letters of the Sanskrit alphabet studied in an alphabet book of three hundred slokas or verses. This primer was to be learnt in six months by heart. At eight a simplified version of Panini's grammar in 1,400 slokas was to be taken up. At ten they were to learn roots, cases, conjugations and the formations of Sanskrit words and at thirteen they began to read the grammar of Panini in its fuller versions. After this they were to compose their own pieces in prose and in verse and study logic and metaphysics.

9

INDIAN CULTURE ABROAD

ONE OF THE myths of Indian history was that the Indians shut up by mountains and seas neither influenced other countries nor were influenced by them, that we were stay-at-home people, unenterprising, timid and unadventurous. That myth is now exploded. The Indians, as we know now, played a great part in moulding the history and civilisation of vast regions in the continent of Asia which lie beyond the Himalayas and the sea. The term 'Greater India' has come into existence to denote the expansion of Indian influences in these countries during the ancient period. We also had great commercial and cultural intercourse with the West broadly including under the term all countries west of India, though in this chapter main attention will be confined to Greece and Rome.

The monumental discoveries at Harappa and Mohenjo-Daro and the discovery of the famous inscriptions at Baughs Koi, mentioning the names of Vedic deities, leave no doubt about a cultural intercourse between India and the western countries more than four thousand years ago. If credence is to be lent to the stories of Mahabharata, we even went to America (so-called patal-loka) and recent discoveries about Maya civilisation, for example, have led many people to trace close connection between the Indian and the old civilisations of America. We also know of close connection between India and Persia reflected in their respective sacred works, the Avesta and the Rig-Veda. Both works contain references indicative of common borderlands or Indo-Iranian domains. The Avesta calls

India Hindu derived from the Sanskrit word Sindhu, denoting both the river and the Country it marks out. By the sixth century B.C. definite political relations can be traced. From Cyrus right down to Darius and Xerxes and Darius III, the Persian kings dominated the North-West of India, the Punjab figuring as part of the dominion of Darius (522-486 B.C.). An Indian contingent fought on behalf of the Persians with the Greeks. Later on, Alexander's invasion (326 B.C.), definitely opened the routes between Indian and the West. From that time right up to the sixth century A.D., there was great intercourse between the two and specially between the Roman Empire and India. Later on, Indian culture entered into Europe through the Arabs.

The intercourse was facilitated by the existence of trade-routes. From pre-historic times, three great trade routes have connected India with the West. The easiest was the Persian Gulf route, running from the mouth of the Indus to the Euphrates and from there to where the road branches to Antioch and the Levantine ports. Another was the overland route, from the North-West passes to Balkh and from there either by river, down the Oxus to the Caspian and then to the Euxine or entirely by land, by the Caravan road which skirts the Karmanian desert to the north, passes through the Caspian Gates and then reaches Antioch. Lastly, there was the circuitous sea route, down the Persian and Arabian coasts, by way of Aden, up the Red Sea to Suez and from there to Egypt or to Tyre and Sidan. Later on, with the discovery of 'Monsoon' this coast voyage was greatly replaced by direct voyage from the Indian ocean to Egypt, avoiding the long coastal track.

Accounts of this vast intercourse have been given by many, the most famous of whom are Herodotus (the Greek historian born in 484 B.C.), Megasthenes, Arrian and Pliny, Strabo, the book Periplus Maris Erythraei, by an unknown author, and Ptolemy (Alexandria).

Historians are not yet agreed about the precise effect of the west on Indian culture and of the latter upon the former and hence the conclusions given here are only tentative.

Intercourse between India and Greece before the days of Alexander, was of an Indirect nature. Indian goods taken by the Indians reached the mouth of the Red Sea, from where others took them to other regions. Greece till then learnt about India from the Persians. The Greeks, therefore, neither knew much nor cared much about Indian culture. Besides they looked upon others as 'barbarians' and treated them with contempt. Nevertheless there must have been some exchange or infiltration of ideas even if in an indirect manner. For instance, the belief in metempsychosis common both to the Indians and the ancient Greeks presupposes some cultural contact between the two. From Plato's writings something very closely resembling the doctrine of Karma has been adduced. The invasion of Alexander did not produce any immediate effect but he left many kingdoms in Asia which formed natural channels of contact between India and the West. We have evidence to show that the Greeks in the Punjab and in western India rapidly became converts to Hinduism and Buddhism and adopted their culture. Specially in the Kushan period the Greek ideas of art and coinage, had great affect upon the north-west India which now produced the Gandhara school of art and purer and more refined coins.

To sum up, so for as Greece and India are concerned the mutual intercourse was not much and the results produced were meagre on the whole except in the realm of coinage, astronomy and sculpture. Though Garbe, a German writer thinks that the historical possibility of the Grecian world of thought being influenced by India through the medium of Persia must unquestionably be granted and with it the possibility of the ideas of Sankhya and Vedanta being transferred from India to Greece. As for the coinage, it is the view of Rawlinson (Intercourse between India and the Western world) that Indians learnt everything from the West in the matter of coinage. But it cannot be denied that the Gupta mint-masters introduced a number of original artistic types, coins novel in their conception, fine in execution and showing no foreign influence whatever (for instance, the Tiger-Slayer type, the Ashvamedha type and the Lionslayer type). Also the Gandhara school of art was confined only to north-west India when independently here schools like those of Mathura and

Amaravati were developing undoubtedly there was some influence of the Greek ideas of astronomy on us. Varahamihira mentions the contributions of the Yavanas (the Greeks) and the Gargi Samhita says, 'The Yavanas are barbarians, yet the science of astronomy originated with them, and for this they must be reverenced like gods'.

With the birth of Christianity and the Roman Empire the cultural contact between India and the West widened, specially as a result of the increasing trade carried on between the Roman Empire and India. It is now accepted that at least some ideas of Christianity are to be traceable to Indian influences for instance, relic-worship and the use of the rosary, popularity of asceticism among many Christian orders, doctrine of the plurality of heavens, practice of non-violence as preached by Christ in 'Sermon on the Mount' and the resemblance between the Christian church and the old Buddhist chaityas. It is curiously interesting how Buddha was passed on to Christianity to be worshipped as a saint under the name of Josaphat. Indian fables and stories were also passed on the West. All this was the result of Buddhist and Brahmanical influences extending over central and western Asia as we know now from recent discoveries. The resemblances between Neo-platonism and Buddhism are very close. The Neo-Platonist strives by meditation to free his soul from the body, and to attain union with the supreme. This is the doctrine of Yoga, also to be found in Buddhism.

Again, during the period of Roman Empire, Alexandria was a great cultural and economic centre and Indians were familiar with it. From Alexandria ideas travelled both ways. Paul of Alexandria and his disciple St. Anthony (who died in 356 A.D.) were influenced by the Indian ideas of monasticism. Christian sects like Manicheism and Gnosticism show the influence of India on ideas. One Abbe Hue visiting Lhasa (Tibet) in 1842 was surprised by the resemblance between the Catholic and the Tibetan ceremonies. 'The crozier, the mitre, the chasuble the cardinal's robe .... the double choir at the Divine office, the chants, the exorcism, the censer with five chains, the blessing which the Lamas impart by extending the right hands over the heads of faithful, the rosary, the celibacy of the clergy, their separation from the world, the worship of saints, the fasts, the processions, litanies, holy water—these are the points of contact which the Buddhists have with us'.

We have already described the migration of folk-tales and our numerals to the West. All these clearly point out that in the ancient period India influenced the West more than she was herself influenced by it. Of course as the facts so far known are few, the picture cannot be clear and distinct. The people in the West have acknowledged the debt they owe to India in the cultural field. Will Durant, the American thinker writes, 'India was the motherland of our race, and Sanskrit the mother of Europe's languages. She was the mother of our philosophy; mother through the Arabs, of much of our mathematics; mother through the Buddha, of the ideas embodied in Christianity; mother, through the village community, of self government and democracy. Mother India is in many ways the mother of us all'.

Coming nearer home, the influence of Indian culture was greatest on countries touching the Eastern boundaries of India as well as the countries in south-east Asia, like China, Siam, Indo- China, Malaya, Eastern Archipelago (Java and Sumatra, etc.) and Ceylon. It should be pointed out here that Indian ideas of colonial empire radically differed from the modern imperialistic ideas of the West. The Hindus went to South-East Asia, established their colonies but did not regard them as an outlet for their excessive population and an exclusive market for their growing trade. They were not regarded as source of exploitation for the benefit of the conquerors. Ours was a cultural mission. Wherever we settled, we introduced our culture and civilisation, were influenced by the native culture and thus evolved a new culture whose dominant note, of course, was Indian because of its richness and depth. Hindus there became children of the soil and not foreigners like the British in India.

The island of Ceylon was the first to open its heart to India. Indian merchants and princes were followed by the Buddhist Monks.

The traffic began briskly from the time of Asoka. From that

time Buddhism has become the main religion of Ceylon. The first people to settle in Ceylon were the Aryans from the north and not the Tamils. The story of Rama and Ravana too well illustrates this fact. In history the Aryan migration began when Prince Vijayasimha of Bengal settled in Lanka in the 5th century B.C. The union of the Aryan and the Dravidian stocks have given us the Simhalese people. Rice cultivation was introduced from India and also all typical Indian arts and crafts like music, drama, dancing, metal-work, building and sculpture. But the great contribution of Ceylon is the zeal, care and purity with which she has retained the Buddhist religion and practices. From Ceylon the world has known about the authentic story of Buddhism kept there in Pali language and script. The Pali Buddhist chronicles of Ceylan, Dipavamsa and Mahavamsa are very famous. A part of Bodhi tree was transplanted in Ceylon and a fragment still exists, the oldest historic bit of tree in the world. Buddha relics also found their way into Ceylon. Rock edicts in Ceylon inscribed in the Asokan Brahmi style record pious donations to the Buddhist monks. Stupas in Ceylon testify to the debt Ceylon owes to the artistic genius of India. Thus, in a word, Ceylon owes the foundation of her culture and civilisation to India.

India's relation with Burma developed more by way of the Bay of Bengal than by the land route. The Pali Jatakas contain references to eastward voyages undertaken by the Indians as early as the fifth century B.C. The voyages were meant for Suvarnabhumi or Suvarnadwipa which may have embraced the whole of Burma and the Eastern Archipelago (Java, etc.). Buddhist legends tell us of two of Asoka's missionaries, Sona and Uttara, despatched to Burma. It is said that the people of lower Burma are racially related to the people of Assam, the Khasis. In Prome (lower Burma) have been discovered ruined Stupas and other objects going back to the sixth century A.D. One of the stupas is a majestic structure rising from five super-imposed terraces. A manuscript of 20 gold leaves in Pyu characters has also been discovered. This script is a direct importation from India with affinities with the Kannada-Telugu script. Kings also in these parts bear the Indian titles of Varman and Vikrama. Later in the 11th century it was conquered by Anawrata, king of the upper Burma, who transplanted to his kingdom from there Buddhist ideas, books, monks, language and all the crafts which had been borrowed from India originally. Metal temple bells and gongs, wonderful carved work, gold and black lacquer illustrations of Buddhist legends, large white bell-shaped pagodas, the sleeping and smiling Buddha images show Burma's adoption of Buddhism with its own additions thereto.

Malaya also received Indian ideas and emigration. Researches so for have yielded stone inscriptions, stupas, monasteries and a number of images of Hindu gods. The Indians went there in greater numbers during the beginning of the Christian era. Both Brahmanism and Buddhism flourished there. The stone inscriptions mention a great sailor 'Buddhagupta' of Bengal who gave certain donations to them. The most impressive monuments are on the Siamese side of the Malayan frontier. They are at Chaiya and Nakhon Sri-Thammarat. These places show temples, stupas and Buddhist images. The style is either that of the Guptas or of the Pallavas of Southern India. Chinese records tell us of embassies coming from Malaya and of Hindu kings reigning there and using the Sanskrit language in the sixth century A.D.

Malaya may be regarded as the main gate of the Indian colonial empire in the Far East. Both Buddhism and Hinduism flourished there. It was a cradle to further Eastern culture inspired by waves of Indian influence spreading across the route from the eastern shores of India. Persons of Indian features are common on the West coast, while colonies of Brahmans of Indian descent survive at Nakhon and Patalung.

Indians also trekked on into Siam and Indo-China. Abraham named Kaundinya landed in Cambodia in the fifth century A.D. and founded the first Indian Kingdom by defeating and marrying the queen of the country. This country was called Funan by the Chinese. Gradually this kingdom reduced the neighbouring kingdoms of Indo-China and southern Siam to vassalage and endured for six centuries. The primitive people were soon initiated into Indian manners, dress, religion, philosophy and arts. One of their missions visited India with the third century of the Christian era. Funan has ruins of sixty Hindus brick temples. Both Shiva and Vishnu worship was performed there as is evident from these ruins. Buddhism also was partially favoured. In central Siam arose another Indian Kingdom named Dvaravati founded by the Mons from Lower Burma in the second or third century A.D. Bronze Buddhas of Amaravati style, Gupta images from the Ganges valley, ruined stupas and monasteries and tablets with the Buddhist creed written in Pallava script have been found there. Dvaravati also converted the Mongolian ancestors of the present day Siamese. Buddhist temples were built by these people. The Siamese lent their own ideas to Buddhist sculpture which are discernible, the famous Siamese Buddha, a slender figure with flame-crowned oval face wearing a strange all-pervasive smile and distinctive Pagoda style often made of broken bits of Chinese porcelain. Siam to this day retains the Hindu manners, fashions and festivals like that of our own Dusserah commemorating the victory of Rama over Ravana.

But the two most famous Hindu kingdoms of Indo-China were Champa and Khamers. Champa now part of Annam lay immediately to the East of Cambodia. The people were subdued by the Hindus in the second century. The Hindus ruled there for centuries and Hinduised the native people completely. During this period were created remarkable sculptures and highly original brick temples. Two temple cities, Mi-song and Dong-duong are very famous. Siva, his Shakti, and his two sons Ganesha and Skanda occupied the first place among the gods worshipped there. Vishnu, Krishna and Buddha were the other deities worshipped there. Champa figure sculpture closely followed Gupta models, not only in subject matter but also in technique. It was simple, natural, strikingly dignified and majestic. Sanskrit inscriptions, one bearing a date in Saka era have also been found. Champa temples are notable for their decoration and ornamentations. The doorways and pillars are adorned with incredible intricate stone foliation of leaf, bud and flower, inset with medallions of adoring anchorites, celestial dancers for ever poised and too intent on charming the gods.

With the weakening of Indian influence the Champa art grew heavier and coarser. This colony probably takes its name Champa from Bhagalpur of today. Thus in Champa both the court and society was thoroughly saturated with Brahmanical culture.

The Cambodian kingdom of Khmers was the strongest kingdom dominating over others right upto the 14th century when Siam destroyed the kingdom. Its capital was Angkor Thom. The ruins of the cities and temple were discovered fully only in the 19th century, in 1861. They have revealed to the world some of the most awe-inspiring ruins to be found anywhere. The Khmers believed that an Indian sage Kambu was their ancestor, so their country was called Kambuja or Cambodia. The Chinese mention it as a vessal state in the sixth century, paying tribute to Funan. The Hindus ruling there conquered Funan. The kings had Indian names ending in Varman. They were very warlike and worshipped both the Hindu and Buddhist religions.

Scattered through the mountains and jungles of Cambodia more than six hundred ruined Khmer monuments may still be counted. They range from temples and palaces to reservoirs and bridges. All the great monuments are near the capital Angkor Thom. Angkor from Sanskrit 'Nagara' (city) and Thom from Khmer, meaning great. Among its temples the most famous is Angkor Wat. It is the largest temple in the world. It was built in the 12th century. It possesses a perfect architectural unity.

A raised causeway of flagstones leads from the main road across a broad moat to the outer entrance gallery or portico of the temple. This portion is a spacious building forming the front part of the wall bounding the enclosure on all four sides. The great temple rises steeply in the form of three concentric rectangular galleries, each doubling in height the preceding one. The galleries are connected by stairs and intervening open terraces. The inner-most gallery is dominated by five tall domes, the central of which dominates the plain below from a magnificent height of 213 feet.

All this vast building has been chiselled into endless beautiful designs and patterns, as if it was not a stone but of wood. Flowers, birds, dancing maidens, temple dancers of the tender sex and ornaments adorn the walls. The Khmer artists who carved the vast panels, 100 yards long, must have spent their whole lives for the work. The themes in the first gallery are taken from the Ramayana and Mahabharata. Vishnu leads but others also adorn the temple with their various incarnations and emanations. Kings are also introduced and Khmer language can also be seen engraved in some places. Philosophy is also expressed on the panels and evils are shown being condemned and merits rewarded by Yama with Chitragupta as the keeper of the records. Another temple Ta Prahm was dedicated to the Buddhist (Mahayana) divinity Prajnaparamita. In the capital was Bayon, the temple second in size only to Angkor Wat. It contains fifty towers. The Khmers also patronised learning in all its branches–Vedic lore, astronomy, grammar, logic and literature. Today the scene presents an unbridgeable contrast between the past and the present. Indignant bats squeak a shrill protest when visitors challenge their supremacy. But in the past everything was great in Khmer. It gave to the world the largest temples the most magnificent detailed stories of India carved on the stone and the brightest testimony of India's cultural conquest of the East.

Indian colonies were also planted in Indonesia, noteably in Java, Sumatra, Borneo and Bali. The whole region has been given the name of Suvarnadvipa. Sumatra has not yet been properly explored but still ruined stupas, Indian images and inscriptions have come to light. The Hindu kingdom of Srivijaya was founded in Sumatra in or before the 4th century A.D. It rose to great power in the seventh century. But from our point of view Java is more important as both inscriptions and architectural remains are plentiful there.

People in Java aver that the Rishi Agastya came over from India and settled there. People from India probably went there in the 2nd century A.D. for the first time. According to the Javanese chronicles, 20,000 Indian families went there. In the second century A.D. The Chinese records speak of an embassy from Java to China in 132 A.D. sent by Deva Varman. Fa-Hien has also described Java in the fifth century as a stronghold of

Brahmanical religion. Later on Buddhism also raised its head there.

In the seventh century Java was conquered by Sri Vijaya of Sumatra, only to be overpowered later on by the Sailendras, a Hindu dynasty probably originating from Malaya. By the end of the 12th century this dynasty had become overlord of 15 dependent states in Java, Sumatra and Malaya. Its supremacy was later challenged by the Cholas of India. A longdrawn-out century of war weakened the people who were crushed by the end of the 13th century.

While the most magnificent temple is found in Indo-China, the most splendid Buddhist monument is to be found in Java. It is the famous Stupa or Barobudur lying in the Kedu plain of Central Java. There are also other famous temples belonging both to Buddhism and Hinduism. Inscriptions engraved in a northern Indian alphabet have been found and records show that Sailendras maintained relations with the Pala dynasty of Bengal.

Barobudur is really a whole mountain-top carried into nine stone terrace's, each of rising height and diminishing size, crowned by a simple Stupa surmounted by an octagonal pinnacle. The terraces have balustrades and there are galleries running around the four lower terraces. The outer side of the balustrades contains niches with images of 5 Dhyani Buddhas. There are 432 such images. Other terraces also have these Buddhas. The most significant feature is the series of 1500 sculptured panels in the four galleries of the lower terraces. They illustrate Buddhist texts of the Mahayana school. The engravings depict the lives of Buddha in his various incarnations, story of the youth Sudhana, his 110 travels all over India till he was enlightened by Maitreya, the Future Buddha and other stories warning the evil-minded and inspiring the virtuous. The sculpture resembles the Gupta one though there is greater simplification and a Javanese atmosphere is created by the introduction of typically Javanese scenes and houses. In Central Java is the Hindu temple of Larajongrang surrounded by smaller shrines. The principal deities are Brahma, Shiva and Vishnu. Episodes from the lives of Ram and Krishna are given. The sculptures are vital and dramatic, superior in their plastic sense to those of Angkor Wat.

In eastern Java also temples and other relics are to be found, the kings were either Hindus or Tantric Buddhists.

Throughout this period India continued to exercise its many sided influence. Javanese languages, arts, law-codes, manners, literature and heroes were modelled on our patterns. Indian themes are to this day witnessed in the Javanese dance, dramas and puppet plays. The people of Indonesia are toady Muslims but they retain their Hindu names, and in Bali the people are still Hindu in their names, dress, religion and manners. The Indo-Javanese culture still lives in dance, music, drama and rituals.

The North-Western Frontiers of India converge upon Afghanistan, Western Tibet and the two Turkestan-Russian and Chinese (or Sinkiang). Passes lead over the Hindu Kush to Samarkand and then to Kashgar while from Kashmir one passes with utmost difficulty to the Pamirs and the Karakoram mountains. These Join the 'Tiger-Dragon Mountains', forming the boundary between Tibet and Sinkiang. Further on the China side is the vast Gobi desert. This vast region was once a thriving centre of Buddhist culture for nine or ten centuries. It is in the twentieth century that we have discovered that some of the early inhabitants of Sinkiang were Indo-Europeans and that under the sands were buried ancient cultural centres built by the Buddhists. The greatest discoveries were made by Sir Aurel Stein in 1908 when he discovered in a hiding place more than 20,000 manuscripts and 55 separate paintings. The collection contained complete Buddhist canonical works, 3,000 works in Samskrit or Brahmi language and other records. Other ruined sites gave up quantities of manuscripts, stupas, shrines and monasteries. Thus in these oases had flourished from 5 th to the end of the 10th centuries Indian religion, art and learning.

Documents of as early a period as second century A.D. were found; some of them bore the Prakrit language written in the Kharoshthi script of Asoka's time. They were written on wood, some an birchbark or palm leaf and others on leather. The Chinese records date to even earlier periods, some are written on bamboo, others on silk and later, on paper.

These kingdoms of Central Asia were, then centres of extraordinary religious, literary and artistic activities. They were reinforced by people from India and they themselves set out on missions, for example, to China. There were Hinduised kingdoms also. There was a great Buddhist translator Kumarajiva, son of an Indian minister of Kusha and daughter of the Kuchan king. The Kucha Dynasty traced its descent from Kunala, Asoka's son; Kunala was not blinded but banished to central Asia, it is said. Fa-Hien and Yuan-Chwang have given invaluable accounts of life in the oases kingdoms of central Asia, the most important of which were Sailadesa (Kashgar), Cokkuka (Yarkand), Khotanina (Khatan) in the southern part and Kuchi (Kuchar) in the northern part of central Asia. In the Southern kingdoms there was a strong Indian element in the population. Indian colonies were established, trade commenced and cultural life followed with Buddhism taking the lead. It was from Khotan that the culture spread towards China. Buddhism also conquered Korea by the end of the sixth century, and also Japan.

The art of Central Asia was first inspired by the Gandhara school and then by the Gupta art. The figures grow more slender, poses are more graceful, draperies are more transparent, heavenly and earthly Buddhas cool their feet on beautiful Indian lotuses, Symbol of purity. Their decoration is magnificent. Princes and princesses exchanged royal robes for the yellow robes of the monk and settled there. Fa-Hien, tells us that the priests numbered thousands, most of them belonging to Mahayana. An annual procession of images like Indian Ratha Yatra used to take place in Khotan. He mentions a monastery which took eighty years to build, 25 feet in height and ornamentally carved and overlaid with gold and silver.

Thus in Central Asia also Indian culture found a lodgement. From there it spread far and wide, converting the whole of the Far East to the Buddhist faith. It also met the same fate which Indian Buddhism met from the hands of the Muslim invaders. The Mangols passed over it leaving death and destruction behind.

Of the neighbours of India, Nepal and Tibet have retained most of the Indian cultural inheritance.

Nepal, five hundred miles long in an east-west direction and one hundred miles from north to south lies between Kashmir and Bengal. Nepal is half owner with Tibet of Everest. Its civilisation has been strongly influenced by India. Its religion, art, literature, language and customs show strong traces of Indian influence. According to tradition Buddhism was introduced into Nepal by Asoka. Guptas also got acknowledgement of their sovereignty from Nepal. Soon intermarriages began between the reigning dynasties of Nepal and those in India and a steady intercourse of all kinds began between the two countries. Nepal has reacted to Indian religions according as they gained ascendancy in the neighbouring parts of India. It took to Hinayana, to Mahayana, to Tantricism and to Hinduism in their periods of ascendancy. The Rajputs and the Brahmans fled to Nepal with the coming of the Muslims and they were also welcomed. In the eighteenth century it was conquered by the Gurkhas who trace descent from the Rajputs and had fled in the sixteenth century to Nepal where they had conquered the little state of Gurkha, from which their name is derived. Their language Khas is a Rajasthani dialect of Sanskrit origin. With the Gurkhas Hinduism became the state religion of Nepal.

It is in the little central valley of Nepal, 15 to 20 miles long and 10 miles broad, with its three capitals lying within a radius of 7 miles of one another (Kathmandu, Patan, Bhatgaon), that India's religious and artistic influences upon Nepal are felt most strongly. One can find there stupas, thousands of temples and other places of pilgrimage. Of these the most famous is the temple-city of Pashupatinath where Shiva is worshipped. In the population of Nepal, the Newars are born craftsmen. The Hindu religious architecture in Nepal is the stone temple with a massive tower above a comparatively small shrine. Nepal has also developed pagoda type of temples made of wood with copper roofs. Nepalese art also shows indebtedness to Pala art traditions of Bengal. Many of the laws of Nepal and its caste system show Indian origin. Thus, Hindu civilisation has conquered Nepal but here also it has evolved a distinct type of its own affected not only by the native traditions but also by those of China and Tibet.

Tibet, Land of Snow, the roof of the world, a land of mystery, encompasses Nepal on the north, touches Assam on the east, Kashmir and Uttar Pradesh on the west. It has been ruled by the Grand Lama though the spectre of communist China has now gripped it. Tibet was the last country to be influenced by Buddhism. It was in the seventh century when the Tibetan King Strong-Chan Grambo was married to a Buddhist princes of Nepal that influences penetrated from India into Tibet by way of Nepal. This king was so strong that he conquered parts of India, Central Asia, China, Nepal and Kashmir. He sent a minister to Kashmir to learn Sanskrit and work out a script for Tibet. He invented the Tibetan grammar and alphabet, the letter based on the Khotanese alphabet, derived from Sanskrit prevalent in the Gupta period. The king's wives, Nepalese and Chinese, brought images of Buddha and since then Buddhism has over spread Tibet. This king also built Jo-I-Hang the most famous temple of Tibet. Tibet had its native religion, mixture of nature worship and necromancy, magic and sorcery and it inevitably laid its influence upon Buddhism.

Further, Padma Sambhava born in Udayana the borderland region between Kashmir and Afghanistan, is said to have arrived in Tibet in 47 A.D. and founded Lamaism or Tibetan Buddhism. He also studied at Nalanda. He took to Tibet Mahayana tinged with Tantric ideas and practices. Hindu deities also like Shiva travelled to Tibet. Buddhist religious books and art began to travel now by way of Nepal to Tibet. Tibetan Buddhism was again renovated by way of Nepal to Tibet. Tibetan Buddhism was again renovated by Santa Rakshita in the 9th century who went from Nalanda for this purpose at the invitation of the King. Later in the 11th century people from Kashmir went there, and the artists beautified the Tibetan temples and monasteries. Thus in Tibet are found artistic creations reflecting the influence of both the Western and the Eastern India. Indian religious literature continued to be translated into the Tibetan language. Two Tibetan scholars converted the grandsons of Jenghis Khan and thus Buddhism was spread among the Mongols also in the 13th century. It is interesting to note that the prefix Dalai before Lama was given by a Mongol chief in 1578 to the head of the Yellow sect of

Buddhism in Tibet. This Dalai Lama is the religious and temporal ruler of Tibet. The rich treasure of Buddhist and Hindu religious literature lying in Tibet is for the most part still untapped and when the thing comes before the world many missing links in our history will be joined. Thus we find that Tibetan language, script, grammar, arts, literature and religion were the product, in the main, of Buddhism that went over there from India.

Indian Culture also penetrated into China and other Far-Eastern countries like the Philippines.

The Manu Samhita mentions the Chinese as mixed Kshatriyas and the Mahabharata calls them allies of king Bhagadatta of Assam. Tantric books also mention China. Historically China comes in contact with India when in the year 60 A.D. the Chinese Emperor Ming-ti-saw sent a mission to India to collect information about Buddhism. After that began the two-way traffic between the two countries and cultural bonds were forged. The first Indian monks to arrive in China were Kasyapa Mantanga and Dhamnaraksha of Scytho-Indian parentage. In their honour the first Buddhist monastery was built in China. Soon other centres were established in China in all of which the main work was the translation of Indian texts into Chinese. Kashmir supplied the bulk of the Indians who went to China for the dissemination of Buddhism. The four centuries of Tang reign in China were the most glorious period of Sino-Indian cultural fellowship during which Buddhism made great headway in China. Thousands of Indian monks and scholars flocked there. Indian influence is also visible in Chinese arts and crafts, in the stone sculptures and bas-reliefs of the Han period and in her music and sciences. Buddhist sculptures in China show traces of Indian art. The eminent artist Nand Lal Bose has pointed out that the figures engraved in the famous Pagoda in Ki-Fong are those of the Bengalis. Inscriptions written in Bangala letters dealing with Tantra have been found in a temple in Peking. The accounts of Chinese travellers to India like those of Fa-Hien and Hiuen-T' Sang have already been mentioned. Study of Indian astronomy and mathematics was also encouraged there. Many Indian drugs also were adopted. Thus, in the culture of China a deep permeation of Indian ideas is unmistakable and much research is being done in this sphere in the Visva Bharati at Santiniketan established by Tagore. From China, Korea received Buddhism about the middle of the 5th century and Korea passed it on to Japan in the sixth century.

Influence in Philippines and Polynesia

Researches into the cultural and racial origins are more and more lending support to the view that the country was once colonised by the people from South India. The scripts of the Filipino have striking resemblances with those of South India. The name of some of the places on the shores of Manila Bay and the coast of Luzon show their Sanskrit origin. The hill tribes of Luzon worship the head gods of the Indian triad and the early Vedic gods. The statue of Ganesh has also been found by a Dutch archaeologist. Handicrafts, coins, folklore and many social and religious customs also show the influence of Hinduism.

The late P. Mitra of the Calcutta University in collaboration with some Polynesian scholars unearthed the story of India's cultural influence over these islands situated in Oceania. The physical appearance of these people is like that of the Indo-Aryans. Their language has affinities to the language of the old Indian tribes like the Santhals. Many of their religious beliefs and social customs are derived from India through Indonesia. Their use of conch shell, nose-flute and musical bone are likely to be of Indian importation. The Hula dance of Hawaii and the Siva dance of Samoa are very similar to some forms of folk-dances of Bengal. Many of their staple food stuffs and animals were indigenous to India. In their traditions and religious lore Purana's idea of Brahmanda and Gita's idea of Aswathth tree are to be found. Many of their decorative designs, crafts, traditions, ideas of phallic symbolism, and images are examples of old Polynesian culture-traits derived from the Brahmanical civilisation.

Indian influence in Asia in Pre-Historic Times

Something may also be said about the influence of Indian culture on Asia in pre-historic times. The extensive maritime activities of India in the ancient world brought her into contact with many countries such as Egypt, Babylon, Assyria, Judea and America. People have traced Indian inspiration in the Egyptian apotheosis of the forces behind natural phenomena, particularly of the solar deities. Their god Osiris and his consort Isis are similar to the Vedic gods Isvara and Ishi. The caste system of ancient Egypt was similar to ours. Herodotus wrote that some of the customs of the Egyptians were essentially Aryan. Statues and other Indian relics have been discovered at Memphis, the ancient capital of Egypt. The Egyptian mummies bore Indian cotton dress.

In Babylonia and Assyria the story of Manu's flood and other legends were current and the Babylonians gave the name Sindhu to the muslin because it was manufactured in India. Their astronomy, their theory of creation, their gods show traces of Indian influence. People have traced the origin of Sumerian culture to the Indus civilisation. Many writers maintain that the Sumerians were an Indian race. There is close resemblance between the Mahabharata war and the central story of the Yahvist sections of the Pentatench, Joshua and Samuel of Judea. Influence of India in Mesopotamia has already been referred to in the chapter on Indus civilisation. In Arabia had lured Brahmins observing the worship of Shiva as Mak-Kesha from which the name of Mecca is said to have been derived. Thus almost from the dawn of her history India has turned on the torch of civilisation to all parts of the world.

We may end this Chapter by a brief reference to the Indian shipping and the travels of the Buddhist art.

Indian Shipping

Indians have been charged with lacking in maritime spirit but the story of their voyages for cultural and colonising purposes disproves this. Further, it has been discovered that they were much advanced in the art of shipping. Sri Radha Kumud Mookerji has shed much light upon this in his book 'History of Indian Shipping and Maritime activity from the earliest times'. Starting from the earliest days he has laid under contribution various subjects like literature, art, epigraphy and numismatics for materials of his subject. He has given us a picture of all ages, illustrating them profusely and showing us that we built ships of all types. These ranged from daintly furnished pleasure-boats to sea-worthy ships both for commerce and fighting. Their tonnage reached upto 1000 tons and they could load even horses and elephants. Minute instructions were laid down about the kinds of wood to be used for various parts and kinds of ships. There were Brahmana ships symbolising lightness, the Kshatriyas indicating strength, the Vaishyas denoting durability and the Shudras with emphasis on weight. The danger of ships colliding with magnetic rocks under the sea was warded off by avoiding the use of iron in the bottom of the craft. Birds were trained to serve as Matsya-Yantra or mariner's compass to determine the direction as well as to detect the approach of land. For the mariners, special coins bearing the name of the ship were also in use. Artistic side of the ship-building was not neglected. Ships were built sometimes with space enough for 700 persons. We have evidence of ship-building even as late as the 19th century when it was finally destroyed by the English.

Travels of the Buddhist Art

The earliest religious art of India is Buddhist to a very large extent. But in the early art there is no figure of Buddha as the Aryans did not believe in idolatry or temple-worship. It was probably Graeco-Buddhist sacred art that introduced the Buddha image. Thus, the first effect of the contact of Buddhism with foreigners led to new changes in art. Then Indo-China introduced flame as surmounting the bun of the Buddha head. The Scythians introduced Buddha as sitting in the European fashion on a seat with his knees wide apart. This figure is found in Dvaravati in Siam and in Java also. Almost the whole expansion of the arts of India can be traced by that of the plastic representations of Buddha. Two different types appear soon, one, a Buddha with the right shoulder uncovered is found first at Amaravati and later in Ceylon and again at Dong-Duong and Dvaravati, in Champa and Siam. The figure with both shoulders covered is found in the Mathura school and is imported as far as China. In the early Javanese art Buddha is clad in an invisible material with one shoulder bare, often inclined to plumpness resembling that of Ellora. Another vigorous type in Java is related to Bengal art. In Siam Buddha is shown seated in European fashion or standing in Gupta fashion clad in transparent material. In Bayon art he is transformed into the type with the closed eyes and the mystic smile. In Siam a new type appears with bow-ridges marked by two convex lines and the mouth is narrow with upturned corners. In China there is another transformation. There are now thick concentric folds arranged almost in steps given over his body, an apparel which later again become light with separate folds indicating thin materials and recalling the Ajanta art. Japan also has this second style. These two types are also introduced into Central Asia and Tibet. Under the influence of Mahayana ornamentation and deities multiplied. This art was much developed in Bengal and from there went to Nepal and Tibet. Finally in Amaravati school two types appear side by side in earlier representations. Buddha is shown himself and he is also not shown in the same relief, his presence being indicated by signs like the vacant throne. The spirit of the art of Ajanta and of Mahayana art is that of the Sanskrit literature and drama and not of the original Buddhist beliefs.

The development of Buddhist art is another indication of the fact that like other aspects of life, art also was based on religion. The artists inspired by spiritual motives and ideas gave out, as it were, their very soul in their artistic creations.

This is in brief, the story of India's cultural conquest of Asia. It was mainly the result of private enterprise. Today again India is given the chance to assume that leadership. 'The ties of the present, as well as the past, are the Buddhist and Hindu legends so beautifully sculptured on temple walls in Java, Cambodia, Burma and Siam, the traditional music, dance and drama enjoyed to this day in the island of Bali, the Buddhist and Brahman priests jointly performing their religious ceremonies in Bali and Nepal, the palm-leaf manuscripts, locked up under triple seals, constituting the treasures of the Tibetan monastic libraries, the living forms of art and craftsmanship in all these

* *The Pageant of India's History*, p. 406.

countries, the symbolism, religious or artistic, which has vital significance for millions of Asiatics. Asia is united at least in its awareness of a common cultural heritage from India'.*

One thing is crystal clear that it was the religious or spiritual inspiration that brought India's Asiatic neighbours into contact with her and in this also India has been true to the basis of her culture, the emphasis on the spirit and India will become great again when this basis, however renovated, is resurrected again.

10

SOUTH AND THE NORTH
(Cultural Assimilation)

SO FAR WE have mainly traced the history of culture in northern India though the important elements thereof are common to both. Some of the main elements and phases of southern culture may, however, be separately given though the North has also influenced them.

Dravidian speaking people in pre-historic times are said to have spread over most of India only to be pressed into south by the Aryans who came on the Indian stage later on. Together with the Aryans, the Dravidians have contributed important elements to the religious emphasis, the social structure, the manners and customs, the arts which constitute the Hindu civilisation today.

There is a tradition that Aryan Rishi Agastya crossed the Vindhyas and spread the Aryan culture in the South. He is revered greatly in south even today. The Dravidians contributed to the Aryan stock a great literature and art, adventurous spirit in industry and commerce, imaginative and deeply emotional religious feeling, great power of mathematical abstraction, well developed village organisation, magnificent temple cities and vast irrigation works besides splendid sculpture in bronze, copper and stone. The various Dravidian kingdoms of the historical period Pandya, Chola, Kerala, Pallavas in the far south, Andhras and Chalukyas in the Deccan, have each left a rich legacy to the Indian culture.

After Asoka, Deccan passed to the Andhras who carved out an important kingdom between the Bay of Bengal and the Arabian sea, ruling there for about four and a half centuries from 225 B.C. upto 225 A.D. Their original home-land was in the Telugu country between the deltas of the Godavari and the Krishna rivers into them were absorbed the Satavahans who had founded a kingdom in the first or second century B.C. in the Western Deccan. Their kings had taken the title of Satakarni. After the Satavahanas we have the Andhras who were replaced by the Vakataka dynasty which in the sixth century gave way to the Chalukyas. In the southern and eastern parts of their domains, the Andhras were replaced by the Pallavas.

The Andhras patronised Sanskrit in the main. One of their kings, Hala, is said to have been a great poet who composed a poem consisting of seven hundred verses on love, in the Maharashtri language. One of Hala's ministers produced a Sanskrit-Prakrit grammar and another the collection of popular tales known as the Brihat-Katha, Great Story Book. Toleration was the great feature of the Andhra rule and both Jainism and Buddhism flourished there. Temples were built though no temple earlier than the fourth or fifth century A.D. has survived anywhere in India. Buddhist monuments have, however, survived giving us the Sanchi, Amaravati and Ajanta schools of art.

Thus, the artistic genius of India first manifested itself on a large scale in Southern India. We have already described the art of these schools but something more may be said about Sanchi.

The early Buddhist tradition was centered in the Supta, or relic mound and was the chief object of worship by the Buddhists. In Sanchi (Madhya Pradesh), besides the great Stupa, the low stone hill is strewn with remains of temples, monasteries and stupas. It was selected as an artistic site by Asoka probably because his wife Devi happened to be born at Vidisa (Bhilsa) five miles from Sanchi. The fame of Sanchi rests above all on the four intricately carved gateways (torana) around the main stupa. These are completely covered with a magnificent series of sculptures in relief. They depict not only religious stories about Buddha and others but also the secular life of the times. The whole contemporary Andhra world of city, village and wilderness lives again in these sculptures. Great realism tinged with moral appeal is the characteristic feature of the sculptures.

In the Western ghats we come across another Wing of religious architecture, namely, the rock-cut caves which in this period were the Bhaja Kordane, Ajanta, Bedsa, Nasik and Karli ones. From the fourth century A.D. we have monasteries of Ellora (Maharashtra), the majority of which belong to the Brahman form of worship. Altogether there are more than 1200 rock-cut temples and monasteries, the greater number of them being located in the Western ghats. We have already described the art of Ajanta which is typical of the cave-architecture.

In the far South (the ancient Tamil country) we have temple architecture only very late after the sixth century A.D. But even this period now survives in ruins and desert. The temple architecture, for example at Madura, Tanjore, Rameshwaram, Srirangam and Chidambaram, belongs to a much later period. But in the literature of the country we get a glimpse of cultural activities pursued by these people.

The Tamil kingdoms (Chola, Pandya, etc.), are first mentioned in a Sanskrit grammatical work of the 4th century B.C. Later on the Artha Shastra of Kautilya makes mention of Pandya pearls. They are mentioned in greater details in Asokan inscriptions and by this time both Jainism and Buddhism had migrated to the south also. Of the dozen Dravidian languages, the chief are Tamil, Malayalam, Kannada and Telugu, the last being spoken probably by the largest number. Tamil is the oldest and purest. It also possesses the earliest vernacular literature of India, apart from Pali. The oldest records are in Brahmi script which was common to all India.

The oldest work that still survives is the famous grammar Tolkappiyam in Tamil, (a work of the first century A.D.) which gives us a veritable storehouse of information. From it we get not only grammar but also religion, love, the art of warfare, social and civic ideals, occupations and geography. We come across tribal chieftains, kings, fishermen, pearlfishers, boatmen, salt and boat makers, workers in shell and merchants engaged in foreign trade. Something like a caste system was germinating, though even now the South has mainly three castes, the Brahmans, Shudras and untouchables. The great literary centre among the Tamilians was Madurai. The great literary schools or sangams are said to have been developed there and from them we get the Sangam classics. These have given us among other things more than 2000 poems, 10 long idylls and other lesser works. Of the main themes of this literature, mention may be made of hero-worship, love, devotion to duty, ethical teachings, honour and friendship. For instance, of the eight classical anthologies, three have love poems, one contains four hundred heroic poems together with fifty lyrics and others contain poems in praise of Madurai, other cities and kings.

Like Sanskrit, Tamil has its own epics, the Silappadikaram and its sequel the Manimekalai. The first was composed in the first or second century A.D., by a monk brother of a Chera king. It has for its theme the love of a wealthy young merchant for a beautiful dancer, the sorrows and self sacrifice of the wife and later in the second epic, her daughter is described as having embraced Buddhism after hearing religious truths from the mouths of teachers of various schools. These epics provide us with prolific details of social and artistic conditions of the ancient Tamilians and on their basis some scholars have evolved an ancient system of South Indian music. Other classical works, mention may be made of the famous and popular work, the Kural by Tiruvalluvar, a poet of genius living in the first century A.D. He deals with the ethical values and problems of the day in terse couplets in which the rhyme as in all other Tamil poetry is found at the beginning and not at the end of a line. Children even today begin their education by memorizing its verses.

The Tamil kingdoms were eclipsed by the Pallavas in the third century A.D. They lost their supremacy only when overwhelmed by the Chalukyas in the ninth century. Throughout this period the Tamilians continued to make cultural progress and their great merchants plied their ships in all parts of the neighbouring seas, trading both with the eastern countries like Ceylon, Indonesia and Malaya and with the West right up to the Roman Empire. The articles most in demand were pearls, pepper and beryls. The Biblical stories of the Old Testament also give us certain articles of commerce which were chiefly of Indian origins, for instance, ivory, peacock, gold, almug trees and precious stones. A great port Ophir is mentioned from where merchandise went to the great Solomon sent by his friend, the king of Tyre. Ophir was probably the Saphir (Sopara) on the West Coast. The Hebrew names for peacock and aloes and the English name for rice, ginger and pepper are of Tamil derivation. Besides cotton cloth and precious woods from Tamilnad adorned the bodies of the Mummies in Egyptian tombs and the places and temples of Babylon respectively in the sixth century B.C. Thus, Indian trade with the West is of great hoariness. This trade became very brisk with the establishment of the Roman Empire. Large Roman coins have been unearthed in the South, one even bearing the fact of Britain's conquest by the Romans. In the Tamilian poems we get stories of these 'Yavana' ships and their crews coming to the Indian ports, some of them even remaining here as mercenaries to kings and trading with India giving wine and gold in return for the precious merchandise of the East. Thus, in the ports there were settlements of foreign traders, all speaking their various tongues. A second century (A.D.) papyrun manuscript found in Egypt speaks of the adventure of a Greek lady ship-wrecked off the west coast of India. The language spoken by the Indian king in this story is found to be Kannada.

Alexandria was the main entrepot for Indian goods for Rome and other countries. Hence people from that place locked to India in sufficient numbers but colonists from other countries also came there like the Jews, the Syrian and the Persian, Christians and the Arabs, the last forming the nucleus of the present Moplah community of Malabar in Kerala. The Malabar Church continues to use even toady Syriac as its liturgical language. Ships also sailed between China and India. As this part of India remained immune from foreign invasion right up to the 14th century, an integrated culture grew up in these parts, even preserving the Aryan elements in their purer forms.

To summarise, what is the picture that we get of the people

of the south in the ancient period ? The people were prosperous and had their communal governments (Megasthenes had heard of the popular assemblies there), their wishes being respected by the governments of the day. The land system was either Ryatwari or the land was the joint property of a group of landlords. In such villages an elected assembly and numerous communities looked after the affairs of the community as a whole. Women also could be members of such bodies which managed all department of communal life. Thus, the people enjoyed many opportunities for self-expression.

In the realm of art, temple building became the most prolific artistic creation. Kings and people vied with one another in endowing these temples with money and land in various forms for their upkeep. Intricate management grew up as temples grew into temple-cities with each such units having their priests, managers, treasurers, musicians, singers, parasol bearers, lamplighters, washermen, potters, astrologers, cooks, gardeners, carpenters, barbers, actors, and dancing girls. Schools and colleges were often attached to these places. Many donations were earmarked for feeding the poor, the Brahmans and for tending the sick. Donations were also given for maintaining a perpetual lamp or offering daily food and for these purposes the grants mentioned details of ghee to be used and food to be cooked and the arrangements thereof. Ornaments were also given and the Tanjore deity of the famous Chola temple is said to have in the crown 859 diamonds, 309 rubies and 669 pearls.

Among the religions, Buddhism died out in most places by the end of the 6th century. Jainism, however, maintained a greater hold. Hinduism had left all these behind in popularity by the end of the ninth century mostly because it was propagated by a number of saints from the 7th to the 9th centuries. These enthralled the people by their devotional songs in praise of Shiva and Vishnu. Thus, the Bhakti form of Hindu religion had a great vogue in the South.

The Vaishnava saints or Alvars were 12 in number and a collection of their hymns the 'Prabandha' is still recited there in the temples. The greatest saint was Nammalvar. There was also a woman saint Goda or Andal worshipping Krishna, a southern counterpart of Mira.

The Saivites number 63 early saints. The four most famous saints are Appar, Sambandha, Sundaramurti and Manikka Vachaka.

While Tamil saints were appealing to the heart of the people in their own language, Sanskrit scholars were attracting the minds of the elite in their colleges and in courts. Indian works like the Ramayana and Mahabharata were being translated. It was in the eighth century that the greatest saint and philosopher Sankaracharya was born in Malabar probably in the year 738 A.D. According to tradition he began ascetic life at the age of eight and wrote works at the age of twelve. He travelled throughout the length and breadth of India and made famous the Vedantic philosophy. He founded the great Hindu centres for Sannyasis at the four corners of India. He is said to have died at Kedarnath in the Himalayas at the age of thirty-two. Sankar's most famous works were the commentaries he wrote on the Upanishads and the Brahma Sutras by Badarayana. The Saivites also accepted him as he paid homage to Shiva and his Shakti but the Vaishnavas did not take readily to him. For them other saints arose into prominence, the greatest of them being Ramanuja in the eleventh century. He accepted God both with and without form, emphasized that salvation could come from the grace of God which could be procured by ardent love and devotion to Him. He did not believe like Sankara that the world was unreal. He organised seventy-four diaceses or districts in different parts of India with a pious householder as the head of each. The head-quarters were established at Sri Rangam in the South.

In the realm of art also, the Dravidian genius made notable contributions, specifically in the cave temples at Ellora and Elephanta and in the open ground temples like those in Tanjore and Madurai. Brahmanical group at Ellora (besides the Buddhist) consists of 16 excavations numbering 13 to 29. The principal examples are Abode of Ravana, ten incarnations of Vishnu, Kailasa or Shiva's paradise, Rameshwara and Sita 'Bath' (Dumar Lena). We may make mention of the Kailasa temple as it is unique and brings out the structural temple of the period, showing that 'the Indian artist had an extra-ordinarily developed plastic sense. No other people have even dreamed of sculpting such great temples out of the solid rock as he has'. (Percy Brown). The temple is one of the greatest examples of our exalted religious emotion. The temple is in four parts, the main structure, the entrance gateway, an intermediate Nandi shrine, and the cloisters surrounding the court-yard. The pillars in the temple add to the ornamental richness of the whole. Kailasa is thus an outstanding monolithic example of a temple and its sculptured figures and other types of decoration mark it out as one of the first examples of Indian artistic genius. The temples at Elephanta resemble those of Ellora, the main shrine resembling the Dumar Lena at Ellora, though it is superior to others of its kind in the character and quality of its sculptures. In the temple Shiva in all his aspects is portrayed, notably Arddhanari, a manifestation of Shiva typifying the male and female energies, and Shiva and Parvati. Both these groups are masterly examples of the plastic art, and pulsate with spiritual fervour, but the most striking is the three faced head of Shiva Maheshamurti, creation of a genius. The whole essence of Shaivism is concentrated in forms of marvellous refinement and subtlety, curved and full and alive, the artist having fused his very soft emotions in the creative sculpture.

The open ground temple at Tanjore built by the Cholas is a magnificent tribute to Shiva. The temple contains among other things, a court-yard measuring 250 by 500 feet and the tower rising to a height of 190 feet. The walls have figures and scenes of exquisite finish showing in its embellishment supremely imaginative quality; thus, it is the finest single creation of the Dravidian craftsman. Another remarkable temple is the one at Madurai dedicated to Shiva and his consort, Meenakshi. The outer area of this temple is 850 feet by 725 feet, with four large gateways. There are gates within gates and court-yards within court-yards and sanctuaries within sanctuaries. There is also a pool measuring 165 feet by 120 feet. There is court of a thousand pillars.

Everything about the temple is gigantic and multitudinous.

The gods, the goddesses, animals and other decorative figures are very life-like showing again the inexhaustible resources of Hindu mythology and artistic genius.

Thus, the early civilisation and culture of the south, a fusion of the Aryan and Dravidian elements contain some of the best features of our ancient heritage in their purer forms. The Dravidians have, in particular, given us great philosophers like Shankara, great products of artistic genius in the realms of dance and temple architecture and also a great sect in Shaivism. Besides in the early period of Muslim invasion of India, they kept intact the products of Aryan thought and culture, thus preserving for the generations to come the bases of our culture.

11

INTRODUCTION TO MEDIEVAL AGE

THE CULTURAL HISTORY of India in the medieval period begins after the death of Harsh in 647 A.D. and ends with the downfall of the Moghul Empire in the eighteenth century. In this introduction, we deal briefly with the political history of India during this period to provide a background to our cultural history.

The unity of Indian history vanishes with Harsh and is not restored to any considerable measure until the closing years of the twelfth century. During this period India was ruled by a number of independent dynasties and so for as north India is concerned these dynasties were mainly Rajput. The transition from Harsh to the emergence of the Rajputs was probably occupied with the absorption into the Hindu body politic of the various hordes of foreign invaders who had come to India during the fifth and sixth centuries A.D. Many of the Rajput clans are said to be the descendants of these foreign tribes.

During the five and a half centuries intervening between the death of Harsh and the Mohammedan incursion into India, India was divided into great many kingdoms where changes occurred so incessantly with never-ending dynastic wars and revolutions that it is not possible to describe all of them in a single continuous narrative arranged in a strict chronological order. Hence, we deal only with certain outstanding features in the history of some of the more prominent kingdoms in India.

The main Rajput kingdoms in the North were Kashmir,

Kannauj, Palas and Senas of Bengal and Bihar, Chandelas of Bundelkhand, Gujarat, Malwa, Delhi and Ajmer.

(1) **Kashmir** - Kashmir was at first ruled by Karkot dynasty and then by the Utpal dynasty whose great king was Avantivarman (855-883 A.D.). Under his minister Suiyya big engineering works were established. Down till the fourteenth century it was ruled by the Hindu kings when it was conquered by the Mohammedans. Its history was written in the twelfth century by Kalhana in the famous book Rajtarangini. The history of the medieval period in Kashmir is very confused with most of the kings ill-treating their subjects and fleecing the peasantry.

(2) **Kannauj** - After the death of Harsh Kannauj comes into the picture again under the rule of Yashovarman who is said to have sent an embassy to Chile in 731 A.D. Both he and his descendants had to suffer defeat at the hands of king Lalitaditya and his son of Kashmir and also the Pala king of Bengal. Finally it was conquered by the Pratihars or Parihars in the ninth century. The Pratihars had come from the southern Rajputana. Among the Pratihar kings, the most famous was Raja Bhoja (c. A.D. 840-890 A.D.) who ruled for half a century and built up an extensive empire including Saurashtra, Avadh and Magadh, under him. Kannauj was governed very efficiently and there was a great cultural renaissance. His son also continued his progressive tradition and patronised the famous poet and dramatist Rajashekhar. Later on Kannauj was occupied by the Gaharwars (or Gahadawala) sometime in 1090 A.D. During the twelfth century the most famous king of Kannauj was Jaichand whose daughter was taken away by Prithviraj for marriage. Jaichand was defeated by Mohammad Ghori and Kannauj was absorbed into the Mohammedan Empire.

(3) **Bengal** - The history of Bengal is obscure immediately after Harsh. Some parts of it are said to have been ruled by the Guptas and the Maukharies. The people were, it is said, tired of the anarchy and elected one Gopal as their King in 750 A.D. He began the dynasty of the Palas which lasted till the conquest of Bengal by the Mohammedans in the thirteenth century. Part of Bengal came under the sway of a new dynasty, the Senas in

the eleventh century. They were also destroyed by the Muslims. The Palas were Buddhists while the Senas patronised Brahmanism.

(4) **Bundelkhand** - Bundelkhand was ruled by the Chandelas who came into prominence in the ninth century when they overthrew the neighboring Pratihar kingdom and extended their sway in Bundelkhand right up to the Jamuna. Their kingdom was called Jajaka-Bhukti or Jijhoti and the important towns were Khajuraho, Mahoba and Kalanjar. The temples of Khajuraho are architecturally very well built. The Chandel king Dhanga in the tenth century and also the king Parmal are well-known in history. After the defeat of Parmal by Prithviraj the Kingdom declined.

(5) **Gujarat and Malva** - Gujarat was occupied by the Solanki dynasty and Malwa by the Parmars. The Solanki dynasty was established by Mulraj in the tenth century A.D. Among the Parmar kings the most renowned was Raja Bhoj (not to be confused with Bhoj of Kannauj) who ruled from 1018 to 1060 A.D. He was an accomplished scholar and a liberal patron of Sanskrit learning. His name has become proverbial as that of the ideal Hindu Prince. After him the Kingdom sank into obscurity.

(6) **Ajmer** - Ajmer and Sambhar had been ruled by the Chauhans for centuries. One of their famous kings was Vigraharaja, a noted patron of Sanskrit literature. His brother's son was Prithviraj who has became famous in Indian History and whose exploits have been the theme of Chandbardai's epic Chand Raiso. After some time in the tenth century Delhi also became a part of Ajmer. And at the time of Mohammad Ghori, Prithviraj was ruling there. After the defeat of Prithviraj by Mohammad Ghori, his empire was also absorbed into the Mohammedan dominion.

While the Rajputs were ruling in the northern India, the southern India was being ruled by a number of other peoples. The medieval history of the southern peninsula concerns itself chiefly with two groups of states, viz., the kingdoms of the Deccan plateau lying between Narmada on the North and the Krishna and the Tungabhadra on the south, and the states beyond these rivers. These kingdoms were so completely isolated from the world that their history in detail cannot possess more than local interest. Hence, we narrate briefly about some of the important kingdoms and personalities.

(1) **Mysore** - It was first ruled by the Kadambas from the third century to the sixth century A.D. and then by the Gangas upto the tenth century who later on went to Kaling, and ruled there upto the fifteenth century A.D. Under their rule was erected the colossal statue of Gomata 564 feet high unrivalled in India for daring conception and gigantic dimensions.

(2) **Chalukyas** - The most prominent of the early medieval dynasty in the Deccan were the Chalukyas who founded their dynasty in the sixth century under Pulakesin I as their king at Badami in what is now Bijapur District of Mysore. His grandson Pulakesin II was the contemporary of Harsh and like him he was the unrivalled ruler of the Deccan. He had defeated Harsh also though he suffered defeat at the hands of the Pallavas, who became paramount in the Deccan about 642 A.D. But the fighting between the Pallavas and the Chalukyas continued and it was only in the eighth century that the power of the Chalukyas was finally shattered by the Rashtrakutas.

The Rashtrakutas continued to rule for more than two centuries and it is said that they had commercial relations with the Arabs also. Both under the Chalukyas and the Rashtrakutas the Deccan was enriched by many temples among which the rock-cut temple of Kailash is very famous. One branch of the Chalukyas was established after the defeat of the main branch, in 973 A.D. in Kalyani. Their most famous king was Vikramaditya whose exploits in war have been narrated by Bilhan. Also in his court was Vighneshwar author of Mitakshara, leading authority in Hindu Law outside Bengal. In the eleventh and the twelfth centuries this branch lost power and was conquered by the Yadavas of Devgiri and Hoyasalas of Dorasamudra.

The Hoyasalas of Mysore first came into prominence in the twelfth century (about 1130 A.D.). They were the followers of Ramanuj and erected many temples in their dominion in the twelfth and thirteenth centuries. Among these temples, the one at Halebid is most famous from the architectural point of view. They and the Yadavas of Devgiri who were descendants of feudatory nobles of the Chalukya Kingdom and had come into prominence in the twelfth century, were defeated by Alauddin Khilji.

(3) Among the kingdoms of the far south the most important was that of the Pallavas who came into greater prominence in the sixth century A.D. though their dynasty had begun in the fourth century A.D. Their capital was Kanchi or Conjeevaram. They were the dominant power in the South from the middle of the sixth century to the middle of the eighth century and had extended their dominion upto Narmada.

They erected splendid monuments in architecture and sculpture among which the most famous are the seven Rathas or temples at Mamallapuram. Their decline came in the ninth century when they were defeated by the Cholas.

The Cholas, the Pandyas and the Cheras have been very famous from times immemorial. They had existed even in the Mauryan period, in the medieval period also they continued to have a well-established state right upto the thirteenth century. The Cholas ruled in a region which is now Madras proper, some adjoining districts of Madras and some parts of Mysore, from Nellore to Pudukottai. The Pandyas ruled over the region which is now in the district of Madurai, Tinnevelly and parts of Kerala. The Cheras or Kerala were mainly in the rugged regions of the Western Ghats to the south of the Chandragiri river. Among these kingdoms the Cholas occupied the dominant position. In the medieval period under Rajaraja the great and his son in the tenth and the first quarter of the eleventh century, they were supreme and had defeated the Chalukyas, Pandyas, Rulers of Ceylon, Bengal, Pegu and Andamans. In the thirteenth century their power declined on account of the establishment of Vijaynagar kingdom, greater strength of the Pandyas and the Muslim inroads. The Cholas were famous for their patronage of art and literature. They had also experimented successfully in the establishment of Local self government or the Panchayat system. Their famous temples are to be found in Tanjore, Chidambaram and other places. The kings were Shaivites.

The Pandyas were always fighting either with the Pallavas or with the Cholas or with Ceylon. They were the leading power in the thirteenth century and their culture has been described by Marcapolo who visited them in 1288 and 1293 A.D. He has described the great commercial activities in which the Pandyas were famous at that time, and has told us about ships coming from Arabia and China.

The Cheras were either allied with the Cholas or with the Pandyas. They did not matter very much. These were the important kingdoms ruled by the Hindus in the medieval period immediately preceding the rise of the Mohammedan power in India. This political history establishes one important fact that there was no sense of political unity, no consciousness that in unity lay strength and therefore, they could not withstand the Mohammedan onslaught. But it would be a mistake to think that whole of India was conquered by the Muslims. The Himalayan states remained independent even at this time. Many states in the interior of India enjoyed independence at some time or other during this period, e.g., states in Rajputana, those in Assam and Orissa and in the far South.

We now come to the Muslim rule in India. Their first attack came in Sind. After the death of Mohammed, the great Muslim Prophet, the age of the caliphate had begun. Under the Caliph Omar the Arabs attacked Sind in the early years of the eighth century. The Hindu dynasty was defeated. But soon after there was trouble in the Mohammedan world and the Arab rule of Sind had, therefore, to end. The next Muslim attack came in the tenth and the first quarter of the eleventh centuries, when Mahmud Ghaznavi invaded India and was active in a large part of North India. His invasion was only for money and he came, looted the various temples and other Hindu Kingdoms and went away. This he did many times but his incursions did not leave any permanent mark except only this that the political conditions of North India worsened, and disunity became greater. It was only from the end of the twelfth century (1193 A.D.) that Muslim rule was permanently established in India. In 1175-76 A.D. Mohammad Ghori of Afghanistan attacked

India and defeated the various Rajput Kings including Prithviraj, the ruler of Ajmer and Delhi. He left his main lieutenant Kutub-ud-din Aibak in India who after the death of his master founded the slave dynasty.

The Muslim rule in India lasted from 1193 A.D. to 1707 A.D. though even after 1707 A.D. some vestige of their rule remained. During the period of the Muslim rule various dynasties arose in India with Delhi or Agra as their capital.

The first Muslim dynasty was that of the so-called slaves. It lasted from 1206 to 1290 A.D. The must famous king of this line were besides its founder, Iltutmish and Balban. In the heyday of their power the whole of the north India had came under their subjection.

The slaves were supplanted by the Khiljis in 1290 A.D. Their rule in India lasted up to 1325 A.D. Their most famous king was Alauddin Khilji who for the first time among the Muslim kings of India made inroads in the Deccan also and his lieutenants conquered the kingdoms of the far south also going down right upto Madurai.

The Khiljis declined after Alauddin and their place was taken by the Tughluqs (1321-1398 A.D.). Among the Tughluqs the two most famous kings were Mohammad Tughluq and Feroz Tughluq. Like Allauddin Mohammad Tughluq conquered the south. Among the pre-Moghul kings he was the most learned ruler. During the rule of the Tughluqs we find once again the centrifugal forces in India asserting themselves and after the death of Mohammad Tughluq many independent kingdoms both Hindu and Muslim arose in all parts of India. Among the kingdoms, the most famous were those of Mewar, Vijayanagar, Bahmani, Bengal, Kashmir, Gujarat and Sind. Later on Malwa and Jaunpur also came into the picture. Bengal remained independent from 1340 to 1540 A.D. Malwa from 1398 to 1531 A.D., Gujarat from 1401 to 1572 A.D., Kashmir from the fourteenth century to 1586 A.D., Bahmani from 1347 to 1580 A.D., when it split up into five kingdoms of Berar, Ahmednagar, Bijapur, Bidar and Golkonda which also lost its independence in the Moghul period. Vijaynagar established its independence from 1336 A.D. and remained so till 1565 A.D. when it was defeated by the offshoots of the Bahmani kingdom. At this time, North India also witnessed the invasion of Timur in 1398 A.D. He laid waste the whole of North India upto Delhi, Meerut and Hardwar. The result of this invasion was the spread of anarchy all over India. Around Delhi the Saiyyids ruled from 1414 to 1450 A.D. They were insignificant and as such their doings do not merit much notice. After some time Bahlol Lodi of the Punjab seized the Delhi throne and inaugurated the Lodi dynasty which lasted till 1526 A.D. When it gave ground to the Moghuls.

The Moghuls under Babar came to India in 1526 on the invitation of certain ladies and some of the Rajputs in order to rescue them from the tyranny of the Lodi king Ibrahim. Ibrahim was defeated and Babar decided to stay in India permanently founding thus the Moghul dynasty. The Moghul dynasty lasted from 1526 A.D. to 1707 A.D. in reality though some weak kings continued to rule over a small territory even later an. The most famous kings of this dynasty were Akbar (1556-1605 A.D.), Jahangir (1605-1727 A.D.), Shahjahan (1627-1658 A.D.), death (in 1665 A.D.), Aurangzeb (1659-1707 A.D.). Under the Moghuls India was once again politically united. They were also patrons of the Hindus as well and specially under Akbar the highest degree of Hindu-Muslim synthesis was achieved. In passing it may be remarked the Akbar's father Humayun had to face opposition from Shershah, the Afghan ruler of Bihar, who between 1542 to 1545 A.D. became the ruler of north India, forcing Humayun to flee India. In his reforms and in his policy towards the Hindus Shershah anticipated Akbar.

Just as the downfall of the Central power in the Sultanate period invited the invasion of Timur, so the decline of the Moghuls also led to the invasion of Nadir Shah and the dismemberment of India into independent political entities. Among the new powers the Marathas were the most virile and established their dominion both in the north and in the south of India. But the various Indian powers took to fighting among themselves and became an easy prey to the British.

The pre-Moghul period of Indian history is known as the age of the Sultanate. Both during the age of the Sultanate and in the Moghul period India continued to make cultural progress. We specially find that after the break-up of the Central power at Delhi in the Sultanate period, the various provinces which became independent continued to patronise the Indian art and other features of our culture and we have as a result of the efforts of these various kings both at the centre and in the provinces the birth of a common Hindu-Muslim culture, which we shall describe in the pages that follow.

12

AGE OF RAJPUTS

WE HAVE TRACED the evolution of the Indian culture from the Vedic age right up to the period of Harsh. This period we have termed the ancient age. We now pass on to the medieval age. There is, however, no fundamental break between the culture of the previous age and that of the medieval age. There is a continuity of culture in this period also. For the sake of convenience we study the culture of this period under the headings of the Age of the Rajputs, the Age of the Indo-Muslim kings and the Hindu-Muslim synthesis. Under the Rajput Age we put the contributions of the Hindus to the Indian culture from 700 to 1800 A.D., while under the Indo-Muslim Kings, we describe the culture which was inherently a contribution of the Muslims, while the Hindu-Muslim synthesis, as is obvious from the name itself, pertains to the joint contributions of the Hindus and the Muslims to our culture.

Coming now to the period after Harsh, we may discuss the fundamental principles and features of the medieval age. We have already remarked that the medieval age is distinguished by the establishment of conventions or regulations. So far as the Hindus are concerned the fundamentals of the Hindu life as established in the ancient period remain. Changes, however, are made in details. Comments and commentaries are written on the religious, artistic, scientific and other types of ancient literature. Some people maintain that this obsession with regulations, laws and standards involved by the end of the medieval age a decline in the cultural genius of the Hindus. We are lost in the wood. Fetishes, superstitions, rites and ceremonies take the place of creative adventure in the varied phases of human life and with the decline of our cultural life politics also presents a bleak prospect and our subjection to the conquerors from across the north-west passes is hastened thereby. Our conservatism in the social and religious fields especially spreads disunity. It is, therefore asserted by some people that India's decline came when she swerved away from an integral conception of life or from that creative spirituality which is a synthesis of the good in materialism and of spirituality proper.

We may now record the salient features of our culture in the fields of literature, religion, art, and economics.

In the field of literature we find in the first place development of the vernaculars. For instance the various 'Apabhramshas' are now developed and cultivated and a vast literature grows up. In this domain the contributions of the Jains and the Buddhists cannot be too much emphasized.

Among the poets who wrote in the literary 'Apabhramsha' resembling Hindi and which was then spoken from the Himalayas to the Godavari and from Sind to Bengal, the most important were Sarhapa (760 A.D.), Swayambhudeva (790 A.D.), Pushpadanta (959-72 A.D.). We have mentioned Sarhapa because he is the first known writer to have written poems in the literary Apabhransha. But the two most famous names are those of Swayambhudeva and Pushpadanta. Swayambhudeva edited both Ramayana and Mahabharata. His narration of these two epics entitle him to be called a great epic poet. His language is characterised by easy flow, sweetness and freshness. His description of nature and of the beauty of women shows the depth of his study and knowledge. His depiction of the joys and sorrows of men is also very touching and inspiring. 'Pushpadanta' specialised in the description of the wrench of pain consequent on separation and his treatment of poverty is masterly. We have also the first Mohammedan writer Abdul Rehman of Multan writing in this language in 1013 A.D.

There was, however, development in other 'Apabhramshas'

also. For instance, in Awadhi, we had Tulsidas the greatest Hindi poet. Tulsidas (1532-1623) who lived in Banaras is said to be 'unapproachable and alone in his niche in the temple of fame'. He was not only the greatest Hindu poet of all times but spiritual teacher of the people of Hindustan where his name has become a household word and his memory is worshiped by millions. The most famous of his works known as Ramcharitamanasa has been described as 'the Bible of hundred millions of people' of Hindustan and his book is in everyone's hands from the court to the cottage and is read, heard and appreciated by every class of the Hindu community, whether high or low, rich or poor, young or old. He also wrote a number of other works among which twelve are at present regarded as authentic. His faith in Rama as an incarnation of God uplifts him and enables him to present a very noble conception of God. His tender love for the humblest as well as the greatest of his devotees, his condescension in becoming incarnate for their sakes, his sympathy and endurance of suffering for those who are devoted to him and his readiness to forgive are expressed with great dignity and power. There is not an impure image or word in his Ramayana from beginning to the end. It is a vernacular Gita. He lived for the people and loved them, and thought the very best he knew in the language of the people and in poetry which reaches the heart in translation. He was truly the 'Valmlki' of Hindi literature.

Another great poet among the Hindus was Surdas. He wrote in Brijbhasha and is probably the greatest lyric poet in the Hindi world. His dates are still unsettled but he was a contemporary of Akbar and is mentioned in the Ain-i-Akbari. His main work is Sursagar which is said to have contained 60,000 verses. Eleven other works are also traced to him. His themes were devotional and centered round the life of Krishna as portrayed by Vallabhacharya. In his works he has portrayed the boyhood of Krishna and his relationship with Yashoda, the foster mother, so wonderfully that their universal appeal will never fade. His psychological depth remains unmatched. He introduced new forms and imagery, giving to Brijbhasha its modern setting, and thus making it a great literary language.

He may well be called the Milton of India, in the world of the Hindi poetry.

The Bengali language also made progress in this period in the realm of poetry. As early as the tenth century we find ballads glorifying kings of the Pal dynasty. We have the Bengali translation of the Ramayana by Krittivasa in 1370 A.D. The Bhagwat Puran was also translated between 1473 and 1480 A.D. by Maladhar Vasu. Religious poetry was also cultivated by great poets like Sanjay and Kasiram. But among the greatest poets of the early medieval age the most famous was Jaideva who adorned the court of King Laksaman Sen. His Geet Govinda is at once religious and according to some people erotic. The poem is a lyrical drama which tells how Radha in jealousy left her faithless lover Krishna, but in her solitude did not cease to think of him and how the two were, at last, united. The poem is composed of songs ('Prabhanda') which are meant to be danced, the sounding lines have the rhythm of ballad and sway like a dance. This poem has been mystically interpreted. Radha is the soul fallen into 'Maya', suffering as soon as it ceases to be in union with the Divine. The return to that union is supreme happiness. Thus, the poem is inspired by bhakti or devotion to Krishna. The poet is magnificent in his descriptions, pouring the fire of passion into a faultless mould. Now soon words follow in quick succession and again there is a slow, measured movement of solemn compounds. Alliteration and rhyme enhance the charm. The nobility of Kalidasa's lyricism comes into fill flower. Other famous Bengali writers were Chandidas who wrote nearly a thousand love songs centering round Radha and Krishna and was a contemporary of Vidyapati, the beginning of the fifteenth century A.D., Mukandaram Kavikankan, one of the greatest poets of Bengal, with his panegyric on goddess Chandi, completed in 1589 A.D., Brindawandas with his book Chaitanyabhagwat, Krishnadas with his work Chaitanyacharitamrit and Ramprasad whose hymns to Durga and other religious songs are deservedly famous.

The Marathi vernacular was also developed during this period. The oldest writer is Jnaneshwar who completed his

Jnaneshwar in 1290 A.D. As a commentary on Gita this book in Marathi can hardly be surpassed in its wealth of imagery. He was followed by Namdev (1270-1350 A.D.) who was a tailor by caste. He was a great devotee like Jnaneshwar, of Vishnu under the name of Vithoba whose image was installed in the temple at Pandharpur. He was a composer of devotional songs called 'Abhanga'. One of his songs runs thus :

The one indeed pervades all things, wherever our glances wander;

But veiled by Maya's magic spell, one is comprehended.

Govinda is the all, without him nothing is, he is the one.

For he is like the cord on which one hundred thousand gems are strung.

As sea and wave, bubble and foam, are not but shape of water, and so on.

The Universe is nothing else but varied forms of Brahma's sport.

Another great saint was Janabai. She was also a great devotee of the Divine. Then came Tukaram (1608-1649). He is said to have written about 4621 'Abhangs' or devotional songs. People of all castes and sex sing his verses in the fields and by the lamplights in their homes. In the same line, we have Ramdas born in 1608 A.D. He influenced Shivaji also and organised monasteries all over Maharashtra, which later on served as revolutionary centers rousing the people against the Moghuls under Aurangzeb. His monumental work is Das Bodha which combines various sciences and arts with the spiritual life as the synthesising principle. It was Ramdas who aroused the Maratha national consciousness and made it a force to reckon with. These were the great names in the field of Marathi literature during the medieval period.

In Rajasthan also we had development of vernacular literature. It is said that the earliest literature in Northern India was the poetical chronicles of Rajputana. In these chronicles we have narration of the deeds performed by the Rajput heroes of the age. The most famous was Prithviraj Raiso by Chandbardai. Another great epic poem was Bishaldeo Raiso.

The Punjabi literature was also developed and we have got

a wealth of popular poetry as a heritage of those times. In these ballads the stories of ancient heroes with their joys and sorrows are narrated, e.g., the story of Nala. One of the forms of the Punjabi was Gurmukhi developed by the Sikhs under Nanak and other Gurus.

In Bihar also the vernacular literature made a marked progress. In particular, we have Vidyapati Thakur who wrote in Maithali in 1409 A.D. His songs are full of the yearning of the soul for God in the form of an allegory portraying the love of Radha and Krishna. We have also the development of the Gujarati language, the lead in which was taken by the Jains, among the Bhaktas we have Narsi Mehta whose devotional songs have got great popularity even now.

Thus, we find that the medieval age witnessed the foundation and the evolution of the modern vernacular languages of India. Specially in the realm of poetry the development was noteworthy. The prose literature was to develop in the modern period. These languages were also provided with grammar and dictionaries during this period. In this sphere the name of Hemchandra Suri, the great Jain sage, is memorable.

The Sanskrit literature also continued to make great progress. In the field of grammar called Vyakaran many commentaries were written. Many of these were the refashioning of the Sutras of Panini. Of these the clearest is the Kasikavritti, the commentary of Benaras composed in the seventh century by Jayadit and Vaman. Bhartrihari also wrote a commentary on the Mahabhashya of Patanjali. Another famous grammar was the Katantra by Sarvavarman used as far as central Asia and in the South it served as a model for works on the grammar of the Dravidian tongues. Dictionaries or the Koshas were also written to explain the meaning of words both old and new. Among these dictionaries the most famous were those of Hemchandra, Bhattachhirswami, Purushottam Deva, Yadava Bhatta, and others. Many works on philosophy were also written. For example, commentaries on 'Nyaya' by Udyotkar, Vachasapati Misra, Udayanacharya and others. Hemchandra wrote Praman Mimamsa on Jainism, Dharmakirti wrote Nyayabindu on Buddhism and Ganesh in Bengal wrote the work Tatvachintamani.

Besides these we had books by Sridhar on Vaisheshik philosophy, by Vachsapati Misra on Sankhya, Yoga and Purvamimamsa and by Sankaracharya on the Vedanta philosophy.

In the field of poetry also many works were written. For instance, there is the composition of Kalhana; the Rajtarangini or 'kings of Kashmir'. This poem is partly epic and partly history. The author living in the twelfth century was a son of a minister at the court of Kashmir. He brought the history of the kingdom of Kashmir in his poem upto 1140 A.D. He paints his characters with rare acuteness. Being permeated with profound sense of morality he tries to show the triumph of good over evil. He is a trustworthy guide to a very large extent for the history of Kashmir at the end of the eleventh century and the beginning of the 12th. His lack of simplicity, of mastery of form and of construction prevent his work from being a true epic. He has poetry in him, but he is not a poet. Other epic poems of the period worthy of note were Amarushatak, Bhattikavya Shishupal-Vadha, Nalodaya, Raghavapandaviya (in this epic stories of Ramayana and Mahabharata are told side by side, each verse having double meaning, one giving the story of Ramayana, the other of Mahabharata) and Parshvabhyudaya by the Jain Acharya Jinasena.

Lyric poetry was also enriched at this time but freshness was giving place to love of clitches. All nature was now classified in metaphors for the use of authors. Among the great poets we have Bhartrihari the philosopher of love who has given us works like Shringarasatak, Nitisatak and Vairagyasatak. To the poet woman is the chief obstacle to the goal of salvation. Unsatisfied in himself, the poet seeks the fault in woman, the eternal culprit. 'In this dirty little girl, frail and liar that she is, what is it that I have adored ?' he cries. His work is full of aphorisms. Another famous poet was Bilhana of Kashmir with his famous work Chaurisuratapanchasika. He also wrote a historical work in verse on the deeds of the princes of the Chalukya dynasty and obtained from the Chalukya king

Vikramaditya (1076-1127 A.D.) the title of Vidyapati. There were various other poets also in this period, e.g., Damodar Gupta, the Chief Minister of Jayapida, King of Kashmir, who wrote the work Kuttinimata in the eighth century. The book was in the form of teaching by an old professional imparting instructions to a courtesan about the art of love. Among others mention may be made of Kshemendra (author of Ramayana-Manjari, Bharat-Manjari Dashavatar), Kumardas and Hem Chandra.

In the field of drama also progress was kept at a high level. The beginning of the sixth century saw the debut of Harsh as a dramatist. His dramas Ratnawali, Priyadarshika and Nagananda are well known.

But the greatest among the dramatists of the century was Bhavabhuti who is regarded as the greatest poet after Kalidasa. In the mastery of Sanskrit language he was without a peer. He lived at the court of Yashovarman, king of Kannauj, who was ruling at the end of this century. Three of his dramas are prominently known, viz., Mahavircharitra, Uttararamcharita and Malatim-adhava. The first two as the name suggests are based on themes taken from the Ramayana while the last is a comedy with a subject taken from a collection of tales and he puts in other accessory details from observation. In his delineation Bhavabhuti excels in the expressian of contrast of light and shade and violent emotions like terror. His vocabulary is inexhaustible, his expression is forceful and even in complicated metres, he does not fail to express harmony. His works demand an audience of connoisseurs. After him, it is said, the freshness in drama diminishes, it becomes prosaic and in place of poetry we have skilled versification. Among other dramatists, mention may be made of Rajashekhar of Kannauj, Anandvardhan of the times of Raja Bhoj with drama Prabodhachandra, which was allegorical in character, the drama Venisamhara by Bhattanarayana, Mudra Rakshasa by Vishakhadutta and Prabodh Chandrodaya by Krishna Mishra. At this time shallow forms of drama like the Bhana (monologue) and the Prahasana (farcical camedy) were also cultivated.

The field of narrative literature was also enriched during this period. There was the famous book Hitopadesh, useful teaching, by Narayana. Another famous book of the times was the Brihatkatha of Gunadhya which has provided models for other narrative stories like the Nepalese Brihatkatha-Slokasangraha of Buddhaswamin in the eighth century, the Brihatakatha-manjari of Kshemendra and the Kathasaritsagar of Somadeva. The Katha-saritsagar with its main theme and 50 stories attached to the main story has become very famous. It might be called an encyclopedia of the social manners obtaining in the eleventh century. It contains tales of morals, novelties, stories of sailars, brigands, vampires (the famous Betalpanchavimsatik, 25 tales of the vampire), myths and legends. Somadeva was a Shaivite and a worshipper of Durga and we, therefore, find the cult of Shakti or power very well described in these stories. Many of these stories have been imitated in the West also. For instance, the story of Shukasaptati (70 tales of the parrot). Of other romance writers the most famous was Dandin, the author of Dashakumaracharit, the adventure of ten princes. The author lived in the seventh century. In his book we are given pictures of the life led by the Princes and the aristocrats as well as by the denizens of the underworld of the city. He is a great realist and at home in Sanskrit. Another writer was Bubandhu, the author of Vasavadatta. The book is a story of a prince who is at last united with his beloved after trials and tribulations through the help of kindly birds. In this story we have very amusing description of birds that talk and horses that are enchanted.

Another great writer of romance was Bana noted for his gift of description, for the art of using contrast and love of color. His books are Harshacharitra and Kadambari. Another great writer was Dhanpala who wrote the novel Tilakmanjari.

We had also many books on sciences. For instance in the field of astronomy we had Siddhanta Shiromani written by Bhaskaracharya. It was the most important book on astronomy next only to Suryasiddhanta and in it we come across the theory of gravitation, eclipses and roundness of the earth. Other great writers were Brahmagupta, Lalla, Sridhar, Brahmadeva and Utapal. In mathematics we have Aryabhatta, Bhaskaracharya and Vachaspati. Aryabhatta, Lilavati and Bijganit are deservedly famous. In medicine (Ayurveda) we had

Ashtangasangraha by Vagbhata and Madhavnidan by Madhavkar, Chikitsasangraha by Chakrapani Dutta and Sharangadharasamhita by Sharangadhar. There were also books on surgery, on love and the science of language like Shabdapradip. Among other books connected with miscellaneous subjects mention may be made by Krishnasangrah (book on agriculture), Prakritaprakash by Vararuchi, grammar of the 'Prakrit' language, also dictionary both of Pali and Prakrit by Maugalayan and Dhanpala respectively. In southern India also great works were edited, composed and written, for instance, Chintamani, Ramayanam, Kalvali narpadu and Vikramasholan ula, the last two were historical poems. All these works were written in Tamil. The Jains were the pioneer in this field. They also developed the Kanarese literature and we had important works in this language like Kaviraja-Marg, Basavapuran, Shatak and Pampa-Bharat. In Telugu language we had the translation of Mahabharata by Nannayyabhatta and others.

Thus, the contribution of the Indians in the medieval period in the field of literature is both significant and praiseworthy. The ancient literature was in danger of being forgotten and be it said to the credit of these writers that they preserved our literature by their comments, editing and commentaries. It may, however, be remarked that during this period creative works became rare. There is greater emphasis on complexities in styles and on verbosity.

This period was also notable in the development of Hindu philosophy. Many commentaries were produced on the ancient philosophical literature. Among the most notable philosophers were Kumarila Bhatta, Sankara, Ramanuja, Madhva and Nimbarka. The beginning of the period also witnessed a philosophical campaign between the followers of Buddhism and those of Hinduism in which the lead was taken by Kumarila Bhatta and Sankara. As a result of this combat Buddhism almost disappeared from the land of its birth and neo-Hinduism was born.

Kumarila Bhatta is the most renowned of the neo-Hindu missionaries. Tradition connects him with a fierce and relentless campaign against the Buddhists.

His faith was in the Karma-Marga, that is, salvation by the sole means of the faithful performance of Karmas or the daily and other periodical ceremonial rites enjoined by the Vedas and the Smritis. Thus, Kumarila Bhatta revived the study and practice of Vedic rites and ceremonies while combating Buddhism by weapons taken from Vedic philosophy.

The greatest philosopher of the age was Sankara. An obscure village, Kaladi, six miles to the east of Alwaye, now a station on the Cochin-Sharanur Railway line, is traditionally mentioned as his birth place. He came from the Nambudri class of Brahmans of Malabar. His parents prayed to Shiva for the birth of a child and hence his name Sankara. His date of birth is not certain some people placing it in the year 788 A.D. It is said he had learnt all the Vedas and the Vedangas by the time he was eight years old. He refused to marry and became a Sannyasin. He travelled throughout the length and breadth of India, combating Buddhism, founding Mathas or monasteries and spreading the gospel of Vedantism. He also controverted the arguments of Mandana Misra, the great disciple of Kumarila Bhatta. He had also a dialectic controversy with Bharati, wife of Mandana. He founded his chief center of learning at the source of the Tungabhadra river and this monastery is famous as the 'Sringeri Math'. He died in Kedarnath at the age of either 32 or 38, probably in the year 828 A.D. Sankara is the greatest philosopher produced by India in the Middle ages. His philosophy acted as the cementing bond of neo-Hinduism. He tried to reconcile all the contemporary Vedic faiths by means of a cardinal co-ordinating idea. His Vedantism supplied this co-ordinating philosophy and later writers tried to write variations on the same theme. Sankara in his philosophy of Vedantism started with the hypothesis of Maya or Avidya (Illusion or ignorance) with his objective. Nothing really exists but the supreme spirit (Brahma) so that what is commonly called Nature is but an illusion, a dream, caused by this ignorance which surrounds the supreme spirit and hides it, even as the smoke that rises from the fire hides the blaze, the rope is mistaken for a snake. In life, therefore, we should cast off the gross sheaths that surround the spirit, within us and realise its identity with the supreme spirit, within us. The chief means of attaining this end is the cultivation of true knowledge that is the study of the Vedanta and the incessant contemplation of its teachings. Thus Sankara emphasized the path of knowledge, the Jnana-marga, and asceticism for attaining salvation. For lesser folk, Sankara advocated both Karma and Bhakti-marga though final salvation necessitated austerity and devotion to the path of knowledge so that man may realize that 'I am Brahman'. Sankara wrote commentaries on most of the ancient Vedic compositions.

The one great weakness of Sankara was to a certain extent neglect of Bhakti or devotion as a means of salvation. To meet this arose other philosophers notably Ramanujacharya, Madhva and Nimbarka. The 'Alvars' of south had already stressed the doctrine of Bhakti as a means to the attainment of salvation and their doctrines were given philosophical expression by Ramanuja and others.

Ramanuja is said to have been born in the year 1017 A.D. His father was Asuri Keshava Bhhattar of Sripereumbuthur. In his youth he lived at Conjeevaram where he studied at the feet of Guru Yadava-Prakasha, an Adwait philosopher. Ramanuja was not satisfied with the Adwait philosophy of Sankara. Renouncing married life he took to the robes of a sannyasi and propogated his teachings which were to be the basis of the new Vaishnavism of India. He also toured India like Sankara and is said to have passed away in the 120th year of his life (1137 A.D.). His chief centre of learning and devotion is Srirangam.

His philosophy is called Vishishtadwaitya or qualified monism, in practical modification of Vedanta and indicates oneness of God, with Visesha or attributes. God alone exists, all else is seen as his manifestation, attributes or Shakti. Such attributes are Chit, the individual souls and achit or matter. Sankara does not posit any attribute, regards manifestation as unreal. Ramanuja regards the world as real and permanent but subject to the control of one Brahman. These attributes do not exist apart and away from Brahman as independent entities and so the oneness of God is compatible with their existence. Ramanuja had felt that the large body of the Hindus could not easily comprehend Sankaracharya's Vedantic religion since it was too philosophical for the common Hindu mind. He needed a personal God to whom he could turn in troubles and difficulties. For this Ramanuja combined the old religious views of the Bhagvatas with the Vedantic ideas of Sankara and emphasized the religious value of devotion and service and self surrender to God. Thus to him Bhakti was the most suitable means to achieve purity, sinlessness and unselfishness in life and was the truest means for the attainment of salvation or Moksha. Ramanuja was the most important founder of the modern Sri-Vaishnava sect.

Another great apostle of Vaishnavism was Madhva who has given us the philosophy of Dualism or Dwaitism. He was born in the year 1238 A.D. According to Bhandarkar he was born in Saka 1119 and died in Saka 1198. He belonged to the land of Tuluva, more or less, now comprising the Kanaras of Mysore. As a youth he distinguished himself in field-games and people called him Bhima. In due course he took to the life of a sannyasin. After studying the Vedas and Vedangas he was given by his Guru the title of Ananda Tirtha and made the head of the math or monastery. He now took to the tour of the country and to dialectical disputation with his opponents. His Vaishnavism is known as Sadvaishnavism and in his Dwaita philosophy he repudiates both the monism of Sankara and the qualified monism of Ramanuja. According to him phenomenal world is real and eternal and not unreal or dependent solely upon Brahman. True perception is only gained when silver is seen to be silver, and not when mother of pearl is mistaken for it. The supreme spirit is Vishnu or Narayana and his consort Lakshmi is also real. Brahma and Vayu were two of his sons. Souls or spirits have forms corresponding to those of animated nature in this universe, and are of three classes : The first class to which belong pitris, sages and kings are alone destined for eternal residence in the abode of Narayana. The second class of which majority of men belong is eternally subject to the ups and downs of samsara, i.e., evil of birth and death. The third class consists of those spirits that are doomed to eternal hell like the enemies of Vishnu. Madhva also was an exponent of Vaishnavism but he assigns a special place to Guru through whose intercession alone salvation is possible, He was specially bitter towards sankara and his followers and in this spirit of intolerance he is almost an exception among the contemporary philosophers. The sect of Madhva is also distinguished by its various festivities all the year round.

In the north of India the first great philosopher of the Vaishnava school was Nimbarka during this period. According to Bhandarkar the date of his death may roughly be placed about 1162 A.D., some time after Ramanuja. He was born in the village Nimba in the Bellary district of Mysore but later went and resided near Mathura. His Vedantic theory is known as Dwaitadwaitavada or both monism and pluralism or dualism. Thus, he has tried to reconcile both dualism and monism. According to him the inanimate world, the individual soul and God are distinct from one another (dualism) as well as identical (monism). They are identical in the sense that the first two have no independent existence, but are dependent on God for their existence and action. But the individual soul is not merely a phenomenon of knowledge as posited by Sankara, it is a substance, an independent entity though its form is distorted by contact with Maya. Its true nature is known by the grace of God. His doctrines gave predominance to self surrender to God as the mode of salvation. He gives prominence to Krishna and his mistress Radha, attended by thousands of her female companions.

These were the main philosophies of the medieval India. All of them were based on the Vedic and Post-Vedic philosophical works. They tried to interpret them and with the exception of Sankara tried to read devotion, Bhakti, into the Vedic theology of the past.

Thus, their greatest emphasis was not on Jnana (knowledge) or Karma (action) but on love, self surrender to God. In this they deviated from true spirituality which is a unified whole, a synthesis of all the three paths. True spirituality ignores none of these elements, the mental, the vital and bodily aspects of man and even rises above them to plumb the supramental whereas these philosophies laid greater emphasis on the vital or emotional aspect of man.

We may now study the essential features of the religious life of the times. The period witnessed the development of popular Hinduism with its symbols and mythology that we have even today. In this popular Hinduism the dominant note was that of the Bhakti cult in which devotion was offered to some personal God whose worship, it was thought, will lead to salvation. Of such Gods, the most popular were Shiva, Vishnu, Ram and Krishna. The female aspect of God or Shakti (Divine energy) or mother power was also worshipped in various forms like Kali, Uma, Durga, Chandi, Lakshmi and Ashtabhuja Devi. It must, however, be emphasized that the development of this cult had its superstitious side also which led a historian to remark 'A careful examination of Alberuni's India leaves upon one the impression that the mass of the people wallowed in mud and mire raising the dirtiest, filthiest and crudest fancies of the day to the dignity of religion'.* But at the same time Alberuni makes it plain that the philosophic, religious and scientific ideas of the educated classes were all they could have been. For instance, the Hindus believe with regard to God that he is one, eternal, without beginning and end, acting by the free will, almighty, all-wise, living, giving-life, ruling, preserving, one who in his sovereignty is unique, beyond all likeness and unlikeness, and that he does not resemble anything nor does anything resemble him. They also continue to believe in the doctrine of human equality defined not from the point of view of citizenship but from the view point of salvation. According to the Hindu philosophers liberation is common to all classes and to the whole human race if their intention of obtaining it is perfect. Alberuni had also observed that the idols were made only for the uneducated, the educated Hindus never made an idol of any supernatural being, much less of God. Also even in the medieval age there was very little dispute about religious differences. 'All their fanaticism is directed against those who do not belong to them, against all foreigners. They call them 'Mlechhas,' that is, impure and forbid having any connection with them. No Conversions to Hinduism were permitted'.* The doctrine of chhut (untouchability) also reached its high watermark in the eleventh

* M. Habib, *Indian Culture and Social life at the time of the Turkish Invasion.*

* *Alberuni's India,* Vol. I, pp. 19-20.

century. Popular religion had become the monopoly of the Brahman and the lower classes were prohibited from studying the Vedas. But in spite of these differences, the Hindu society continued to be cemented into unity under the influence of Bhakti. At this time the two most important Schools of Bhakti were Shaivism and Vaishnavism. We may briefly review the history of the two.

Shaivism is a many-branched system and contains Shaivism proper, Shaktism and other minor systems. It is also sometimes known as the Vratya or Dravidian system. According to A.P. Karmarkar, in his book, the *Religions of India*, Volume I, Shaivism is the oldest religion in India. In its elementary form it is found in the Indus valley civilisation. In the Vedas also the non-Aryans are designated as Sishnadevah, which according to Karmarkar refers to God Shiva who is represented nude in the Indus valley civilisation. This sect was first known as Vratya who is exalted in the Atharva-Veda to the position of the Supreme Being, Mahadeva. The inscriptions of Mohenjo-Daro as interpreted by Heras speak of the divine Triad consisting of Shiva, Amma (Parvati) and Muruga (Karttikeya). This Shiva was three-faced or Trimurti, a conception later borrowed by the Brahmans.

There is no mention of Ganapati or Ganesh in the earlier period, he being mentioned only by the end of the period of the Harivamsha. He is not mentioned even by Patanjali. The Vedic God Rudra was an attempt to present a new personality. Later there is an amalgamation of Shiva and Rudra and finally he is assigned a place among the three Gods, Trimurti, namely, Brahma, Vishnu and Shiva. Further, during this period Shiva was also called Pashupati, this Supreme Being with the whole of humanity as his folk. In the epics and the Puranas the Shiva of the Indus valley people and the Rudra of the Vedic period are finally merged. The Mahabharata and some of the Puranas give a long list of the 1008 names of Shiva. With Shiva is also associated the phallic cult and the worship of the Mother goddess Amma, the supreme creatrix of the universe, the basis of the Tantric cult of later times. As Woodroffe observes 'when we throw our minds back upon the history of this worship (mother worship) we see stretching away, into remote and fading past the figure of the mighty mother of nature, most ancient amongst the ancients, the Adya-Shakti, the Dust-Divinity, many breasted, crowned with towers, whose veil is never lifted, Isis, the one who is all that has been, is and will be, Kali-Hathor, Cybele, the cow-mother Goddess Ida, Tripura-Sundari, the Ionic mother–Kundalini, Guhyamahabhairavi and all the rest'.* Archaeological evidence points to mother worship not only in the Indus valley civilisation but also in the Mauryan and the Sunga periods. Later on, of course, the evidence is plentiful. During the Puranic period this worship was monopolised by a separate cult, the Shaktism, according to which God is the supreme mother and is called Mahadevi, consort of Shiva, sometimes also conceived as the creator of Shiva and superior to him. She was variously known as Adya Shakti, Maha-Shakti, Jagadamba, Lalita, Mahatripura-Sundari and Mahakundalini. King Harsh, it is said, used to practise Shaktism or Tantricism. During our period the elements of Shaktism spread here and there in the Vaishnava and other sects.

The Shakta cult took different forms and shapes in different localities and provinces in India after the Vedic period. They are divided into two main sects, the right-hand (Dakshinachara) and left-hand (Vamachara). The latter is condemned for its most obscene and immoral practices of the Chakrapuja and other rites. In the right-handed sect, worship is offered to Devi. Certain rituals are performed at night. Magic powers are obtained by the use of a rosary of human bone. The highest stage is that of Kamla or Divya who 'sees the imperishable in all things and all things in the self,' Shaktism is also known as Tantricism and their literature is called Agamas. As a result of the study of Shaivism and Shaktism we can say that there is much truth in the dictum that, 'while the Dravidians were Aryanised in language, the Aryans were Dravidisnised in culture'. The worship of these sects, it is said, had originated with the Dravidians who were probably first to be found in the Indus valley. The main Shaiva sects are the Yatis, the Arhats, the Ganagirs, the Pasupatas, the Lakulisas, the Kapalikas, the

* *Sakti and Sakta*, p. 128.

Kalamukhas, the Nathas, the Resesvaras and some other minor sects like the Lingayats and the Aghoris.

During our period Shaiva philosophy and devotional worship were firmly evolved mainly in the south by the efforts of the four Acharyas and sixty-three wandering saints (Nayanars) corresponding to the Alvars of Vaishnavism. The Shaiva philosophy is that Siva is beginningless, free from defects, the all knower. His body is all energy (shakti) it is composed of the five aksharas. The three fundamental principles or categories of Shaivism are the Lord (Pati), soul (Pasu) and the world (Pasha).

Siva-shakti is a category intermediate between Siva, who is pure consciousness and matter which is unconscious. She is the cause of the bondage of all beings and also of their release. Man is bound by many fetters mainly of ignorance, Karma and Maya which are broken by the Shakti evolving into Anugraha, the grace of the Lord, leading gradually to liberation or identity with Siva. Various Shaiva sects differ in details and there is a division between the northern or Kashmir schools and southern or the Tamil schools. There is also the Lingayati sect worshipping Siva alone and proclaiming equality for all classes.

Like Shaivism, Vaishnavism also claims hoary antiquity. It is true that in the early ages of the Rig-Veda Vishnu (The Supreme God of the Vaishnavas) was not a separate deity but only the sun in the capacity of the lord of unceasing activity. Varuna was the head of the Adityas. But as Vishnu was associated with him and also with Bhaga, the lord of bounty, it is easy to see that the conceptions of Varuna and Bhaga were transferred to Vishnu in course of time. Vishnu was also said to take three strides across the universe. From the above we have the terms out of which the doctrines Puranic Hinduism were eventually developed. The idea of three steps led to the conception of the avatars, Vaman and Trivikrama, the idea of supporting the universe led to the prime function of Vishnu as one of the Trimurti and the idea of bountifulness led to the development of Ananda or Bliss which formed the basis of the theory of Vaikuntha, the highest abode of Vishnu, where his devotees live in the eternal bliss of companionship with him and in service to him.

In the later Vedic age, the conception of Purusha or cosmic man–the Supreme Being was developed and associated with Narayana and Nara. Later on, the whole thing was elaborated and given a distinct place in the religious development of the post-Upanishadic period by a member of the Satvata-Yadava clan, who had the patronymic name Vasudeva and the proper names of Krishna and Devakiputra. Krishna Devakiputra figures as a disciple of Ghora Angirasa in the Chhandogya Upanishad.

He advocates there the offering of worship to God in the name of Bhagavan, the Adorable. Later on Vasudeva and Bhagavan came to be identified and in Panini's grammar we find Bhagvatas being identified with Vasudevakas and Arjunakas. All these developments find their final evolution in the Bhagavata which gives great details of a thorough theory of Vishnu's avataras. The Bhagavata is, therefore, 'the earliest exposition of the Bhakti system or the Ekantika Dharma'.*

It was during the first four centuries after Christ that to the above elements of Vaishnavism was added the story of Krishna, the cow-herd. The whole creed of Bhagavatism was also known as the Pancharatra Agama (or popular method of worship). Thus during this period the basic works of Vaishnavism, the Pancharatra Samhitas were formulated. During this period was also developed the association of Rama with this cult. He was also regarded as the 'Avatar', incarnation, of God or Vishnu. Thus by the end of the ancient period all the main elements of Vaishnavism had been developed and the chief 'Avatars' enunciated, namely, Vishnu, Narayan, Vasudeva, and Krishna. In the medieval period the philosophy and practices of this sect were further developed. Ramanuja, Madhva, Nimbarka, and Vallabhacharya among others greatly contributed to the evolution of Vaishnavism during this period. We have already referred to the contributions of Ramanuja, Madhva and Nimbarka. We may now note the contribution of Vallabha in this domain.

Vallabhacharya (1479-1531), a Brahman belonging to the Telugu country was born in Banaras. He received Sanskrit

* Bhandarkar, *Vaisnavism, Shaivism, and minor religious systems*, p. 19.

education and later travelled throughout India meeting scholars and other interested persons. He now called himself an incarnation of the God Agni (Fire) and acknowledged no human teacher saying that he had learnt his system direct from Krishna. Philosophically his school is called Shuddhadvaita (pure monism). He tried to correct Sankara who had not sufficiently stressed Bhakti. To him. Bhakti was not only a means but an end. True devotee will live and sport for ever with Krishna. According to him, Shakti is given by God, by his grace called by him Pushti. Released souls rise to Krishna's heaven (Vyapi Vaikuntha) which is far above the heavens of Vishnu, Siva and Brahma. In heaven there is far above the heavens of Vishnu, Siva and Brahma. In heaven there is also Vrindavana where reside Radha, Gopis and Gopas. They sport with Krishna there eternally. The loftiest aspiration of a Vallabha is to become a Gopi and sport with Krishna in his heaven.

The cult is called 'Seva' or service or Krishna (also known as Pushtimarga). There are eight times of worship daily in each temple and the mantra of the sect is 'Sri Krishna Saranam mama'. Guru is always to be regarded as God. They are now known as maharajas and this sect is very popular among the rich business class of Western India.

The Bhakti Cult

We may, therefore, say that during the medieval period the religious life of the times centred round Bhakti (devotion, piety). The word Bhakti is not found in the Vedas or the Upanishads except in a verse in Satarudriya but its ideas are present in these works. The word etymologically signifies resorting to, and then loving, the thing resorted to. Bhakti also developed as a counterdose to asceticism emphasised by older Buddhism and Sankara. The development of the Bhakti schools led also to the evolution of iconography and temple worship in India. The various followers of the several schools of Bhakti had their separate rituals, forms of worship, paraphernalias and painting of symbols on their bodies.

In the Bhakti cult the impersonal Brahman is converted into the personal God or Isvara. God cannot be apprehended by the senses. He is beyond the ken of logic or argument and is attained only through whole-hearted devotion. God is pleased with self– surrender. As the Gita puts it, 'Give up all religious paths and take refuse in me alone. I shall deliver thee from all sins. Sorrow not'. (xviii. 66). Thus taking refuse in God is the highest goal of men.

In the Bhagavata or Bhakti cult great stress is laid on the grace (Anukampa) of God. Religion is the elevation of man to God and the descent of God to man. God can be attained only by his grace or kindness.

According to Narada, Bhakti is of the nature of intense love for God. It is of the nature of love (prema) which reaches its acme of perfection (parama). In such a devotion we are loyal only to Him. This loyalty is incessantly expressed in all our words, deeds and thoughts. Various attributes of Bhakti are described. It is of the nature of attachment (Raga), of love (Rasa), of nectar (Amrita), it is unmotived devotion (ahaituki-bhakti) to God, 'It is not of the nature of knowledge but an emotion of affection and it depends upon faith, appreciation and love (shraddha, anuraga and prema)'. Bhakti is not moved by desire. It is free from desire. We live for God alone. According to Shandilye, Bhakti involves Yoga or concentration of mind and cultivation of the intellect for the culture of devotion. The Gita also preaches the cult of devotion enlightened by knowledge though in many cases one develops pure Bhakti without knowledge. Devotion also involves renunciation. Devotion, again, does not mean giving up of action. We should do our duties without any attachment. All our actions must be dedicated to God and be for Him. We must take care even of our bodies so long as we live in order to live in and love for God. We should perform social duties and religious rites so far as they help us in acquiring the love of God. In this connection various rites and observances have been elaborated so that our devotion may be constant, continuous and absolutely intense. Thus we have washing, dressing and offering food to the Lord, Bhajans and Kirtans for Him and to Him.

Various types of salvation in Bhakti are described for example Salokya, living in the same world with God, Sarshti, enjoying supernatural powers of God, Sameepya being near to God, Sarupya equality with God and sayujya union with God.

In the primary devotion there is only one end in view, namely, God, who is to be the be-all and end-all of our life. Narad also describes eleven forms of devotion. In the final form the devotee feels His living presence everywhere, feels the pang of separation from his Beloved and is eternally united with Him even in separation. The Lord is viewed in various personal forms. He is regarded by the devotee as either a lover or beloved, Prabhu lord or dasa (servant), Sakha (friend) or Janaka or Janani (father or mother) and even in the form of wifely love (madhurya).

To attain such Bhakti various practices or means are enjoined. The devotee should shun evil company of all kinds, avoid talks about women, wealth and the atheists, give up egoism, pride and passions, shun vain discussion about God, renounce all attachments to man, study the treatises on devotion, cultivate virtues, hear and sing of God and incessantly pray to Him. We should seek the company of great souls or gurus through whom the grace of God may come to us and he may guide us. By following sincerely these means we can attain liberation and freedom from birth and death. The cult of Bhakti is open to all irrespective of their birth in any class.

Thus in the Shakti cult, the devotee by attaining love of God sees Him alone, hears Him alone and thinks of Him alone. He belongs to Him, and not even to himself. The only end of his life is the service of God. (See Narada Sutras 55, 67, 70, Bhagavata Purana II. 29-13-14).

Shaivism and Vaishnavism may have their different branches, philosophies and practices but during the present period they were all united by the cementing bonds of Bhakti. Thus, the dominant features of the religious life in the era before the advent of the Muslims was the evolution and practice of the cult of Bhakti which received further impetus from the contact between the Muslims and the Hindus. But in the sphere of religion also we forgot true spirituality in the long run. In Bhakti more stress was laid on devotion to external rites and observances than on inner development or union of the soul with Brahma. Hinduism in becoming popular in assimilating foreign cultures lost for the time being its healing and refreshing touch with the Vedic synthesis.

Arts

In the sphere of art also the period witnessed further evolution and development. The greatest development during this period took place in architecture, namely, the evolution of temple-building or iconography. Before dealing with this topic something may be said about painting, dancing and music.

Rajput Painting

In the sphere of painting we had the development of the Rajput and the Pahari (hill) schools, notably after the advent of the Muslims, in the fifteenth century. In this century two things revolutionised the practice of painting in Northern India; these were the rise of a vernacular literature consequent upon the development of Bhakti and the introduction of paper. At this time the stories of Rama, Sita, Krishna and Radha were popularised by bards, poets and others in the vernaculars spoken by the people. These stories became the themes of pictures. Further the change of medium, specifically from stone to paper, in painting, added new styles, new colours and designs to the existing Rajput art. Also, the patronage of the Moghuls infused a new strength to this school. The Rajput school had its predecessor in the Western or Gujarati school as also the decadent Classical art. The Gujarati school showed a linear vividness and vigour developed with great virtuosity, also fine draughtsmanship combined with bold massing of vibrant colours and highly decorative designs in clothes and other textiles. These can be still seen in the Jain manuscripts of Gujarat. Very little Rajput paintings of the pre-1600 period survive. These illustrate Gita-Govind of Jaideva, Chaura-panchasika of Bilhana and some also illustrate Krishna-Lila (sport of Krishna). Afterwards we have plentiful illustration of Rajput paintings.

The Rajput art was patronised by the Rajas and Maharajas. Every ruler had his own artists. The main centres of this art were (1) Malwa, (2) Mewar - Udaipur, (3) Ajmer-Jaipur, (4) Marwar-Jodhpur and Bikaner, (5) Kishangarh, (6) Nathadwara, (7) Kota-Bundi (8) Banapur, (9) Datia, the last two were in Bundelkhand. This art reached its zenith by the end of the seventeenth century. Much of its fastidiousness and finish was derived from the Moghuls.

The main subject matter of Rajput paintings is Ragmala. The various 'Ragas' (melody-types) have almost been personified in the paintings. Although the form of these Ragas and Raginis was determined and pictures were made on the basis of these forms, the other themes were Krishna-Lila, Nayika-Bheda (depiction of the beloved in various moods), Ritu-Chitra (pictures of the seasons), court scenes, rulers' portraits and scenes of royal pursuits, such as festivities, processions and hunting.

The outstanding features of the Rajput paintings may be briefly summed up thus (i) Primitive-vigour and strength; (ii) Directness and simplified formula of expression; (iii) Traditional motifs; (iv) Gay and brilliant colour-scheme and (v) Decorativeness.

The Rajput art in common with other Indian arts probes the innermost self. The artist is not satisfied in painting as much as he sees with his own eyes.

Within him–in his inner world– there are other shapes, other visions and scenes. These he tries to paint with his brush and thus he differs from the Moghul painting which is generally concerned with this world.

The developed Rajput paintings in the seventeenth century have 'forms as definite as those of the sonnet or the novel, it portrays the states of love or the type of hero and the heroine, generally in illustration of theoretical or systematic poems treating of these themes'. (Basil Gray). The Rajput paintings are distinguished by their gorgeous colour-schemes. In them gestures are means of expression and colour combinations form the elements of composition. They are part of the national art of India.

'Himalaya' Painting

Allied with this school we have the 'Kangara' or 'Pahari' or Himalaya school of painting. The area of this painting spreads from Jammu (in Kashmir) to Tihri-Garhwal and from Pathankot to Kulu in the Punjab. The pivot of the painting of the school is the beautiful damsel. Around her are depicted the various scenes and imageries. Her emotions, moods, gestures, beauty of the limbs and devotion are depicted in thousands of ways. 'But the herd-girls of the Pahari drawings have eyes for none but Krishna, the singers and dancers are as much absorbed in their service and their art as any of those at Borobadur; none, are aware that they are overlooked. There is no more single-minded painting in the world'.* These paintings also illustrate the themes of devotional love, Bhakti centering round Krishna and Radha. We also get stories of Ramayana and Mahabharata treated in these paintings. Some of the important paintings are Nal-Damayanti (marriage-scene), Go-charan (Krishna as the cowherd), Krishna and Radha in the rains and Govardhan-dharan (Krishna supporting the mountain on his finger). Like the Rajput paintings, these are also distinguished for their colour-schemes and depletion of inner feelings. The originality of this school lies in the sense of bliss or ecstasy which they infuse into the heart of a sympathetic onlooker or artist. Both these schools registered a decline in the 19th century.

Dancing and Music

The medieval period is also remarkable for development of dancing and music. In dancing we had the evolution of 'Kathak' style in Northern India as a result of the contact of the Muslims and the Hindus. This style is distinguished for its movements specially the footwork. To a certain extent, however, it was a hothouse plant being confined to the Courts of the Mohammedan and Hindu Kings, and gradually it degenerated into the performance of nauchgirl (dancing girl).

Similarly in the south Bharat-Natyam became the affair of the Deva-Dasis (temple girls) and remained to contribute to the merry-making of the Rajas. Still both in the south and in the north, there were certain families where the pure lamp of these schools continued to be lit down till our own times and some of their traditions have also percolated through the folkdances even now extant. Kathakali and Manipuri systems retained more of their purity than the two above mentioned.

But the period was most remarkable in the development

* A.K. Coomarasvami : *The Art and Crafts of India and Ceylon*, p. 90.

of the Indian music. It was really the formative epoch of the modern system of Indian music. For the first time we hear of the 'Ragas', and the 'Raginis'. The modern musical instruments were evolved like the Sitar, the Tabla and the Sarangi and books were written about the principles and methods of our music. The most important authors were Dantila, Kohala, Sarangadeva, Haridas Swami, Damodar, Somnath Pundit Ahobala, Vyankatamakhi and Purandara Vitthala. As a result of the efforts of all these writers, musical notation was evolved, musical instruments were classified, melody types were classified. Melody types were set to music and the various notes were described in terms of the lengths of the speaking wire of Veena (the main musical instrument of the Hindus). During this time there was also the evolution of new melodies as a result of the contact between the Muslims and the Hindus. One result of this contact, however, was the sundering into-two-of the musical system of India, the division into the Northern and the Southern schools. The Northern became a mixture when it assimilated Muslim styles whereas the Southern retained its classical, pure style to a very large extent. The period was also remarkable for the existence of a number of famous musicians who have become almost legendary.

They were Gopal Nayak (said to have been taken away from South by Alauddin Khilji to his court), Nayak Bakhshu (in Gwalior), Swami Haridas with his pupils Tansen and Baiju Baware, Jagannath Lal Khan, Adaranga and Sadaranga. Many kings also became famous as patrons of Indian music. The most notable of these were Mansingh (of Gwalior), Akbar and Mohammad Shah.

But like other arts music also declined in the 18th century. One reason was the loss of royal patronage, another was the conservatism of the various 'gharanas' or schools of music and lastly the teacher in music was loath to impart his knowledge to all except to a favourite or two so that the whole thing remained like a cloistered virtue.

Temple Architecture

We may now review the salient features of temple

architecture which was the rage of the day. The principal architectural features of the temple are as follows. Throughout the greater part of India, the sanctuary as a whole is known as the Vimana, of which the upper and pyramidal or tapering portion is called the Shikhar, meaning tower or spire. Inside the Vimana is a small and generally dark chamber are cella, called Garbha griha, for the reception of the divine symbol. In front of this is the Mandap, actually a pavilion for the assembly of the devotees. There are various other subsidiary structures. The most complete illustrations of the fully formed temple structure are the tenth century examples of Khajuraho, in Madhya Pradesh. There are marked resemblances between the Indian temple on the one hand and the Greek and the Christian temple and church. It may be remarked here that there are certain differences both in nomenclature and designs between the Northern and the Southern temple architecture while the Orissa style is a class by itself. In the southern style there is a difference in the shape and design of Vimana and Shikhar, in the general formation of the structure and also in the 'order', expressed in the shrine-like niches on the walls of the temple. The northern Shikhar is monolithic while the southern is pyramidical. There are a series of such towers. Further the temples in the South have Gopuram enclosure with a number of gateways and in same there are more than one Gopuram so that in the developed styles we have rather temple cities with tanks, enclosures, gates, towers and mandaps, profusely ornamented and decorated with gods, animals and inanimate objects. The temples have long corridors, big court-yards and hall with numerous ornamented pillars. In Orissa the generic name for a temple is 'deul' which is also the name given to the Shikhara, the mandapa is here called Jagmohan there is further the dancing hall called Nat-Mandir in front of which is the Bhag Mandir or hall of offerings. The lower portion of the Shikhara is called Bada, the flatfluted disk at the summit is known as the Amla and its final Kalasa. The Orissan temples have rich carvings outside and featureless treatment inside, a contrast from other Indian styles.

With the establishment of the temple type about the eighth

century A.D. the people proceeded to embark on an era of temple building, which can have few equals. It was an epoch of Bhakti corresponding in same respects to that wave of passionate building which swept over much of Europe in the Middle Ages. In the temple architecture the religious motive was predominant and the best temples were inspired works of art. Attempts have been made to trace the ancestry of the temple style and various theories have been evolved, some observing their indebtedness to the Buddhist chaityas and viharas, some Peaking of the Shikhara being evolved from the peaked or domed huts of Eastern and Central India, others observing the resemblance between Ratha (Chariot) and the Shikhara and Havell points out that the Southern style took its cue from the Aryan village whose cattle forts with their four gates lead, for example, to the evolution of Gopuram.

Although emphasis has been laid on distinctions in style, as a whole the art of building was based an certain common fundamental principles. There is a standardisation of procedure, artistic and structural, implying that the master masons were working not only with one general understanding, but also by means of some comprehensive and well-established technical code. This was brought about by the guilds of craftsmen with their Shilpa Shastras or canons of art. The Indian masons showed Judicious observance of the laws of gravity, an appreciation of the grandeur of mass and the rich value of shadows. In the words of Percy Brown 'every portion, every effect, was the product of long years of application. Wherever it was to his advantage the Indian builder made the climate his hand maid, when this was impossible he used his artistic ingenuity in providing against it'.*

We may now mention some of the important temples built during this period. The rock temples at Ellora, Elephanta, the temples of Tanjore and Madura have already been referred to in the previous chapters. In Northern India, the temples at Khajuraho (Madhya Pradesh) are a class apart. Then there are the famous temples of Orissa in Bhubaneshvar and some miles from the place the temple of Jagannath at Puri and the remains

---

* Percy Brown, *Indian Architecture*, p. 80.

of the temple of the Sun at Konarak. The Lingaraja or Great temple of Bhuba-neshvar ranks as one of the finest architectural productions of the country. The temple occupies an area measuring 520 feet by 465 feet. Round the main temple are many shrines and chapels. The most impressive feature of this temple is the great tower of the Sri Mandir, dominating the whole town with its height and volume. At its base it measures 56 feet wide while in height its merely middle portion is 125 feet from the ground. The tower is decorated very finely and the whole conception presents an effect of exuberance evidently expressive of the luxuriousness prevailing in the existing social environment. The Jagannath temple is 310 feet by 80 feet while the tower is nearly 200 feet in height. Its elevated position makes it singularly commanding in appearance. The greatest and grandest achievement of the Eastern school of architecture is the Temple of the Sun at Konarak, some 20 miles from Puri. Much of it has fallen by now. The conception of this temple was that of a genius. The temple is dedicated to Surya to whom other famous temples dedicated are Martand in Kashmir and Modhera in Gujarat. The masons tried to represent the traditional description of the sun-god as given in the Vedas visualising the deity standing in time, in winged chariot urging on his team of seven horses, with which he blazes his way through the heavens. These he unyokes at sunset. The building was to be fashioned like a chariot whirled along by the seven horses. The base is an immense terrace with 12 giant wheels, each nearly ten feet high fixed on either side and in front is a wide flight of Steps, its sides supported by seven richly caparisoned steeds, rearing and straining in their harness to drag the great bulk along. On this platform, the large hall or Jagmohan was 100 feet wide and 100 feet high while the tower was 225 feet from the ground. There were other shrines attached to or near this main building. The immense surface was filled without stint by sculptured forms and intricate designs, some of them erotic. Only the assembly hall remains intact while the whole building was never completed. Few buildings can boast of such an unrestrained abundance of plastic decoration as this structure. Each portion is finely balanced and well proportioned. The temple marks the evolution of Tantricism in Orissa.

In the temples at Khajuraho we come across one of the most refined and finished manifestations of Indian architecture. They have been deserted for centuries but are still intact. They are in what was formerly known as the state of Chhatarpur, 100 miles south-east of Jhansi. They were erected in the tenth century mostly, being 30 in number.

They are distinguished by their elegant proportions, graceful contours and rich surface treatment. The halls are richly decorated with sculpture. They are dedicated to Mahadeva, Vishnu, Jagdamba and to the Jain deities.

In Rajputana and Central India there are various dismantled and fragmentary temples owing to the onslaught of the Muslim iconoclast; similar is the fate meted out to most of the buildings in Gujarat and the West. Still many temples survive in these places. Mention may be made of Maha-Mandir of Jodhpur and Eklinga temple of Udaipur. Again the Sun-temple at Modhera 18 miles South of Patan (Gujarat) is very remarkable, a monument of incomparable beauty even in its ruins, the entire composition being lit with the living flame of inspiration.

There is an atmosphere of spiritual grace. On Mount Abu besides other Jain temples, there is the temple of Vimla built at this period. Practically every surface is elaborated with sculptured forms. Its dome of eleven concentric rings is superb in showing the inventiveness of the artist. Not much of the original fabric of Somnath remains to speak of its architecture. In the Deccan there are a number of temples of this period notably temple of Ambarnath in Maharashtra state, the Sas Bahu temples in Gwalior and the Gondeshwara temple at Sirnar in Nasik. Further in Kathiawar, there are temples with gabled or multiple roofs as found in Kashmir. The temple cities on the mountains of Kathiawar, on the Sitrunjaya and Girnar hills, were built by the Jains. The brick temples of southern Bengal are native to the soil.

Lastly, there is the art of Kashmir, quite distinctive from the designs and styles so far treated and resembling both the Gandhara school and the Gupta school. Kashmir developed its artistic genius mostly during the reigns of Lalitaditya and Avantivarman in the eighth and the ninth centuries. The best style is that of the great temple of the Sun at Martand. It is a comprehensive central structure standing within a rectangular courtyard surrounded by a cellular peristyle which is entered by an imposing gateway all occupying a superb site five miles from the ancient town of Anantnag. It is the skilful manner in which all its parts are adjusted and treated that gives the temple its supreme aesthetic and architectural character. There is balanced plastic decoration and there is nothing small or sparing in its composition. Its beautiful simplicity and balanced perfection are heightened by its surroundings, symmetrically elevated against mountain background, and looking out on the lone splendour of the everlasting snows.

Architecture has been called the matrix of civilisation and is the principal record of man's intellectual evolution. Each great cultural movement has made its own particular contribution to the art of building. In India the basic principle of architecture has been its spiritual content. In the period treated in this chapter this characteristic remains, however decayed it might have become. The principles of Bhakti developed in this period found their expression in the temples erected from the seventh century onward. Specially during the heyday of Bhakti movement in the eleventh and twelfth centuries the temple architecture received its most pronounced perfection.

Social and Economic Conditions

Hindu Society, as in the past, continued to be cemented by the caste-system.

The Caste System

Brahmans commanded the greatest respect. They specialised in learning and knowledge. They were also the advisers or the ministry of the king. In some cases they also acted as Commanders-in-Chief. Their chief work was as poet, astronomer, philosopher or priest.

They were mainly engaged in study, teaching, performing sacrifices and charitable functions. On account of the rise of Buddhism they had lost many of their functions and had, therefore, taken to some of the work performed previously by Vaishyas and the Shudras. Commentaries or Smritis were written now to justify the assumption of these functions, for example, the Parashar Smriti allows all to join the profession of agriculture and even to take to the profession of arms. Brahmans now engaged, at least a fair number of them, in business, trade, and also worked as an artist. But they were to be particular about the rules of honour, cleanliness and touch (chhut). They could. not sell milk, honey, wine, meat and salt. They enjoyed many facilities denied to other castes, e.g., they could not be awarded capital punishment. During this period sub-castes begin to appear in greater number among them. For instance, in the inscriptions of the twelfth century we have mention of sub-castes like Dikshit, Pathak, Upadhyaya, Patwardhan. The sub-castes probably originated in differences about food (meat-eaters and vegetarians), professions, customs, philosophy and religious practices. In the fourteenth and fifteenth centuries the Kanyakubja Brahmans had many new sub-castes and further acquired 'bigha,' 'biswa' divisions. Similarly we now hear of the divisions of the Panch Gours and Panch Dravids

The next in social status were the Kshatriyas. They occupied a high position in society and supplied the rulers of the Hindu States from amongst themselves. Their main functions were government, defence, charity, sacrifices and study. Many of them were men of learning, e.g., Harshavardhan, Chalukya king Vinayadityat, Raja Bhoja and the Chauhan king Vigrahraj, the fourth. During this period they also began to be divided into sub-castes and took to other professions. Evils of drink and gambling began to develop among them.

Below the Kshatrityas we had the Vaishyas whose main functions were agriculture, cattlerearing, charity, sacrifice, study, trade, business and money lending. They were now discarding agriculture as it was regarded a derogatory work by the Buddhists, and were taking mainly to business. Some of them were ministers and commanders also. They also split up into subcastes in the medieval period.

The service class was named the Shudras. This Varna or caste was, however, not untouchable. They had the right to

Panch-Maha-yajnas. Their main functions were now agriculture, artisanship, smithy, carpentry, cloth-washing, dyeing and pottery. Besides these there were the untouchables living outside the city, on the borders, chief among whom here shoe-makers, hunters, butchers and weavers.

Besides these there was one special caste, namely, the Kayasthas. Previously persons of the castes doing clerical work were called Kayastha. But during this period they began to develop into a distinct caste.

This caste is, therefore, a mixture of all castes. Even now Surajdhwaj Kayasthas call themselves Shakdwipi Brahmans.

During the early medieval period the relations between all the castes were very cordial and marriages could also take place between them. Bana mentions Parshava as the son of a Brahman by a Shudra woman. In the Pratihar inscription of 861 A.D., Harishchandra, a Brahman married a Kshatriya girl Bhadra. A Kshatriya could marry a girl belonging to the lower castes but not the girl of a Brahman family. The caste of an issue was determined according to that of his or her father. By the end of our period all these customs disappeared and we had strict enforcement of the rules of the caste. Similarly there was inter-dining in the earlier part but it also disappeared later on.

Women also occupied an honoured position in society. They received proper education. We have references about women engaging in philosophical disputations with men, for instance, Sankaracharya had to argue with the wife of Mandan Misra. The famous poet Rajshekhar had also an educated wife whose opinion he has quoted. There were many poets among them. For example, Indulekha, Marula, Subhadra, Madalsa and Lakshmi. They were also trained in fine arts. They did not observe Pardah (veil). Harsha's mother used to meet the courtiers and Rajshri had paid visit to Huien-T-Sang, the Chinese traveller. In the Deccan Akkadevi, the sister of Solanki king Vikramaditya, is said to have laid siege around the fort of Gokage (now Gokak in Belgaum district of Maharashtra). Thus the Pardah system developed in India only after the advent of the Muslims. There was polygamy also but child-marriages were rare in the earlier part of the medieval age. Instances of

Widow-marriages are also on record. Sati (widow-burning) was not much prevalent. Women could inherit property also. We thus see that the early days of the Hindu rule in India present a progressive society as compared with the later period of the Medieval Age.

The Hindus were not completely ascetic. The upper classes used to have palatial buildings with provision for music, hospitality, library and disputation. All the year round there were festivities and fairs which attracted people from far and wide. There were amusements and entertainments like music, dancing, drama, animal-fighting, open-air dining, boating, swimming, chess and dice. Dress was of various kinds and suited to all occasions. Needle and thread are mentioned even as early as the Vedic times what to say of now. Attention was paid to the variety, design and beauty of clothes. Ornaments were used both by men and women. Particular purity was maintained about food not so much because of untouchability but because the laws of health and cleanliness so demanded. The articles of food were wheat, jowar, bajra, milk, ghee, gur and sugar. Non-vegetarian diet also prevailed specially among the Kshatriyas and the lower castes. Sacrifices or Yajnas were in vogue and hospitality was strictly enjoined upon. There were slaves also maintained by the kings and the rich people. People had also developed faith in magic, ghosts and spells.

Economic Conditions

Agriculture was the main occupation of the people. The agriculturists were well looked after by the government concerned. Irrigational projects of all sorts existed. We have in Rajtarangini, a mention of Suya, an engineer who built a dam on the river Jheulum and thus helped the agriculturists. Big reservoirs, canals, tanks and wells were also dug and maintained. The land was surveyed by the government, village areas were demarcated, fields for pastures were left and the agriculturists were helped in times of dire necessity like the famine. The land provided the main income in the form of land-tax to the powers that be. It was generally 1/6 of the produce, taken in kind.

Trade and commerce were the next main occupations. Cities were the centres of these. Among the famous cities of the age were Madura, Vanji (Vanchi) in Malabar, Vatapi, Tamralipti, Kannauj, Ujjaiin, Broach and Pataliputra or Patna. Commerce was both by land and sea. The commerce of India was particularly with Arabia, Phoenecia, Persia, Egypt, Greece, Rome, Java, Sumatra, Indo-China and China. There were many important roads connecting the cities in India. One road 1,200 miles long connected Coromandal coast with Kanya Kumari, another 1,100 miles long had connected Patna with Afghanistan. The main articles of export were silk, bleached cloth, muslin, gems, pearls, spices, ivory and diamonds.

India also specialised in metallurgy. Steel and iron of the finest type were manufactured. The iron-pillar at Delhi near Kutab-minar is illustrative of Indian skill in this field. Gold and silver utensils and ornaments were also made of excellent design and suited to all tastes. Glass-work was also to be found during this period. Pliny, (the Roman Historian), regarded it as the best of its kind. Trade and manhood commerce were monopolised not so much by any individual capitalist as by the guilds of traders and manufactures. Trade was generally by barter and hence the comparative neglect of coinage by the kings of the Hindu period. Thus economically India was a wealthy country and that is why it invited the cupidity of the iconoclast like Mahmud Ghaznavi.

This is in brief the survey of the Hindu India during the Medieval Period. We see remarkable developments in various fields of life. Philosophically the key-note is provided by the rise of scholasticism as in medieval Europe. The Vedic works were annotated, compiled and edited and on their basis we had commentaries galore in this period. All the main philosophies were further commented and debated upon. The field was dominated by Sankara whose theory of illusion or maya-vada led to a reaction in the form of Bhakti. But the dominance of maya-vada or illusoriness of this world had so much stamped itself upon the people that they developed a certain unbalanced outlook upon life, forgetting the good in materialism for the sake of virtue in asceticism. Much of this confusion was due to the rise of Buddhism. Before the Gita with its wide synthesis of knowledge, action and devotion had time deeply to influence the national mind, the heresy of Buddhism captivated the Indians. Buddhism with its exaggerated emphasis on quiescence and the consequent virtue of self-abnegation, its unwise creation of a separate class of quiescents and illumination, its sharp distinction between monks and laymen implying the inferiority of the latter and its relegation of worldly action to the lowest importance led to confusion and destroyed the people. Half the nation moved in the direction of passivity and negation, the other by a natural reaction phunged deep into a splendid but enervating materialism. Our race lost three parts of its ancient heroic manhood, its grasp on the world, its magnificently ordered polity and its noble social structure. Sankara tried to salvage some things from the ship-wreck. But he could not shake off the deep impress of the religion he had combated. The old vitality could not be recovered. The old Kshatriya class disappeared or became degraded. The Brahmans remained the sole interpreters of the Gita. They being men of knowledge laid stress on quiescence and did not echo Krishna's call to action. The disinterested and desireless pursuit of duty is a gospel for weaklings. Babes and sucklings may practise it, because they must, but with others it is a hypocrisy. Thus Sankara, taking his cue from Buddhism, deviated from the supreme truth of Indian culture, the harmony between life and spirit and paved, partially at least, the way for the downfall of the Hindu India.

In the religious field the age witnessed the rise of the Bhakti school just as in Europe we had the rise of piety symbolised by the Cathedrals. The good in this was that the Hindu society was cemented by the bond of devotion to a common, personal Godhead and the canker of untouchability was shorn off its poison. But here also partial vision developed; emphasis was laid on the external aids to devotion and worship and it was not realised that the mystical experience by living inward and through the fervour of devotion was the only way to discover harmony and concord. Besides Bhakti also savoured of quiescence or inaction. It emphasized the vital at the cost of the physical and mental aspects of man.

In the literary and artistic fields also the Hindus continued their old traditions but there was a decline in the creative urge. In the field of literature, we had the evolution of the Vernaculars. The architecture and sculpture of the period seem decadent when compared with the Gupta art in these fields. The period was noteworthy for the standardisation of rules and laws of music and dancing. It also witnessed the rise of the Rajput school of painting. Further the advance made in the scientific field specially astronomy and mathematics was noteworthy. Socially and economically the Hindu India continued to be progressive till the seventh century. Even afterwards in the social sphere the caste distinctions and other inequities were few and far between but as we enter the eleventh century and onward inequalities increase, pardah comes in vogue, untouchability arises, superstitions become rife and poverty for the masses is stamped upon the age. There is a close connection between economic life and culture.

During this period wealth was concentrated in the hands of the few. They spent it on unproductive purposes, on palaces, dances, animals, favourities, pastimes and on wards. The Hindu kings of the period gradually became seekers after self-interest and naturally the masses remained passive spectators when the night of foreign invasion descended upon India. Thus economic inequality made for an unbalanced culture, led to the rise of class-culture and break-up of Indian harmony achieved in the previous age. We had evolved a harmony of interest, desire, religion and liberation (Artha, Kama, Dharma and Moksha). It was disturbed now. Fundamentally thus the root of the malady lay in the partial vision of the people who mattered during the Medieval period. With the loss of concord between spirit and matter the decline of India was inevitable. We bacame prisoners of the fetters we had ourselves fashioned.

13

CULTURE DURING THE MUSLIM RULE

WE HAVE SO far traced the purely Hindu contribution to the Indian Culture in the Medieval Period. We now describe the contribution of the Mohammedans who became the main ruling class in India towards the close of the twelfth century. In this connection it will be worthwhile pointing out that the ruling classes among the Muslims were generally the foreign Muslims and the so-called Indian converts hardly counted in the counsels of the powers that be. Further in the initial period of the rule of the Sultans India was in the grip of a military occupation and there was hardly any Hindu-Muslim rapproachment. Only when the angularities of the foreign rule had been softened by environment, climate and circumstances of the times that a realisation dawned that only by placating the Hindus could an endurable peace and concord be established in India. Consciousness of this came late, mainly during the Mughal Period. Also the culture of the Muslims was for long either an exotic one or a class culture confined to a certain group that basked in the sun-shine of the King's favour.

Certain enduring aspects of Muslim contribution to our culture may be emphasized. The monotheism of Islam led to the birth of a similar movement among the Hindus also. Certain aspects of 'Bhakti' movement among the Hindus were coloured by the iconoclastic character of Islam. Kabir was the most representative figure in this sphere. Further the need to approach the Hindus for the purposes of conversion led to the development of the vernacular literature for only in their languages could the Muslim saints make themselves intelligible to the masses. In the field of fine arts also the Muslims carved a niche of their own. Muslim architecture, painting and crafts had a certain originality which enriched the fabric of our culture. In the literary field the development of Urdu, use of prose for secular purposes and the birth of historical writings are some of the monumental Muslim contributions to our culture. Further in the externalities of life also the Muslims left abiding impressions. Our dress, manners and food, for instance, specially among the aristocracy in Northern India, underwent a certain reorientation in imitation of the Muslims. We shall now describe the Muslim culture with particular reference to social and economic conditions, religion, literature and fine arts, taking first the conditions under the Sultans and then under the Mughals.

Social and Economic Conditions under the Sultans

The State in India was feudal despotism and the King was more or less co-terminous with it. He was the apex of the whole system, the keystone of the arch of government and his example was literally followed by those under him as far as possible. They (kings) thus set the tone of the upper social classes. The ambitions of the Sultans of Delhi set in the direction of building lofty palaces, holding grand levees, enjoying the spectacle of a world prostrating itself before them, accumulating vast treasure, concentrating all financial powers in their hands, carrying on incessant wars of conquest and maintaining a large establishment of domestics and 'harams' (seraglio). We hear of Sultans like Alauddin and Firoz maintaining 50,000 and two lac slaves respectively while even a minister of the King of Malwa had 2,000 women in his seraglio. Consider also the wailings of Sultan Ghiyas-ud-din Khilji of Malwa who maintained a whole department for female supply but died in the grief that he never met a woman exactly to his choice. The king had also his favourites of all sorts, astrologers, poets, musicians, clowns and others. Among the refined courtiers the most influential were the 'Nadims' a class intellectually well-equipped, in manners sophisticated, in dress most up-to-date and conversationally very pleasing and adaptable to the moods of the sovereign. They had hardly any official position and were in the nature of boon companions of a monarch. The Sultans had also a vast household staff organised into departments. For instance there were the 'Sarujandar' charged with the duty of personal protection of the king, the 'Sarabdar', looking after the royal toilet arrangements, the 'Chashnigir', supervising the royal kitchen, and 'Saqi-i-khas' providing wines and other drinks to the royalty. These functionaries had a regular subordinate establishment to help them. The Sultan as a public person was surrounded by pomp and ceremonies. Among the ceremonies marking the enthronement of a new king were those of the 'Khutba' and 'Sikka'. The 'Khutba' was the recitation of the public servant in the name of the new king and the 'Sikka' was the issue of money bearing his superscription. Strict etiquetie was prescribed for these functions.

Below the sovereign came other social classes. The chief among the upper classes were the proper ruling class (Ahl-i-daulat) comprising the members of the royal family, the nobility and the army; the intelligentsia comprising the theologians (the 'Uslama', the Judicial Officers (the 'Qazis'), men of learning and piety; and lastly came the class (Ahl-i-murad), catering for pleasure like the musicians and the dancers.

Then came the masses both among the Hindus and the Mohammedans. These enjoyed very little either of pleasure or of profit. Their function was just to pay the taxes, till their fields or work in the urban areas and allow themselves to be oppressed by the officers concerned. Power was therefore monopolised by the aristocracy in which the foreign element consisting of the Turks, the Persians, the Arabs, the Abyssinians, the Egyptians and the Afghans predominated.

During the period of Alauddin Khilji Indian converts also found a chance to be in the governing clique. The nobility was united only in war; in peace it was torn by particularistic and personal jealousies, ambitions rivalries and interests. As the Muslims were surrounded by a sea of non-believers, the influence of the 'Ulama' was great. This class monopolised Judicial ecclesiastical and educational services. The 'Ulamas', were consulted by the sovereign both on important points of law and on matters of state policy. Their influence was not always healthy or beneficial. In particular they always showed inclination towards a 'Jehad' (war) against the infidels.

The Hindus formed the bulk of the population. They were (a majority of them) hewers of wood and drawers of water. Of course, the Muslim masses were hardly better. But they carried an additional stigma of being non-believers. Hence, neither their property nor their person was safe. Most of the land was held by them. Some among them manned the lower branches of administration like the revenue and finance, supplied the bulk of the financial, trading, business and commercial classes and even acted as merchants (Banjaras) to the Muslim army as there was no regular commissariat arrangements, partisan reading of Indian history may result in the judgement that the Hindus were either deprived of all privileges or that they enjoyed comparative freedom and social amenities together with the Muslims. The truth lies in between. By their religion and beliefs they were naturally suspect to the powers that be. The ruling classes were in the minority and had to stick together. It was easy to unite them under the cry or pretext of 'Jehad'. Hence the pages of Indian history are disfigured by onslaughts and oppressions against the Hindus. But with the firm establishment of the Muslim rule in India, the rulers discovered that permanent peace could only be secured in co-operation with the majority in India and, therefore, we find them seeking the help of the Hindus also in various functions and departments. Specially in the provincial courts or administration the treatment of the Hindus was not on the whole oppressive.

Socially, therefore, the Muslim society under the Sultans was feudal. Social privileges, amenities of life, wealth and honour were the monopoly of the king and those surrounding him. The masses lived in comparative poverty and were looked down upon.

Economic Conditions

It has become proverbial that India was a land flowing with milk and honey. Certainly in the Medieval Age she had enormous wealth of all kinds and attracted the covetous eye of the foreigner.

The first Muslim attack came in the eighth century and then after the tenth century a series of invasions followed leading to the occupation of many parts of India by the Muslims. They naturally became the heirs to the wealth of India. As compared with the British it can be said to their credit that they did not drain away the wealth of India and did not uproot the sources of our production.

Agriculture

As at present India was predominantly and agricultural country; the source of production was land; ploughing and animals were the main power to draw out the potential wealth and the implements were the conservative and time-honoured plough, harrow, the pick, the hoe, spades, rakes and such like. Produce was generally sufficient unless insufficient monsoons or famines, locust pest, epidemics and invasions intervened. Life was stereotyped. The villages were peopled by inhabitants claiming common descent, caste-wise, and united by traditional tics of religion and customs. The village was a self-sufficient unit, organically united. For instance, the husband man took to the tilling and harvesting of crops, the women folk lending their hands to various functions like the care of the animals; the carpenters made and mended the implements for which the wood was supplied by the husbandmen; the blacksmiths supplied the iron parts of the implements and repaired them; the potters made the household utensils; the cobblers mended or made the shoes and the plough harness and the priest performed the marriage rites and other ceremonies. There were also the subsidiary functions of the moneylender, the washerman, the sweeper, the cowherd and the barber. Thus land was the pivot around which the whole village life revolved.

Production was mainly for local consumption. Some people in the cities, in the main, lived on the income derived from industries for which raw materials could be imported by way of the rivers washing the boundaries of these cities and some classes living in the ports lived on the fruits of foreign commerce. The towns also served as centres of distribution of agricultural produce and industrial goods. The state took a large share of the produce mainly in kind and in return provided some security and also some irrigational facilities. There was no fixed standard of comforts and the people were accustomed to comparative poverty, a course sanctioned by their traditional religion also. The chief crops were pulses, wheat, barley, millet, peas, rice, sesame and oilseeds, sugarcane, jute and cotton. Medicinal herbs and spices were also grown and exported to a certain extent. Some new crops were now introduced like tobacco, tea and coffee. Among the finest we had mangoes, grapes, dates, pomegranates, plantains, melons, peaches, apples, oranges, figs, lemons and jack-fruits. The Sultans took pains to develop orchards and gardens. We had flowers remarkable for their charm, smell and variety. There were also great varieties of animals, both domestic and wild.

Industries

There were first of all village and cottage industries and the crafts necessary for the work of the village husbandman already mentioned. The labour employed was hereditary, the technique was conservative and traditional. Among other industries we had sugar, scents and spirits. These together with varieties of oil were also made in the cities. Among the cottage industries the most important, however, were those of weaving and spinning of cotton. The processes were the same as are employed today. We had also small arms making industry. There were also goldsmiths and silversmiths, within their limitations the village-products were both artistic and cheap. The husbandman had very little left to him after paying the various craftsmen, the taxes, and the ceremonial expenses. Their lot was not, therefore, enviable. In common with them the standard of living of other people in the villages was hardly better.

There were no factories or big enterprises in the modern sense, usually either there was exchange between the small producer in the town and the distributor in the big cities or the producer disposed his stock at the periodical fairs. The Sultans also took a hand in building up big enterprises known as the 'Karkhanas'. Here craftsmen were employed under the direct supervision of officials to manufacture articles fashionable among the aristocracy. For instance, the royal factories at Delhi employed for silk manufacture above 4,000 weavers. It is said that Mohammad Tughluq used to distribute 2,00,000 complete robes of honour twice every year and for this purpose he had to import goods from China and Iraq also. This can give an idea of the royal demand for goods.

The manufacture of textiles was the biggest industry of India. The textiles included cotton cloth, woollens and silks. There were the allied industries of embroidery, gold thread work and dyeing. The home demand was fully met and some quantities were also exported notably by Bengal and Gujarat. The fine cloth was of excellent variety and the rich people dressed themselves in varieties of silk, muslin, linen, brocade, satin and furs. The famous centres of cloth manufacture were Deogir and Mahadeva Nagri in the Deccan, Delhi in the North, Cambay in Gujarat and places like Sonargaon, Dacca and Banjala in Bengal. Bengal in particular led in the manufacture of cotton textiles. There was also the manufacture of carpets, cushions, coverlets, beadings (durries) and bedstrings. We had also the dyeing industry and calico painting.

After the textiles we had the metal work. Our workers were expert in handling metals like iron, brass, silver, zinc and mica. We had various metal industries like the sword making, steel making, manufacture of basins, cups, knives, scissors and even guns.

India had also made great progress in inlay work of all sorts. Inlay work on gold and silver ornaments and utensils, embroidered work of various kinds on belts, dress, dish covers and work of enamelling reached a high water-mark during this period. There was also the stone or brick work. The fine buildings erected by the sovereign needed excellent artisans and masons and as is well known they were plentifully supplied by the medieval India. Alauddin Khilji alone is said to have employed 70,000 workers for the construction of state buildings. Other minor industries were those of the coral-work, ivory, imitation jewellery, leather, paper and sugar. The workers were organised in guilds and had considerable artistic abilities but the traditions of secrecy and exclusiveness led to the dying cut of the skill which was peculiar to them.

Trade and Commerce

Both the king and his nobles were always in need of luxury goods and this necessitated extensive trade and commerce. Both inland and foreign trade flourished, voyages by sea and travel on land were frequent.

As for the internal trade we had the various classes of merchants and shop-keepers. The Gujaratis of the North, the Chettis of the South and the Banjaras of Rajputana were famous. Besides shops we had movable stalls, pack horses, peddlers and other itinerary dealers. Bigger deals in commodities were made in special market towns or 'mandis'. Connected with the merchants we had the class of carriers of goods, the brokers. The Banjaras (spoken above) carried on the business of conveying agricultural and other produce from one part of the country to another. The native bankers used to give loans and receive deposits or 'hundis'. These bankers, Sahus and Mahajans, were always helping the upper classes with money. Alauddin Khilji instituted special officers and laid down strict rules to control the operations of markets, adulteration of food and fraudulent weights. The towns were the focus of the internal trade.

As in the ancient past, even now India had substantial commercial relations with the outside world. Indian goods were carried by the Arabs to all parts of Asia. Caravans of merchants were a familiar sight. The sea-routes were in the hands of the Moorish merchants. The chief articles of import were silks, velvets, embroidered stuff, horses, guns, gun-powder and some precious metals. The chief items of export were grain, cotton, precious stones, indigo, hides, opium, spices and sugar.

The countries attracted by India in commerce were, in particular, Iraq, Persia, Egypt, East Africa, Malaya, Java, Sumatra, China, Central Asia, Afghanistan, Islands in the Pacific and countries round the Persian Gulf. From Alexandria in Egypt goods went to Europe.

In foreign trade the coastal cities took the lead particularly those of Gujarat and Bengal. The share of the Indians in the carrying trade on the Indian coast was very small. The foreign merchants had no love lost for India. They were interested only in carrying on their business and making profits. The volume of foreign trade was however, comparatively not very significant. On account of the luxurious life of the king and his retinue most of India's wealth from the industries was spent on the maintenance of a parasite class leading naturally to the impoverishment of the masses. Prices of commodities were cheaper than those obtaining today but the masses could not benefit much on account of the filching by the powers-that-be and the aristocracy.

Economically, therefore, the age of the Sultanate presents a vivid contrast between affluence and poverty. Material wealth was concentrated in the hand of the few. The pattern of spending was set by the Sultans to whom prestige and honour demanded huge expenditure and luxurious living.

The culture and refinement of a very small upper class had no relation to the life of the common people. The life of the majority was stereotyped, unrefined and represented a very low stage of mental culture. In this period, therefore, economic conditions, had a very close bearing on our culture. The kings became corrupt, luxury-loving and inefficient. They represented in course of time an effete culture not related to the needs and demands of the masses and as such their downfall became inevitable. The sturdy Moghuls now trampled over their freedom and established their own rule in India.

We shall now describe the social and economic conditions in India under the Moghul Kings.

Social and Economic Conditions under the Moghuls

As in the previous period, society continued to be divided into the haves and the have-nots with power and wealth concentrated in the hands of the king and a small class of aristocracy. We had already traced the various divisions of society and need not linger over this. Two new factors, however, entered during this period and influenced the social development. In the first place the kings became national monarchs. Akbar especially inaugurated a policy of reconciliation, concord was established between the Hindus and the Muslims. Consequently we had now social solidarity and cohesion. The Hindus manned the administration of the empire in collaboration with the Mohammedans and also became ornaments of the royal court, contributing their share in the literary and artistic developments and by their inclusion widening the ranks of aristocracy. Secondly, the Mughal kings were secular in outlook and refused to be guided by the 'Mullas' or Ulamas. As a result the influence of sacerdotal class, which had so far been exercised in the direction of religious fanaticism, was curtailed and in this sphere also the initiative was taken by Akbar.

Women and wine continued to be the pre-occupation of society or the aristocracy. We have Abul Fazl volunteering the information that Akbar had a seraglio of 5,000 women supervised by a separate staff of female officers. In the reign of Jahangir wine flowed freely in the court. We, however, find the kings attempting various social reforms. Evils like Sati and female infanticide were banned or frowned upon, widow-remarriage was encouraged, and female education was imparted. Dowry system was discouraged and attempts were made by Akbar to secure consent of the bride and the bride-groom also to their marriage. He also tried to check eariy marriages, polygamy and promiscuous wedding, in spite of these reforms the fundamental question of the deep social gulf between the few and the masses remained unsolved and society continued to be feudal, conservative and reactionary.

Economic Conditions

In the economic life of this age a new factor emerged, namely the advent of the Europeans on the stage of Indian politics in the closing years of the sixteenth century and the Portuguese became masters of the Indian seas. Akbar tacitly recognised the position of the Portuguese by taking out licences for ships sent by him to the Red Sea, and the Moghuls made no attempt either to free or to command the water. There was no realisation on the part of the Moghul Kings of the nature of sea-power or its role in the future military strategy. The result was that by the close of the reign of Aurangzeb the influence of the European merchants had extended over the greater part of India. On the coast, from Sind to Bengal, Dutchmen and Englishmen were to be found wherever there was trade worth having while in the north they were active over large portions of the areas now known as Bihar and the Uttar Pradesh; their presence was familiar on the roads leading from Agra to the seaports. It may fairly be said that, with the exception of the Punjab, every important part of India was affected by the new conditions which had come into existence. In other words as the Indian rulers could not change society in a progressive direction, nature sent foreign rule to effect the change over from feudalism to capitalism.

Economically the most important feature was the top-heavy expenditure of the government which remained despotic in character though like Europe in the eighteenth century it was benevolent despotism.

The expenditure mainly related to personal demands of the king, army and the administration. To meet these needs recourse was had to a system of taxation. The taxes could be classified into two main divisions, namely, the Fa's and Zakat, the former being secular and the latter a religious one. The Fa's included such taxes as Khums, Jezia and Khiraj. Zakat was mainly levied on property. Khums, meaning one-fifth, was a tax levied on war-booty acquired by a Muslim soldier and on mine or treasure. Jezia was levied an the nonbelievers (discontinued by Akbar and his successors till Aurangzeb) in return for protection and Khiraj was a land tax ranging between 1/2 to 1/5. Zakat was a religious tax levied on the Muslims possessing free property, exemption being granted to infants, invalids, insolvent debtors and lunatics. Ushr (Tithe) was another religious tax levied on the Muslims, it was levied on the actual produce of the soil and the minors were not exempted from it. In other words the main sources of income were land, customs, mints, inheritance and presents. Land, however, remained the main source of support to the King.

Under Akbar various revenue reforms were carried out

to stabilise this source of income, to give chance to the cultivator to increase his produce and be sure of the state demand and prevent fraud and corruption in the revenue service and administration.

Todar Mal helped Akbar in building a scientific land policy. The revenue payments were set by the Zabt (regulation system of assessment of Todar Mal) which fixed cash rates and took one- third of the gross produce as the share of the crown. The charge was on cultivation and not on occupation. The revenue officials were to be paid in cash and dealt directly with the peasants. It was laid dawn that the collector 'must consider himself the immediate friend of the husbandman; he must not require any intermediary, he must assist the needy husbandman with loans of money, and receive payments at distant and convenient periods; he must reward skilful management; let him see that his demands do not exceed his agreements, let him collect the revenue with kindness; and vexatious taxes must not be exacted'. Akbar's settlement was based on measurement, classification and fixation of rates. The land was measured by a 'Jarib' or chain equal in length 60 yards and the chain consisted (in the developed form) of bamboo's joined by iron rings which remained in all seasons of constant length. The unit of land was the 'bigha' equal to 3600 square yards. The land after measurement was divided into 4 classes, namely, Polaj (continually cultivated), Parauti (land laid fallow for a year or two), Chachar (land lying fallow for 3 or 4 years), and Banjar (land uncultivated for five years or more). Each of the first three classes was sub-divided into three grades and the average was then calculated.

Of this averages, government took one-third as its share. Land revenue could be paid in kind. Payment of revenue was to be based on solar Years called the Ilahi era. These lands were kept separate from the exchequer and the jagir lands, belonging respectively to the king and his feudal lords. Plurality of post was abolished and each officer was assigned a particular post and a salary. Thus, the land policy of Akbar was essentially sound and was applied irrespective of caste, colour or creed.

Thus was ensured the prosperity of the peasants who

formed the backbone of the economic structure of India. This system was continued by Akbar's successors though from Shahjahan's time evils began to creep into it and it is said that farming system was resorted to in various ways, and the powers of the settlement officials were increased. The agricultural crops were the same as those mentioned in the earlier period and the method of cultivation also remained similar. The self-sufficient village unit remained as of old. The plight of the peasants used to worsen some time on account of the famines which now occurred in the reigns of all the Moghul Kings.\

Industries

The manufactures were at the artisan stage, the cottage industry was the rule and not the exception. The state remained as of old the biggest entrepreneur.

The king advanced big loans and financed industries. As he was a great patron of arts, the best skilled workers were monopolised by him. The demand for silk, cotton goods and perfumes had grown. Akbar was of a mechanical turn of mind and his Karkhanas, or workshops, catered to his tastes. The manufacturer conducted his operations in his house and belonged to castes in which the occupation had become hereditary. The empire was self-supporting, producing enough necessaries and luxuries. Foreigners were attracted by Indian textiles, indigo, opium, pepper and spices.

The textiles were exported to Burma, Malacca, Persia, Egypt, Arabia, China, Africa, to Europe and to Brazil. Calico was the most important of cotton products, that of Calicut (Kerala) being most famous. There were various kinds of Calicos and long cloths. The calicos were given various names by the foreigners like the Semianoes, Pintados, Necanies and Percalles. The coasts of Bengal, Bombay and Madras contained ports from where these goods went outside. In the Punjab the district of Hoshiarpur was famous for the production of varieties of cotton goods. From Gujarat silk went to Peru, East Africa, Turkey, Tartary, Syria, Barbary and Ethiopia, silk was also imported into India from the Far East, Central Asia and countries along the western coast. Bengal, Bihar and Ahmedabad were centres of silk manufacture. Kashmir specialised in woolens, carpets and shawls.

Indigo was extensively grown in the Doab and had a great foreign market specially after Akbar.

Fine arts were also developed. Ice was supplied in the summer from Sirmoor, a hilly state. It was transported by coolies and boats.

The big industries were financed by the king. For the small industries we have the development now of banking houses (called Kothees) whose business was lending of money, exchanging old with new coins, issue and discount of hundees (Promissary Notes) and depositing of money at a certain rate of interest. The persons engaged in this work were called Sharrafs (Shroits) and the manager was called Muneemji (agent of the financier). These Kothees opened their branches in various places in India and took up other business also besides banking. For proper trading and financial purposes of the state good coinage is a necessity and Akbar adopted measures to have a reformed currency. The coins were brought to a fixed standard of purity and their shapes were improved. The coins in regular use were silver and copper. Gold coins were rarely used. The chief silver coin was the rupee of 172.5 grains : the chief copper coin was the 'dam', equal to 1/40 of the rupee; l / 8 of a dam was known as 'damri' and one 'paisa' or dam fetched 72 'cowries', while for imperial purposes 'Jitals' were also in use, being 1/28 of a dam. The gold 'mohur', was equal to 10 rupees. The rupees was equal to 2 shillings and 3 pence, roughly calculated. The normal rate for an unskilled worker was 2 dams and for a skilled worker 7 dams.

The unskilled worker could obtain for this money 9 pounds and 4 ounces of wheat for example, and a skilled worker could obtain 32 pounds and 6 ounces. Thus, the food was extra ordinarily cheap. There was no principle of taxation and no mobility of labour. Foreigners were taxed less than the natives and were given concessions which hit the native industries, for instance customs duties or inland transit duties on their goods were hardly any as compared with those levied on the merchandise of the Indians. There was also the evil of farming taxes. Thus uncertainty of the taxes, their wide range and frequency, insatiable greed of the officials and weak protection of life and property on the king's highways killed enterprise and initiative in trade.

The transport system operated through land, rivers and the seas. There were various roads converging on Agra the capital which was connected with all places of India like Dholpur, Delhi, Lahore, Kabul, Surat, Broach, Ahmedabad, Ajmer, Fatehpur Sikri, Kannauj, Lucknow, Ayodhya, Faizabad, Jaunpur, Allahabad, Patna and others. The Punjab conducted a considerable trade via Kashmir and Ladakh, Yarkand and Kashgar. There was also the connection of Agra to south via Burhanpur, Daultabad and Golkunda. Inland navigation was confined to the Ganges and the Indus. Boats used to come from Bengal to Banaras and Allahabad. Bullock-carts and pack animals besides boats transported goods. At every 5 coss (Kos) posts were established with horses and a set of footmen maintained there (one coss = 5000 yards). To convey special papers 50 coss was travelled in 24 hours or a letter reached Ahmedabad from Agra in five days. Travelling was not always safe.

Trade and Commerce

So far as the inland trade was concerned the conditions remained the same as before but there was a new development in the foreign trade, namely, the incursion of the European merchants. We should have taken a warning and a lesson from them. All the factors in favour of India being a great trading country—natural wealth, extensive sea-board, teeming population with artistic skill were present but the kings did not care about these and neglected the sea-trade and commerce.

The Portuguese and later the Dutch and the English controlled our foreign commerce. Among the Indians (to lend help) were the Moslems of the coastal areas, the 'Banias' of Gujarat and the 'Chettis' of the Coromandel coast. The important sea-ports were Lahari-Bandar (near Karachi), Diu, Broach, Surat, Daman, Bassein, Chaul, Goa, Mangalore, Calicut, Cochin, Negapatams, St. Thome, Masulipatam, Hooghly, Chitagong and Satgaon. Foreign goods came through Persia and traders exported horses, pearls, incense, gummastic and Jew's stones. They also exported sugar, butter, olive oil, cocoa and textiles. To Surat came ships from many parts of Africa, Europe and Asia laden with spices, silks, sandals, ivory, velvets, pauvina, wines, precious metals and African slaves. They imported cotton goods, in-laid works, silk, daggers and weapons of Somnath. Bengal supplied rice, sugar, cotton, silks and slaves. Lahore and Multan gave sugar, textiles, paper and steel-weapons. Agra supplied indigo, Kashmir gave fruits, shawls, borax, silk and woolens. The frontier trade was also with Bhutan, Nepal, Kumaon and Burma. Persia sent us wines, Arabia sent us horses and Africa sent us slaves among other things. India became rich in silver and gold for merchants brought coins and carried away goods. In the Moghul times new commodities for foreign trade came into existence like the saltpeter, sal-ammoniac, sandalwood, indigo of Bengal and spices. Shops were not open throughout the day or the week. They opened twice a day, for instance, in the summer, in the morning after sunrise for 3 hours and in the evening after sunset for 2 or 4 hours. Indian merchants were clever and an European Pyrard de Laval observed, 'for they are all cunning folk, and owe nothing to the people of the West, themselves endued with a keener intelligence than is usual with us'. In carrying trade they acted as the middlemen and even royalty engaged in these enterprises. Agricultural wealth and foreign trade made the Moghul kings fabulously wealthy. It is said that Akbar left 40 million pounds sterling in coined money to his successor, which would be equal to 200 million pounds sterling of the present.

But the splendour of the Moghul Court was based on the ruin of the nation. There were hardly any social amenities or comforts for the masses. There were no middle classes consisting of the lawyers, the teachers, the journalists, politicians or the engineers. Money was hardly available for productive purposes because of two factors one, the dominant care of the upper classes was the consumption and hoarding of gold, silver, pearls, diamonds, etc., and two, the uncertainty of reaping where one has sowed for the law was that the king could seize the wealth of the deceased.

The Moghul economic prosperity reached its greatest height in the reign of Shahjahan and the same reign witnessed its decline also. While Shahjahan was draining the Empire in order to build magnificent palaces and mosques, the foreigners were fixing their tentacles deep into the heart of the empire. The 'Deccan' policy of Aurangzeb completed the economic ruin. Absorbed in the conquest of the Deccan he neglected the economic interests, trade languished, roads became unsafe, provincial and the Hindu powers raised their heads, land was rockrented, labour was sweated and sea piracy developed. It was a sign of the times that the English minted coins without the royal permission in Bombay. The royal boat was looted and the chastity of women was violated. National bankruptcy brooded like a dark cloud over the whole period of Aurangzeb's rule, and eventually in conjunction with other factors, brought about the ruin of the empire.

It must not, however, be supposed from these observations that the lot of the masses was completely bleak, monotonous and uninteresting. In the first place there were all sorts of sports in which the masses either took part or were interested spectators. There were the outdoor sports like the chase, swimming, hawking, animal-fighting, Gladiatorial contests, wrestling, polo, and pigeon-flying. Among the indoor-games we had chess, 'Chaupar' or backgammon and dice. Then there were the musical and dancing performances. Besides there were numerous fairs and festivals and many occasions for pilgrimages. The villagers had their evening amusements or engagements like the story-recitation or folk-dances on festivals like Holi. All these extenuated the bitterness of economic life. These amusements had their fashion among the aristocracy also who further enriched the social fabric by new fashions in manners, dress and goods.

This ends our brief description of the economic and social conditions of the people under the Muslim rule. The points that emerge from this description are the wide gulf between the few who own the wealth and the majority who produce the wealth, the unproductive nature of the enterprises undertaken by the state, absence of a middle class, poverty of the masses, lack of appreciation by the rulers of the importance of foreign trade and the estrangement between the highly cultured aristocracy and the untutored masses. The redeeming feature was that the wealth was not drained away from the country and skilled work continued to have a wide field. It is also said that the Moghuls restored our connection with outer Asia and provided work to the Hindus also.

Religion

The question of religion can be looked at from various points of view. Some of these are : the religious policy of the Sultans or the Mughal kings, the relationship between the king and the 'Ulamas' or the ecclesiastical class, the non-social religious movements during the period and the tone of the current morality among the people. So far as the religious functions of a Sultan are concerned, it is said, they were confined to the following duties, namely, the reading of the Khutba for the Friday and Id' prayers; the fixing of the extent and the limits of religious prohibitions; the collection of taxes for charitable purposes, the waging of wars in defence of the faith; the adjudication of disputes and suppression of innovations in religion. The Sultan further set apart funds from his treasury for religious and charitable purposes, as a matter of grace. Further from the conversations between Barani and Iltutmish the Sultan and between Sultan Alauddin and Qazi Muglis-ud-din of Biyana it is crystal clear that the Sultanate was an essentially secular institution with no room within it for a dogmatic attitude towards religion and no scope for the established religion to usurp the authority of the civil functionaries who derived their power from the king. The 'Ulamas' discovered great possibilities in the Quaranic injunction 'Obey Allah and Obey the Apostle and those in authority from among you'. The Sultans were identified with those in authority,' and were later invested with divine attributes and disobedience to them was to be regarded as sinful. In short, the Ulama, subscribed to the proposition, 'He who obeys the Sultan, obeys, the Lord Merciful'. The claim of the Mughal King Akbar to be both the secular and religious head of the Indian Muslims must, therefore, seem a logical development. So far as the Sultans and their Hindu subjects were concerned it must be conceded that initially they were suspected and persecuted; how far it was a matter of policy and how for a question of conviction, must remain a controversial question. But when the militant fury of the invader cooled down, the warrior learned to turn his sword into a plough-share and the normal functions of administration began to demand greater attention, it was realized that even-handed justice and redress for every wrong committed against anyone were essential to promote peace and prosperity. Hence towards the close of the Sultanate we find a more tolerant attitude towards the Hindus and this was specially true in the case of many kingdoms which arose in the provinces with the weakening of the central authority at Delhi.

As for the relationship between the religious class and the Sultans it varied according to the personage who happened to be the king. The religious class consisted of the theologians, the ascetics, the Sayyids, the Pirs and their descendants. Of these, officially the theologians or the 'Ulama' counted most. They manned the judicial and religious offices in the state. They had tended to acquire undue importance in the state, were becoming fanatical and often forgetful of the tenets of their faith. It was Sultan Alluddin Khilji who put a curb to their over weening ambitions. They were to decide only on judicial questions and strictly religious problems. Mohammed Tughluq went even further and completely secularised the state. Firoz, however was more lenient. But their former supremacy was gone for ever. Thus, the ecclesiastical class became a handmaid of the Sultan's political policy and administration.

So far as the non-official religious movements are concerned we find the development of Sufism among the Muslims and the Bhakti movement among the Hindus. The latter has been treated both in the previous chapter and the one that follows some notice may now be taken of Sufism in India.

The period of individualistic missionary activity begins from the eleventh century onward. Of the earliest missionaries of whom we have any record was Shaikh Ismail who came to Lahore about the year 1005 A.D. Among others who came now mention may be made of Abd Allah. In the twelfth century we have an important missionary in Gujarat, namely, Nur-ud-Din. From the thirteenth century their numbers increased and we had important missionaries like Khwajah Muin-ud-Din Chishti of Ajmer, Jalal-ud-Din of Sind, Sayyid Ahmad Kabir of the Punjab and later on others like Baha-ul-Haqq, Baba Farid-ud-Din and Ahmed Kabir. From the fourteenth century the missionaries spread into Western India and the Deccan.

Islam has its monastic orders and saints, the underlying basis of which is the mystic role of the religious life known as Sufism. Sind was the first province to be the home of Sufism. Largely by means of poetry, Sufi ideas have been spread throughout India. They have modified some schools of Hindu mysticism which has also affected Sufism in India. The Sufis have split up into a number of sects which have been referred to in the next chapter. We shall now discuss the main principles of Sufism.

Sufism is devotional, pietistic and a natural revolt against the cold formalism of a ritualistic religion. Naturally it found a congenial home in India with its warm, mystical yearning after union and fellowship with God. Their faith may be thus summarised. God has given all his sons or servants the capacity for union with Him.

This capacity is potential, hidden within us and can be developed with the help of a guide who should be one illumined by divine touch and light and so qualified to initiate people into the divine mysteries. To perform these spiritual functions various illuminated souls have come into this world dowered with the gift of miracles (Aromatic). These men, out of their practical experience in the way— tariqah, of coming into union (wasi) with God, have defined the stages of progress and laid down rules for the guidance of all men who desire to live on terms of the closest intimacy with God and His saints (walis). The spiritual guide is known as the 'Murshid,' 'Pir' or Shaykh, and his disciple is called a 'Murid'. Various ceremonies have been prescribed for the initiation of a disciple. After-initiation he becomes a 'Salik,' traveller on the way and must carefully observe the rules and the ritualistic practice of 'dhikr' besides strictly obeying the master till he has attained illumination (khatrat). The various stages of illumination are 'Nasut' when the law of Islam is the guide; 'Malakut' when one develops the nature of an angel and becomes pure; 'Jaborut' when powers descend and 'Lahut' where one has absolute truth and is absorbed in divinity. The religious practices to attain these stages are of vital importance. There is the practice of 'dhikr' or remembering Allah, bringing Him to mind. Either His name is quietly repeated or other thoughts are loudly suppressed. Further the disciple shuts his eyes, closes his lips and fixes his attention on his inhalations and exhalations, saying La ilahah (there is no God) when the breath goes out and saying illa Allah (except Allah) when the breath comes in. He should practise this so that ultimately this becomes automatic and he need not think at all of the process or practise it. Sometimes in the practice of 'dhikr' ecstasy is induced and one loses consciousness. It can also be performed in groups. The master or the 'pir' becomes hereditary and has his headquarters called 'Khanaqah' (monastery). It is often built over the tomb of the founder pir. The members are both laity and the clergy. Among the latter are these who collect gifts from the country, divided, for this purpose into circles (halqahs), for the order and those who constantly reside in the monastery and are of various groups according to their spiritual development. These orders exercise extensive influence in the religious life of the Indian Muslims.

The Sufis in India were not characterized by religious fanaticism. They adopted many Indian rites and principles into their faith. They approached the Hindus with artlessness, simplicity, love, kindness and benevolence and tried to appeal to them in their own language. They gave to the Bhakti movement various devotional exercises and charted it with their own experiences of mystic and divine love. Their Love was of various kinds as that of the wife towards the husband, of the beloved towards the lover, often servant towards the master. The pain of separation was forcibly expressed and was a sign of intensity of love towards God. Later on the two, man and God were looked identical. But very few reached this conception or regarded it as worth adopting. The separation between God and man was maintained in consonance with the principles of Islam.

As for the moral life of the people was concerned, on the whole it was marked by faith, love and piety. Loyalty and charity were appreciated and adhered to, courtesy and hospitality were enjoined upon and properly observed. But as compared with the masses the aristocrats or the upper classes were not morally praise-worthy. Excessive sensuality, unnatural love, gambling and drinking and personal jealousies disfigured their lives. They took their cue from the sovereign and even the 'Ulama' had swerved from the path. Amir Khusaro finds that the only distinguishing feature of the theologians as a class was their hypocrisy, vanity and conceit. Balban complained of the want of truthfulness and courage among them. The only redeeming feature was the intense love of religion among the masses and the development of devotional sects like those of the Sufis.

These were the main features of the religious life of the age of the Sultanate, so far as the Moghuls are concerned we need not dilate upon their policy here as it is extensively treated in the next chapter. It may be emphasized that the developing spirit of tolerance in this age crystallised itself in the reign of Akbar. We have the testimony of Abul Fazl who observed in Ain-i-Akbari that Akbar tabulated the causes of difference between the Hindus and the Mohammedans and exerted all the authority of the State to remove them. These causes were :

(a) diversity of tongues and misapprehension of mutual purposes;
(b) the distance that separated the learned men of the two communities;
(c) the absorption of mankind, in the delights of corporeal; gratification and unwillingness to hear praise of another;
(d) insolence, no intention to understand one another;
(e) the blowing of the chill blast of inflexible custom and the low flicker of the lamp of wisdom;
(f) the uprising of the whirlwind of animosity and the

storms of persecution (Understanding each other an impossibility); and

(g) the prosperity of wretches without principles.*

Akbar, therefore, strove to reconcile the two communities. He gave the first place to reason and not communalism and thus laid the foundations of a national and secular state in medieval India. His example was followed by his successors. Aurangzeb deviated from it with consequences too well known to merit detailed narration. The priestly class was given a short shrift, devotional movements like those of the Sufis and others were encouraged and the moral tone of the people was raised when the Emperor Akbar developed his scheme for a common religion for the people and regulated his moral life. The contribution of the Moghuls in the religious field form abiding monument of Indian history.

Literature

In the field of literature three important developments may be noted. The period witnessed the introduction and development of Persian literature, it saw the rise of vernacular literature and also the foundation and growth of secular writings in prose in which chronicles or historical literature predominated. In fact the Indian culture was enriched by the growth of historical form of literature which was a Muslim contribution. The Sultans were busy in wars of conquest but they did not neglect the arts or the sciences altogether. They extended their patronage to men of learning. Conditions in many parts of Asia were unsettled and men of parts flocked from those places to India where they found a ready welcome. Thus, India became a centre of Persian literature. Delhi became an international literary home for the learned and the artist.

Education

No medieval government had a regular department of public instruction but Muslim India could claim to possess one which looked after religious as well as educational institutions. As a result of this we have the foundation of schools and colleges, establishment of libraries and literary societies and

* *Ain-i-Akbari*, Vol. III, p. 24.

patronage of scholars.

Apart from houses where individual instructor privately imparted education after receiving payment from pupils, there were three types of institutions namely : primary, secondary and university. Both in the villages and the cities we had the 'maktab' a primary school, then there was the 'madrasa', the secondary school, lastly in important centres we had the universities. Very often mosques and 'Khanqahs' or shrines of Muslim saints served as centres for the disseminations of knowledge, both spiritual and secular. Here they were taught reading, writing and arithmetic besides making them familiar with the rudiments of religion. Education of girls was also provided for. The university centres were, for instance, at Delhi, Jullundur, Firozabad and Jaunpur. Literary societies were first started by Prince Mohammed, eldest son of Balban. These societies became the centres of literary discussion, poetical recitation, musical and dramatic entertainments. Libraries were also built up to preserve for posterity the best thoughts of learned men.

Technical education was provided in 'Karkhanas' or workshops through a system of apprenticeship. The trading classes maintained their own schools where knowledge in business and accounts was imparted. Development of arts and crafts points out to the high quality of technical education. In education morality was also emphasized and discipline and devotion were insisted upon. Thus, the age of the Sultanate had its cultural tendencies. We had a growth of Persian literature also during this period. Among the most notable writers mention may be made of Lusher and Shaikh Najim-ud-din Hasan also known as Amir Hasan Dihalvi who migrated to Daultabad where he died in 1324-1325 A.D. Khusroo was a prolific writer and is said to have written more than four lakhs of couplets. He was undoubtedly the greatest of the Indian poets writing in Persian. His important contributions are Qiran-us-Sadain, the Miftah-ul-futuh or Fath-ul-futuh, the Nuh Sipahr, the Khaza-in-ul-futuh, Dewalrani, Khizr Khan and Tughluq-nama besides his Diwan and numerous other poems. Many of his writings are historical. For instance in Khaza-in-ul-Futuh he gives a systematic account of the first fifteen years of Sultan

Allauddin Khilji. As a poet he is refined, puritan and lofty when he sings of the court but when he sings of the people he becomes homely and tries to be congenial sometimes even borrowing the commonness of the undeveloped mind. He lived in the reigns of four kings, namely, Balban, Jalal-ud-din and Alauddin Khilji and Ghiyas-ud-din Tughluq. Amir Hasan was also a poet of internatianal repute. With the exception of Amir Khusrao most of the writers took their themes, phraseology and styles from Persia and Arabia and as such their contributions were of limited value. Moreover, the cultural activity was confined to the court and the aristocracy, the people had hardly any share in it.

Among important chronicles or historical writings of the period, mention may be made of Tajul-Maasir by Hasan Nizami, Tabqat-i-Nasiri by Mihaj-ud-din Siraj, Tarikh-i-Firozshahi by Zia-ud-din Barani, Tarikh-i-Firozshahi by Shams-i-Siraj Afif, Tarikh-i-Mubarakshahi by Yahya Bin Ahmad and Futuh-us-Salatin by Isami.

We have also books on fiction, folklore and practical arts and compendiums. Mention may be made of Jawami-ul-Hikaya by Muhammad Awfi, Matla-ul-Anwar of Khusrao, Tufa-it Nasa'ih of Yusuf Gada, Kitab-i-Ni'mat Khana-i-Nasir Shahi giving a description of culinary art and recipes for making scents, cosmetics and Hidayat-ur-rami, gives a guidance in archery, Futewa-jahandari of Barani giving political advice to the princes and lastly Figh-i-Firuz Shahi begun by Yaqub Karrani and finished by orders of Firoz Tughluq. It is a compendium of civil and ecclesiastical law and much social history can be gleaned from it. We have also a number of travellers during this period whose accounts throw much light on the history of this period. The most important of them were Marco Polo, Ibn Batuta, Mahuan, Aiadur-Ra-Zaq, Conti, Nikitin and Stephans, Varthema, Barbosa and Sidi Ali. Reis and so also in the Moghul period. The most complete and learned account is that of Ibn Batuta (1325- 1354). His account is a life-like picture of India. He married in India, had children and got employment in the state. He, however, believed in marvels and was led into many misstatements and errors of observations. We have also collections of official and private letters among which mention may be made of Riyaz-ul-Insha of Mahmud Gawan.

There was also the development of vernacular Literature, birth of Urdu and further growth of the Sanskrit literature. We have traced these developments in the other two chapters on the medieval period. Here some reasons may be given for the development of the indigenous literature. In the first place the demand of the new revival in religion among the Hindus could only be met if appeal was made direct to the people in their own Languages which had begun developing from 'Apabhramsha'.

The preaching of 'Bhakti' or devotion necessitated this development. Secondly, when the Muslim preachers came to India they felt the necessity of a language in which they could speak direct to the people and this explains the origin of Urdu and the Muslim contribution towards the development of provincial languages. The Muslim kings in the provinces encouraged translation of the Sanskrit works in provincial language. Thus, the patronage of the kings or Rajas was another reason for this new development. It is possible that an economic cause also may have operated in the moghul period, namely, the development of foreign trade. The Europeans established their trading centres inland also, came in touch with local producers and the merchants and felt the necessity of conversing with them in their own language. This also might have given an impetus to the development of the vernaculars. Rulers in provinces declared their independence of the Central government and felt the necessity of rallying to their cause the support of the people whose literary renaissance they, therefore, encouraged. Again, the brilliant development of original Hindi poetry in the time of Akbar may be ascribed partly to the toleration and peace enabling the poets to work in a congenial atmosphere. Akbar also extended his patronage to the Hindu literatures. Thus religious, political and economic causes combined to produce a whole crop of literatures in the provincial languages.

We may now take up the development of literature in the Moghul period. In this field also the reign of Akbar forms the focus-point of the various tendencies which had been developing during the former period.

We have also the reform of education. The author of *Ain-i-Akbari*, Abul Fazl mentions that in every country especially in Hindustan boys are kept for years at school, where they learn consonants and vowels. A great portion of the life of the students is wasted by making them read many useless books. His Majesty, therefore, ordered that every school boy should first learn to write the letters of the alphabet and also learn to trace their several forms. The shape and name of each letter is to be learnt in two days. Then Joined letters should be written. Afterwards some selections from prose and poetry should be learnt by heart. Self instruction instead of tutoring should be the rule. The teachers should look specially after five things namely, (i) Knowledge of letters, (ii) meaning of words, (iii) prose; (iv) verse, (v) former lesson. Each boy ought to read books on morals, arithmetic, notation, agriculture, menstruation, geometry, astronomy, physiognomy, household matters, government, medicine, logic, music, history and mechanics. All these should be gradually attempted. Study of Arabic and Persian was compulsory.

In the primary school the curriculum comprised learning of sections of Quran by rote necessary for the five compulsory prayers, the practice of reading and writing the alphabet and other lessons on wooden boards called 'Takhtis' and reading of the primer as well as some Persian books such as Sadi's works. In the secondary institutions art of administration, arithmetic, algebra, sciences, accounts, economics, history, law, morals, literature and philosophy were taught. But all Subjects were not taught in any particular school. Much depended upon the staff and the principal. The aims of education were to bring out the latent faculties of the students, to inculcate discipline, to mould character, prepare for life and equip them for the professions. Religion was at the root of all studies. In every 'Madrasa' there was a mosque and every mosque had a 'maktab' besides a library. Teachers were held in high esteem and provided judges and ministers of religion from amongst themselves. Universities were of the residential type. Monitorial system was in vogue, education was free and scholarships were granted. Estates were attached to the schools and colleges for maintenance. Examination was conducted by the teacher in charge of the subject. Certificates, diplomas and medals were awarded. Truants were physically punished and not fined. There were Hindu institutions also corresponding to these. Thus, we had a reformed system of education in the Moghul times.

The literature of Akbar's reign may be classified under the heads of translations, histories, letters and verse. Translations were made from Sanskrit books which we mention in the next chapter. The famous historical works of the period are Tarikhi-i-Alfi of Mulla Daud, the Ain-i-Akbari and Akbarnamah of Abul Fazl the Muntakhab-ut-Tawarikh of Badauni, the Tabaqat-i-Akbari of Nizam-ud-din Ahmad, the Akbarnamah of Faizi Sarhindi, and the Maasir-i-Rohini of Abdut Baqi. The most accomplished writer of the reign was Abul Fazl, a man of letters, a poet, an essayist, a critic and a historian. His Ain-i-Akbari is deservedly famous. It was a work of encyclopedic character, where useful information of all kinds is to be found and to which people in every walk of life could resort to for reference, instruction and amusement. For the first time life of the people is put before us. Abul Fazl took great pains to collect his information. He, however, betrays unbalanced judgement when he gives Akbar all the credit of originality and wisdom.

Among the principal collections of letters those of Abul Faiz may he mentioned.

Poetry reached the pinnacle of glory under the Moghuls. Babar and Humayun were also poets and Akbar continued the tradition. Among the poets we had Abul Faiz (Faizi) the Persian poet-laureate, Abdur Rahim, Abdul Fateh, Ghizali, Mohammad Hussain Naziri and Sayyid Jamal-ud-din Urfi of Shiraj. More than 70 versifiers are mentioned by Abul Fazl. Many of these prostituted the word love in the service of unholy passion.

Jahangir possessed an excellent literary taste and his autobiography is second only to that of Babar in matter and style. His court was adorned by many literary gems like Ghiyas Beg, Naqib Khan, Mutamid Khan, Niamatullah and Abdul Haqq Dihlawi. Some historical works were also composed during this period, for instance, the Maasir-i-Jahangiri. Shahjahan was a lavish patron of arts and literature. By this time two distinct schools of writers had come into existence, the Indo-Persian school and the purely Persian school. The first outstanding representative of the former school was Abul Fazl. In this reign this school had a number of representatives, namely, Abdul Hamid Lahori Md. Waris, Chandra Bhan and Md. Salih. This school was absorbing Indian ideas and thoughts. It was also grandiose in style. The Persian school attracted men like Aminai Qazvini and Jalal-ud-din Tabatabai. A number of foreign poets came in this reign. The poets wrote 'Ghazals', Qasida, Masnavi, and poems of adulation. Among great poets mention may be made of Gilani, Kalim, Qudsi, Saib, Rafi, Munir, Brahman (a Hindu), Haziq, Khiyali and Mahir. Among the historical works mention may be made of Padshahnamah by Abdul Hamid Lahori, Shahjahannamah by Inayat Khan and Amal-i-Salih by Muhammad Salih. There were prose writings of other types also for instance 'beilis letters,' dictionaries, medicinal and religious books, astronomy, mathemetics and translations from Sanskrit. Aurangzeb had no taste for poetry Among the famous works were Alamgir-namah by Mirza Muhammad Kazim, Muntakhab-ul-Lubab of Khafi Khan, Khulasat-ut-Tawarikh of Sujan Rai Khatri and Fatuhat-i-Alamgiri of Ishwar Das. Dara Shikoh encouraged the translation of Sanskrit works into Persian.

We had the greatest development of provincial languages during this period so that it may well be called the classical age of Hindustani literature. Hindi owed its greatest development to a number of saints and poets. Beginning from the Buddhist schools of Mantrayan and Vajrayana and Siddhas a long line of saints contributed to the development of the vernaculars. During this period we had great writers like Tulsidas, Kabir, Surdas, Sundar Das, Chintamani, Kavindra Acharya, Keshava Das, Matiram, Bhushan, Bihari, Deva, Padmakar, Alam, Ghananand and others. Religion, heroism, human love and praise of the king were some of the themes touched by these writers. We have discussed some of them in the other two chapters. In Bengal also there was a great development of the

Vaishnava literature and we had many writers like Krishnadas, Jayanand, Trilochan Das and Mukadaram. Women also participated in the literary activities and mention may be made of Gul Badan Begum (sister of Humayun), Nur Jahan (wife of Jahangir), Mumtaz Mahal (wife of Shahjahan), Jahanaera and Zeb-un- Nisa, sister and daughter of Aurangzeb respectively.

Literary activities did not cease with the death of Aurangzeb but the cultural decay is apparent from the character of the literature now produced. It was erotic, devoted to praise of passion and female forms and dress. Style had also degenerated.

We thus come to an end of our brief survey of the literary activities of the period. The survey shows the development of Persian and vernacular literatures and the birth of Urdu. It also shows that the kings extended their patronage profusely to this activity. It may be remarked that during the Mughal period Urdu developed more in the Deccan than in Hindustan where its development began only in the reign of Aurangzeb. Finally a tendency in Persian literature must be pointed out. The social content of the literature is meagre. Life is unattractive for them unless it is played out in the courts. At most they will extend their inspiration to the cities and some religious themes. They are neither interested in the life of the Hindus nor even in the life of the Muslim masses. We have a static society and a stereotyped narration of that Society. Themes are often taken from outside India. It may well be that such a literature was a necessary outcome of the medieval feudalism and aristocratic life. Finally the contribution of the Mohammedans in the evolution of historical writing and prose-narration cannot be over emphasised. We shall end this chapter by describing the development of fine arts during this period. We shall take for study dancing and music, architecture, painting and some crafts under this section.

Dancing and Music

Dancing of the traditional type continued in this period both in the north and in the south. We had now the evolution of a new type of dance, namely, the Kathak. But the art was not pursued purely from an aesthetic point of view. We had the corruption of the art on account of the vogue of 'the dancing girl', the courtesan. The kings and the Rajas either encouraged dissolute practices or were indifferent and so the art became a prisoner in the hands of the professional pimp and the courtier. This was the case both in the reigns of the Sultans and the Moghuls.

But in music India reached a noon-day splendour during this period. The orthodox Muslims had no love lost for this art but contact with Iran and development of Sufism with its religious fervour expressing itself in dance and music made the Muslims appreciate music. In India contact with the music-loving Hindus further stimulated the growth of music among the Indian Mussalmans.

The Sultans had a regular company of musicians and instrumental performers. Khusrao was both a singer and a dancer. We have a story which shows the love of the Sultan Alauddin for music. It is said that the Sultan found the South more advanced than the north in music and singers both male and female were taken away to Delhi. The greatest singer Gopal Nayak was taken away, it is said, to Delhi and a musical combat took place which is thus related by Capt. Williard in his Treatise on the music of Hindustan, 'It is related that when Gopal visited the court of Delhi he sang that species of composition called Gita, the beauty of which style enunciated by the powerful and harmonious voice of so able a performer could not meet with competition. At this the Monarch caused Umeer Khusro to remain under the throne, whence he could hear the musician unknown to him. The later endeavoured to remember the style and on a subsequent day sang Khayal and Turana in imitation of it which surprised Gopal and fraudulently deprived him of a portion of his due honour'. Khusrao also introduced Sitar and Tabla besides 'quavali' mode of singing as well as several 'ragas' like Zilaph, Sazagiri and Sarparda. Prince Bogra Khan, son of Balban founded a dramatic society whose members included musicians also. Jalal-ud-din Firoz Khilji was a musician and also used to dance with his companions. Firoz Tughluq was also a patron of music. In the provinces also the art was highly appreciated and we have Hussain Shah Sharqi of Jaunpur, who is said to have invented 'Khayal'.

Further we have the Gwalior school of music dating from the time of Raja Man Singh (1486-1518) whose wife is also said to have been a musician. The Raja also called conference of musicians, it is said, to properly classify Indian music. During his reign lived the famous Nayak Bakhshu whose melodies are only second to those of Tansen. Raja Man Singh is supposed to be the author of the 'Dhrupad' style of music. Other musicians of the period were Baijoo, Bhonoo, Pandvee, and Lohung. Rag Darpan a book on music was translated into Persian from a Hindi book on music compiled by order of Man Singh. Thus music flourished in the age of the Sultanate and there was interaction between the Muslim and the Hindu music producing fresh melodies.

The Moghuls were also patrons of music and in their reigns it attained great perfection. Babar was well-versed in it and one of the classes of society mentioned by Humayun was Ahl-i-murad, consisting of musicians and dancers. The reign of Akbar was the focal point for this art also. Akbar took special delight in music and song, and had a considerable knowledge of the technicalities of those arts. In 1562 he asked Raja Ram Chand of Rewa to send to his court Tansen who was universally recognised as the premier musician of the age. Tansen or Tanna Misra was the son of a Hindu and his father is said to have left him to a Muslim saint who is said to have kissed him blessed and thus polluted him. He, therefore, became Muslim. His Guru was the Saint Haridas Swami. In Akbar's court there were more than thirty musicians arranged in seven divisions one for each day of the week. There was Baz Bahadur of Malwa, a singer without a rival. Akbar was taught Hindi vocalisation by Lal Kalwant or Madan Lal and Baiju Bawra. Among Persian and Indian musicians mention may be made of Ram Das, Subhan Khan, Daud Dhari and Mian Nanak. At this time in Khandesh we had Pundarika Vitthala Karnataki who is said to have written books on Indian music. There were a number of instrumental performers like Ustad Dost Mohammad, Bahram Quil and Qasim. Abdur Rahim Khankhana was a liberal patron and is said to have given Rs. 100,000 to Haridas and Ramdas for their musical performance. In Jahangir's reign we had Jahangir Dad, Khumam, Dad Makhan and Chhatar Khan.

Shahjahan also patronised music and had notable singers like Ramdas, Mahapattar, Lal Khan, Gun Samudra and Jagannath. Sukh Dev was a master player on 'Rubab' (guitar), and Sur Sen on the 'bin' (Zither). He also used to hear daily songs from women. In Aurangzeb's time music was banned and the musicians celebrated the event by taking a funeral procession of music. In later reigns, however, there was a revival and we had numerous families (gharanas) or schools of music. During this period instrumental music was also cultivated and new instruments like the Sitar, Tabla and Rabab were introduced. The instruments were of four types, namely, stringed, those played with a bow, drum-like instruments and wind instruments. Of the first the most representative were Vina, Sitar, Tambura and Rabab the second was represented by Sarangi, Dilruba and Mayuri, the third consisted among others, of Pakhwaz, Tabla, Naqqara, Dholak and Mridanga; and the fourth had such types as the Bina and the Bansuri. Cultivation of music brought the two communities together and fostered national unity.

Architecture

We may now study the architecture of the period. It is not proposed to discuss the designs and characteristics of the various buildings for they have been discussed in the following chapter. Here certain general questions are touched upon. In the first place what is the relationship between the Muslim art and the Hindu art and how the two have been assimilated. This question is also touched upon in the next chapter. We shall give opinions of certain authorities on this question. 'The essential features of their own tradition, inherited from ninth century Baghdad included the dome, painted arch and minar or tower these in India, fused with the already motifs of the same character. The peculiarities of the Moghul architecture, so far as they are foreign, originated (as in the analogous case of Moghul painting) in Samarqand'.* It is more noteworthy that the form of the dome (of the Taj) is characteristically Indian,

* A.K. Coomarasvami, *The Art and Crafts of India and Ceylon*, pp. 215-218.

the lineal descendant folder Dravidian and Buddhist types, while the ground plan is that of the old Hindu panch-ratna-one, central dome with four small cupolas. Mr. Havell utters no paradox when he says that the science of Muhammadan art in India as well as the inspiration of it, came from the Hindu Shilpashastras'.* The Moslem architecture of India, like the Muhammadan style in other countries is primarily derived from the ancient vaulted architecture of Mesopotamia, as modified by later developments under the Sassanids, and is therefore, closely related to the style in vogue at Baghdad in the days of the Abbassid Khalifas'.** The most important factors Common to both forms of architecture (Hindu and Muslim), specially in respect of mosques and temples, were that to both the styles ornamental decoration was very vital and that the open court was in many cases surrounded by colonnades. But the contrast was equally striking; the prayer-chamber of the mosque was spacious, whereas the shrine of the temple was comparatively small, the mosque was wide and open, whereas the temple was dark and rather closed; and the Muslim style of construction was based on arches, vaults and domes, whereas the Hindu was based on columns, architraves and pyramidal towers or slender spires'.*** Finally we may quote the opinion of Dr. H. Goetz of Leyden University, Hollands whose opinions on the subject were expressed before the Allahabad University students in a lecture in 1942. His conclusions seem to clinch the issue. 'The idea of a decline of Hindu art during the Muslim period is not true. The creative spirit of India assimilated the new inspiration brought by the contact with Islam, incorporated them into the Indian tradition and gave them back, enriched to the Muslim world. The presence of this living Hindu tradition reacted on Muslim art in two ways. One was a mixture of formal elements which was prepared by the system of Hindu tradition because of its application to Mohammedan purposes in Bengal and Gujarat of the fifteenth century and its new crystallisation into a natural style among the Rajputs of the 16th century. The other was the slow transformation of the constructive

* *Ibid*, p. 221.

** Edwards and Garret, *Moghul Rule in India*, p. 302

*** *Archaeology in India*, Government of India Publication, p. 109.

Mohammedan architecture into the sculptural Hindu conception as in the Deccan of the sixteenth century and then in the northern India of the eighteenth century'. The same writer points out that the Rajput architecture originated in the Jahangiri Mahal. Its central hall, its square pillars, bracket capitals and rows of small arches are built according to the Hindu designs. Fergussan justly observed that it would hardly be out of place at Chitor or Gwalior. Other buildings, reminding us of the Hindu designs are the Diwan-i-Am, the Panch Mahal, Akbar's Mausoleum at Sikandara, tomb of Itimad-ud-daulah at Agra and Jodha Bai's palace at Fatehpur-Sikri. Certain other examples may be cited to show that the Mughal style was more sumptuous and decorative than the styles that preceded it and its delicacy and ornamentation furnish a striking contrast to the massiveness and simplicity of the art of pre-Mughal days. For instance the dome of the tomb of Humayun with an arched alcove, the interior arrangements and the complex of rooms in the tomb were foreign to the pre-Moghul style. The Agra Fort of Akbar and the buildings in Fatehpur-Sikri display originality and spontaneity of a new style. The minarets of Akbar's mausoleum were also foreign to the pre-Moghul style. In Shahjahan's reign we have the introduction of a new style of building - art of exceptional elegance and splendour. The robust and exuberant style of Akbar gives way to an elegant and effeminate style while the red sandstone is replaced by the white marble. The arch became multifoil, usually containing nine cusps, so that arcades of engrailed arches came to be the order of the day. His dome is bulbous but high-drummed and constricted at its neck involving the building of double-doming. His pillars have foliated bases, tapering shafts and vaulted capitals and the introduction of double columns add much to the grace of the buildings. An artistic treatment of marble inlaid with semiprecious stones exquisitely blended in colour to represent the petals and tendrils of flowers is a characteristic feature of his decorative art. All these features were perfectly blended in the Taj. Thus, it can be safely asserted that in design, in the use of materials, in delicacy and grace, in ornamentation and carving the Moghul buildings were radically different from those erected by the Sultans and had more of the Persian and the Hindu elements in them than the former buildings. Some European influence may also be traced specially in the buildings of later Moghuls. The salient features of Moghul architecture were the pronounced dome, the slender turrets at the corners, the palace halls supported on pillars and the Indo-Saracenic gate.

Painting

The art of painting did not receive the attention and encouragement which the other arts did at the hands of the early Muslim kings of India. This was mainly because it was tabooed on account of its close association with idolatry. Hindus embracing Islam spread it and the Moghuls brought it from Persia. We have, however, Sultan Jalal-ud-din Firoz Khilji embellishing his Muizzi castle with paintings.

Babar brought choicest specimen from the library of his ancestors—Timurids— and was also inspired by Bihzad and his school in Persia. This art was mainly manly and vigorous scenes of battle, sieges and gladiatorial combats predominated. There were romantic and mystical themes also. Humayun brought from Persia two master-painters of the Neo-Persian School. In Akbar's time there was greater advance. He used to say, 'It seems to me that a painter has, as it were, peculiar means of recognising God; for he, in painting anything that has life is ultimately convinced that he cannot bestow individuality on his creation and is thus forced to think of God, the giver of life'. He founded and endowed a State Gallery where painters came from far and wide to emulate one another. The mural decorations of Fatehpur-Sikri are splendid specimen of the art of painting. Jahangir was the Prince of Artists and a most fastidious critic of art.

Moghul painting consists almost entirely of book illustrations and portfolio pictures, usually called miniatures. It is a courtly and aristocratic art, realistic and romantic, almost wholly secular, and quite remote from folk-sentiment. It is profoundly interested in individual character, and the splendid ceremonial of court life. Its keynote, accordingly, is portraiture, actual likeness, verisimilitude.

The elements in the painting were derived from Bukhara,

Samarquand and China. Some Persian and European elements also entered. It has, however, an individuality of its own and also takes some features of the Rajput art, for instance, the moonlit terrace is fundamentally Rajput. Moghul painting was never deeply rooted in the soil but rather a purely artificial product of the court and the connoisseurs, a fact which fully accounts for its rapid decline after Shahjahan. The paintings have, however, a historical value preserving to us many scenes of the period.*

Minor Crafts

We may now describe some of the minor arts and crafts. There was the art of illuminating books with gold borders and bindings were also adorned with gold. Books were also illustrated with drawings and pictures. There were also the art of calligraphy, beautiful writings in book, in coinage and on buildings. Nasir-ud-din, Mohammad Tughlaq and Aurangzeb possessed this skill in a very high degree. Abul Fazl speaks of eight modes of calligraphy being in vogue in Akbar's times.

Decorative relief carving reached a high pitch of excellence in the reigns of Akbar, Jahangir and Shahjahan. The carving consisted of calligraphic ornamentation, representation of clouds, plants, flowers, butterflies, insects and vase designs.

Traceries, Lattice-work, screen-work, inlay decoration and mosaics attained great perfection during this period. The style 'pietro dura' (inlay of precious stones) now developed after Akbar. There was also the work in enamelled or glazed tiles. The arts of lapidary and the jeweller benefited from the love of ostentation cultivated by the Moghuls. The Koh-i-nur and the Peacock Throne are symbols of the age of magnificence. The art of dress, with embroidery and chicken work as examples, the culinary art and lastly gardening also attained the height of perfection. Gardens according to Havell were the greatest contribution of the Moghuls to Indian art. Many of the gardens were designed as pleasance to accommodate the Imperial Court on its frequent progresses through the country. Many of the phases of paintings and gardening are discussed in the other

---

* Please also see the next chapter.

chapters on the medieval period and we, therefore, end our description of Muslim fine arts.

Our discussion shows that the Muslim contribution to our culture was second to none in the medieval period. The Mussalmans were great builders, creators of new melodies in music, makers of new rhythms in dance, moulders of new styles in literature, inheritors of a religious tradition which blossomed into Indian Sufism, originators of new styles of painting and reconciliation of rival faiths. It is particularly from contemplation of the architectural and artistic legacies of the Moghul age that we receive the most vivid impression of the rulers of the period. Of course they had their faults and shortcomings and particularly they ignored the question of economic welfare of the masses but this partial or biased outlook was the result of the conventional age when the minds of men worked in traditional and set grooves and an integral outlook was foreign to the spirit of the times. We should, however, agree with the dictum of a French lady quoted by Edwardes and Garret : 'Depend upon it, Sir, God thinks twice before damning a man of that quality'.

We shall end this chapter by certain observations as to why the Hindu-Muslim cultural reconciliation could not be perfectly achieved. In the first place, the religion of the two could not be reconciled during this period. Again and again we have the eruption of religious fanaticism during this period and the cultural synthesis is given a shock which takes decades to die down. Secondly, the social practices of the two faiths clashed. The Hindus refused either to dine or marry with the Muslims. The Muslims on their part stuck to many things foreign to India. If like the Chinese they had been Indian in everything but religion probably a reconciliation might have taken place.

Also the converts to Islam generally belonged to the have nots and they took with them a hatred towards the Hindu aristocracy which remained like a perpetual ulcer on the Indian body-politic. Further, the Muslims could not reconcile themselves to the idol-worshippers. The caste-system of the Hindus was a perpetual deterrent to social solidarity. The

Mussalmans could not also forget that they were conquerors and looked down upon the Hindus. Thus a wide gulf existed between the two communities and it was widened whenever political partisanship entered the field. In our own days the British policy of divide and rule fanned the embers of discord which were there beneath the soil and the Muslim aristocracy in particular exploited the situation to create Pakistan.

What is the remedy ? We have generally solutions which may be called external solutions. Cultural assimilation, adoption of common names and language and customs, mingling in each other's joys and sorrows, in fairs and festivals, inter-dining and inter-marriages and such like are the remedies that are proposed. The Mussalmans are asked to look upon Indian history of the ancient period as their own and shed all extraterritorial patriotism or inclinations. But some or all of these solutions have been tried. We had Akbar's attempts in this direction. Many Indian Mussalmans retain their Hindu names and customs and in the villages we had common fairs and festivals. Inter-dining has become a fashion among the educated and civil marriages are permissible. But the reconciliation did not take place. The fact is that the solution should be attempted on psychological lines or spiritual lines if it is to be a success. External differences do not matter if the souls are attuned in common love of God. Only when there is an integration of the values of life and humanity with those of mystic realisation and spiritual self-perfection, can there be a true reconciliation. All other solutions are temporary and will fail.

14

AN ATTEMPT AT HINDU-MUSLIM SYNTHESIS

IT HAS BEEN shown in the previous chapters that Hinduism in all its cultural aspects had been consolidated and synthesized by the end of the reign of Harsh. The new Hinduism that developed during the later period had its essential moorings in the ancient past and the various reformers only claimed to reinterpret the Vedas, the Upanishads and the Epics. It has also been remarked that on account of Sankara's philosophy of Maya (illusion) a certain other worldly outlook had permeated the masses, fatalism had flowered, spirit and matter had been sundered and with the rise of Bhakti there was a corresponding decline in the progressive development of all aspects of life which was so characteristic of the ancient Mauryan and the Gupta civilisations. The growth of spirituality in ancient India had not meant the sacrifice of the demands of life. World and spirit both belonged to Brahman. The age which gave birth to the Upanishads, the Epics and the Gita also witnessed the flowering of Indian genius in literature, arts and other aspects of life. We even went abroad on cultural missions to various parts of Asia and the surrounding seas and islands, though our missions were never the prototype of modern imperialist adventures.

But during the middle ages gradually we lost sight of this synthesis of life and soul, spirit and matter. Asceticism grew up, Bhakti was evolved, ritualism was perfected, caste-rigidity became pronounced, adventures abroad were banned, we lost touch with the developments in the outside world, life change from creative to regulative, daring speculation gave place to conservatism, while our enjoyment of security from foreign attacks from the sixth century to the eleventh century bred an easy acceptance of life and made us an easy prey to the invaders who came from the North-West.

Culturally, therefore, as compared to the ancient period the medieval period does not give us a profound and synthetic view of life. But that is not to say that this period gives us nothing new or significant in the field of culture. Specifically this period witnessed the compact and the impact of two cultures, the Hindu and the Islamic and as a result a new pattern was evolved to which we have so far paid scant attention. Our history books specially those written by the Britishers have fostered the belief that sabre-rattling, blood-shed and unmitigated tyranny were the hall marks of the bloody rulers who ruled over India from the thirteenth century onward. But the historical perspective is now changing, and a more integral conception of Medieval Indian history has emerged.

It is, therefore, now agreed that the medieval period witnessed a great interaction between the Hindu and the Islamic cultures.

There is, however, a variety of opinion among scholars about the degree of this influence or interaction, some maintaining that Hinduism was fundamentally affected by the new culture, while others maintain that Hinduism did not take much from Islam but instead put its own stamp upon Islam in India. To the first school belong men like Dr. Tarachand who observes that 'not only did Hindu religion, Hindu art, Hindu literature and Hindu Science absorb Muslim elements, but the very spirit of Hindu culture and the very stuff of Hindu mind were also altered'.* Others maintain that medieval Hindu India, despite her political weakness, was culturally so full of vitality that, to use the great Bengal saint Chaitanya's simile she was like the tree which gives shade even to him who cuts its boughs or in the words of E.B. Havell, 'Islam seized her political capitals,

* Dr. Tarachand, *Influence of Islam on Indian Culture*, p. 137.

controlled her military forces, and appropriated her revenues, but India retained what she had lost on the battle-field'.

The truth is that the synthesis between the two cultures was never whole-hearted, that Hinduism in its deep foundations was not transformed by the Islamic culture, that the effects of the two were more on the externals of life rather than on the spirit or soul of India and that before Akbar the interaction was largely unconscious or subconscious, in that it was confined mostly to cities and the upper classes and that Hinduism had greater effect upon Islam in India than the latter had upon the former.

Still the truth of great interchange or interaction or attempts at synthesis cannot be denied. The reasons why the Muslim rulers could not always be in a war-like mood are quite easy to understand. In the first place the Muslim rulers with their limited means in men and materials could never subjugate permanently the vast country of India. Willy-nilly, they had to seek the consent of the people if they wanted peace and order in their realms. Again psychologically bellicosity is not a constant quality of man's mind. The kings had to revert to the pursuit of arts of peaceful life after a brief indulgence in the gray activities of life. Islam in India was not spread by the sword so much as by peaceful persuasion and influence of her saints and thinkers. Further, the employment of the Hindus was a necessity of their rule. When Qutb-ud-din Aibak decided to stay in Hindustan, he had no other choice but to retain the Hindu staff which was familiar with the civil administration, far, without it all government including the collection of revenue would have fallen into utter chaos. Their buildings were erected by the Hindus, their coins were struck by the Hindu gold-smiths, Brahman legists advised the king on the administration of Hindu law and Brahmin astronomers helped in the performance of their general functions. Thus, the structure of economic life in the country forced even the most zealous and fanatical of kings to moderate the policy of persecution of the Hindus.

Agriculture and commerce continued to be in the hands of the Hindus. In administration the lower ranks of the bureaucracy had to be the Hindus. Besides the masses converted to Islam, for the most part, retained their old customs and thus in all these ways Hinduism forced the Muslim rulers consciously or unconsciously to become pro-Hindu, to a more or less extent. The Hindus also must have felt the loss of their freedom. In their searchings of heart and mind they must have been led to seek for the good points in Islam, adopting them for their own benefits. For all these reasons a fusion or synthesis of the two cultures began in the medieval period which might have been possibly completed but for the advent of the Europeans in India. It is, therefore, wrong to emphasis the record of difference and conflict between the Hindus and the Muslims in this period while forgetting the story of fusion or synthesis. Besides it is doubtful if any of the Muslim invasions was a purely religious invasion undertaken by religious fanatics. Like all conquests they were actuated by temporal and material motives rather than by religious zeal. These Muslim invaders had often to fight the Muslims who had settled in India. In India, again, many independent local Muslim kingdoms had grown up and they were fighting not only against themselves but also against the central Muslim authority at Delhi. The Hindus enlisted on both the sides. Again, when Babar fought Rana Sanga of Mewar the latter was assisted by Hassan Khan of Mewati and Sultan Mahamud Lodi.

Of the 35 monarchs who sat on the throne between 1193 and 1526 no less than 19 or a majority were killed or assassinated not by the Hindus but by the Mussalmans. If in his wars Aurangzeb employed Hindu generals, his Hindu rival Shivaji also had in his employ quite a number of Muslim military officials. Some of them held important positions, like the General Siddi Hullal and Nur Khan. In his navy there were three Muslim Admirats—Siddi Sambat, Siddi Hasri and Daulat Khan. Thus all through the six hundred years of Indo-Muslim rule in India, Muslims fought Muslims more than they fought Hindus and not that they were constantly engaged in oppressing and persecuting the majority of the country with which they had cast their lot. They even went further, evolved a national state of India, encouraged art and literature and established a spirit of toleration at a time when Europe was disfigured by the wars of religion.

It is usual to trace the effects between the two cultures from the establishment of the so-called slave Dynasty in India but the intercourse between the two, the Islamic peoples, and the Hindus, had begun even earlier. Reference has been made to the settlement of the Arabian traders in Malahar, Umar, the Khalifa, was told by an Arab sailor that 'India's rivers are pearls, her mountains rubies, her trees perfumes'. People had asked Omar to permit an invasion of India but he refused. Early in the ninth century we find that the last of the Cheraman Perumal Kings of Malabar became a convert to Islam. Mosques were built in his kingdom and the Travancore ruler used to say in his oath 'I will keep this sword until the uncle who has gone to Mecca returns', thus recalling the fact that a certain Travancore ruler had gone to Mecca. The Zamorin of Malabar became a patron of the Arab traders. In Gujarat also the Arabs built mosques and received protection from the King. In Sind after the first flush of invasion, the Hindus were left to command the administration and worship freely in their own manner. The Arab geographer Astakhari visiting Sind in the middle of the tenth century observed that in their social intercourse the Hindus and the Muslims were tending towards a harmony of their manners and customs.

The Abbasid Court of Baghdad was famous for its patronage of learning and had invited Hindu scholars, appreciating highly their incomparable gifts in medicine and astronomy. Works on medicine, philosophy, religion and astronomy were translated into Arabic and Persian languages. Al-Beruni's visit to India is a notable event in the history of Indo-Muslim friendship in the world of learning. Al-Beruni was a contemporary of Mahmud. He wrote a history of India in which he described the social and religious life of the country. He wrote that, 'the Hindus believe with regard to God that He is one, eternal, without beginning and, acting by free will, almighty, all-wise, living, giving life, ruling, preserving, One Who in His sovereignty is unique, beyond all likeness and unlikeness, and that does not resemble anything nor does anything resemble Him'. He praised the Hinaus and also pointed out their defects, their conceit and self sufficiency and thought that if they travelled abroad they would not be so norrow-minded. At this time many Muslim Saints or Sufis also visited India and preached their teachings. Their piety, liberality and religious sobriety had its effects and brought many converts. They influenced Hindu philosophy and were influenced by it. The earliest of the Sufis to settle in India was probably Al-Hujwiri who died in 1072. Thus through the Arabs and through the Sufis Indian philosophy and religious thought percolated to many parts of Asia. India's contact with the outside world was re-established. Thus the story of India's contact with the Islamic culture is very old but its secure foundations and development may be traced only after the establishment of the Indo-Muslim kingdoms in India. For our convenience we may study this cultural contact under the categories of religion, arts, society, literature and education, describing first the progress made in the so-called Sultanate period and then in the Moghul period.

Religion

In the sphere of religion the first fruits of the cultural contact are to be found in the religious poetry of Kabir. Kabir was the disciple of Ramananda who has been called the bridge between the Bhakti movement of the South and the North. 'There is still some uncertainty about the time of Ramananda but he may be said to have lived in the fourteenth century. He belonged at first to the Ramanuja sect of Vaishnavism. But after coming into contact with learned Mussalmans in Banaras he modified the system substituting the worship of Rama for Vishnu and opening the doors of his faith to all classes and castes, even the Muslims could join his school of Bhakti. Restrictions about inter-dining were modified. His teachings gave rise to two schools, the conservative and the progressive. The latter tried to create a creed acceptable to both the Muslims and the Hindus. Of this school Kabir was the most shining example in the fifteenth century. His life is shrouded in mystery. Nothing is certain about the date of his birth and death. It is said that he was the son of a Brahmin widow who in order to hide her shame left him on the side of a tank in Banaras. A Muslim weaver found him and brought him up.

The religious atmosphere of Banaras deeply affected him. Ramanand became his Guru and initiated him into the knowledge of Hindu philosophy and religion. Tradition speaks of Kabir associating with all sorts of religious ascetics and saints of all classes. Kabir was not a learned man in the accepted sense.

After some time he settled in Banaras but his independent mode of thought aroused the hostility of Hindu and Islamic preachers and he was exiled, later we find him returning to Banaras. He led a married life and did not believe in asceticism. He practised the art of weaving. He died at Maghar which is on the railway line between Basti and Gorakhpur. His body was claimed both by the Hindus and the Muslims, thus showing the breadth of his vision. What was Kabir's message ? He refused to bow down to the Hindu distinctions of caste or recognise the ritualism of Brahmanism. To him Bhakti or worship of God was the supreme thing. He rejected all those features of Hinduism and Islam which militated against the spirit of love and brotherhood that he wanted his disciples to develop. He took his ideas from both the religions and his language also was a mixture of Sanskrit, Persian, forms of vernacular like Rekhta and Bhasha. He condemned formalism and placed the greatest value upon the inwardness of religion, upon being true to the soul within, to God within rather than being true to ritualism and external mode of worship. He said 'Be truthful, be natural. Truth alone is natural. Seek this truth within your own heart, for there is no truth in the external religious observances; neither in the sects nor in the holy vows, neither in religious garb nor in pilgrimages. Truth resides within the heart and is revealed in love, in strength, in compassion. Conquer hatred and extend your love to all mankind, for God resides in all. The difference among faiths is only due to difference in names, everywhere there is yearning for the same God. Why do the Hindus and Mohammedans quarrel for nothing? Life is transitory, do not waste your time, but take refuge in God', Kabir did not favour useless mortifications of flesh. He was both a great poet and a great singer. His influence permeated through all the religious and intellectual movements of Medieval India. He calls God by various names but his favorites name is Sahib. To quote some of his verses. 'Where dost thou seek me, O slave. I am indeed near thee, I am not in the temple, nor in the mosque, neither in Ka'ba, nor Kailas. If thou art a true seeker I shall meet thee immediately in a moment's search, says Kabir, hear, ye, Sadhus, He is in the breath of breaths'.

Thus Kabir's was the first attempt to reconcile the two religions of Hinduism and Islam. His influence spread far and wide and many saints arose all over India inculcating the same teachings in various garbs, languages and forms of thought. It may be here remarked that Sufism provided many elements in the teachings of Kabir and this movement of Sufism was, therefore, a factor in the new synthesis that was being attempted. A few remarks about Sufism are called for 'Sufi mysticism has its roots in Mohammed's experience and teaching but the leading elements of the system came from two external sources. The first was Neoplatonism which came into Islam through Greek philosophy and Gnosticism. The other source was Indian thought which flowed through Buddhism and Vedantism'. The Sufi conception of God tends to be immanental rather than transcendental. He works everywhere but especially in the human heart. Many Sufis visualise a state of bliss called Fana, which resembles Hindu belief very closely. In order to reach illumination and union with God (called a Haqa) it is necessary to walk the paths, a way of life divided into stages. Such a life can be lived according to some on ascetic basis, according to others by the householder earning his daily bread. The teacher (Shaikh, Pir or Murshid) has to be obeyed implicitly. The details of Sufi practice resemble those of our yoga, the purpose being to realise that God is the only reality. To the Sufis all religions are of equal value.

The influence of Kabir is traceable into many sects which arose after him, a list of 11 such is given by Farquhar in his book, The Religious Quest of India (p. 334). The common features of these sects are (1) Worship of God alone, idolatry being prohibited. (2) Men of a caste are allowed to come into the fold. (3) Following is attracted both from the Hindus and the Muslims. (4) Great stress is laid on the value of the Guru. (5) The literature is in vernacular verse. We may mention so specially two saints who put into practice the teachings of Kabir, namely, Dadu and Nanak. Dadu was born in 1544 A.D. in the village of Narana or Narayana in Rajputana. He wanted to unite all the divergent faiths in one bond of love and comradeship and founded the Parabrahma Sampradaya for this purpose. He believed not in the authority of scriptures but in that of self realisation. To attain this realisation we must purify ourselves of all sense of the ego, and surrender our lives entirely to God. His disciples made a collection of the devotional writings of all the different sects calculated to help men in their striving towards God. His prayers and poems were full of love and devotion towards God.

Nanak, the founder of Sikhism, was born in 1469 A.D., in the village of Talwandi, in the Tehsil of Sharkpur, in the district of Gujranwala. He was a Bedi Khatri by caste and his father was an accountant of a zamindar. He learnt Hindi, Sanskrit and Persian. He had been married but at the age of thirty renounced life and became a faqir or Sanyasi. It is said that he wandered not only throughout India but also went to Ceylon, Persia and Arabia gathering mystical or spiritual experience. Like Kabir, there was a dispute over the disposal of his body also and we find both the Muslims and the Hindus erecting memorials for him.

His mission was to unite the Hindus and the Muslims. He taught that 'there is one God in the world and no other, and that Nanak the Caliph (or son) of God speaks the truth'. His God is exalted above all. But he is within all as well. Nanak does not worry about ritualism or God with forms or idolatry. 'The Hindu and Muslim saints are the diwans in attendance upon the preserver (parvardigar), the great Pirs are magistrates (Siqdar) and collector (Karoris), the angels are accountants and treasurers (botedars). The gentleman trooper (ahadi) Izra'il binds and arrests, and degrades the ignorant and beastly men'. He decries the superstitions and formalism of all whether

Muslim or Hindu.

'Hadst though the eighteen puranas with thee,
Couldst thou recite the four Vedas
Didst thou bathe on holy days and give alms according to men's castes,
Didst thou fast and perform religious ceremonies day and night.
Like a qazi, a mulla, or a Shaikh,
A jogi, a Jangam, didst thou wear an ochre colored dress,
or didst thou perform the duties of a householder.
Without knowing God, Death would bind and take all men away'.

To the Mussalman he says

'Make Kindness thy mosque
Sincerity thy prayer Carpet.
What is just and lawful by Qoran.
This modesty thy circumcision.
Civility thy fasting, so shalt
Thou be a Mussalman'.

Nanak always harps upon two themes - praise of virtue and condemnation of vice. The stern ethical tone and vigorous puritanism of his teachings stamped themselves upon his followers who proved a tough nut for Aurangzeb to crack but it is an irony of fate that Sikhism was at war with Aurangzeb, the protagonist of Islam which was also loved by Nanak, the founder of Sikhism.

Another contemporary of Kabir was Raidas, a worker in leather, chamar. He was born in Banaras. Mirabai is said to have been devoted to him. His hymns breathe a spirit of humility and self surrender. 'Hari is in all and all is in Hari', observed he. Give up all egoism and all ritualism, betake to the devotion of one only, by losing the self in Him, as the river loses itself in the sea', were his teachings. His disciple Mirabai is very famous in the devotional religious history of India. He became the wife of the heir apparent of Mewar who was the son of the great Kumbha Rana. She was ungraciously treated by her brother-in-law and left Chittor, becoming a disciple of Raidas. Her Radha Krishna lyrics in Brijbhasha are very famous.

There are numerous songs in Gujarati attributed to her. She lived in the second half of the fifteenth century.

In Bengal also many syncretic cults and practices arose as a result of the interaction of Hinduism and Islam. The Hindus offered sweets at Muslim shrines, consulted the Quran, celebrated Muslim feasts and the Mussalmans responded with similar acts. But out of this close comradeship grew the worship of common God, adored by Hindus and Mussalmans alike, namely Satya Pir. The Emperor Hussain Shah of Gauda is supposed to be the originator of the cult. But the greatest influence of this synthesis is to be found upon the movement inaugurated by Chaitanya. He was born of Brahmin parents at Nadia in 1485 A.D. He set up as a teacher at the age of twenty. But later he renounced this life and become a wanderer over the whole country. The essence of his teachings is adoration of Krishna, and serving his Guru. All religious systems based on caste are meaningless. Worship consisted in love and devotion, song and dance, producing a state of ecstasy in which his presence was realised. He became to his followers Shri Gauranga, the supreme God-head, Hari of Krishna of the Bhagavad and like him he performed Rasa-Lila, the highest stage of ecstatic joy. Three of his great disciples were Muslims. He taught that universal love is the keynote of world-religion. Through his example he showed how God could be realised by the individual. He was thus one of the makers of great synthesis which was worked out in medieval period.

In Maharashtra also the Bhakti movement in this synthetical form was spreading. There the Bhakti movement began with Jnaneshwar whose commentary on the Gita is very famous, the commentary being completed in 1290 A.D. But the first great name in the long line of Maharashtrian saints who rose above ceremonies and formalism like Namdev, born according to tradition in 1270 A.D. Namdev was averse to idol-worship. Says he, 'Vows, fasts and austerities are not all necessary nor is it necessary for you to go on a pilgrimage. Be you watchful in your hearts and always sing the name of Hari'. His disciples included Muslims and members of depressed classes.

Another instrument in this religious synthesis was the

religious orders belonging to Sufi schools of thought. The Sufi saints were worshipped by both the Hindus and the Muslims and this led to a common religious outlook and common forms of worship. Their tombs have become places of pilgrimage for all sorts of devotees. The oldest of these Darwesh fraternities is the Chishti order which traces its descent to Abu Abdal Chishti who died in 966 A.D. In India it was introduced by Khwajah Muin-ud-Din Chishti who was born in Afghanistan in 1142 A.D. He came to India in 1192 A.D. and in 1195 went to Ajmer which he made his headquarters. He died there in 1195 A.D. His tomb in the famous Dargah of Khwajah Sahib at Ajmer is the centre of attraction for tens of thousands of Muslims and hundreds of the Hindus who annually visit the city on the occasion of the 'Urs' or festival which celebrates the anniversary of the death of the saint. The Chishti order counts many famous saints in India among whom is Nizam-ud-din Auliya born in 1238 A.D. and Shaikh Salim Chishti who died in 1572 A.D. and had exercised great influence upon the Moghul Emperors. Other famous orders of saints are those of the Suhrawardis, the Chattris and the Qadiris.

Besides these there are innumerable Pirs or Sadhus worshipped by the Hindus and the Muslims. There is Madari order founded by Shah Badi-ud-Din Quth-ul-Madar who is said to have exercised a Hindu demon, by the name of Makana Deo. His tomb in Makanpur in Kanpur district attracts thousands of Hindu and Muslim pilgrims. Thus owing to the Hindu practice of Guru-chela bhakti which was the heritage of the majority of the Muslims of India through their Hindu origin it became easy for saint-worship to become a fixed part of Muslim religious life. Islam may have repudiated image-worship but in its Indian environment it took to saint worship with all the paraphernalia of worship familiar to the Hindus and was thus greatly modified. Titus in his boak Indian Islam mentions many Hindu Muslim saints. One such saint is Ganga Pir, a Hindu convert to Islam. His devotees are to be found in many parts of Northern India.

Lal Beg is another saint worshipped by the sweepers. Then there is a following of a group of saints known as Panj Pir. There is Khwajah Khidr celebrated now by burning lamps (chiragh) and placing them on rafters at the fair.•

Provincial Development

It should be, however, made clear that the Muslim rulers of Delhi before Akbar made very little contribution to this synthesis in the religious sphere. It was mainly the work of saints, thinkers and mystics. Of course, there were a number of rulers in the provinces who showed great respect for the Hindu saints and religion and so the synthesis was worked more there than at the centre of Indo-Muslim empire. The provinces were those of Gujarat, Jaunpur, Malwa, Bengal and Bahmani Kingdom. Some instances are now given of Hindu-Muslim concord in the provinces.

Bengal became independent in 1345 A.D. In 1412, it is said, a Hindu Zamindar Raja Ganesh seized the throne in Bengal and his son ruled for nineteen years having become a convert to Islam under the name of Jalal-ud-din. He was accepted by his Muslim officers without demur and they had even told him that they were not concerned with his religion. The culture that spread now was essentially Hindu. The Muslim kings in Bengal patronised the Hindu saints and got Hindu religious poetry translated into Persian and Bengala. Further, under state patronage comman worship was evolved, the saint being named satyapir (the true saint) thus anticipating Akbar. Hussain Shah (date of accession 1493) of Bengal was most indefatigable in this work of Hindu-Muslim renaissance.

The province of Jaunpur became a centre of culture under the Sharki dynasty. According to Havell, 'The Muhammadan colleges of Jaunpur may, therefore, be said to have assisted in preparing the way for the great Vaishnava revival in the beginning of the sixteenth century'.

In the Bahmani Kingdom the Brahmans controlled the finances of the Mussalman kings. Firoz Shah (seated in 1397) extended his patronage even to the Hindus, married Hindu women from many parts of Deccan and tried to avoid religious fanaticism.

In the middle of the fifteenth century Gujarat and Malwa

played the most important part in the politics of India for the Sultanate had fallen upon evil days. Many of their Kings were Hindu converts. Leaving aside their wars with the Hindu or Muslim neighbourly rulers they kept alive the spirit of religious toleration. Similarly Kashmir under Zain-ul-Abdin kept us the traditions of religious toleration. Ibrahim Adil Shah of Bijapur was called Jagadguru by his Muslim subjects for his patronage of the Hindus in the state.

We have thus far traced the interaction of the Hindu and Islamic cultures in the field of religion upto the end of what is called the Sultanate period. It is clear from the above that slowly and imperceptibly a fusion or a synthesis was being evolved.

The rulers in Delhi may not have consciously directed or helped this movement but they cannot be said to have obstructed it. The religious synthesis led to the newer developments in Bhakti movement inspired by great saints like Kabir, Nanak, Rai Das, Dadudayal and Namdeva. But not only Hindus, Muslims also were affected in various ways. One interesting development of this interaction may be pointed out. During this period there began to develop the Punthi literature under the Muslims. Among the Hindus the epics and the Puranas provided great and inexhaustible materials to the story-teller. The Muslim story-teller was at a disadvantage for the element of myth and legend is negligible in pristine Islam. So if the Muslim history did not supply the Muslim story-teller with a mythology, it must be invented. If the Hindu could sing of Rama and Lakshman and their devotion to each other, the Muslim would retort with the deeds of Hanifa, a legendary brother of Hassan and Hussain Ali. He became a mythical hero combining the tales of Bhima and Arjun. The character of Amir Ummiya was invented to serve as the counterpart of Hanuman. These tales varied from province to province and the story-teller was often a historian of contemporary manners.

Various endowments and grants were made to the Hindu temples and religious shrines by the Muslim kings, specially in the provinces. The nucleus of the large Zamindari of the Mahant of Bodh Gaya was a grant made by Mohammad Shah.

Sher Shah granted wakfs to his Hindu subjects for the

encouragement of education. Sultan Zain-ul-Abdin of Kashmir used often to visit Amarnath and Sharda Devi's temple, and had built houses there for the comfort of pilgrims.

All these tendencies found their fruition in the reign of Akbar who may rightly be, therefore, regarded as the first great national monarch of India in the Medieval Period. He was almost the first great ruler to abolish all distinctions between the Hindus and Mussalmans, thus modifying the character of the Muslim state. Ray Choudhury in his book, the Din-i-Ilahi has traced the evolution of Akbar's religion, pointing out the influence of Central Asia, Persia, Indian religions, Christianity and Islam upon the development of Din-i-Ilahi. Akbar was the product of the age and not an accident. The evolution of his religion had a long ancestry in which India of the past provided a notable element. Choudhury also refers to the notable part played by Abul Fazl, Faizi, Birbal, Man Singh and Todar Mal in the evolution of the religious synthesis aimed at by Akbar. The Hindus were admitted into Ibadat Khana, the hall of worship for discussion. The books of the Hindus were translated. Faizi translated Yoga-Vashistha, Lilavati, Nala-Damayanti and Singhasana Battisi; Haji Ibrahim translated the Atharva Veda; the Ramayana and the Mahabharata were translated by a group of schalars; Hindu scholars like Madhu Saraswati, Narayan Misra, Damodar Bhatta, Ram Tirth and Aditya came to his court. Tansen, the great musician adorned his circle of nine gems. Stories are told about his connection with Tulsidas, Surdas, and Dadu. The very presence of the Hindu wives in Akbar's harem was responsible for the introduction of many Hindu customs into the Chagtai harem. To quote Choudhury, 'The road connecting the Mahal of Yodha Bai and the apartment of the Emperor was entirely separate and could not be used by others and she had in her Mahal a Tulsi plant, a place for Hom and Yog'.* Akbar's long and varied experience had proved to him that Hindu help was essential in the administration of the land of the Hindus. Akbar was not blind to the faults of the Hindus, the reforms he introduced

* Roy Choudhury, *The Din-i-Ilahi*, p. 143.

amongst the Hindu community sufficiently illustrate the breadth of his views, and the wisdom of his conception.

The Sufi creed of Din-i-Ilahi was promulgated by Akbar in the beginning of the year 1582. It has been called the 'Monument of Akbar's folly'. It was nothing of the kind. In a way it was the climax of the attempts at religious synthesis that had been going on in India since the advent of Islam. Others would call it a new order of Sufism within the fold of Islam. Akbar did not desire to found a new religion, they say.

Akbar in the inmost core of his being was a seeker, and his seeking deepened with age. Abul Fazl says that Akbar used often to pass the morning alone in meditation sitting on a large flat stone of an old building which lay near the palace in a lonely spot, with his head bent over his chest and gathering the bliss of the early hours. In matters of religion he had been following the footsteps of his grandfather Babar, who in his will to Humayun had asked him to be tolerant towards the people of Hindustan. Thus while Catholics were being murdered in England and Protestants in France, the Jews in Spain and Bruna being burnt at the stake in Italy. Akbar invited the representatives of all the religions in his empire to a conference, had their honour pledged to peace and issued edicts of toleration for every cult and creed. Akbar felt that the king should be the symbol of national unity, loyalty to whom would prepare and perfect the people's loyalty to harmony and unity and a concordant mutuality in the country. It was this conception that took shape in his mind and ripened into Din-i-Ilahi or the Divine Faith. It was an order whose members were required to be always ready to sacrifice all they had and all were for the padishah who was regarded as their sole protector. Thus, the Divine Faith which included the truths of various religions, assured that honour should be rendered to God, peace be given to the people and security to the Empire. But Akbar did not force his views upon his subjects and his Din-i-Ilahi remained confined to a very select circle. To Akbar's intuition the country was one, indivisible, and one people and even one race and he was daring enough to encourage racial intermingling, so that a new type of humanity might be produced by this fusion. Akbar caught the imagination of his Hindu subjects who used to hail him with the cry of 'Dillishwao va Jagadishwaro va' (the Lord of Delhi is the Lord of earth).

Akbar thus dreamt a great dream of a united India, united in faith and culture, in all the teeming diversity of a richly flowering national life. To quote the writer of The Vision of India, 'Akbar's was the greatness of vision, the largeness and nobility of the conception, the intrepidity of the first decisive formation. The kindliest of political dreamers, the mightiest of political architects, the most humane of legislators and administrators, Akbar stands unique in history. Neither Alexander nor Caesar, nor Napolean was endowed with such an amplitude and depth of humanity combined with such quiet strength and far seeing constructive genius'.* Din-i-Ilahi was thus the crowning expression of the Emperor's national idealism.

From Babar to Shahjahan this religious synthesis or spirit of toleration continued in its broad streams fertilising the religious field of India leading to peace and amity among the followers of all religions here. But suddenly Aurangzeb decided to break away from this tradition. He dealt sledge-hammer blows at the tradition of religious toleration. The effects of this have been far reaching.

The decrying of Akbar and the eulogy of Aurangzeb by the followers of Mr. Jinnah is an event of recent times and thus once again a feeling has been aroused that the medieval religious synthesis was not full-fledged or complete. To quote Sir Jadunath Sarkar 'The Indian Muslims have, throughout the succeeding centuries, retained the extra-Indian direction of their hearts. Their faces are still turned, in daily prayer, to a spot in Mecca before English education modernised India, their minds, their law-code, their administrative system, their favourite reading sought models from outside India, from Arabia and Syria, Persia and Egypt. All Muhammedans have the same

---

* *The Vision of India*, pp. 114-15.

sacred language, literature and arts, teachers, saints and shrines, throughout the world, instead of these being restricted to India, as is the case with the Hindus'.* Some people feel that the Muslims in India minus Pakistan must learn to regard India as their homes and Indian culture before the advent of Islam as part of their patrimony to which they must pay due homage while the Hindus should abolish distinctions and restrictions in dining, marriage and social customs and thus only a true synthesis will be evolved. We may now describe the synthesis that was attempted in the field of arts.

Arts

In the field of arts, architecture occupies a special place because it symbolised the united genius of the Hindus and Muslims most completely. In this sphere again the Sultanate period shows a well-defined development and a distinction from that later evolved under the Moghuls. How much precisely this Indo-Islamic art (sometimes called Indo-Saracenic) owned to India and how much to Islam, has been a moot point. There is the school of Havell with the pronounced views that the Islamic art in India is just a variation on the theme of the Hindu art while others treat the Indo-Muslim architecture as having been essentially derived from outside. In a vast country like India evidence can be adduced in support of both the schools. We may, therefore, conclude that the Indo-Muslim architecture was indebted to both the sources and the buildings erected show this, some leaning heavily towards the foreign motifs, others hardly distinguishable from the old Hindu art.

By the time Islam came to India, it had evolved well-developed types and designs in architecture having taken under contribution the developed arts of Greece, Rome, Spain, Northern Africa, Persia and Egypt. The Muslim rulers who established themselves in India were endowed with remarkable good taste and a natural talent for building. On account of their inborn artistry coupled with a natural catholicity of taste, they were quick to appreciate the talent and adaptability of the

* Jadunath Sarkar, *India through the Ages*, p. 41.

Indian craftsmen and to turn these qualities to account on their own buildings.

For it should be remembered that originally there was the greatest contrast between the Islamic and the Hindu religious architectures. The Hindu system of construction was trabeate, based on column and architrave; the Muslim was arcuate, based on arch and vault. The temple was crowned with slender spires or pyramidal towers, the mosque with expansive domes. Hinduism produced great sculptures and well-developed idols. The Muslims loved rigid simplicity and were idol-breakers. Nevertheless, there were certain common features which helped in evolving a common type. For example, there was the open court encompassed by chambers or colonnades while decorative element was adopted by both. The Muslims borrowed many features of the Hindu art. According to Marshall two of the most vital elements borrowed from us were the qualities of strength and grace. In no other country except India are strength and grace so superbly united and harmonised, further, the Islamic architecture in India varied according to local surroundings. In Delhi it was more pro-Muslim while in provinces like Jaunpur the local styles enjoyed greater ascendancy and specially in Bengal the rulers not only adopted the established fashion of building in brick, but adorned their structures with chiselled and moulded enrichments frankly imitated from the Hindu types. In Gujarat and Kashmir also the same imitation can be read in the prevailing architecture. The Muslims gave breadth and spaciousness to Indian buildings endowing them with new beauties of form and colour. Before their advent, concrete had been little used in India and mortar scarcely ever but now these were fitted into our system and thus space, arch and dome became new additions to the Indian art besides the minars and the minarets. In ornamentation the Muslims introduced the flowing arabesque or intricate geometric devices and sometimes supplemented them with the graceful lettering of his sacred texts and historic inscriptions. Stones of various hues supplied the element of colour. Later on a glistening surface of enamel was evolved to produce brilliant effects.

Further, Hindu ornament invaded the Islamic forms. The plain severity of the dome submitted to the imposition of the Kajasha or ornate lotus-cresting and its metal finial gave place to an elaborate carving in stone. Moreover, the Mohammedans learnt from us the proportionate massing of buildings and the disposition of their parts. There was thus given to US a splendid synthesis of Muslim ideals and Hindu methods of treatment. We may now take a few buildings to illustrate the principles stated above.

In the city of Prithviraj, in Delhi, the conquerors erected one of the most splendid series of monuments. The central piece of architecture was the Quwwat-ul-Islam mosque founded in 1191 by Qutb-ud-din Aibak to commemorate the capture of Delhi and show the might of Islam. The building as originally designed showed Hindu influences very perceptibly. Half of the plinth on which it stood had actually been the basement of a Hindu temple and the rest of the structure, walls, columns, architraves and ceilings, was composed of materials stripped from the Hindu shrines. Later on arched screen of Muslim design was thrown across the whole front of the prayer chamber. The facade of this screen has superbly ornate carvings. Such superb ornamentation was a tribute to the Indian genius. Connected with this building is the famous Qutb-minar begun by Aibak and completed by Iltutmish. The minar according to some people was built at first by Prithviraj or his grandfather as a tower of victory but the weight of opinion inclines to its having been built by the Muslim rulers. The Qutb-minar seems to have been intended as a ma'zina or tower from which the mua'zzin could summon the faithful to prayer though it soon came to be regarded as a tower of victory. Originally designed it stood some 225 feet in height comprising four storeys with richly decorated balconies on each storey and in addition there were bands of inscriptions with foliate designs. In the reign of Firoz Shah Tughluq the minar was struck by lightning and the fourth storey was divided into two smaller ones. Inside the building there are certain Nagari records.

Nothing is more imposing or fittingly symbolic of Muslim power than this stern and stupendous fabric, nor could anything be more exquisite than its rich but restrained carvings. The only thing it lacks is the mystery or romance surrounding towers like those of Gratto or the Tower of victory in Florence and Chittor respectively.

From the time of Iltutmish right down to that of Alauddin attempts were made to react against Indianisation but the result was to give us a vacillating and nerveless style, for example, the tomb of Iltutmish. The most famous building associated with the name of Iltutmish is Arhai-din-ka-jhaupra at Ajmer built in two and a half days according to traditions and hence this name or probably it commemorates a fair held for two and a half days in Maratha times. It was built by Qutb-ud-din and ornamented with a screen by Iltutmish. The mosque contains a hall of really solemn beauty. This building was also built out of the spoils of Hindu temples. The Jama'at Khana Masjid at the Dargah of Nizam-ud-din Auliya was built in the reign of Alauddin Khilji and shows a great reaction against Indianisation. The Aloi Darwaza also built in the same reign in the Qutb is one of the most treasured gems of Islamic architecture. The orthodox Tughlaqs sedulously tried to eschew Hindu influence and produced at their best a stern, gloomy and puritan architecture. Still they could not wholly divorce the Hindu designs of art and this is evident from the pillars, brackets, windows and other features of the buildings erected during this period.

But under the Saiyyids and the Lodis the latent genius of Hindustan was once more revived. The best buildings of this period are the tombs of kings and nobles. The Hindu features of the gate, the external dripstone or the mosque, and the plaster decoration on the interior of the dome of the tomb, bespeak the passing of the Puritan period of art at Delhi. The buildings of this period prepared the way for the Moghul architecture and are thus a transition from the Sultanate to the Moghul styles of architecture. The famous buildings of this period are the Mausoleum of Sikandar Lodi and the Moti-ki-masjid built by the prime minister of Sikandar Shah.

We may now mention some important buildings in the provinces as illustrative of the influence of Islam on Indian architecture. In Bengal the most perfect example of Indo-Muslim architecture is the Dakhil Darwaza built by Barbak Shah (1459-74) at Gour. It is a superb example of what can be achieved in brick and terracotta. Sixty feet in height by 113 feet from back to front, it consists of a central arched passage with guard rooms on either side. At each of the four corners is a five-storeyed tapering turret, once crowned by a dome. Walls and turrets with courses, mouldings, panels, niches, rosettes, the chain, the bell, battlement and quatrefoil remind us of their Hindu origin. The whole structure shows a surprising boldness of design and masterly skill. Another building is the Bara Sona Masjid in Gaur which Fergusson calls the finest memorial now left in Gaur.

In Gujarat there was a perfect blend of the Delhi and local Hindu styles. The breadth, the spaciousness, the chaste and graceful elegance of the Hindu style were combined with the sense for symmetry and proportion together with the faultless sense of the Islamic style at Delhi. The effects of such a blending are evident in the buildings like those of Jami Masjid at Cambay (1325 A.D.) and of others erected in Ahmedabad. The latter city was founded by Ahmad Shah who commemorated the beginning of his dynasty by founding this city. The most famous buildings are the Tin Darwaza (Triple Gateway), the Jami Masjid, the mosque and tomb of Shaikh Ahmad Khattri at Sarkhej, the mosque specially having a hall built on purely Hindu principles and the buildings built by Mahmud Begarha who erected the most magnificent structures of the period. Jami Masjid at Champanir is the most striking edifice. The stepwells designed during the period were also a copy of the Hindu style. Further the mosque of Rani Sipari built in 1514 in Ahmedabad is regarded as one of the most exquisite structures in the world.

There is also the mosque of Sidi Sayyid with magnificent traceries, a world-famous structure. Its methods of screening window openings have never been surpassed. The buildings in Dhar and Mandu, 200 miles from Gujarat are more illustrative of the Islamic art than of the blend of the Islamic and the Hindu arts.

Jaunpur was another province, the city being founded by

Firoz Shah Tughlaq, showing the blend of the two arts in its architecture. The finest example is the Atala Masjid founded in 1137 and completed in 1408. The screen of the mosque is so massive and imposing as to overshadow all else in the quadrangle. Its propylan screens and surface decorations bespeak of the local style. There are few mosques so imposing in their proportions and so arresting in style. The style of Lal Darwaza is markedly Hindu.

In Bahmani kingdoms down till the beginning of the fifteenth century, the Persian and Delhi styles played more prominent part than the local styles though the Jami Masjid at Daulatabad and the Deval mosque at Bodhan are adaptation of a Hindu shrine. The monuments are mostly found in Gulbarga and Bidar. In Gulbarga the splendid mausoleum of Firoz Shah bears witness of the steadily growing strength of the Hindu influence shown in the carved and polished blue stone plasters and in the drip stones and elegant brackets that support them. Above all in Bijapur the Hindu genius rose superior to foreign influence and stamped itself more and more deeply on these creations but the story belongs to the Moghul period and is reserved for treatment below.

In Kashmir Zain-ul-Abdin stuck to the old Kashmiri art in the wooden architecture. The tomb of Madani and that of his mother are famous buildings. The most imposing of the wooden structures is the Jami Masjid at Srinagar. According to Marshall, however, the Kashmiri architecture exhibits the same fusion of Hindu and Muslim ideals.

Thus in the field of architecture the early Indo-Muslim kings made notable advances. In the words of Fergusson, 'Nothing could be more brilliant and at the same time more characteristic than the commencement of the architectural career of these Pathans in India. The simple severity of the Muslim architecture was toned down, and the plastic exuberance of the Hindu was restrained. The craftsmanship, ornamental richness, and general design remained largely Hindu, the actuated form, plain domes, smooth-faced walls and spacious interiors were Muslim superimpositions'.*

---

* Dr. Tarachand, *Influence of Islam on Indian Culture*, p. 243.

In the sphere of other arts also there was the same attempt at synthesis. To take music, for example, the Islamic peoples had not advanced very much in early days because Islam in its severe monotheism had a depressing effect on exuberance of feelings but later on music began to be cultivated specially after the Sufis developed devotional songs and poetry. When the Muslims came to India they found this art very well developed and took to it readily and also the majority of the converts being Hindu continued the practice of their devotional songs and other types of music, thus further adding to the musical richness of the Sultanate society. While the Hindus gave to the Muslims their instrumental music and Dhrupad, the Muslims led by the great poet Khusrau invented the quawwalis and the Khyal, also introducing Sitar and Tabla. Music, in short, opened a new channel of intercourse between the two communities of India. It is said that Alauddin had sent for Hindu musicians from the Deccan and used to hear their songs. Numismatics also point out towards this developing synthesis. The earliest coins bear an inscription in Nagri also. Gold coins of Mohammad Ghori struck in imitation of the Hindu Kings of Kannauj with the goddess Lakshmi on the obverse are without a parallel in Muslim history. There were other coins called Delhiwala with humped bull of Siva and the sovereign's name in Nagri on the obverse and the Delhi Chauhan type of horsemen on the reverse. On some coins of this class Iltutmish's name is associated with that of Chahada Deva of Narwar. A unique specimen bears the name of Mohammad Bin Sam and Prithviraj on the obverse and reverse sides respectively. During this period we also find the introduction of paper, calligraphy, illumination of manuscripts and improvements in the implements and arts of war. As in other spheres, in the fields of arts as well the greatest development took place in the Moghul period climax being generally reached in the reign of Akbar. We may study the arts under the headings of architecture, painting and music.

We have referred to the differences of interpretation of the Islamic architecture in India in the pre-Moghul period. Similarly with regard to this period, one school places great emphasis on Persian and European ideas in the Moghul architecture while the school led by Havell sees nothing radically different in the Moghul architecture from the Hindu art or from the Indo-Muslim one developed by the end of the fifteenth century. The truth lies somewhere in between.

It is said that Bijapur art, together with that of Gujarat and Rajputana forms the three planked bridge whereby earlier Indian art passes into that of Moghul India. We have already referred to the Rajput and the Gujarat arts. We may now describe the Bijapur architecture which is regarded as of rare architectural merit. The Adil Shahi dynasty made their capital Bijapur one of the most magnificent cities in the whole of India.

The Bijapur Kings made their courts centre of learning and arts attracting scholars and artists from Persia, Central Asia, Constantinople, Portugal and many parts of India. Thus the art developed there may well have furnished the basis of the Moghul architecture. Two of its famous buildings are the Gol Gumbaz and the Mihtar Mahal. The former building contains a dome larger than that of the Pantheon at Rome, the total area covering more than 18,000 square feet. Seen in the gathering dusk of the evening its great bulk rises above the surrounding plain like a mountain hardly looking as the product of the puny hand of man. The Mihtar Mahal is one of the richest gems of the builder's art. It is a tall graceful building with an upper storey containing an assembly room, and above this is an open terrace surrounded by a high wall with oriel windows and a perforated parapet. On each side of the facade are two slender minarets but it is the projecting balcony window which is most striking. Its stones are so finely wrought as to have the appearance of wood. Its delicate prettiness has a uniqueness of its own showing the exuberance of the artist's (tomb and mosque) and rivals even the finest buildings of the Moghuls. The mausoleum shows exceptional artistic magnificence.

The greatest buildings of the Moghul period were erected in the reigns of Akbar and Shah Jahan. Akbar had a thorough understanding of architectural details and his open assimilative and synthetic mind gathered together artistic ideas from all sides. At Fatehpur Sikri the most famous structures the Bulund Darwaza, Diwan-i-Khas and the Panch Mahal, are very excellent.

The Diwan-i-Khas contains the central Lotus Throne pillar of Hindu conception and the Panch Mahal (five-storied pavilion) is a continuation of the plan of the Indian Buddhist 'Viharas'. The tomb of Itimad-ud-Daulah built by Nurjahan reminds one of the Gol Mandal at Udaipur. The Moghuls also lent the elements of grandeur and originality to the grace and decoration of Indian art. We may remark that the Mausoleum at Sasaram built by Sher Shah is thoroughly Indian in conception and construction. The Moghuls also introduced the innovation of placing Mausoleums in the centre of a large park-like enclosure, a formal garden with its paved pathways, flowered parterres, avenues of cypress trees, ornamental water courses, tanks and fountains. They also changed the designs of the dome, specially constructing a double dome, an outer and an inner one, the latter forming the vaulted ceiling of the mortuary chamber below. In Gwalior was erected the tomb of Muhammad Ghaus in Indo-Muslim style. The forts of Akbar in Agra and Lahore also show the grandeur of style and it is said that the stones are so closely joined that even a hair cannot find its way into their joints. Within the Agra Fort, Akbar built many buildings after the Bengali and Gujarati styles. Percy Brown also observes that in this fort Rajput citadels were used as models. Again in Fatehpur Sikri many buildings contain decorative features which are copies of those seen in the temples of the Jains and the Hindus.

'Augustus's boast that he found Rome of brick and left it of marble has its counterpart in the building productions of Shah Jahan, who found the Moghul cities of sandstone and left them of marble'. - (Percy Brown)

The building art acquired a new sensibility to correspond with this change in material. Instead of the rectangular character of the previous period there arose the curved line and flowing rhythm of Shah Jahan, while the chisel of the stone-carver was replaced by the finer instruments of marble cutter and polisher. The most striking innovation was the change in the shape of the arch, which in almost all buildings of Shah Jahan's reign is foliated or cushed in its outlines. Thus was inaugurated the Golden Age of the Moghuls. At Agra and Lahore the palaces within the forts were reconstructed and all the cities were enriched by his buildings. Lovely things reached the zenith of perfection. In Agra we have the famous structures of his reign, namely, the Diwan-i-Am, Diwan-i-Khas, the Khas Mahal, the Shish Mahal, the Musalman Burj, Anguri Bagh, the Machhi Bhawan and the Moti Masjid. He also built a new capital in Delhi. Much of the description of Asoka's palace given by Dhammapala might apply to Shah Jahan's fortress at Delhi. The beauty of the Rang Mahal baffles description. He also built the Jamia Masjid in Delhi, the largest and most eminent in the whole of India.

But the most magnificent of all works of art was the Taj Mahal built to commemorate the love of the king for his queen Mumtaz Mahal. Her remains were put in this monument of matchless beauty to the making of which went ideas and artists imported from many parts of India, Asia, and possibly Europe. It may be noted that the decoration was mainly the work of Hindu craftsmen, the difflcult task of preparing the pietra dura especially being entrusted to a group from Kanauj. The chief supervisor was one Ustad Isa.

The whole scheme including the garden, is laid out in the form of a rectangle with its long axis lying north and south, the Mausoleum standing at the north end. This rectangle is enclosed by a high wall with broad arcaded turrets at each corner, and is entered on the south by a monumental gateway. The plan of Mausoleum is square with chamfered corners, each side being 186 feet long, so that the width of the facade is equal to the entire height of the building. Its crowning glory is the great dome which hangs in the sky like a shapely white cloud. Principal embellishment is obtained by arabesques of inlaid coloured stones. The share of Indian artists is mainly in the scroll work in the spendrels above the great arches, in the minute flowers on the cenotaphs and the perforated marble screen enclosing these. All this is a work of art of entrancing beauty.

The building is the finest example of not only magnificent artistry but also of superb technique. Its cupolas are derived in design from those of the Hindu temples. Further, the building owes not a little of its sensuous charm to the extraneous effects of the atmosphere, and the variations in the light on its marble surfaces. In the light of full moon, 'it seems as the hand of nature and the hand of man had united and done their utmost to produce a spectacle of supremely moving beauty'.

And here we may stop in our discussion of the synthesis of Hindu and Muslim architectures during the Moghul period. With Taj Mahal we have reached the finest synthesis of the two Hindu and Muslim elements coalesced to form a new type. The severity of Muslim architecture was mellowed down and the plastic exuberance of the Hindu was curtailed. The Saracenic emphasis on harmony and form blended with the Indian emphasis on splendour and decoration. The Rajput buildings of this period also show this fusion.

Painting also received the greatest impetus during the Moghul period and shows a perfect blending of the Chinese, Persian and Hindu arts in the period of Akbar's reign. By the time of Shah Jahan the Chinese influence disappeared, the Indian style becoming predominant. It has already been shown that in ancient India this art had reached the greatest perfection, the supreme example of which can still be seen in the Ajanta Frescoes. Abul Fazl mentions sixteen artists as being pre-eminent and of them thirteen are Hindus. The paintings of the Hindus as shown in Ajanta exhibit delight in the pomp and splendour of the royal state, in the pride and triumph of war and chase, and people are eagerly interested in the daily concerns of life, in the romance of love-making, in the delights of feasting, singing and dancing and in the busy hum of the market and at the same time there are pictures with religious themes showing 'Yogic' tranquillity and serenity, pictures of Buddha's life and teachings in the form of allegories. In a word, the Hindu religious ideal of one in the many is again stressed in the form of pictures. The medium through which this intense feeling is expressed is the line. The artist employs it with the same knowledge and success whether he has to render the tenseness of sight through the air, the upward spring of plant and tree, the waving trunk of an elephant, or the wonderful gestures of the hands, and he is equally at home in creating with it types or individualities, forms of man or of nature. In their suppleness, sinuousness and delicacy of charm the paintings share the plastic character of Indian architecture. Babar brought in India the artist Bihzad who was regarded in the sixteenth century as the greatest painter of the Timuride school which was also indebted to the Chinese through Central Asian paintings.

This art is intensely individualistic. It is not interested in masses and crowds. It pays homage to grand simplicity and rigidity at the cost of plasticity. Later it showed some elements of romance and self abandonment or Sufi mysticism. The line is used as the medium but it bends and breaks, thins and broadens in surprising manners.

Under the Moghuls these two met to form a new synthesis. Upon the plasticity of Ajanta were imposed the new laws of symmetry, proportion and spacing from Samarqand and Herat. To the old pomp new splendours were added, and to the old free and easy naivete of life a new sense of courtly correctness and rigid etiquette. 'In the result a stiff dignity was acquired, but along with a marvellous richness of colour and subtlety of line'.

Thus arose the new school of Indian painting which was cultivated both by the Muslims and the Hindus, many of whom like Daswant, Keso Lal, Madho and Ram are mentioned in Ain-i-Akbari. Many others appear on the contemporary paintings preserved in the Khuda Baksh library at Bankipore, Patna. Most of them came from Gwalior, Gujarat and Kashmir thus showing that the Indian school must have flourished in these places and that the Moghul art was related to the Indian art. Jahangir was a connoisseur of painting and under him the Indian school completely freed itself of imitation, portrait-painting acquired unusual fitness and scenes of hunting became popular. In the reign of Shah Jahan the portraiture was further developed. It is said that this school threw many offshoots of which the most prominent are the Rajput and Pahari styles of Jaipur, Kangra, the Hindu states of the Himalayan hills, the 'qalams' of the Deccan, Lucknow, Kashmir, Patna and the Sikh 'qalam'. Some people, however, maintain that the Rajput school is of independent origin.

Two different and contrary tendencies rule all art. One aims at decoration, proximity and splendour; the other is dominated by the ideal of simplicity, economy and sobriety. In perfect art these two are blended. The Indian and Saracenic styles supply complementary elements whose fusion created not only a great art but a deep abiding culture.

In music again this fusion or synthesis was continued. Abul Fazl tells us that Akbar paid much attention to music and patronised those who practised this art. It became customary to have musical performances on festive occasions. Semi-religious congregations began to assemble to hear songs of divine love sung by professional singers. Instruments like Rabab, Sarod, Tans and Dilruba were either invented or refashioned. Akbar patronised numerous musicians of whom Tansen is the most famous. There were others greatly famous like Haridas and Ramdas. The art of music now reached its noonday splendour. Shahjahan was a great patron of music and could himself sing well. His two great singers were Ramdas and Mahapattar. Music also flourished in provincial kingdoms and Baz Bahadur of Malwa was described as the most accomplished man of his day in the science of music and in Hindi song. Another great patron of music was Raja Man Singh Tanwar of Gwalior whose school of music was famous at the time. In Golconda, it is said, as many as 20,000 musicians were maintained. The classical Hindu ragas were modified by the Muslim singers. One interesting development of this musical contact may be noted. Hindu music was pre-eminently a religious art and, therefore, all classes of the Hindus were its devotees. In Muslim courts, however, it became for many a degraded profession specially when it took to romantic or erotic themes, further in courts the main body of the singers were females often of ill repute and as a result of all this a gulf arose between the higher classes who could afford such music and the ordinary people who took to folk songs. In the South, however, music continued to be the common heritage of prince and peasant alike. Thus, the history of music after the advent of the Muslims unfolds a chapter of Hindu-Muslim Co-operation. The Moghuls have also bequeathed to us well-ordered gardens as places in which to find repose, beauty, recreation and protection from the heat of the day.

Flowing water was an essential feature of these gardens. The Moghuls had a great feeling for natural beauty and beautiful gardens in Kashmir (Shalimar and Nishat), in Lahore (Shalimar) and elsewhere are a sign of this. These gardens inspired the Hindus and others in India and evoked rich poetry.

The arts of illuminating books and calligraphy continued to flourish, Aurangzeb being one of the best calligraphers. Workshops or Karkhanas were built by Akbar. Abul Fazl gives a list of more than a hundred, and these fashioned new designs in arts and crafts. Hindu temples built in this period show the influence of Islamic art, notably in Vrindaban.

Thus in the sphere of art and architecture the Moghul period showed the assimilation of the two cultures at its best. Both the Hindus and the Muslims lived and laboured to evolve joint culture in which arts occupy a prominent place as being the most visible and appealing symbol of such a synthesis.

Social Conditions

Early Muslim occupation in India has been compared to a military camp, the rulers being military despots living exclusively with the retinue surrounding them, while their Hindu subjects were the helots of the empire. Such a view is untenable, specially in the light of what has been said above.

There were various reasons why social intercourse between the Hindus and the Muslims should develop and evolve common ways of living in all its aspects. Firstly, at a certain stage even conquests begin to exact too high a price and peace becomes inevitable. Peace needs proper governmental organisation or administrative apparatus. This is only possible when same adherence to standards of Justice between various classes is observed. For the collection of taxes and government dues, it was essential to give security and protection to the vast masses of peasants and craftsmen, even against the members of the ruling classes, which further implied an outward, respect for, and tolerance of their deep-rooted sentiments. The Muslims may not ridicule Hindu manners in public, much less supplant them. As a matter of fact, the Muslims soon learned to admire and to assimilate Hinduism and Indian customs to such a degree that the pious Muslim invader Timur made it an excuse for attacking the territory of the Muslim kingdom of Delhi. Secondly, the Sultans demanded loans for the government, they wanted commerce to develop not only for income but also to get amenities of civilised life from outside, the Hindu took the lead in these transactions and thus provided another channel of social intercourse. Thirdly, the Muslims had not come here in large numbers, specially they had not brought females with them. Naturally marriages became frequent and we even find Allauddin marrying the Hindu princess Kamla Devi, wife of the Raja of Gujarat and later the daughter by the first marriage was wedded to his eldest son, Khizr Khan. Hindu women introduced their social customs in their new homes. Further, the village people inspite of their conversion continued to follow their customs and mix freely with their Hindu brethren. Fourthly, Muslim and Hindu saints attracted followers from the two creeds and this also led to exchange of social courtesies and customs. Lastly, the artistic and literary patronage extended by the Kings, specially in the provinces, to Hindu scholars and others inevitably led to social intercourse. By the end of the Sultanate this rapprochment had proceeded so for as to call from Babar the term 'Hindustani' way for the social cohesion that he saw among the ruling classes and people. As a result of the Muslim impact, social divisions were levelled, religious tendencies took a new direction and force and the conception of India as the common motherland was made possible. These formative forces of Indian culture in this period were the result of the Muslim impact so by the time of Akbar the ground work was completed and the Emperor as well as his successars followed the pattern, their Turkish and Afghan predecessors had shaped for them. This early period, therefore, is a landmark in the synthesis which developed as a result of the Hindu-Muslim contacts.

There were various features that were adopted both by the Muslims and the Hindus. Some of them may be mentioned here. In the early period we find many features in court ceremonial and life being taken by the Muslim kings from the Hindu customs. There was for example the superstition of 'the evil eye' resembling the Hindu custom of Utara and the ceremony of Arti. This was termed 'nisar' and consisted in taking platefuls of gold and silver coins or other precious jewels and scattering them to the poor or to any other assemblage after being passed over the head of the monarch a number of times. Further the court etiquette led to the evolution of seating arrangements for various classes or order who were classified into Ahl-i-daulat, the ruling class proper, Ahl-i-sa'adat, the intelligentsia, Ahl-i-murad or the class catering for pleasure. These were adopted by the Hindu states also. Hindus were gradually taken into higher services as well. Babar speaks of a Hindu who bore the title of Khan-i-Jahan, creating troubles for the Moghuls. Hemu was the general of the Afghans and when he returned after defeating a section of the Afghans, his Sultan heaped many favours upon him and conferred the title of Vikramaditya. Rajput chiefs and nobles became friends specially at the close of the Sultanate.

The hereditary Hindu maths with their gurus and chelas gave the idea to the Muslims to develop not only the office of the Pir or Shaikh but also Pirazadas and Mukhdumzadas or the descendants of the Pirs and Shaikhs. Muslim Kings like Muhammed Tughluq began to approach Hindu yogis and sadhus for aid in the fulfilment of their inmost desires.

The Hindu Rajas adopted some of the features of the institutionalised slave system of the Muslims. The Muslims began to develop a caste system. The various classes of the

Muslims began to live aloof from one another, in separate quarters even in the same city. To quote the writer in the Gazetteer of India, 'In India, however, caste is in the air, its contagion has spread even to the Mohammedans, and we find its evolution proceeding on characteristically on Hindu lines. In both communities foreign descent forms the highest claim to social distinctions and just as in the traditional Hindu system men of the higher groups could marry women of the lower, while the converse process was vigorously condemned, so within the higher ranks of the Mohammedans, a Sayyid will marry a Sheikh's daughter but will not give his daughter in return. The lower functional groups are organised on the model of regular castes, with councils and officers which enforce the observance of caste rules by the time-honoured sanction of boycotting'.* Mutual contact developed new castes and sub-castes. We find mutual jealousies among the foreign and Indian Muslim nobles of the Sultans and when Mohammad Tughluq in disgust took to extreme democratisation in administration he drew the wrath of the contemporary historian Barni and others.

The impact of the Muslims on the caste system was two-fold. In the first place it led to the revival of a popular, liberal religion and concessions were granted to the higher classes who were reclaimed to the Hindus. Secondly, it led to rigidity in the caste system and specially the lower castes found their lot more miserable. Further, society was now divided vertically instead of horizontally as before Islam, it is said, split Indian society into two sections from top to bottom and what has now come to be known in the phraseology of today as two separate nations came into being from the beginning.

While the Hindus gave to the Muslims their caste system, the latter gave to the former their strict form of purdah system. People have tried to discover this system among the Hindus and Mr. Jaffar quotes Draupadi from Mahabharata as having observed the purdah but it cannot be denied that 'the present elaborate and institutionalised form of purdah dates from the

---

* *The Gazetteer of India*, Vol. II, p. 329.

time of the Muslim rule'.* The example of Razia is well known and proves the existence of purdah in the Royal Harem. Firoz Shah forbade the visit of Muslim women to mausoleums outside the city of Delhi. Women went in covered litters and we find the wives of Raja Rudra Pratap of Puri, for example, going to visit Chaitanya in 'covered' litters.

There were Muslim nobles who adopted even the custom of Jauhar. For example Kamal-ud-din, the Governor of Bhatnair and his retainers burned their women and their property and then proceeded to fight Timur.

There was interchange in dress also. The Hindu turban became popular among the Muslims of the upper classes while the Hindu aristocracy took to Muslim dress. Hindu personal hygiene specially bath and ceremonial ablutions were adopted by the Muslims. The Muslims adopted many features of the Hindu festivals. Shabe-Barat, the 'Guy Fawkes Day of Islam is, according to Ashraf, probably copied from Shivaratri. The Sultans readily took to it and it spread quickly. There were some evil customs which were also adopted by many among the Hindus. For example, there was the development of unhealthy sex-complex. The relations of Alauddin with Malik Kafur are too well known'.

Thus we find that by the close of the Sultanate period social relations between the two communities were developing, the upper classes and the lower classes mingling with their opposite numbers in the two communities. Further, the effect of Islam on Indian culture was to make rigid the caste system and institutionalise the Purdah system. But all these tendencies were only in their formative period. During the Moghul period they crystallised into their present form and therefore this period is more important from the social point of view also.

Society in the Moghul period reached its highest watermark from the point of view of affluence and comforts. The nobles were rolling in wealth and indulged in luxuries. The fleshpots of Arabia and Egypt became dear to them but the lot of the lower classes was comparatively poor.

---

* K.M. Ashraf, *Life and Condition of the People of Hindustan*, p. 244.

Akbar's religious policy of appeasement and the desire to weld the peoples into a unity or social cohesion led to exchange of views between the two main communities and the Hindus were now consciously given share in the seats of power. Thus, the earlier fanaticism of Islam was shuffled off. Both the Hindus and the Muslims began to appreciate and adopt each others customs as for as possible. Akbar discouraged the Hindu or Muslim customs of marriage before puberty, marriage between near relatives or taking of plurality of wives. He maintained that the consent of the bride-groom and bride should also be taken for marriage. He discouraged dowry and the Sati system. The Hindus and Muslims freely participated in each other's functions. More and more Hindu women were married to the Muslim rulers. He even wanted the Hindus to allow widow remarriage. He put an end to cow-killing and abolished the hated Jizyah. He even offered worship to the Sun, sometimes marked his forehead like a Hindu and celebrated the festival of Raksha Bandhan and Diwali, also refraining from eating meat on certain days.

His policy of toleration and love towards the Hindus were followed by his successors and this intimate social relationship reached its climax with Dara Shikoh. During his life he sought knowledge about the religion and philosophy of the Hindus, particularly on the mystic side, and to this purpose he not only got translated Sanskrit books into Persian but assiduously saught the company of Hindu ascetics. He believed that there were only verbal differences between Hindu and Muslim mysticism and wrote his Majma-ul-Biahrayn to show where the 'two seas' of mystic thought meet.

As a result of this close contact between the two communities, common social customs developed. There are also survivals of the Muslims upto recent times with customs brought from their Hindu ancestry. Jahangir while visiting Kashmir had found Muslim groups with their chiefs styled as Rajas and following Hindu customs such as the burning of widows and inter-marriage with the Hindus. There is a community of Malkana Rajputs belonging to Agra and adjoining districts with Hindu names, worshipping temples, using salutation of Rama, practising circumcision, burying the dead and preferring to be addressed as Miyan Thakur. In Gujrat there are the Memons of Kutch eating no flesh, practising no circumcision, worshipping Hindu triad, Brahma, Vishnu and Siva and they consider Imam Shah who converted them as the nation of Brahma. Same sort of conditions can be found in other parts of India. Many Muslims worship Kalka Sahja Mal in U. P., the Mirasis of Amritsar worship Durga Bhawani, the Turk Nawas of Bengal worship Lakshmi Devi and among the Muslims of Mysore the joint family system of the Hindus obtains in the rural areas. There are sects with common religious beliefs and observances, for example, the Pirzadas founded in the seventeenth century had in the religious book selections from the Hindu scriptures and worshipped Vishnu in his tenth incarnation. The Shamsis in the Punjab are outwardly Hindu but worship Agha Khan as an incarnation of Hindu Trinity.

Islam with its clear, definite and simple creed appealed to many among the Hindus and with its social democracy was a welcome release to others from the bondage of caste but when all is said there seems to be little doubt that Hinduism has wrought a greater change in Islam than Islam has wrought in Hinduism.

The Hindus took readily to Muslim dress and ways of preparing food specially the upper classes.

Rich and spiced preparations, the pulaos, birianis and other varied foods of the Middle East were adopted. Rare fruits, mysterious decoctions, refinements of the culinary art to suit jaded palates, which the cosmopolitan society of Persia, long in contact with Rome, China and Egypt had evolved found their way into India and soon gained popularity with the richer classes among the Hindus and Muslims alike. Nanak had bewailed that the Hindus had adopted the dress and manners of the Muslims. The pyjamas and the chapkans were adopted by the elite. Even 'hookah' was accepted in the Hindu families. In short, the dress, manners and social amenities which the Moghuls introduced ceased to be foreign and were accepted by the higher classes everywhere.

Thus the influence exerted by the Hindus on the Muslim social life and custom and vice-versa was remarkable. Dr. Rajendra Prasad in his work 'India Divided' quotes instances from Bihar to show how close the two communities had come in their social functions connected with birth, marriage and death. To give a few of these examples. The birth of a male child leads to singing of songs called 'sohar'. Women of both the communities sing them. During confinement the mother is not to touch food to be taken by others, spirits are supposed to haunt the house, hair of the baby is removed. All these customs are observed in the Muslim household also.

Among the Hindus marriage is celebrated with great eclat. Islam had enjoined simplicity but the pomp, ceremonies, procession, festivities and even jokes of the Hindu's marriage have been copied by the Muslims. For example, when people of the bridegroom's party proceed to the bride's house they carry a kind of basket called Sohagpura, containing spices, fruits, sweets, coloured yarn, rice, etc., exactly like that of the Hindu's. Similarly after death certain ceremonies are performed resembling those of the Hindus. The Moplas in Malabar are governed by the Hindu law. Ornaments worn by women are in many ways common to both the peoples. It will thus appear from the above description that there has been considerable influence exerted by the two communities on each other.*

As in other spheres in this field also Akbar's contribution was greatest. He endeavoured to create an Indian nation in place of the two differing communities. To quote Bartoli, 'for an Empire ruled by one head, it was a bad thing to have the members divided among themselves, and at variance one with the other. We ought, therefore, bring them all into one, but in such a fashion that they should be one and all, with the great advantage of not losing what is good in any one religion, while gaining what is better in another. In that way honour would be rendered to God, peace would be given to the peoples and security to the Empire'.

---

* Dr. Rajendra Prasad, *India Divided*, pp. 38-48.

Literature and Education

Lastly, we may see how far in the literary field the two communities influenced each other. In the first place, the Muslim invasion before Akbar was in the main politically oppressive. The people (Hindus) sought relief in religion, especially of an emotional kind, which is always the anodyne of a people in distress. This development of Bhakti led to a great crop of religious literature which in order to appeal to the masses had to be written in vernacular languages of the people in various parts of India. Thus one effect of Islam on Indian culture in the literary field was to provide a stimulus to the growth of provincial languages and literature. It should also be understood that many Muslims also began to write in popular languages so that the masses may be attracted towards their teachings. This led to the growth of Hindvi language which later on changed either into Urdu or Hindi. We have a poet Masud writing in Hindvi as early as the eleventh century.

In the second place, Islam gave birth to what is known as the Urdu language which was evolved as a common medium of expression between the Hindus and the Muslims.

Thirdly, the Muslims had brought with them the traditions of historical writings. The Persian chronicles which were written under every Muslim dynasty in India and in every reign under the Moghuls not only served as materials of study in themselves but furnished an example which Hindu writers and rulers were not slow to develop themselves. Thus a new and very useful element was introduced into the Indian literature and in the seventeenth and eighteenth centuries it formed a magnificent body if we take all the histories, biographies and letters into account. In fact the history of medieval India would not have been written properly if these materials were lacking.

Fourthly, the lower ranks of bureaucracy developed an official prose style, lead being taken by the Kayasthas and the Kashmiri Brahmans, and this was followed even by the Maratha Chitnivises for their own vernacular.

Fifthly, many Muslims in order to understand Hindu culture encouraged translation of Sanskrit works not only in

Persian but also in vernaculars, for example, the Muslim rulers in Bengal. Thus a new renaissance of Indian literature broke forth in India after the thirteenth century accompanied by a Reformation, the Bhakti movement, inaugurated by Hemananda.

Lastly, the Muslims with their introduction of paper and calligraphy and the system of illumination of manuscripts encouraged the art of writing.

In short, the advent of the Muslims in India had the same profound effect on Indian literature which happened in Europe when the Turks drove out the Greeks from Constantinople, forcing them to eke out their living by opening the treasure-house of their literature to the rest of Europe.

We may now give some instances to show the fillip given to the Indian literature by the Muslims. In the field of Indo-Muslim literature the most important personality before the Moghuls is Khusrau. Khusrau (1253-1325 A.D.) was the first great poet of Hindvi, a mixture of many dialects specially Khari boli and Brij Bhasha. He was a man of versatile genius being a musician, poet, historian and prose writer. Khusrau is regarded as a courtier, a man of letters but he came from the people and felt at his best only when he moved among the crowd. Hence his Hindvi poetry is simple and directly appealing to the people. He also wrote a number of riddles in the form of verses. His greatest contribution in this sphere has been to give not an ornate style but simple style of poetry indicating also the form of language popular with the masses of those days. He wrote also a lexicon giving Arabic, Persian and Hindvi equivalents. Khusrau may, therefore, be regarded as the father of Urdu.

Under Sher Shah flourished the famous poet of Oudh, Malik Muhammad Jaisi who wrote and sang in his sweet native Awadhi. In some ways, he was greater even than Amir Khusrau for while the latter has more or less confined in his treatment to Muslim society, the former had drunk deep at the springs of both Hinduism and Islam. He is the oldest vernacular poet of India of whose work we have any uncontested remains. In his well-known book Padmavat he deals with the events of the popular story of Raja Ratansen of Chitor, the marriage of the Raja with Padmini, a princess of the distant Ceylon, his battle against Alauddin Khilji, his imprisonment by the latter and finally his thrilling escape through the device of his queen.

Behind the mask of his love story Jaisi drove home the principles of Sufism. The style inaugurated in the main by him had other followers also, for example, Qtban Sheikh who wrote Mragawati. There were other Muslim poets writing in vernaculars of their times like Abdur Rahman, Babbar and Daud. In the field of religious literature besides these we had the greatest name of Kabir about whom we have already spoken.

But all this encouragement of Indian literature was mainly the result of private initiative, the Sultans of Delhi had no love lost for the Hindu culture or literature. Only in the provinces did some rulers give fillip to Indian education, the most notable being the rulers of Bengal. We may here quote from Law's book, (Promotion of Learning in India), 'The efforts of the rulers of Bengal were not confined to the promotion of Muhammadan learning alone, for they also directed their fostering care for the advancement of letters into a new channel, which is of particular interest to the Bengali speaking people.... It was the epics, The Ramayana and Mahabharata that first attracted the notice of the Muhammadan rulers of Bengal, at whose instance they were translated into Bengali, the language of their domicile. The first Bengali rendering of the Mahabharata was ordered by Nasir Shah of Bengal (1282-1325 A.D.) who was a great patron of the vernacular of the province and whom the great poet Vidyapati has immortalised by dedicating to him one of his songs'.* Again, 'Emperor Husain Shah was the great patron of Bengali. Matadhar Basu was appointed by him to translate the Bhagavata Purana into Bengali'. One of his generals Paragal Khan and his son have made themselves famous by getting some portion of Mahabharata translated into Bengali. These examples were followed by the Hindu Rajas and thus through the efforts of these Muslim rulers Bengali came into its own.

---

* N.N. Law, *Promotion of Learning in India*, p. 107.

In the field of education the rulers did not maintain any separate establishment but kept it in charge of the religious department. They, however, made grants to scholars and for various schools and colleges called Maktabs and Madarsas. The Madarsas founded by Firozshah and that in Jaunpur were the most famous. It does not seem that Islamic institutions of education produced any effect on Indian education as a whole. Nevertheless there was great similarity or correspondence between the two. Just as the Hindu pundits used to teach pupils at home so also the Maulvis used to take classes in their houses, again the temples had pathshalas associated with them, similarly the mosques had Maktabs in their buildings and just as in the field of education private initiative was great among the Hindus, so also was the case with the Muslims. There was also broad correspondence between the courses specially in the primary stage when the three R's were taught by both. Females were also taught at home. It does not seem, however, that during the Sultanate period education of Muslim and Hindu boys in the same institution was encouraged.

Nevertheless by the time the Sultanate period ends we find a welcome change in the attitude of the Muslims towards Indian education and literature, a great contrast from the posture of affairs when Bakhtiyar Khilji, the lieutenant of Qutb-ud-din Aibak destroyed the Buddhist university of Nalanda and of Nadiya, massacring scholars and burning books. Thus, through long association, the growth of the numbers of the converted Indo-Muslim community, and the influence of several liberal movements in India, the Hindu and Muslim communities came to imbibe each others thoughts and customs. Famous Muslim scholars and saints lived and laboured in India during the medieval period, and they helped the dissemination of the ideas of Islamic philosophy and mysticism in this land. It was out of the desire for mutual understanding that Hindu religious literature was studied and translated or summarised in the Muslim courts like those of Zaln-ul-Abdin in Kashmir and Husan Shah in Bengal. Further, Muslim courts and Muslim preachers and saints were attracted to the study of Hindu philosophy like Yoga and Vedanta and the sciences of medicine and astrology. The Hindu astronomers similarly borrowed from the Muslims technical terms, the Muslim calculations of lattitudes and longitudes, some items of the Calendar (Zich) and a branch of horoscopy called Tajik, and in medicine the knowledge of metallic acids and some processes in Medico-chemistry. The growth of Urdu, out of the mingling of Persian, Arabic, and Turkish ideas with languages and concepts of Sanskritic origin, is a proof of the linguistic synthesis of the Hindus and the Muslims. This assimilation between the two cultures led also to the springing up of new styles of arts, architecture and music in which the basic element remained the old Hindu, but the outward form became Persian and the purpose served was that of Muslim courts. Further, while there is no Averroes or Avicenna, no Tabari or Masudi to illumine the pages of Islam in India, still the Indo-Persian literature has undoubtedly a few great names and their works are a part of the heritage of India.

Thus in the Sultanate period we find a formative epoch in the field of literature and education, the fruits of which were garnered in the Moghul Age. The Moghuls inaugurated a conscious policy of religious toleration. In this particular the influence operated from the very beginning. To give a quotation from Babar's will to Humayun (a copy of which is in Bhopal State library), 'O my son, people of diverse religions inhabit India; and it is a matter of thanks giving to God that the King of Kings has entrusted the government of this country to you. It therefore behoves you that :

1. You should not allow religious prejudices to influence your mind, and administer impartial Justice, having due regard to the religious susceptibilities and religious customs of all sections of the people.
2. In particular refrain from the slaughter of cows.
3. You should never destroy the places of worship of any community'.

Humayun consciously followed this policy and for the first time Hindu Raja of Kalinjar was made a nobleman of the empire. Under Akbar this policy was fully implemented and the influence of Islam on Hindu literature and vice versa was the greatest thing that one writer calls this period the Augustan Age of vernacular literature. All those influences which we have mentioned in the beginning of this section fully operated now in their rich diversity.

To give some examples - Akbar patronised Hindu litterateurs like Manohar, Jayat Ram, Birbal, Hol Rai, Todarmal, Raja Bhagwan Das and Man Singh, Nar Hari, Gung and others. His encouragement of Tansen and other Hindu singers like Bilas, Nanak, Sur Das and Rang Sen is worth mentioning. There were Hindu painters also like Mukund, Mahesh, Jagan, Haribans and Ram.

Works from Sanskrit were now translated in plenty, for example, the Mahabharata which was translated by Naqib Khan, Abdul Qadir, Haji, Faizi and others, Ramayana by Abdul Qadir, Atharva Veda by Haji Ibrahim, Lilavati by Faizi, Panchatantra by Nasrullah Mustafa and Husiani Wa'iz, also Nala and Damayanti into Persian Verse. Simhasana Battisi, Rajtargini and some astronomical works besides a history of 1000 years were also translated or written. Many Muslim writers wrote in Hindi or about Indian topics for example, Alam, Jamal, Qadir, Mubarak and Rahim. The last was the most famous of all. His full name was Abdur Rahim Khankhana. He was at home in Persian, Arabic and Sanskrit. He was a great Hindi poet. He was so generous that once he gave the great Hindu poet Gung thirty-six lakhs of rupees. His didactic verses are very popular.

He has compased about eight books in Hindi besides some in Persian and also some verses in Sanskrit. In his poems he shows perfect acquaintance with the problems of life. He was a master of Brij Bhasha and Awadhi and also of various styles of Hindi poetry. Even great Hindi poets like Bihari plagiarised many of his verses. Thus after Kabir he was the greatest master in Indo-Muslim literature.

All the emperors were great collectors of books and encouraged all sorts of writings. There was a great vogue of memoirs and histories or chronicles. Books were richly illumined by painters and calligraphy received great excellence.

We see in Akbar, for the first time, a great Muslim monarch of India sincerely eager to further the education of the Hindus and the Muhammedans alike, both studying in the same school with improved methods of education suggested by the king and his advisers. Madarsas and Maqtabs multiplied like anything under state patronage. Stipends and endowments were granted to all regardless of creed or class. We have already referred to Dara's patronage of the Hindus and their literature. He engraved in Hindi letters the word Prabhu upon his rings. Jahangir and Shahjahan, of course, continued the patronage of litterateurs writing in Hindi, for instance, Ahmad, contemporary of Jahangir and Sunder Das who was given the title of Maha Kaviraj by Shahjahan.

During this period Hindi prose writing also began to develop having come from the Deccan where it was first taken by Gesu Daraz Banda Nawaz Shahbaz Buland in 1393 of the Vikram era.

The first prose works in the North were written in Akbar's time namely, Bhuvan Dipale and Chand Chhand Barnan ki mahima.

Female education was also encouraged and we have great names like Gul Badan (sister of Humayun), Nurjahan, Mumtaz Mahal, Jahanara and Zibunnisa, eldest daughter of Aurangzeb. Thus during the Moghul period Indian Islam made an outstanding contribution to the general treasury of Indian culture. Akbar's patronage of the Hindus made the Hindu Rajas also emulate him and so this period witnessed the flowering of Hindu genius in all spheres of life. We have now come to an end of this chapter devoted to the description of the influence of Islam on Indian culture. It is now obvious that Islam was not merely a destroying agency but a civilising mission also. To quote Sir Sultan Ahmad, 'The Hindu-Muslim differences of today threaten to undo the historic fellowship between the two communities that beginning under the Moghuls has existed for centuries. It is seldom realised that to disunite Hindustan would be to work against the one constructive factor of the history of Muslim rule in this country. Indian leaders and thinkers of a remoter age sought to establish harmony between the two religions. Prince Dara Shekoh compared them to two fluent rivers, Majma-ul-Bahrein; Kabir and Nanak tried to fuse them together and imported into their prayers the names of both 'Allah the Bountiful and Rama'. The Hindu and Muslim masters were inspired to bring into existence common arts and crafts that touched the souls and satisfied the utilitarian need of both the Hindus and Muslims. Common notions of Joy and beauty were involved.

The Muslims in India had become sons of the soil. But Aurangzeb turned the clock back and the politics of today administered the last kick, yet Indian Political unity is as necessary as cultural unity and in their accomplishment will lie India's salvation. We shall end this chapter by referring to certain general features of Indian renaissance during this period. The later middle ages dominated as they are by the Muslim kings may at first seem to have produced a depressing effect upon the Hindus but facts do not warrant such a Conclusion. If not at the centre, Hinduism remained strong at the periphery and gradually won back its position even at the centre. In this Hindu renaissance and reformation, policies of many enlightened Muslims, kings, nobles and plebeians, were a helping factor and specially with the advent of the Moghuls we have splendid monuments of Hindu or Indian culture. We may briefly study some of these in the fields of religion, literature and arts.

It has already been remarked that in the sphere of religion the middle ages were dominated by Bhakti or devotionalism. Writers contend that this devotional movement is directly traceable to the influence of Islam in India but we have shown that it was an independent movement and could be traced to Bhagavadgita though it cannot be denied that one aspect of this movement or one school of it owes its inspiration to Sufism and yet even this school has elements common to other schools of Bhakti. It differs only in greatly emphasising monotheism or one God without any equality or form, in rejecting the theory of incarnation, in decrying ritualism including idol-worship and in rejecting the taboos of the caste-system. But even these elements can be found in the broad-based philosophies of Upanishads. We have aleady referred to the main propounders of this school.

During this period (1200-1700) Bhakti school continued to flourish in all its aspects and multiformity. Recently another sect has come to light known as the Siddhas who were regarded as the precursors of the Santas (Saint) of Bhakti schools. These Siddhas were related to Nath Panthis whose main teacher is Gorakh Nath, a very famous figure in the Sakta school. Again while in the south generally Bhakti school continued mainly to be the favourite of the elite, here in the North it spread to the masses and partook of certain impurities.

Another outstanding movement to arise during this period was Sikhism. We have already referred to Nanak. He was followed by a number of Gurus, notably the most famous Guru Govind Singh, who put the doctrines of this sect on firm foundations. Guru Arjun Das, the fifth in the order, was the first to transform his followers into an organised community. He completed the Tank of immortality at Amritsar, collected the writings of earlier Gurus and many Hindu and Muslim saints, the whole being called the Holy Granth, an authoritative scripture for the Sikhs. He had to suffer martyrdom at the hands of Jahangir and this aroused the wrath of the Sikhs who now began to be transformed into a military community. The ninth Guru (Teg Bahadur) also suffered martyrdom at the hands of Aurangzeb. The tenth Guru Govind Singh now organised his people on proper military lines, giving birth to 'Khalsa' by instituting the baptism of the sword. The cry of the militant Sikhs Sat Sri Akal (God is true) was now heard in the Punjab from thousands who joined in battle with the Moghuls and later carved out a kingdom for themselves under Ranjit Singh. Guru Govind Singh died in 1709.

Just as militant Sikhism was rising in North as a counter-blast to the fanaticism of Aurangzeb, similarly in the Deccan was arising the militant nationalism of Marathas. Behind both there was religious inspiration. We have already referred to the religious movement in Maharashtra under Jnaneshwar, Nam Dev, Tuka Ram and Ramdas. It was Ramdas who aroused the Maratha consciousness and made it a force to reckon with.

The Marathas developed their own literature and encouraged research into our ancient past. They discovered political devices and terms which they used for their own government.

While in the North and in the Deccan, the Rajputs, the Marathas and the Sikhs organised national resistance against the religious persecution of Aurangzeb, the same work was performed by the Vijaynagar dynasty in the pre-Moghul period. The great kings of this kingdom stood as guards over the southern bastion and kept alive Indian culture in its pristine purity. It was the centre of a Hindu revival, of the rejuvenation of the Sanskrit and the vernacular languages, the proclaimed successor of the orthodox doctrine of Hindu Empire. The growth of later Vaishnavism is closely connected with the dynasty and the temples they built and endowed over the length and breadth of the country are evidence of the great religious feeling that animated the people at this time. With the court were associated great commentators and thinkers like Sayana, the last great commentator on the Vedas and Madhavacharya, the great Jurist whose Parasara Madhaviya is considered a work of authority. Queens also figure as authoresses like Ganga Devi the authoress of Madhura Vijayam. The greatest king Krishna Deva Raya was himself a scholar and writer. Telugu and Kanarese also developed under their patronage. The court poet Pedanna is still considered one of the fathers of Telugu.

This kingdom provided thus, in more ways than one, a synthesis of South Indian culture. Similarly in the north the Rajputs of Mewar continued to be patrons of Hindu culture and there were many famous Ranas like Kumbh and Sangram who provided an armour plate, so to say, to Hinduism against Muslim invasion. Kumbh himself was the commentator of Gita Govind and author of Sangitaraja, an encyclopaedic work on music and numerous other poems in Sanskrit. The climax was reached in the reign of Maharana Pratap who remains the idol of Hindu India.

In the literary field also Hindu culture produced some of

the greatest names in India and this period also witnessed the foundation on firm footing of the modern vernacular literature of the various parts of India. In the realm of Hindi we had Tulsidas and Surdas, in Bengal we had Chandidas and Vidyapati and similarly in Urdu, Marathi and Gujarati great names like those of Khusrau, Tukaram and Narsi Mehta respectively.

Hindu culture was great not only in the field of religion or literature but also in the field of arts and this was true in this period also. Great temples were built in Vijayanagar, Rajputana and Vrindaban and a new school of paintings arose which has been aptly called the Rajput painting by Ananda K. Coomaraswamy.

We have not written much about Sanskrit literature durıng this period but it does not mean that Sanskrit was a dead language. Jainism was vigorously flourishing and we have great writers like Hemachandra Suri of Gujarat who wrote in Sanskrit. Besides Banaras was the centre of a notable revival in Hindu intellect in the Moghul period as well. New schools of Dharmashastras and Nitishastra sprang up and scholars came from all parts of India. One notable name is that of Kavindracharya whose friendship was cultivated by Bernier. He was a great poet and a scholar and also held in high esteem as a Yogi. He was one of the gurus of Dara and a friend of Shah Jahan. He was the most famous teacher of his time. There were also during this period commentaries on law which led to the development of the Mitakshara and Dayabhaga schools. Thus during this period Sanskrit also received a great impetus.

We have now come to the end of the medieval period after having surveyed the main cultural tendencies of the period. Our survey makes it clear that the medieval period in India was not synonymous with obscurantism. It was no dark age. Religious persecution so Rampant in Europe was conspicuous by its absence in India, otherwise how can we explain the presence of only 14 percent of Muslims in India where they ruled for about six hundred years. The effect of Islam on Indian culture was thorough and of far-reaching implications. It gave birth to a school of Bhakti, emphasized. monotheism, led to new forms of architecture and painting, modernised Indian society and secularised Indian literature besides furnishing ground for the growth of vernacular literatures. It gave us the Urdu language and sophisticated manners at the table and in the court. But it would be also true to say that if outwardly or materially Islam seemed to dominate over India, inwardly it failed to subdue the Indian soul and it was itself transformed so that the Indian Muslim today has more points of contact with his Hindu countrymen than with his Muslim comperes outside India. But the medieval period also ended on a tragic note. The policy of Aurangzeb sounded the death-knell of the Moghul Empire and the eighteenth century in India specially its second half was the gloomiest and darkest age in Indian history. That alone shows that something was still wanting in our culture. The balance and synthesis, the unity of spirit and matter which we had secured in the ancient period had been disturbed and it needed another cultural force to fill up the lacuna.

15

MODERN CULTURE

BEFORE DESCRIBING THE Modern Indian Culture we may briefly review the political history of the period. While the Moghul empire was being established in India, Europe was waking up from its medieval slumber and nations like Portuguese, the Spaniards and the English were moving out of Europe for adventure, for material wealth or commerce and for territory. The Portuguese were the first to arrive in India in the fifteenth century. They supplanted the Arab traders so far as India's carrying trade was concerned and established their settlements in places like Goa.

Soon in the sixteenth century the Portuguese had to compete with the Dutch and the English for the trade of the Indies. They lost ground to both these nations. The Dutch, however, confined their main interest to the spice islands, etc., and the Indian trade was monopolised by the English. Through Hawkins and Sir Thomas Roe, the British secured some concessions from the Moghul emperor Jahangir and established their main settlement in Surat. The English were followed by the French who began their commercial operations in Surat.

Politically however, the British raised head in India only with the decline of Moghul Empire after Aurangzeb. In this attempt they came in conflict with other Europeans specially French and with the Indian rulers who had become independent after the decline of the Moghul Empire. The French were defeated after a series of wars between 1744-1763. After this their opposition had only a nuisance value and that too disappeared in the regime of Wellesley and after the defeat of Napolean-I. So far as the Indian states were concerned, India had once again become the battleground between the various ruling powers among the Marathas, the Nizams and the rulers of Mysore, Haider Ali and Tippu, were the foremost. They did not realise that only in unity lay their salvation. The result was that one by one they were all defeated by the British and by the end of the first half of nineteenth century almost the whole of India lay at their feet, the Sikh being the last to be defeated. All the disaffected elements in India tried to combine against the British and raised the standard of revolt in 1857 but this attempt miscarried and for the next 90 years the British were to remain Supreme in India. The Moghul Emperor had become a nonentity specially in the time of Wellesley. Upto 1857 the East India Company governed India through a Governor General. Among them we had many important personalities as Governor - General. Among these the makers of India were Clive (1757 as first Governor, and in 1765, as Governor for the second time), Warren Hastings (as Governor 1772, as Governor General 1774-1785), Wellesly (1798-1805) and Dalhousie (1848-1856). The last Governor-General before the mutiny was Canning who also became the first Viceroy after 1857. During the premutiny period there were reforming Governor-General also like Cornwalis and Bentinck.

After the mutiny the Government of India was taken over by the Crown. The main interest after mutiny lies firstly, in the consolidation of the Indian Empire economically, politically and administratively and secondly, in the beginning of the Indian Renaissance. During this period Parliament governed India through the Secretary of State for India, a member of British Cabinet and he controlled the Governor-Generals among whom the most conspicuous were Ripon (1880-84) and Curzon (1899-1905). The contact of the Indians with the progressive West bred in them a desire to free themselves for only in that way they could realise their aspiration in every field of life. Here in the political field the main interest lies in the political struggle between the Indian National Congress (founded in 1885) and the powers that be. The British tried to meet this demand by conceding certain political and constitutional reforms from time to time (1861, 1892, 1909, 1919, 1935) but they failed to meet our aspirations and from 1905 recourse was had to direct method like terrorism and Satyagraha or Civil Disobedience Movement, the latter being associated with Mahatma Gandhi who became the most important Indian leader in 1920 with the death of Tilak.

The Congress did not represent the Muslim middle classes sufficiently as they were loyal generally to the British and had their own political body in the Muslim League. The League and the Congress became bitter opponents after 1937 and we find after a certain time the demand for a separate homeland for Muslims. The League achieved this in 1947 when India and Pakistan became Sovereign powers and the British withdrew. Pakistan was born in strife and even now the two countries are at loggerheads thus exemplifying the lessons of Indian history that only by unity permanent welfare of the whole of India can be achieved.

16

THE WEST AND INDIA

IN THE MODERN Age the West had entered into India mainly through the British and so the story of Indians-contact with the West is woven round the Indo-British relationship that began developing after the fall of the Moghul Empire. This relationship has had three main phases or periods with three attitudes so far as the ruling power was concerned. For the first fifty years of the British Raj, after the early excesses of a period of conquest had finished, the attitude was one of indifference towards the Indians. There was no desire to raise storms against themselves by interfering in social or religious fields and also because this period produced notable scholar administrators who had a certain tender respect for one of the centres of world civilisation. This mood changed as the nineteenth century advanced and under the stress of the utilitarian and liberal philosophy born of the rising material and scientific progress in England; it was realised that the Indians were very superstitious and uncivilised, that nothing good could be salvaged from the Indian culture and therefore they must be reformed. Macaulay represented this school. In politics and administration this school found its culmination in the rule of Dalhousie. But the Mutiny of 1857 appalled the Britishers and thus began the third period when zeal for innovation was checked.

The British in India looked at us with a mixture of toleration and contempt. Therefore, the direct contribution of the British administration in India in bringing to us the benefit of the western civilisation has not been very significant in recent times.

Nevertheless, the British power in India has acted as a dissolvent. In the words of Sir Henry Maine, 'It is by its indirect and for the most part unintended influence that the British power metamorphoses and dissolves the ideas and social forms underneath it. We rather change because we cannot help it. Whatever be the nature and value of that bundle of influences which we call Progress, nothing can be more certain than that, when a society is once touched by it, it spreads like a contagion'.

British action in India was both destructive and constructive. It hammered, pulverised and disintegrated the old Indian Society, breaking many of the links of the past that had bound us and left us as so many atoms with the result that we are still struggling with the problem of uniting India by a new set of principles. The prince disappeared or became ineffective; the aristocracy went down in influence and power; singers, artists, craftsmen and all the traditional charms of the courtly life disappeared or collapsed. The very roots of national life were affected when the villages also were caught in the storm. The new government with its paternalism and its easy accessibility to the rural areas on account of the developed means of communications reached everywhere, touching, destroying and uproating, though unintentionally, the age-old village institutions. Violent play of new and almost uncontrolled economic forces blew and scattered the old world apart. Such were the new economic forces summed up in the world capitalism with new markets, new techniques, communications and rapidly changing prices, of course, the old was not completely destroyed and many things have remained, good on archaic, adding to our troubles and perplexity. We have still the caste system, the linguistic divisions, the communal problem and many invidious, religious and social customs.

British rule had also its constructive side. Politically the conception of Indian unity was reborn and re-emphasised. Further a modern machinery of government was created and in place of personal loyality we had an institutional loyality.

Rule of law was established though under its mask the administration often acted high-handedly. The rule of law operated by means of the law codes and the courts. We can contrast this with the medieval times when the strong had justice invariably on his side. The British also gave us representative institutions. In the cultural fields the use of the English language and the setting up of Anglicised schools and colleges had also incalculable effects.

Through these institutions were planted in the minds of the younger generations the various ideas associated with the European liberalism—ideas like individualism, romanticism, humanitarianism and nationalism.

Economically, peace fostered trade and private enterprise leading to the growth of commercial, banking and industrial concerns. New classes appeared. Specially momentous was the rise of a middle class which had not existed in the medieval times. This class acted as the main source through which western influences poured into India. The press in India helped it to propagate its views and cement it by common bonds. It also acted as the spear-head of social movements like abolition of untouchability, widow re-marriage, widows' homes, girls' schools, asylums for the blind and the orphans, abolition of purdah, raising of the marriage age, forbidding polygamy and abolishing caste.

Such was the hotchpotch of actions, prohibitions and influences which determined Indian destiny under the British rule. Recently attempts have been made to draw up a credit and debit side of the British achievements in India but we are too near the event to draw up a correct balance-sheet. We can only make a rough estimate of the British achievements in our country. So far we have discussed in a general way the effect of the British rule in India. We shall now make a detailed study of some of the results brought about by contact between the two civilisations or cultures.

Our culture had become by the end of the eighteenth century almost moribund, decadent and effete. It seemed that a period had dawned marked politically by the anarchy which gave Europeans adventure its chance, inwardly by an increasing torpor of the creative spirit in religion and art, science and philosophy and intellectual knowledge which had long been dead or petrified into a mere scholastic Punditism all pointing to a nadir of setting energy.

So just as in the thirteenth century we needed a foreign attack to jolt us into proper consciousness similarly we needed the shock of foreign conquest in the nineteenth century to rouse us from our cultural inertia and torpor.

Economic Results

We may now analyse the results of the Western impact. Economically, the West introduced capitalism in India though here also we supplied the wealth from Bengal which enabled the growth of capitalism in England on the basis of industrial revolution.

At that time our country was just emerging from rural economy. She was developing commerce, trade and industries. But our immature and undeveloped industries had to face the vigorous and hungry capitalism of the West. Indian industries were destroyed and the country was forced back to the rural economy from which it was seeking to emerge. The reversion to an agricultural way of life coupled with enforced peace increased existing difficulties and created new problems. Population increased but the country was denuded of its wealth. Land can never provide for the whole population adequately, except in societies that are still primitive in organisation. In India, thus, the British tried to put the clock of civilisation back. But our contact with the West revealed to us a panorama of immense possibilities. In our own day we witnessed the rise of Japanese and American capitalism and how these countries came into the vanguard of civilisation. Thus our economic situation and our material potentialities roused the Indian intelligentsia and the middle classes to demand self government so that industries might be introduced here as well and the country be made rich. In other words the higher standard of material civilisation achieved by the West served as a challenge and an irritant.

Further from the West we have got economic theories of Socialism or Communism. A new awareness of Indian poverty has become the stock-in-trade of both our politicians and thinkers. The new generation has taken to these theories stock, lock and barrel. In the past 'the condition of the people' question had been almost relegated to the background and the historians of economic theories are to a certain extent justified in charging the ruling class in India with indifference so far as the question of improvement of the material conditions of the people is concerned. This economic backwardness was one of the irritants producing communalism in India. Because the Hindus had grown rich earlier or had become the landlords (as in Bengal) it was easy for the upper class Muslims to incite the poor Muslim against them under the pretext of Islam in danger. Every age or period has certain emphasis or some dominating tendency. The modern age is marked by an economic emphasis and naturally economic questions loom large on the Indian social horizon.

In this sphere, therefore, our indebtedness to the western civilisation is unmistakable. Though how far we have been able to dovetail these economic theories into our social and cultural traditions, is another question. The West today teaches us that, if we do not modernise our industries, art, transport, banking and armaments, all other avenues of progress will be blocked. The rural economy of the past must be, if not supplanted, at least supplemented to a large measure by industrial economy.

How best we can do it is another question where differences arise and we have become a cockpit for the contending theories of Capitalism, Socialism and Communism.

Social Results

In the social field, the influence of the West has either produced defensive complex or accelerated the process of social change. We have our conservatives, revivalists or 'back to the past' school who warn us of the insidious encroachments by the West on our social structure that has withstood the assault of time and man for so long and maintained social solidarity and cohesion. On the other hand we have the advanced schools of social thought which warn us of the dangers that come from perpetually stamping a major class of people with the stigma of untouchability or denying equality to the Indian women. In other words our social consciousness has been aroused. Besides, the West has given a new shape to our middle classes. The unbalanced growth of the middle class is the most significant fact of Modern India. They are restless, critical and individualistic. Today they are compelled either to move upward into the ranks of the capitalists or to relapse into the ranks of the proletariat. Those who cannot accommodate themselves to either of the two situations become either fascists or escapists. They have adopted the manners and the snobbishness of the west without understanding the reality of western society.

Scientific Aspects

In the scientific field the West has given us a dynamic outlook of life, a scientific and detached way of thinking and scientific education. As we have seen by the end of the middle ages our society was becoming static. The group ideas as represented by more or less autonomous castes, the Joint family and the communal self governing life of the village were the main pillars of our social system, and all these survived for so long because, in spite of their failings, they fulfilled some essential needs of human nature and society. They gave security and stability to each group and a sense of group freedom. But these ideas and systems continue so long as they adapt themselves to the changing environment. This did not happen in our recent history. We became prisoners of social routine. The very thing India lacked, the modern West possessed and possessed probably to excess. It was dynamic, it was progressive and full of life and bent upon scientific progress in all fields. Science, therefore, has opened up innumerable avenues for the growth of knowledge. It has given us a spirit of enquiry, a method of experiment and boldness of adventure and imagination to which we had become foreigners. All that is good as far as it goes. We must develop the scientific approach, the search for truth and new knowledge, the hard discipline of mind and capacity to probe into uttermost mysteries of life. All these things have come back to us from the modern West.

Literature

In the literary field also the West has made its contribution in various ways. In fact it would not be an exaggeration to say that we discovered our ancient heritage through the efforts of a group of Europeans who took to Indian history and literature for sheer love of adventure, of speculative thought. In the eighteenth century we had forgotten our ancient past almost completely.

It was through the efforts of Warren Hastings, Sir William Jones, Sir Charles Wilkins, Colebrooke, Horace Wilson, James Prinsep and others that the ancient Sanskrit classics were introduced not only to the Western world but also to India herself. The years 1828-70 saw the flowering of oriental scholarship. Hodgson discovered the literature of Northern Buddhism during his residence in Nepal from 1833-1844. Roth published his epoch making treatise on the Literature and the History of the Veda in 1846 and in collaboration with Bohtlingk began the issue of the great Petersburg Lexicon in 1852. Max-Muller's tract on Rig-Veda was issued between 1849-75. Prinsep and Cunningham laid the foundation of our knowledge of Indian art, epigraphy and archaeology. Between 1870-1900 we had other flowers of oriental studies like Sacred Books of the East, Trubner's Oriental Series, the Harvard Oriental Series, Childer's Dictionary of Pali besides works from other Indologists like Rhys Davids, Weber and Buhler of Vienna who began the Encyclopaedia of Indo-Aryan Research from 1897 and to which more than thirty scholars from different countries have contributed.

The English and other Europeans also led in the fields of archaeology, numismatics and other sources of history laying bare the skeletons of our history. Indians thus discovered themselves through the agency of the West. Again the West gave us the printing press which has been another instrument of our national awakening. The introduction of English as a medium of education has also been a tremendous factor in the growth of our modernism. The English literature is a literature of freedom. We have drunk deep from this fountain and nothing is more illuminating than the speeches of the Indian politicians before 1915, in this respect. They consciously modelled themselves after the British leaders of thought and action. It was through this language that the West was opened to us and incalculable consequences have flown therefrom. The Western literature in all its branches provided set models which were sometimes sedulously aped. English books let loose a flood of new ideas, Sanskrit works were translated and gave us an inkling into our ancient thought. A prose literature came into existence in the vernaculars of India. Newspapers were started and brought us into contact with not only the outside world but also with the political, economic and social ills of our country. Of course, labouring under the theory of filtration, our educational structure became top heavy, the education of the masses was neglected and even the people from villages, who came for studies did not return the fruits of their education to their native places. The decision to give education through the medium of English was, therefore, not an unmixed good. In the field of arts also the West gave us great incentive and inspiration, while on the one hand writers like Havell aroused in us the consciousness of the value of our arts, others encouraged us to study the western art for models and thus we had different schools of art, originating specially in the present century.

Philosophy and Religion

In the philosophic field the West gave us new philosophies of materialism, realism and idealism, fruitful sources of intellectual ferment and restiess questionings. Many of us indoctrinated with the western rationalism became iconoclastic. Critical of authority and tradition, old beliefs were denounced and even the good was rejected because it came from the past encumbered with effete traditions and practices. This produced a reaction and a revivalist mentality set in but there still remained a school begun by Raja Ram Mohan Roy, which sought only to reject the evil, to reform old abuses and renovate our religious and social life on the basis of principles not militating against the true traditions of our religion. Further, European philosophy became a subject of study in itself in our colleges.

Politics

In the political or administrative field Western civilisation gave us unity, a rule of law and constitutional freedom. By various agencies, the press, the developed means of communications, capitalism and other forces developed leading to India's unification. The nascent spirit of nationalism was fostered by the establishment of Indian National Congress and heroes like Mazzini and Garibaldi of Italy became our guides in the political sphere. We developed the feeling that all were equal before the law. But here also there was no unmixed good. If the British enabled us to appreciate the value of freedom, they also gave us the policy of communalism. The Mohammedans of India developed a communal mentality as a defensive mechanism because firstly, their Hindu brethren had got the loaves and fishes of office and secondly, because only by this could they gain the favour of the powers that be and oust the Hindus from the offices and seats of power.

To sum up, the British gave us peace, contact with the outside world, science and all that it led to in the shape of inventions, scientific, technical and mechanical. They gave us unity and uniformity of administration. In other words they prepared the ground for the Indian renaissance. Just as the Western Europe woke up from the lethargy of the middle ages and turned to the literature of Greece and Rome for models of thought and style, so India was roused from its intellectual coma by contact with the West and turned to it for inspiration in many fields, specially economic and scientific. But as we have emphasized all this was no part of the policy of the British rulers in India. They even tried to block our path to progress, consciously or unconsciously. Various reactionary forces were either consolidated or given birth to, our growth was stunted and we are still paying the price of this unnatural blocking of our progress. Nevertheless the West was knocking at our doors and its entry could not be denied. World-unity could not be a practicable proposition till India and other oriental countries had been brought into contact with western civilisation so that out of their mutual impact same comman civilisation and culture may emerge. That alone explains the historical process that brought India and England together.

India and the West

India also influenced the West in many directions. The cultural interactions of India and the West go back to remote times. We have aleady referred to India's contact with the West in her ancient period of history. Even in the medieval period Indian goods and ideas passed into Europe mainly through the Arabs and the Italians who controlled the carrying trade between Asia and Europe. Later on we have a number of travellers besides the Portuguese and other trading missions that came to India. Sir Thomas Roe is said to have provided inspiration for Milton's picture of Satan sitting exalted.

High on a throne of royal state, which far
Outshone the wealth of Ormuz and of Ind.

There was also the drama 'Aurangzeb' written by Dryden.

But so far the ancient literature of India and her civilisation had been a closed book to the Europeans. The first attempts were made by the Jesuits who obtained some knowledge of Sanskrit through a study of the Indian vernaculars. Through them a book went to Europe and made great impression on Voltaire. A Jesuit compiled the first Sanskrit grammar in 1732. Through Duperron, a Frenchman, Dara's translations of Upanishads reached Europe and influenced the German philosophers notably Schopenhauer and Von Hartmann.

But these were individual attempts. The first systematic study of our culture by the Europeans began when our works in Sanskrit were translated by a group of orientalists encouraged by the initiative of Warren Hastings. In 1785, Sir Charles Wilkins, the first European really to understand Sanskrit, published a translation of the famous philosophical poem, the Bhagavadgita. In 1784 was also founded the Asiatic Society of Bengal by Sir William Jones. From this society arose those valuable translations of the Indian classics which have reverberated the fame of the Indian culture throughout the whispering galleries of Europe. Sir William Jones translated the works of Kalidasa and also Manu-Smriti. He also made it known that Sanskrit was the most scientific language and contained words common both to Latin and Greek languages. He thus laid the foundations of the science of comparative philosophy and provided the seeds for the theory of Max Muller to grow, about the common home of the Aryans. Europe owes the study of phonetics to the ancient Sanskrit grammarians whose works thus became known to the West. In this field of translation the greatest work was done in the early years of the nineteenth century by H.C. Colebrooke who made epoch-making Studies of the Hindu law, philosophy, grammar, astronomy and religion. Thus for the first time Vedas were revealed not only to Europe but also to most of the Indians, for the Pandits had jealously concealed the secret of the Vedic lore. One Englishman, Hamilton, taught Sanskrit to some Frenchmen and Germans and this led to vigorous researches in our culture by France and Germany. Max Muller was the first to translate completely, after a labour of thirty years, the text of Rig-Veda in 1875. His work was epoch-making, something like the translation of the Bible for the Vedas had never reached the people who would now be able to study it. Like Charles Darwin in the physical world, he inaugurated a revolution in the realms of philosophy and religion, giving us subjects like comparative philosophy and comparative religion. He made the Europeans feel something of the majesty and splendour of Indian culture. India also, it is said, influenced the romantic movement in England and Germany.

Shelly, Wordsworth and Carlyle are full of the traces of the Vedanta, which reached them through German or Platonic sources. Goethe's praise of Shakuntala is well known. Moreover, India influenced the Americans also like Emerson and Thoreau. Tennyson also referred to Indian topics in some of his poems. Hindu philosophy exercised a considerable influence upon the poets of the Celtic Revival in Ireland especially Yeats and Russell. Anglo-Indian literature is really a subject in itself. Many Englishmen connected with India have given us their own books on Indian history like Wilks, Elphinstone, Tod, Mill and others. Sir Edwin Arnold was the greatest Anglo-Indian poet. As an interpreter of the East to the West he stands unsurpassed as his book like the Light of Asia and we have also a school of Anglo-Indians who presented a romantic and often indefensible caricature of Indian life, of whom Kipling is the best known. India supplied many of the manners, words and dishes of the English society. The 'nabobs' with their hookah, polaw and chutney were well known in the nineteenth century. The great English novelist Thackeray was born in India and many Anglo-Indian characters found place in his novels. In the present century also the Europeans have written much about India either in praise or in condemnation. Forster's works are well known, specially his novel 'Passage to India', condemning the ways of the Indian station life. Besides in the field of Theosophy Madame Blavatsky and Mrs. Annie Besant have given their best to India. Europe also has known the works of Swami Vivekanand, Rabindranath Tagore and Mahatma Gandhi. In the field of art also Indian influence is permeating Europe and Europe has developed a taste for the Indian artistic works. Many societies in Europe and America have sprung up catering to the demand for information about our culture.

We shall end the chapter by a brief reference to the development of what is called the Indo-Anglican literature, that is, the works of those Indians who have written mainly in English. The class includes a variety of poets, novelists, essayists and critics.

Among the most famous of the poets were the late Toru

Dutta, Mrs. Sarojini Naidu and Sri Aurobindo. Among the second class of modern poets we have Manmohan Ghosh, Harindranath Chattopadhyaya, S.R. Dongerkery, K.D.' Sethna, Dilip Kumar Roy, Lalita Devi, A.K. Seth and Subho Tagore. Sarojini's lyrics are master-pieces of Indo-Anglican poetry. To quote some of her lines

Spring time, O Spring Time. What is your essence,
the lilt of a bulbul, the laugh of a rose,
the dance of the dew on the wings of a moon-beam,
the voice of the Zephyr that sings as he goes,
the hope of a bride or the dream of a maiden
watching the petals of gladness enclose? Behold
The rise to meet the destined spring,
And scale the stars upon my broken wing.

Sri Aurobindo is one of the futurists, the poet of the world-literature of tomorrow. His dramas, lyrics and epics are all of a piece, profound, sweet, melodious and inspiring. His last work was Savitri an epic-poem consisting of more than 25,000 verses. To quote some lines from this master-piece.

A mystery is this mighty Nature's birth :
A mystery is the elusive stream of mind,
A mystery the protean break of life,
What I have learnt, chance leaps to contradict
What I, have built is sieved and torn by Fate,
I can foresee the acts of Master's force,
But not the march of the destiny of man;
He is driven upon paths he did not chaase,
I feel trampled underneath the rolling wheels.
My great philosophies are a reasoned guess;
The mystic heavens that claim the human souls
are a charlatanism of the imagining brain,
All is a speculation or a dream,
In the end the world itself becomes a doubt;
The infinitesimal's jest mocks mass and shape,
A laugh peals from the infinite's finite mask.

Among the novelists we have Dr. Mulk Raj Anand, Manjeri S. Isvaran and K.S. Venkataramani. Mulk Raj with his novels, Coolie, Untouchable, Two leaves and a Bud enjoys world-wide fame. Isvaran is among the foremost writers of the South while Venkataramani is regarded as the Tagore of South India. All these have evoked appreciation from the West. Lastly we have a group of essayists and critics among whom we may list persons like M.M. Bhattacharji, V.N. Bhushan, Sukumar Dutt, Amar Nath Jha, U.C. Nag, I.H. Zubeir, Satyendranath Ray, Sri Aurobindo, Tagore, Mardhekar, Jawaharlal Nehru and Humayun Kabir. We have also a notable class of writers and speakers on political and philosophical topics like Mahatma Gandhi and S. Radhakrishnan.

Thus, the West has entered into India through many doors and window. Indian life, literature, philosophy, society, politics, religion and arts have all felt the impact of a vigorous and adolescent culture and we have been jolted into a new awakening and a new sense of our responsibilities as well as of our weak-nesses while the West also as of old has realised anew the glory that was India.

17

THE INDIAN RENAISSANCE

INDIA IN OUR own day is in the throes of a crisis which has so far baffled all solutions. Indian independence has let loose, as it were, the Pandora's box. Political, economic, social, religious and psychological problems and questions have gained an intensity we missed before. Yet the solutions so far offered or attempted hardly seem to be so comprehensive, integral and synthetic as to meet the requirements of the situations. Indian statesmanship lacks vision and where the people are wanting in vision, the nation perishes. May it not be that our solutions fail because the problem of India has not been grasped in its entirety or that we fail to see that the 'Indian problem' is to be visualised in the context of a world-crisis and its solution is, therefore, part of a universal resolution of the world-problem. It is possible also that we may discover some key to our problem by analysing the Indian Renaissance of modern times, which has been ushered into by contact of the two civilisations of the East and the West and therefore, a right understanding of it may enable us to appreciate in its proper significance the world-crisis as well.

India in the eighteenth century had become moribund and her aristocratic and feudal culture had fossilised leading to a failure of inspiration and vision. We had been seized by torpor and lethargy.

At this momentous period of our history nature sent, as it were, foreigners to apply the shock of conquest and subjection so that we may be awakened into a newer understanding of our short-comings and difficulties. The West has had its renaissance or awakening and the Indians of the nineteenth century eagerly seized upon the chief features, or elements of the Western renaissance and proceeded to apply them to the Indian setting also. The Western renaissance in its latest phase was a revolt of reason and science against religious dogmatism and we also took up the cudgels for secularism and reason against the popular superstitions of the day.

Indian youths avidly seized upon the discoveries of science and threw all caution to the winds just to mock the religious sensibilities of the Pharisees of the India as witness, for instance, the rush of the Bengali youths of the middle classs to qualify for a degree in medical.

Science where the dissection of animals went against the susceptibilities of the believers in non-violence. The Brahmo Samaj in Bengal was a symbol of this revolt or awakening. This was the first phase of the Indian renaissance. Soon, however, this onesided appraisal of the Indian situation, this extreme drift towards the Western scepticism produced a reaction which was symbolised in the religious messages of men like Dayanand, Ramakrishna and Vivekanand. But, as it happens in a crisis, the moderate elements in these phases were swamped by the exrtremists and while Brahmo Samaj degenerated into formalism, the religious awakening either passed off into revivalism or losing its initial fervour became a matter of outward creed and ritual. So long, however, as it retained its potency and vigour it led to a rediscovery of the past and a refashioning of our arts, literature, philosophy and society.

There was however, no proper appreciation of the needs and demands of an awakened India and possibly could not be because of our obsession with politics, a subject India could not think independently. Freedom was an imperative necessity and we got it in 1947. But the bloodshed it involved and the economic troubles that it let loose swamped us off our feet and there could be no time to go into the fundamentals of our problems. It was easy to seize upon the solutions that the West could offer in the realm of politics, or in the departments of life or in the domain of economics and apply them to the Indian situation. Thus, the Indian renaissance after freedom is in an inchoate stage and we have adopted a policy of drift. The influence of the West in morals, in social attitudes, in artistic principles, in literary fashions is so overwhelming that we have lost our bearings and become 'pedulous apes'. The cultural crisis in India needs a synthetic approach and not an uncritical adoption of all that the West offers. It would, therefore, be well to delve deep into the fundamentals of the Western and the Eastern cultures and see where they err and in what way they can be harmonised, for, only in such a harmony can the present Indian renaissance find its historical justification.

The two fundamentals of the Western culture as it has developed in its modern setting are reason and science. Their development was a historical necessity for religion in Europe had tended to crib, cabin and confine man into narrow grooves of formalism, dogmatism, superstitions and religiosity blocking all progress. Reason cleared the way. It was the highest developed faculty of man. On account of reason man was prevented from being carried away by the exigencies of the moment. Reason is science, it is conscious art, it is invention. Through its help man could sift and arrange truth of facts; could launch upon constructive work, could extricate and forecast truth of potentiality and regardless of the passions or the utilities of the hour seek disinterestedly Truth for its own sake. 'It has been the Prometheus of the mythical parable, the helper, instructor, elevating friend, civilizer of mankind'. Reason in politics discovered democracy, rationality in economics discovered socialism and it found in science the key to unlock the treasures of nature. Yet mankind remained as far away as ever from discovering lasting solutions of the ills it was suffering from. Reason has been used to justify all sorts of ideas and nostrums. In philosophy it could advance valid reasons for monism, pluralism, idealism and realism. In religion it could satisfy the atheists and propitiate the God-lover. It could justify both asceticism and hedonism. It could be a convincing champion of dictatorship as well as democracy. It was a prophet both to communism and anarchism. In short, it can place itself at the disposal of any combinations, harmonies and theories according as the spirit in man is attracted to or withdraw from it. For it is really the spirit in man which decides and reason has proved to be a brilliant servant and minister of this veiled sovereign.

Though reason led man to democracy which was mainly political in character, it failed to meet the demands of the situation, it was said that political democracy had become the servant of capitalism. Socialism was, therefore, born as a revolt against capitalism and was compelled to work itself out by a war of classes and had also to take the shape of an industrial and economic creed. Its real basis, however, is the demand of human reason to carry on the rational ordering of society for its fulfilment and get rid of all parasites. Competition should be replaced by co-operation and capitalism by social regulation of our economic life.

This involves initially atleast, curtailment of individual liberty which had led to economic malaise of competitive capitalism. Property is to be vested in the community and even man in all his social functions as a father, as an educator, as a worker, as a citizen belongs entirety to the society. The individual has failed to reason out properly and must be guided by the reason of the community which finds its dynamic will in the state or its apparatus, the government. Thus freedom is supplemented or supplanted by the slogan of equality. Some people try to steer a via media. The socialists in Germany did it and were supplanted by the Hitlerites, the Labour Party in England attempted it and has fallen into the lap of the American capitalism for logic of socialism is on the side of communism or collectivism. Equality in practice means the rule of the few for the good of all, the majority of whom are to be raised sufficiently high mentally and culturally before they can be allowed to rule themselves or enjoy freedom. Yet this socialism also involves contradictions and conflicts. With absolutism in politics comes a tendency to brush aside reason and crystallise all social, political and economic life of the people into a new rigid organisation. In such a situation when the mind of man is denied freedom to think or freedom to realise its thought by action in life, reason fails to perform its office.

Man in the absence of such freedom will become a stunted and static being. Men may bear the economic despotism for a time in consideration of the visible new benefits but in course of time its defects become more and more realised and prominent, dissatisfaction and revolt are sure to set in the clearest and most vigorous minds of the society and propagate themselves through the mass. This is the central defect through which a socialistic state is bound to be convicted of insufficiency and will have to pass away before the growth of a new ideal. Life abhors mechanisation, the basis of socialism, and will break away from it when opportunity offers. Thus socialism is also a partial solution and cannot satisfy the demand of the hour as we have seen now in Russia.

We have another instrument of reason, namely, science. In the nineteenth century science seemed to promise cure of all human maladies. It seemed to fulfil impeccably the two supreme demands of the age of reason. It was a truth of things which depended for its veracity or authenticity neither on any scripture nor on the whims of any human authority. Its book was nature, its instruments were experiments and intellectual honesty and its results were abiding. It was the sovereign panacea for all the diseases of the human organism. It was the key to unlock the treasures of Progress.

For a time it worked wonders but soon a nemesis seemed to overtake mankind. Science had unleashed weapons which seemed to destroy mankind. For ultimately science led to a mechanistic way of thought and an atomic view of the homosapiens. It had overpassed itself and its shortcomings became patent when a mounting flood of psychological and psychic knowledge pouring into the Western culture as a result of the researches of men like Freud and Jung brought into clearer perspective the complex nature of man. Thus reasan and science, the twin-gods of the Western civilisation are not alone sufficient to solve our troubles. But they have given us two valuable discoveries which we can discard only at our peril. The first is the democratic conception of the right of all people in any country to the full life and the full and complete development of which they are individually capable. Social development cannot be at the expense of the masses. Privileged class is an anachronism.

Secondly, the individual is not merely a social unit; he is something in himself. He has a personality of his own. He has an individual worth, an individual truth and law which can be fulfilled in his own way and in consonance with his own nature. He demands freedom, thought, space and initiative to fulfil the laws of his self, to discover his soul.

The West has grasped this idea intellectually and in this its kinship to the Indian way of life can be feasible.

While reason and science have been the master ideas of the modern Western culture, spirituality has been the master idea of the Indian Culture. But in the long run this idea has been the servant of religion which has been so applied as to lead to decadence and demoralisation. There are two aspects of religion, true religion and religionism. True religion is spiritual and its attempt is always to find habitation in the spirit, in what is beyond the intellect, beyond all borders of the aesthetic, ethical and practical sides of man but not away from them. These too have to be informed by the higher light and law of the spirit. Religionism, in India, on the other hand, is characterised by two main features in the first place it has been identified with cults, systems of ceremonial forms, narrow pietistic exaltations, intellectual dogmas, rigid moral code, religio-social systems and various superstitious rites and ceremonies. These things can be aids and supports; they may sometimes be needed by the less cultured to pave the path for the higher things and they posses utility only so long as their true nature is understood, provided also they are not forced upon any individual. The spiritual essence of religion alone matters and not its paraphernalia. Secondly, religionism has been identified with indifference towards earthly life. The material aims of life are either condemned wholesale or their subordination is so emphasized that the spirit becomes same thing ethereal, otherworldly, heavenly which man can only attain by discarding the ordinary life and taking to an ascetic withdrawal from this illusory world. We develop pessimism, a gospel of the vanity of life and decry all attempts to seek beauty in life. In the long run such an attitude bred fatalism and inertia. The indifference of the village-folk in India to the change of rulers is explained partly at least by such a philosophy of life. This leads to a truncated life and a partial vision. Our narration of India's culture has revealed this major defect in Indian life, this confusion of religion with religiosity and the consequent imperviousness to the demands of life. True religion is synonymous with spirituality which affirms that only by the light and power of the highest can the lower be perfectly guided, uplifted and accomplished. 'Spirituality respects the freedom of the human soul, because it is itself fulfilled by freedom; and the deepest meaning of freedom is the power to expand and grow towards perfection by the law of one's own nature, dharma. This liberty it will give to all the fundamental parts of our being. It will give that freedom to philosophy and science which ancient Indian religion gave freedom even to deny the spirit, if they will as a result of which philosophy and science never felt in ancient India any necessity of divorcing themselves from religion, but grew rather into it and under its light. It will give the same freedom to man's seeking for political and social perfection and to all his other powers and aspirations. Only it will be vigilant to illuminate them so that they may grow into the light and law of the spirit, not by suppression and restriction, but by a self searching, self-controlled expansion and a many-sided finding of their greatest, highest and deepest potentialities'.

We have made an analysis of the fundamentals of the Western and Indian cultures to find out light for the third phase of our renaissance which is now in the formative stage. We find that reason and science can be harnessed into the service of man so long as they remain the servants of the spirit and not instruments of our passions or prejudices. We should also learn from the West respect for the individual and solicitude for the welfare of all. The West will have to learn that reason and science with their emphasis an external remedies, on the setting up of institutions and systems of thought will be convicted of nullity unless they are guided by the true light which will descend into man when he seeks a larger affirmation, a greater harmony and a more complete union with the Divine.

This is our understanding of the drift or significance of the Indian renaissance of modern times. The renaissance stimulated by contact with the progressive West began as a recoil against the Indian life as lived by the majority. But it developed a defensive mechanism, a revivalist mentality as a reaction against the extreme positions taken by the modernists in India. Together with these we had another mentality which sought some synthesis of the two, some compromise or middle path represented by persons like Vivekanand, Tagore and Annie Besant. But the synthesis was neither whole-hearted nor comprehensive. The masses remained unaffected and our preoccupation with politics did not allow us time to think out a new synthesis. This explains why we have lost the original fervour which threw up on the stage of the Indian life men like Tagore in literature, Vivekanand in religion, Abanindranath in painting, Tilak and Gandhi in politics, Radhakrishnan in philosophy and Udai Shankar in dancing. The age of giants seems to have passed away. But such a view will be a misreading of our cultural history. We are on the threshold of a new awakening. Freedom has given us new opportunities and if we develop the inner vision the outer too will be set right.

We have discussed the fundamental basis of the Indian culture and its reflection in our renaissance. We shall now describe the chief features of the new awakening in the various fields of religion, social and economic life, arts and literature.

Religion

The first contacts of the West with Indian cultural life led to the adoption of the western ways of life, rejection of what were called the dogmas and rituals of Indian religions on the part of some Indians but there were at the same time many religious movements aiming at the revitalisation of the Indian religious and social life, like the Brahmo Samaj in Bengal, the Prarthana Samaj in Maharashtra and later the Arya Samaj, the Theosophical Society, the Ramakrishna Mission and others.

Brahmo Samaj

The founder of Brahmo Samaj was Ram Mohun Roy who may well be called the father of the Modern Indian Renaissance. Born on 22nd May, 1772 he began writing about Indian conditions at a very early age. He was well-versed in English, Persian, Arabic, Sanskrit and Bengali. His earliest publications were his studies on the Upanishads and Vedanta. At the same time he was engaged in controversies with many people, on religious and social problems since he settled in Calcutta after 1792. He engaged in religious bouts both with the traditional Hindu Pandits and with the Christian missionaries. He advocated the abolition of the cruel rites of Sati. He was a zealous advocate of the adoption of the Western scientific studies in our educational institutions.

He was also a great patriot with a penchant for politics and publicity. He represented the cause of Indian liberty both at home and abroad. Probably in the year 1815 he founded the Atmiya Sabha for purposes of religious discussions. In 1819 he founded the Calcutta Unitarian Committee. Finally, on 20th August, 1828 he established the Brahmo Samaj. The Samaj was to aim at the propagation of true Hinduism as Ram Mohun Roy understood it, purged of social evils and idol-worship, yet he was not a fanatic as is obvious from the following words written by him in 1830 in connection with worship in Brahmo Samaj.

"And that in conducting the said worship or adoration no object, animate or inanimate, that has been, or is or shall hereafter become, or be recognised, as an object of worship, by any man or set of men, shall be reviled or slightingly or contemptuously spoken of or alluded to either in preaching, praying, or in the hymns, or other mode of worship that may be delivered or used in the said message or building. And that no sermon, preaching, discourse, prayer or hymn be delivered, made or used in such worship but such as have a tendency to the promotion of the contemplation of the Author and Preserver of the Universe, to the promotion of charity, morality, piety, benevolence, virtue and the strengthening of the bands of union between men of all religions, persuasions and creeds". The Raja died at Bristol on 27th September, 1833.

Ram Mohun Roy and his Brahmo Samaj form the starting points for all the various Reform movements whether in Hindu religion, society or politics, which have agitated India during the past hundred years and which have led to her wonderful Renaissance in our own days. To the present generation he is only a name, a memory but to his contemporaries he was a great beacon light, a tower of philosophical wisdom, a constructive genius, a champion of liberty and the first great Reformer of modern India. His advocacy of reformed Hinduism threw a veritable stone in the stagnant pools of Indian waters, beginning a process of self introspection and analysis that has gone far in purging Hinduism of its grossest superstitions.

The leadership of Brahmo Samaj was taken up by Devendranath Tagore and later by Keshub Chandra Sen. Under these personalities the Samaj began attacking abuses of Hindu society like intemperance, polygamy and caste-tyranny while widow remarriage and female education were vigorously advocated. The Samaj had such leading lights as Raj Narain Bose and Ishwar Chandra Vidyasagar. In 1867 the conservative group in the Samaj formed the Adi Brahmo Samaj. The advanced section accepted the lead of Keshub Chandra. He had begun advocating a movement which would reconcile all the apparently conflicting creeds and this was misunderstood.

Still Keshub was at heart an Indian as can be gleaned from his writings about Swami Dayanand and Ramakrishna Paramhamsa. To quote some lines from his Asia's message to Europe - 'I am a child of Asia; her sorrows are my sorrows, her Joys are my joys. From one end of Asia to the other, I boast of a wide nationality and an extended friendship'. Keshub died in 1884 at an early age of forty-six. In 1878 the Brahmo Samaj had a further split, a younger group forming the Sadharan Brahmo Samaj. The venerable Maharshi Devendranath sent a message of blessing to the new group. By this time the Samaj had got branches in Assam, Bihar, Uttar Pradesh, South India, Maharashtra and Sind. The Samaj catered to the educational needs also of the people by opening various schools and in other ways its leaders were to be in the forefront of the Indian awakening. As a pioneer in the field of our cultural resurgence the contribution of the Samaj cannot be too highly assessed.

Arya Samaj

Like the impact of Islam, influence of Christianity in India inaugurated many Protestant movements here in this period, of these the most famous is Arya Samaj. Its founder, Rishi Dayanand's interpretation of the Vedas has given a new orientation to the Hindu faith. First scoffed at and ridiculed, the view point of the Rishi has of late been hailed by savants of both the East and the West, says Sri Aurobindo 'There is then nothing fantastical in Dayananda's idea that the Veda contains truths of science as well as truths of religion. I will even add my own conviction that the Veda contains other truths of a science which the modern world does not at all possess and in that case Dayanand has rather understated than overstated their depth and range of the Vedic wisdom'. Thus Dayanand's interpretations gave us a real scripture. Swami Dayanand Saraswati lent his powerful voice against social evils, against attachment to the shell of idol-worship, losing sight of the substance there of, and saved the Hindu from being engulfed by Christianity or Islam. But he was not a fanatic and had even mooted the idea of a conference of representatives of all religions on the occasion of the Delhi Darbar in 1877. Rishi Dayanand (1824-1883) formally started the Arya Samaj as an organisation to propagate Vedic religion in Bombay in 1875 and also published there his most famous writings in *Satyartha Prakash*.

His preaching took the strongest root in the Punjab and in the Uttar Pradesh. Like every reform movement, the Arya Samaj set itself first to purge the Hindu society, of its rampant evils. The worship of one God, the abolition of castes to be replaced by true Varna-Vyavastha based on character, performance of religious ceremonies as enjoined in the Vedas, freedom of women, abolition of untouchability, education through Sanskrit or Hindi and conversion of even non-Hindus to Hinduism or Vedic-Dharma were some of the principles of Arya Samaj. Members of the Arya Samaj, 'The Church Militant' had to suffer martyrdom for the sake of their convictions both at the hands of the superstitious Hindus and at the hands of fanatical Mohammedans.

The contribution of Arya Samaj in uplifting the Hindus is indirectly testified to by the rulers imprisoning its followers merely because they were Arya Samajis as can be read in Lady Minto's diary The Hindus at that time had become weak-kneed, spineless and feeble-minded. They lacked the stamina to fight the social abuses. With the advent of the Arya Samaj this mentality of undisturbed indifference is gone for ever. Faith is again a living thing with the Hindu. The Arya Samaj men appealed to reason, to the best in our scriptures and its founder set an ideal of self sacrifice which has few equals in the annals of history, under the Arya Samaj schools have been opened, Gurukuls started on the analogy of old Ashrams, Seva Samitis opened for the service of all and even outside India its branches have been opened for uplift work and social regeneration. Truly the Arya Samaj cemented the Hindu society when it was disintegrating during the years following the so-called mutiny of 1857. Democracy is the God today but we find Swamiji practising it as early as the eighties of the nineteenth century when he refused to advise the Lahore Arya Samaj unless he was made its member. He was a saint of a dynamic order and derived inspiration from personal communion with the Divine.

The Theosophists

Another group of thinkers in the religious line who made the West realise the truths of the Indian culture and civilisation, was the Theosophists. The name Theosophy is an exact translation of the well-known Sanskrit term Brahmavidya, for it is made up of the two Greek words, Theos—God, and Sophia—wisdom. This word has been popularised today by the Theosophical Society founded by Madame H.P. Blavatsky, Colonel H.S. Olcott and others. The knowledge of Brahman or Absolute has been gathered by the Theosophists from many sources notably India, Egypt, Greece and mystical teachings of early Christianity. In India we remember it because of its connection with Dr. Annie Besant whose advocacy of Indian freedom is well known. Her luminous touch and magnetic personality attracted many Indians towards Theosophist. The Theosophist holds that all religions are derived from one source, and that, therefore, there is no one religion which is the exclusive road to salvation. Each religion is considered by the Theosophist as having its role to fulfil in a great plan for all men just as the seven rays in solar spectrum have all new distinct functions in fostering the growth of living.

Since all men have the divinity in them, Universal Brotherhood becomes a fact of nature. The Theosophists have gathered valuable data concerning life beyond death. Thus the Theosophist is characterised by a profound belief in the existence of a divine wisdom and by a determination to be an agent in God's plan for men. He, therefore, serves all men regardless of their colour, caste or creed. The Theosophists have also helped in the spread of the Indian culture.

Ramakrishna Mission

Reference may now be made to the spiritual movement inaugurated by Sri Ramakrishna Paramahamsa. This movement has played a decisive part in the Indian Renaissance. We have to assess its importance against the background of cultural debacle that overtook India in the seventies of the nineteenth century. During this period India had been wading through a bewildering welter of cultural ideals. Politically overthrown by the British, she had been fast coming under the sway of an exotic civilisation. Nurtured upon English education, the Indians began to believe that India had no culture worth the name and that she would have to remould herself thoroughly in the lathe of European civilisation. Further a tidal wave of atheism swept over the land through the medium of the English language.

But Western materialism was accompanied by Christian evangelism which would have swept Indians off from their old religion if Hinduism had not been succoured by the reform movements culminating in the Ramakrishna Mission.

This movement differs from those above to a great extent because it attempted to reform Hinduism from within without attempting to set up an independent doctrine or order. The Brahmo Samaj and the Arya Samaj did not secure the adherence of the vast majority who remained wedded to their old faith. These were served by Sri Ramakrishna whose phenomenal life of intense spirituality, a remarkably broad and synthetic vision of Hinduism and an extraordinary, simple and illuminating exposition of all the ideas and ideals of Hindu theology were perfectly in tune with the whole tenor of Hindu thought and aspirations and as such harmonised completely with the lives and teachings of the sages, seers and prophets who had preceded him. In the words of Mahatma Gandhi, 'The story of Ramakrishna Paramahamsa's life is a story of religion in practice. His life enables us to see God face to face. No one can read his life without being convinced that God alone is real and that all else is an illusion. Ramakrishna is a living embodiment of Godliness. Even intellectuals like Narendra Nath (later Swami Vivekanand) humbled themselves at the feet of Paramahamsa. Through Swami Vivekanand the message of Paramahamsa spread both in the East and the West'.

In the words of Romain Rolland, 'The man whose image I here invoke was the consummation of two thousand years of the spiritual life of three hundred million people. Although he has been dead forty years, his soul animates modern India'.

Ramakrishna came from the people. He was born in the early dawn of the 15th February, 1835, in the village Kamarpukur in the district Hooghly of Bengal. He belonged to a Brahman family. He was given the name of Gadadhar. From early age he began to have ecstatic visions. He was an ardent lover of music and poetry and took great delight in singing songs and reciting verses from the epics. During this period while enacting the part of Siva in a drama or worshipping goddess Visalakshi we find him swooning with sheer joy and ecstasy. Meditation on a deity would call up the real form before his mind's eye and immediately his outward consciousness would be sucked in a whirlpool of surging emotions. At the early age of nine he had to shoulder the family task of worshipping the family deity and this gave him intense pleasure or bliss.

When his elder brother went to Calcutta to officiate as a priest in a temple nearby in 1855 he also went to stay there though at first reluctantly.

Next year his brother died and he got the Job of the head priest of the temple. This temple continued to be his abode down till his death. The temple is commonly known as Dakshineshwar Kali temple, situated in the village Dakshineshwar, four miles to the North of Calcutta. It stands directly on the Ganges on the eastern bank. Within the compound there was one temple dedicated to Krishna and in twelve temples were installed the images of Siva. But it was to Kali, the Divine Mother, that Ramakrishna was attached most. From now on he had many religious experiences, for example, he wanted to see Kali face to face. For this he began to cry, beseech and bemoan. He suffered great anguish and torment and decided to end his life but the Mother relented and the beatific vision was unfolded before his eyes, he became bathed in an ocean of ecstasy. He emerged out of this trance after two days. By degrees he developed a consciousness in which he could always see Kali and be guided by Her. Later he wanted to see God in other forms like those of Ram and Krishna. He realised these wishes also. In 1859 he went for sometime back to his village where he was married but all through life he remained a Brahmachari. After this he came back to Dakshineshwar. Here, again he underwent various spiritual realisations and took to the religious practices of Tantra, Vaishnavism, Advaitism, Islam, Christianity and Buddhism, from all these he emerged a seer, a realised saint and was now ready to shower his teachings upon those who sought him for salvation. By his spotless purity, absolute unassuming pose and overflowing love for humanity, he attracted all and sundry like a mighty magnet. His wit and parables charmed all. In simple language he could explain an abstruse philosophy, specially by means of stories. Soon he gathered a band of followers. His attitude to mercy is thus finely expressed. 'They talk of mercy to the creatures How audacious it is to think of showering mercy on the Jiva, who is none other than Siva. One has to regard the creature as God himself and proceed to serve it with a devout heart, instead of taking up the pose of doling out mercy'. It was this message of divine worship through service of suffering humanity as a veritable manifestation of God that Swami Vivekanand the most well-known disciple of Paramahamsa spread throughout the world and left it for generations to follow by the institution of Ramakrishna Mission. Before his death on 15th August, 1886 Sri Ramkrishna entrusted to Vivekanand the task of consolidating the holy brotherhood and looking after their spiritual welfare.

To Ramakrishna religion was the breath of his life, religion in the sense of all-embracing spirituality. Realisation of God was the worthiest object of life, and devotion, purity, sincerity, selflessness, love and humility constituted the real wealth of man. 'From his life it discovers the meaning of the scriptures, through his life and teachings man has got an opportunity of learning the old lessons afresh'.

Vivekanand (1863-1902) spread abroad the message of his Guru, verifying it by his own experiments and observations. Vivekanand was the monastic name of Narendra Nath who was born in an aristocratic Kayastha family of Calcutta on the 12th January, 1863, in physique he was strong and of athletic build. He was at home in manly exercises and also a master of music. He received full-fledged College education. He had joined the Brahmo Samaj but not being satisfied he went in search of other religious worthies and met Sri Ramakrishna in 1881. This was like a meeting of the religious and mystic East with the sceptic and rationalistic West and the latter was conquered completely, of course, by stages.

When in his first interview he asked Sri Ramakrishna if he had seen God, the reply came pat, 'Yes, I see Him just as I see you here, only in a sense much more intense'. He further observed, 'God can be realised; one can see and talk to Him as I am doing with you. But who cares to do so ? people shed torrents of tears for their wife and children, for wealth and property, but who does so for the sake of God? If one weeps sincerely for Him. He surely manifests Himself'. All this had a profound effect upon Narendra Nath and he was so attracted towards him that he began to visit him daily. He changed his views and became a 'Sadhak' of spirituality. After his Guru's death, Narendra Nath decided in 1886 to found the Ramakrishna Mission and he together with a band of co-workers became Sannyasis. Thereafter they took to wanderings all over India. By degrees he developed the conviction that 'if the Hindu were to rise to the height of glory, it was absolutely necessary that the faith of ancient rishis must be made dynamic 'Hinduism must become aggressive'. The world must know the spiritual treasures of India'. He decided to attend the Parliament of Religions to be held in Chicago (USA) in 1893. But when he reached there he could not at first be allowed to attend the Parliament for he had no credentials. However, a Professor in Harvard recommended him in these words, 'Here is a man who is more learned than all our learned Professors put together to the chairman, of the committee for selecting delegates and he was admitted'. His speech on the very first day captured the imagination of the audience which listening to the age-old message of unbounded Catholicism of the Hindu seers, saw new light beyond the misty hedges of sects, communities, churches and denominations. His message was of peace, universality, of brotherhood and tolerance towards all religions. 'The Lord is in every religion'. He now took to a tour of USA.

He was full of praise for America's love of liberty, industrial organisation, educational system, devotion to progress, science, organised social welfare but at the same time he criticised the American love of luxury, vanity, religious and cultural intolerance violence and economic exploitation of the weak. He gave discourses to many people who took to his teachings permanently and thus he set up a nucleus for future branches of Ramakrishna Mission to grow in USA. In 1895, he went to England, via Paris where also he was respected and honoured. Later he returned to USA. There in New York he organised the Vedanta Society in 1896. He came back to England and there he met Margaret Noble who became a devoted lover of India and is known to us as Sister Nivedita. In 1897 he arrived back in India. By his work abroad he had raised India high in the estimation of the world. Hs defined religion as the manifestation of divinity that is already in man. 'This pursuit of the Infinite, this struggle to grasp the Infinite, this effort to get beyond the limitations of the senses, out of matter, as it were, and to evolve the spiritual man, this striving day and night to make the Infinite one with our being - this struggle itself is the soundest and the most glorious that man can make'. The Swami was emphatic in his enunciation that the value of the life of an individual or a society was to be assessed on its spiritual progress and not merely on its material possessions or intellectual attainments.

He made an extensive tour of India before sailing again for USA in 1899. The people in India saw in him a redeemer of India's honour and called him the 'patriot saint of India'.The Swami announced, "The flat has gone forth, India must rise. None can resist her any more; never is she going to sleep any more, no outward powers can hold her back any more; for the Infinite giant is rising to her feet." But he also denounced the poverty and superstitions of India for which he held the Indians also responsible. He asked his countrymen to develop 'muscles of iron and nerves of steel, gigantic wills that nothing can resist'. Again in India religious life forms the centre, the key-note of the whole music of national life; and if any nation attempts to throw off its national vitality, the direction which has become its own through transmission of centuries, that nation dies, if it succeeds in the attempt. 'Our life blood is spirituality. If it flows clear, pure and vigorous, everything is right, political, social, any other material defect even the poverty of the land will be all cured if that blood is pure'. His prophecy that 'Europe, the centre of the manifestation of the material energy, will crumble to pieces within fifty years if she is not mindful to change her position', has proved true. Socialism can only succeed if it is based on spiritual ideals. He wanted all to work for the poor, the down-trodden humanity. 'Him I call a mahatma whose heart bleeds for the poor, otherwise he is durama (wicked one)'. 'No amount of politics would be of any avail until the masses in India are once more well-educated, well-fed, and well-cared for'. In 1897 the central offices of the Ramakrishna Mission were established at Belur, five miles up Calcutta.

The Swami again toured USA and established centres there, the one at San Francisco being very prominent. He left America in 1900 to attend the Congress of the History of Religions in Paris. From there through Central Europe and Egypt he came back to India in 1900. He passed away in 1902 at an early age of 39.

The Ramakrishna Mission has branches all over the world. It trains aspirants for spiritual progress and puts them for service to man in various fields of life, for educational, missionary, social and philanthropic purposes. Sri Ramakrishna Paramahamsa and Swami Vivekanand opened the floodgates of Indian spirituality and prepared the foundations for the Indian Renaissance which has flowered so richly in the beginning of the twentieth century in the figures of Rabindranath Tagore, J.C. Bose, Tilak, Sri Aurobindo, Mahatma Gandhi and others.

Radha Swami Movement

Another catholic movement of the times has been the Radha Swami Satsang or brotherhood. The Radha Swami faith derives its name from its original founder, the Supreme Being, Radha Swami, who appeared in the world in human form and designated Himself Santa Satguru or perfect Saint or Guide. According to Radha Swami Mat Prakash, published by the second guru, 'This Holy name Radha Swami signifies both the Supreme Being and the original Spirit or Sound Current (word) which emanated from his Holy Feet and which is the prime factor and principal agent in the whole creation'. The Supreme Being manifests in the world in Sant Satguru or through his emanations like Sadhu Guru and a devotee wanting salvation must get the assistance of the above. Under his instructions Surat Sabd Yoga is to be practised to approach the Supreme Being. No intoxicating drink or animal food are to be taken and immoderate indulgence in any desire is to be avoided.

The Guru is everything in this faith. He is the centre of the whole. The first Guru was an Agra banker of Kshatriya caste born in 1818. He is known as Siva Dayal Sahib. He publicly proclaimed his doctrines in 1861. He died in 1878 and his ashes lie buried in a sacred tomb in the Radha Swami Garden, Agra. The second Guru Rai Saligram Sahib Bahadur, a Kayastha, was born in 1828 and later became the Postmaster General in U.P. He became Guru in 1878 and continued so till his death in 1898. The sect owes a great deal to his clear intellect and power of expression. He has written several works. The third Guru was a Bengali Brahman, Brahma Shankar Misra, born in 1861, was an M.A., of Calcutta University . He became the Guru in 1898. He created a constitution for Satsang, setting up a Central Administrative Council. His title was Maharaja Sahib. He died in 1907. After him some signs of disunity appear in the sect and same other branches are set up but the central and main branch remains in Agra where its most famous Guru of recent times 'Sahib ji', late Sir Anand Swaroop, presided over the affairs of the sect. Under him a colony called Dayal Bagh has grown up. It is an up-to-date colony with houses for the devotees, schools, business and industrial concerns and a temple for devotion. Most of its conceptions are derived from Hinduism. The practice of the sect is summed up in the phrase Surat Sabd Yoga, that is union of the human soul (Surat) with the Spirit-Current or word (Sabad) coming from the Supreme Being. The methods are imparted by the Guru secretly to each devotee or group. The followers need not give up their domestic life. There are no caste restrictions and no strict separation of men and women.

There is no proselytism and no breaking away from Hinduism. They have to perform works of faith and charity, and should be moved by a spirit of service and prayer. Their teachings have affinity with those of Kabir. The ordinary disciples are also known as Satsangi or Sadhu. In the main it belongs to the Bhakti School. Its esoteric teachings, absence of Hathayoga and refusal to embrace sheer asceticism have made it popular.

The Prarthana Samaj

In the analogy with the Brahmo Samaj we had the establishment of other religious and Social Societies in India, in particular the Prarthana Samaj in Maharashtra. It, however, remained part of Hinduism, just a reforming movement from within. It came into existence in 1867. Its ideals were national worship of one God and social reforms. They also drew their inspiratians from their own saints like Namdev, Tukaram and Ramdas. The realism in Maharashtrian character expressed itself in the emphasis which they placed upon the eradication of social evils like untouchability, illiteracy, cruelty to the Hindu widows, inequality between the sexes and advocated inter-dining and inter-marriage among different castes, remarriage of widows and provision of asylums for the dawn trodden and the orphans.

The leader of this movement was Justice Mahadev Govind Ranade. The famous Deccan Education Society owes its origin to his inspiration. He was one of the prime movers of the idea of starting a political institution for demanding political reforms which led to the establishment of the Congress and he also began the practice of holding a social conference when the sessions of the Congress were held. He was a clear thinker and a realist who felt that the susceptibilities of the masses must be taken into account of in matters of social reform. But at the same time there could be neither a tinkering with the problem nor a partial vision. All aspects of reform—political, social, economic and religious must be tackled with thought not with the brain of a zealot. In the words of C.F. Andrews, Ranade comes nearest to Raja Ram Mohun Roy and Sir Syed Ahmad Khan among the reformers already mentioned in the largeness of his range of vision and the magnanimity of his character; but he was more advanced, than either of them in the width of his constructive aim, his grasp of the principles underlying Western civilisation, and his application of them to Indian conditions'.

Another religious reformer belonging to the Punjab may be mentioned. He is Swami Ram Tirth who voluntarily drowned himself in the Ganges. He was a well-read man and had taken M. A. degree. At the age of 24 he renounced home and took to a missionary life and went abroad also. Many missions have been established to propagate his teachings but he himself was against setting up any society. As he had said all societies in India belong to Ram who will work in all of them and all Indians are one with him. He was a great devotee of Ram but not of the traditional one. To him Ram was an endearing name of God. He often passed into ecstasy which he called 'A state of balanced recklessness'. In his teachings emphasis was laid on truth, knowledge, right conduct, selflessness, equipoise and thought of the Supreme Reality. Man should become Ram. His teachings were expressed in beautifully simple prose and poetry. He was truly a realised soul. More recently we had Raman Maharishi and Sri Aurobindo as great spiritual teachers.

We find that modern religious movements have not been purely orthodox. They have developed critical. outlook, have laid emphasis both on individual and social developments, stressed liberty of thought and instead of devoting attention to paraphernalia of religion have directed attention to practice of morality and spirituality.

Religious Awakening among the Muslims

Along with the Hindus other sections of the Indians also felt the influence of the new awakening and attempted to set their house in order. We may note the religious awakening among the Muslims. Here also prevailed either a spirit of revivalism (or Puritanism) or reform in keeping with the modern trends. The first school had its prominent initial advocate in Sayyid Ahmad of Bareilly. He stood for Puritanical reform in Muslim manners, customs, practices and wished to sweep away the superstitions and innovations which had sapped the purity and vigour of Islam. Then there was Maulana Qadir of Delhi, who translated Quran into Urdu, enlightened thus the ignorance of the masses and through public preaching and discussion in vernacular prepared the ground for the reform of his co-religionists. But the most prominent literary apostle of the new movement in the early sixties of the nineteenth century was Maulvi Karamat Ali of Jaunpur (death 1873). His main work lay in Eastern Bengal where he preached in Urdu and by his energetic religious propaganda he stirred the Muslim masses and was a factor in the cultural evolution of Muslim Bengal. He tried to combat the superstitions that had crept into Islam and waged war against certain new heterodox schools which had recently come into vogue. He disowned Wahabi doctrines and upheld the Sufi schools.

There was also Maulvi Chiragh Ali (1895), a man of learning and a research scholar, who wrote mainly in English, addressing his appeal to all. He worked in various capacities in Government service in U.P. and later got employment in Hyderabad. The Muslims had not taken kindly to the Western education and had also developed many social evils. Chiragh Ali by his library work was instrumental in calling their attention to the true spirit of their marriage laws in favour of monogamy, to the true relation of Islam to the modern sciences and to the portion of women. He, therefore, belonged to the second school which sought a reconcilation with the Western Civilisation. The most effective work in modernisation of Islam was done by Sir Sayyid Ahmed (1817-1898), a man of action, education and a reformer. He was the Grand old man of Aligarh. Long before he had written on the abuses of the system of Pir and Murid as practised in India and now he wrote against the religious objections to not dinning with the Europeans or not taking to the Western education. He was against slavery, favoured the emancipation of women and leaned towards a modern interpretation of Quran. He also went abroad.

He devoted himself to the promotion of English education among the Muslims and founded in 1875 a school which soon developed into the Muhamedan Anglo Oriental College of Aligarh, the nucleus of the Aligarh University. He also started Mohammedan Educational Conference in 1886 as a rival body to the Indian National Congress as he did not want the Muslims to lose themselves into the Hindu-fold or be disloyal to the British. His slogan was 'reason alone is a sure guide'. He preached against polygamy, fatalism and formalism. He wrote commentaries on Quran to prove the truth of his contentions. Thus the educational progress of the Muslims and their adaptation to the new conditions in India were the chief contributions of Sir Sayyid. He was ably seconded by others among whom the most notable were Sayyid Amir Ali, Iqbal, Professors S. Khudabakhsh and AM. Maulvi.

In recent times we-have another movement which has sought to work out a synthesis of Islam, Christian and Hinduism, namely the Ahmadiya Movement, started by Ghulam Ahmad of Qadian in the Gurdaspur district of the Punjab. Mirza Sahib was a vigorous exponent of religious goodness and from 1889 he began to accept disciples like the Sufi teachers. In 1891 he claimed to be the promised messiah as prophecied in Muslim theology. He called himself the second Ahmad. This led him into bitter controversies with others. In 1904 he claimed to be a manifestation (Avtar) of the holy Krishna. In 1913 there was a split, the branch in Lahore cut itself off and refused to acknowledge Sahib as a Messiah. The Ahmadiyas have become a strong group with their main centre at Qadian. They have also done much educational and social work. They have established their missions outside India also. These were some of the prominent movements for religious reforms that gripped the Muslim Community in the modern age.

After having discussed the religious movements in Modern India, we shall now proceed to the consideration of the social and economic aspects of modern Indian culture.

Social Conditions

The protests against the Hindu Code Bill which sought to place women on a footing of equality with men, providing for divorce, monogamy and inheritance by women also of their father's property have once again brought into lime light the conservative core of the Indian society. Religion has again been used in defence of the vested social interest. But this is a misreading of India's cultural history or the spirit of the Dharma Shastras as we understand them. We have shown that in ancient India the spirit mattered and not the form and even as late as the tenth century there was inter-marriage between a Brahman bridegroom and a Kshatriya bride and so on.

New Smritis were written to justify the changes in social customs necessitated by circumstances. Where spirit rules freedom was inevitable. Our customary laws evolved indeed, but by a natural development of the body of social habits in obedience to changing ideas and more complex necessities. There was no single or fixed authority to determine them. The King in India was an administrator of the laws and not the legislator. In fact, even Manu stands more for a legendary figure, a symbol of the mental demi-god in humanity than an actual living personality. But gradually the sacerdotal class acquired power, the balance in the caste system was upset and the Muslim rule in India forced the Hindu Society to a defensive position which led to the crystallisation and solidity of the vested socially privileged class. The caste system which had begun in a natural manner providing for freedom and development according to the nature of man petrified leading to a static society, conventionalised and stereotyped.

The dynamic West has forced us to re-examine the postulates of our social thinking and laws. In this endeavour the main incentive has been provided by the social and religious reformers of the modern India. The state has been for the most part neutral. Sometimes the state has intervened either as a result of the liberal movement that swept over England in the days of Governor-General like Bentinck or Ripon or on account of agitation by an enlightened body of public opinion in India. We have got such laws as the prohibition of Suttee (Sati). The word means a chaste and virtuous woman but had by a curious process been applied to the practice of burning chaste women along with the dead bodies of their husbands. By the regulation of 1829, Sati was declared illegal. Other laws passed related to the banning of infanticide, throwing of children into the sea in fulfilment of a religious vow or killing them because they were girls and could not be easily married as in Rajpuṭana (regulations of 1795 and 1802), the suppression of the thugs (organised band of criminals) in 1831-1837, the abolition of slavery (1843), discontinuance of the state lotteries in the Presidency towns, stoppage of Human sacrifice in Orissa (1847-1854), prohibition of gross obscenities under the garb of religion on the streets (1855), legislation of widow marriage (1886), passing of the Age of Consent Act (1891), prohibiting cohabitation with girls under the age of 12, amended by the Act of 1893, which raised the age to 14 for girls and the Civil Marriages Act. Both through the Courts and legislature the state has thus made some attempt to suppress social evils or bring social customs in line with progressive ideas.

But the greater share in rousing public opinion against social inequalities and iniquities has been taken by private individuals and bodies. In the very beginning we had Ram Mohun Roy and his band of followers protesting against the social abuses like the rigours of caste, the degrading position of women, the 'Sati' custom and the degrading position of the peasantry. We had the Prarthana Samaj ably led by Ranade, who inaugurated an yearly Social Conference alongside with the session of the Indian National Congress. The Samaj established founding asylums and orphanages, night schools, Widows' homes, Depressed Classes Mission, Widow Marriage Association and the Deccan Education Society, the latter two were inspired by Ranade. Corresponding to it we had the Brahmo Samaj which struggled for the removal of the purdah system, introduction of widow re-marriage, abolition of polygamy and early marriages, provision of higher education, inter-dining, inter-caste marriages and removal of social barriers to foreign travel, under the Deccan Education Society (1884), the famous Fergusson College in Poona was started with the teachers taking a vow not to take more than Rs.75/- as the starting salary. This society included Gokhale as one of its members. Ishwar Chandra Vidyasagar and Malabari were foremost in the cause of the uplift of women. Gokhale founded in 1905 the Servants of India Society with the object of training national missionaries for the service of India. Its members were to accept nominal salaries, were to be servants of the motherland in a religious spirit.

There was to be no personal self aggrandisement. As a result of the efforts of these missionaries Social Service leagues were started, boy-scouts were trained, libraries, night school, co-operative societies, nurseries, entertainment for the poor, sanitation, medical relief, trade unions and newspaper were provided for.

The Parsis also went in for social and religious reforms and the Sikhs under the Chief Khalsa Diwan advocated liberal reforms in society and culture. Under the inspiring lead of Mahatma Gandhi all these tendencies received further impetus and in particular the conditions of women and the untouchables vastly improved. Since 1904 we had Indian Ladies Conference at the same place as the Social Conference. Karve organised a school for women in 1906 which was the nucleus of the later Indian Women's University, salvation army began to work for reform of the criminal tribes. In 1923 a Women's Indian Association with many branches was started. An All-India

Women's deputation waited upon the Secretary of State for India, Montagu, in 1918 to press for Franchise for women while Sarojini Naidu became the first woman president of the Congress in 1925. Seva Sadan Societies were started to train women for medical relief and service.

Depressed classes started their own associations to further their interests while health and sanitation were looked after not only by semi-official societies like St. John's Ambulance Association but also by the state when in 1920 popular ministers had under their charge the department of public health. Thus right from the third decade of the nineteenth century Indians of light and leading were awake to their social duties and as a result of the cumulative efforts of the Indians for the last hundred years Indian social environment has undergone a radical transformation. If conservatism still rules it is the last flicker of the fading lamp.

Economic Conditions

Indian poverty is the most glaring phenomenon of recent times and the causes of this unhappy state of affairs are historical. We have seen how in the Moghul times India was not only the nursing mother of Asia feeding its different countries with rice, wheat, sugar, raw cotton, but also the industrial workshop of the world producing a prodigious quantity of cotton and silk goods for the markets spreading from the Indian Archipelago in the east to Europe in the west and from the shores of the Caspian Sea to the coast of Mozambique and Madagascar. The trade with Europe by land, however, began to shrink in the opening decades of seventeenth century as a result of the growth of sea-borne trade of the Portuguese, the Dutch and the English. The sea-borne trade in the Asian waters was still shared by the Bengalis, Gujaratis and Malabaries. But gradually they were also squeezed out. The Western traders established their trade in the East by a regular system of piracy, which they earned on seizing every Arab or Indian vessel they met. The Portuguese annihilated the Indian traders, were themselves destroyed by the Dutch who were supplanted by the British between (1650 and 1700). The East India Company acquired superior trading privileges in comparison with the Dutch in the Coramandel Coast at Masulipatam in 1634, in Bengal and Orissa in 1656 and in Western India at Surat and the Deccan in 1716. Further they secured preferential treatment from the Moghuls and this hit hard the Indian traders. The vast profits of the expanding trade of India with Europe in cloth goods and other manufactures did not improve the economic conditions and standard of living of the Indian artisans and handicrafts men because of the vicious system of monopoly and trade privileges which severely handicapped the Indian merchants or made them contractors and later on mere gumashtas of the Company, on the one hand, and the system of dadani advances, as a result of which the workers were ruthlessly exploited. To take the example of Bengal. Even in the year 1756 there was a brisk trade between Bengal and the countries of Asia but the defeat of the Indian ruler Siraj-ud-daula at the hands of the British turned the tables. Bengal became poor for several reasons. There was a large drain of wealth due to the so-called presents given by the puppet Nawabs to the British and even the surplus revenue of Bengal was invested in purchasing the articles exported from India by the East India Company. It is estimated that in the course of twenty-three years (1757-1780) Bengal was filched to the extent of nearly sixty crores. All this money went to England and helped in the spread of the Industrial Revolution. Further there was the exploitation of the permit for trade (Dastaks) given to the British by which they obtained complete freedom of trade though the Indian merchants had to pay the duties. The permit had been to the Company but its servants used it for their private trade and even sold them to the Indian merchants who thus evaded payment of duties. Not only that, soon this permit was utilised in the internal trade also and further the servants dispossessed the artisans and producers of their goods by force, paying nominal money while they forced their own goods on the ryots at excessive rates. Various other devices came into existence to fleece the weavers who were forced by fear of violence to sign bonds to supply goods at fixed prices and stated intervals. They were not paid well and could not sell their goods to other parties. Thus Bengal continued to be exploited.

The opening years of the eighteenth century also saw the beginning of protective legislation in England against the importation of the Indian manufactured products. The prohibition of the import of all Indian calicoes and silk in 1701, was followed up by the prohibition of their wear and use in 1720, and this contributed not a little towards stimulating the mechanical inventions and discoveries in the textile industry, just as the wealth brought by the commercial classes from the Indies furnished the capital for both the transition from the handicraft to the large scale industrial enterprise in England and for the development of her trade with the New world. Later on the Company established a permanent market in India for British woollens, metals, stores and provisions, also prohibiting the manufacture of silk fabrics in Bengal. The gradual conquest and consolidation of British power in India saw a complete, revolution in the commercial relations between England and India. The balance of trade which had been in her favour turned against her. Our best industry, weaving, was crushed as a result of the imposition of British taxes and the loss of continental markets due to the French Revolution and the Berlin decrees, of the introduction of mechanical inventions in England and of the competition in India herself with the products of the power loom. Even the export of yarn to England ceased. Thus the national enterprise of Indians which had supported the artisans, the rural workers and women (who in their spare hours took to weaving and spinning) and had held the monopoly of markets in Asia, Africa and parts of Europe went to ruin. Indians began to lean more heavily on agriculture.

Further laws were passed in England between 1811 and 1814 by which the Indian mercantile marine was also ruined. India was started on the road to transformation from being an industrial country to one of the raw-material producing countries of the world. While agriculture was overcrowded there was no attempt to reform the land policy or increase agricultural wealth. The landlords were grafted on the soil and the villagers were rack-rented. Unemployment and poverty became unprecedented in the history of any modern civilised country. England during her industrial revolution prohibited the export of machinery and even artisans so that India could not get valuable experience in new methods. There was also the fact that the aristocracy in India did not give wealth for productive enterprises. The dwindling of the Indian merchant and middle class in strength and influence prevented the development of industrial capitalism on modern lines as in the West, while the change in the system of land-tenures encouraged investment in land. There was further a wide gulf between the intellectual class and the artisans and there could not be any scientific inventions where scholasticism prevailed. But the key to India's ruin lay in the policy of the state. The industries were not encouraged to develop by the policy of free trade adopted by England in the nineteenth century while the feeding of the British industries by the raw-materials of India further tended to impoverish not only the nascent industries but also to cast a burden on Indian agriculture which it staggered to support when it was already feeling suffocation by the rise of population in India. New classes intervened between the actual tillers of the soil and the state and these intercepted the profits from the land, landless proletariate multiplied while heavy assessment drew almost the last penny from the pockets of the ryots, introduction of railways and wrong exchange policy further crippled the inland industries and agriculture.

But this state of affairs could not last long. So far as industries were concerned the rise of the middle classes in India after the introduction of Western education led to the realisation of the need for industrialisation and private initiative notably by the Tatas who took a hand in the development of factories specially cotton, iron and steel while the British started plantation industries, those of tea, coffee and indigo. But the state continued to be indifferent or sometimes hostile, as for instance, when the duties on Indian goods were also levied together with those on British goods. Only in agriculture the State moved in to a certain extent to redress the wrongs of the ryots for otherwise they would not have got raw materials and would have killed the hen that laid the golden eggs. We shall now make a brief review of the evolution of the Indian capitalism, agriculture and commerce right down to our times.

Factory industries arose in India after the mutiny of 1857 for a number of reasons. In the first place there was an increased introduction of foreign enterprise or capital which was facilitated by the introduction of railways and we find the first factories started by the British. But increasing knowledge, establishment of peace and order, improvements in transport and the examples of the Europeans induced the Indians also to invest in the Indian enterprises. Further the Crimean War and the American Civil War stimulated the rise of the jute and cotton industries because the Russian hemp and the American cotton were not available in England. The gradual growth of these industries and of the railways stimulated directly or indirectly the rise of other industries, like engineering, workshops, iron foundries, subsidiary cotton and jute industries and woollen mills. The first cotton mill was started in 1851 and today a century after we have about 420 cotton mills with a paid up capital of about Rs. 60 crores employing over 8,00,000 skilled and unskilled workers. The first jute concern was established in 1854 and in 1947 we had 104 jute mills in West Bengal. Between 1880 and 1895 the woollen industry was also established on a firm footing while foundation of mining industries was laid between 1850 and 1880. We had coal, petroleum and the manganese industries initially developed. Iron and steel industries followed after 1880. Salt, mica and gold mining also attracted the attention now. Attempts were also made to start other industries like leather, paper, cotton ginning and pressing, But as the examples of Germany and Russia in Europe show in the pre-war (1914) period, proper development is only possible when the state encourages, guides and helps. Here in India there was no such course possible in the presence of an alien government. The drain continued and the investment policy of the Britishers led to further exploitation of the Indians. Figures speak for themselves. The British Government took over from the company a debt of ..70 millions. This included money spent on wars against Afghanistan, China and other countries which had nothing to do with Indian interests. This debt increased to ..884.2 millions in 1939. The increase was due to costs of establishing ways, public utilities and charging to India every conceivable charge that could be levied. To quote Jenks, 'The Sultan of Turkey visited London in 1868 in state, and his official ball was arranged for at the India office and the bill charged to India. A lunatic asylum in Ealing, gifts to members of a Zanzibar Mission, the consular and diplomatic establishments of Great Britain in China and in Persia, part of the permanent expenses of the Mediterranean fleet and the entire cost of a line of telegraph from England to India had been charged before 1870 to the Indian Treasury'. During the same period British investments operated in India, foreign banks started working and by 1913 they controlled over three-fourths of the total of bank deposits while this British investment operated only in things connected with Government, transport, plantation and finance. The state did not help the Indian financiers while the masses or the middle classes stuck to their old habits of hoarding rather than investing. Further by their tariff and exchange policy the Government helped more the British than the people in India. All these reasons combined together to retard India's industrial development and increase her poverty. Shah and Khambata calculated in 1924 the average income per head per day at for a majority of the Indians which meant that, 'the average Indian income is just enough to feed two men in every three of the population .... on condition that they all consent to go naked, live out of doors all the year round, have no amusement or recreation, and want nothing else but food, and that the lowest, the coarsest, the least nutritious'.

The state of affairs should be contrasted with the potential wealth of India. She possesses abundant supplies of coal, iron, oil, manganese, gold, lead, silver and copper.

The American Technical Mission sent by Roosevelt to India (Aug. 1942) estimated 'India's bauxite deposits at about 25,00,00,000 tons. India accounts for about 30 per cent of the world's output of manganese ore, three-fourths of the world's supply of sheet and black mica and is the world's largest producer of lac'. The Industrial Commission of India reported (1918) that our mineral wealth was sufficient to maintain key-industries. The two world-wars forced the British government to revise their economic policy and ultimately grant us freedom. But their help has been too niggardly to benefit us. India remains a land of missed opportunities. But things are changing after independence.

The same tale is unfolded in the case of agriculture. Before the British came Indian villages had enjoyed some prosperity. To quote Tavernier, 'Even in the smallest villages rice, flour, butter, milk, beans and other vegetables, sugar and other sweetmeats, dry and liquid, can be procured in abundance'. But by 1929-30 the official publication of the Indian government, India in 1929-30, had to report that 'a large proportion of the inhabitants in India are still beset with poverty of a kind which finds no parallel in Western lands'. The government appointed commissions like the Famine and the Agricultural Commissions or issued reports now and then, Agricultural departments were organised and then in 1919 placed in charge of the Indian ministers while finance remained in the Britishers' hands. All through the period there was only a tinkering with the problem. The result is an agricultural crisis with these features. In our national economy it occupies an unbalanced position. There is over-crowding and under-development at the same time. There is stagnation or deterioration with low yields, waste of labour, fragmentation of holdings, subdivision of the fields, multiplication of sub-letting, absentee landlordism or rack-renting, increasing indebtedness and increase in the landless proletariat. Thus Indian independence has only meant that the ball has been thrown to our side of the net.

The scene is no better in commerce. In the post-Mutiny period the most important development in connection with the

Fiscal policy of the country is the establishment of Free Trade. The government in 1859 laid down the rule that the import of raw-materials for purposes of Indian industry should be facilitated and at the same time exports from India had to pay an increased duty. In 1874 The Manchester Chamber of Commerce put in a plea for the abolitian of the 5% import duty on cotton manufactures. Accordingly, after sometime the import duty was abolished at first on certain coarser cotton goods and then on goods of less than 30 counts. The Britishers took to producing goods which could come under these categories. Between 1882-1894 the Indian cotton mill industry remained without protection. In 1894 the duty on cotton imports was again levied but it was coupled with 5% excise duty on Indian mill-yard of over 20 counts. The Indian leaders and manufacturers protested but nothing could move the government and the excise duty was only abolished in 1926. In 1926 the import duty was reduced to 3% while all Indian mill products except yarn had now to pay cess and all this because Lancashire so demanded. As R.C. Dutt declared, 'as an instance of fiscal injustice it is unexampled in any civilised country'. After 1923 the Indian government adopted a policy of discriminative protection and a tariff board was set up to recommend protection for industries when called upon to do so. But the concession was neutralised by the grant of what is known as the Imperial preference since 1927 which became general after the Ottawa conference in 1932. A further blow was struck by the decision to fix the rupee exchange at the high rate ls.6d in 1927 in the teeth of Indian opposition. We were also denied almost all share in the carrying trade of India. Foreign commerce was thus monopolised by the British or other Europeans. To sum up in the words of Prof. Adarkar, 'Apart from protection, western countries have, through their governments, taken active measures such as bounties, state aid, experimental and demonstrational undertakings, foreign trade commissions, industrial research, and active control and guidance of industrial concerns. The discriminative protection, on the other hand, has vouchsafed nothing better than a perfectionary assistance'. Thus, economically we became just suppliers of anything and everything, menders, repairers of all things on earth, but the makers of none. Two further developments in the situation are the inability (or inertia) of the labourer to work and the partnership between the Indian and the foreign capitalists to exploit the country. The evils connected with capitalism have been intensified here because public opinion was not strong enough; the racial question was involved, foreign rule and capital making many questions political; the workers were neither educated nor very efficient or properly organised; the idea of joint-stock enterprise being new to India, proper safeguards against its abuses could not be developed; old crafts decayed rapidly but the new industries did not grow in proportion to the void created or the expanding needs of the people; capital was invested in things where either high remuneration could be secured or safety could be guaranteed and finally foreign capital meant even greater want of contact and sympathy between capital and labour. Added to these troubles and the arrested economic development of India we now have the International tension and differences with Pakistan so that we are like men in a hurry who have hardly any time to plan out coolly and execute smoothly. In short India's economic troubles are a legacy of the past. Nature has dealt generously with us but man has not behaved justly.

The free Indian government is trying to plan out an economic regeneration of India; in agriculture it is trying to increase the supplies by multipurpose projects, various hydro-electric schemes, providing better seeds, fertilisers and advice from the agricultural departments. Land-lordism is being abolished. 'Grow more food' campaign has been launched. Collective farming and use of tractors are other devices for improvement. Improvement of live-stock is also being attempted. Rural education is being hastened by the use of radios. In industrial field we have the Planning Commission and its continuous work and advice. The government has taken over, some industries, in others it is sharing with private agencies and in some it is allowing full scope to private industries. Laws have been passed to regulate banking, insurance and the system of managing agency. Condition of labour has been improved. Trade agreements with various countries have been signed. The Export Promotion Committee was constituted in 1949 to submit recommendations for development of Indian exports. There was unfavourable balance of trade but that too has disappeared and we had in 1950 a favourable balance.

Our markets have expanded. Railways are being integrated. Indian shipping has developed and civil aviation has came into prominence. We are developing key-industries as well through the help of the sterling balances we had accumulated in the war-period. Nevertheless, certain basic troubles still haunt us. There is no parallel in history to the grave situation especially in matters of necessities such as food and clothing. Taxes are high and black-market prevails. Import of goods is eating away our cash balances. Capital remains shy, inflation continues and development schemes are either utopian or are executed by corrupt agencies so that we have many scandals. Thus we have a picture where shade predominates. Above all, there is suspicion all round, the labour suspects the industrialists, the capitalists suspect the government and the public suspects the administrator. We need a proper social philosophy. In ancient India economically also we had organised into groups or guilds which looked after our material and even ethical welfare. Hence a certain decentralisation in industries is called for. This will also obviate the danger of the rise of monopolies and cartels, make the labourer feel an interest in his work, and link the village with their cottage industries to the cities where big industries may be concentrated. Thus the advantages of such groupings are worth exploring. We have to discover how larger aggregates with their means of defence and opulence can be combined with smaller centres with their creative life in which all could participate. Let us remember that 'smell is beautiful'.

We have discussed the social and economic aspects of our present culture. We shall now take into consideration the artistic life of the times.

Development of Arts

Indian arts had fallen upon evil days with the loss of patronage by royalty and the nineteenth century was a dark age for our arts but by the end of the nineteenth century certain personalities began to ,work for the revival of our arts which have now received recognition both from the government and from the intelligentsia. In particular, our age has witnessed a great revival in dancing, music and painting. We shall study these in great details.

Dancing

The medieval age had ended in the development of erotic dances and dancing was now a preserve of seductive pupils. Dancing girls monopolised all attention and classical dancing had become decadent. When Krishna Iyer of Tamil Nadu state began his attempts to revive dancing he was met with rebuff and rebold comments. He could not get co-operation even from educated women. He however, persevered. By lectures, through films and on public platforms he spread his message. He went to the extent of dressing himself as a woman and performing classical dances. Slowly he met encouragement and got co-operation from Varalakshmi and Jayalakshmi. He also got co-operation from Bala Saraswathi who is regarded as a veritable dancing goddess, a direct descendant in traditian of the magical sculptures of dancing found on our art-monuments. Musical Societies now sprang up and educated class adopted the fashion. Thus Bharata Natyam was revived as a counter-dose to the old dancing suggestive with its lewd looks and gestures of back-streets after mid-night. Others took up the refrain in South India notable among whom were Menaka, Rukmini Devi, Gopi Nath, Gopal, Meenakshi Sundram Pillay (teacher of Ram Gopal) and Mrinalini Sarabhai. We now have vigorous training and new experiments in the various dance-systems of South India, in particular Bharata Natyam, Kathakali and Mohini Natyam. Folk-dances have also been revived. Some of the dance-centres now well established are Darpan (Ahmedabad), Kalakshetra (Adyar, Madras) and Kerala Kalamandalam.

Dancing also revived in the North. Bengal led the way inspired by Rabindranath Tagore who encouraged it in Shantiniketan from 1917. In Lucknow the traditions of Kathak were revived by Kalka and Binda followed by Achhan and Shambhu Maharaj. Above all we had the emergence of Udai Shankar who was the most famous and widely travelled of Indian dancers. Udai Shankar was born in a Bengali family connected with the court of the Maharaja of Udaipur. His father, a Brahman, was very cultured, well-versed in our ancient learning and a master of Sanskrit. From his very childhood Udai Shankar showed an artistic genius and the Maharana of Jhalawar sent him to the London Royal College of Arts for training at his expense. There he became a favourite of Sir William Rothenstein who wanted him to be a painter. But his inclination were towards dancing and his mind was made up when he met famous Russian dancer Anna Pavlova. She took him away and taught him the art of dancing. She danced with him as Krishna in London meet.

They came to India in 1927 and here also they got great acclaim and fame. But he did not rest on his spurs. He took further training from men like Sankaran Nambudri, travelled through the ancient art galleries of India like the Ajanta imbibing classical dancing spirit and coining new forms based on the assimilation of the best in the East and the West. He also travelled in European countries like France, Germany, Austria and Hungary learning their art forms. He developed great skill which is manifest from his dances like Shiva-Nritya and Kalia-Nritya which symbolise unity of man with God and control over the tussles of the world. He travelled all over the world.

There has also been a revival of the ancient dances of Manipur. These dances contain elements from their ancestors (ruling race of the plain who, it is said, came from the Himalayan region to Manipur before the time of Mahabharata) as for example the 'Khamba' dance is meitie. Manipur is regarded as the traditional home of the Gandharvas, the celestial dancers. In their dances the work of the drummers and dancing-cymbal players is unique. The dances are of the rhythmical variety and we have them on the occasions of festivals of gods, military festivals and other religious occasions. The Assamese name of this dancing is 'Jagol'. Raj Kumar Priya Gopal is the leading dancer of this school in its pure form. Other non-Assamese dancers of this school are Brajabashi Singh and Mani Bardan.

We have now all over India establishment of centres where one or more schools of dancing are in vogue. For Kathak we have the schools at Lucknow, Banaras, Jaipur and Raigarh where new experiments in this art are being tried. For Bharata Natyam we have Adyar and Kerala Kalamandalam and in Malabar we have teaching of the Kathakali School. Other cultural centres are Purva Parishad (Calcutta), Shantiniketan (founded by Tagore) and Bhartiya Nritya Kala Kendra (Patna). Since the dawn of freedom small centres have sprung up all over India.

Music

In music also, India has witnessed a great renaissance. We had a movement of learned scholars from all parts of India meeting in national conferences with a view to focus attention on, and co-ordinate the results of, research grappling with the technical side of the question, such as for instance, the working out of a uniform system of notation, systematisation of the 'ragas' sung in North India so as to make the same easy of instruction and assimilation. We had also the growth of music clubs and schools of music offering facilities for serious study of the art and lately its introduction in our schools and colleges.

All this has been the work of the Indians in the twentieth century. Previous to this music had declined in our country with the downfall of the Moghul Empire. The first steps were taken by Maharaja Pratap Singh Deva (ruling about 1791) of Jaipur and Mohammed Raza of Patna, a nobleman. Maharaja Pratap Singh called a conference of musicians and attempted to get a standard work on Hindustani music written. The book was named Sangeet Sara and gives valuable guidance about the melodies present today. Mohammad Raza wrote in 1814 Nagmai-e-Asaphi with the purpose of simplifying the classification of the Ragas of his day. The great principle which he clearly stated was that there should be same similarity or common features between the Ragas and the Raginis. But the most monumental work in the nineteenth century was that of Raja Sir S.M. Tagore whose History of Indian Music and other works like Sangeet Sara and Kathakaumudi put modern Indian music on its feet. Europeans also wrote upon our music, as for instance, Williard, Wilson and Clements. Music also flourished through in a very conservative state in various places. We had musicians like Ustad Abdul Karim Khan, the best Khayal singer of his times, Alauddin Khan, Professor of music and master of 18 musical instruments, Chandan Chaubey of Mathura, Dilip Chandra Vedi of the Punjab, Ustad Faiyaz Khan, one of the foremost singers of his times, Raja Bhaiya Poonchhwale of Gwalior, and others. Some of these like Alauddin and Faiyaz Khan survived the nineteenth century.

But so far we had no system or fixed principles of music and the 'Gharanas' or schools of music did not part with their secrets. A proper notation and a scientific scale was the need of the hour. This work was performed mainly by Vishnu Narayan Bhatkhande who deserves, therefore, to be called the father of modern Hindustani music. Bhatkhande was a member of the Jnanottejak Mandali of Bombay, a dramatic and musical society. His lectures there provided the nucleus for the new education in music which he introduced all over India. In his book Lakshya Sangitam published in 1910 he gave a practical basis for the Hindustani music of North India providing a practical system of notation. In his book the Hindustani Sangeet Paddhati he gave the theory of the Indian music. He classified all the 'Ragas' under ten 'thatas', or 'melas' (previously called Jatis) putting all the Ragas under them on the basis of their affinity with the parent 'Raga'.

His associate Appa Tulsi translated his system into Hindi also in the book called Ragachandrika Sara. Thus he did much to record accurately, exhaustively and definitely the 'Ragas' as sung at the present day while at the same time making their study and singing a matter of easy self-application. He redeemed music from the hands of the illiterate singers whose methods of teaching were unscientific. His works were translated into other languages. He called the first All-India Music Conference at Baroda in 1916, where his system was approved. The following words of his speech there are prophetic, 'I feel happy at the thought that I have been able to mould a model for my successors to improve upon and to perfect; and I cannot but hope that in a few years more there will be an easy system for the instruction of our music, which will lend itself to mass education. Then will the ambition of India be fulfilled for then the Indians will have music in the curricula of their universities and music instruction will be comman and universal. And if it pleases Providence to so dispense that there is a fusion between the two systems of the North and the South, then there will be a national music for the whole country, Nation will sing one song. This system has been adopted in many places like the Morris College of Music in Lucknow. His disciples are teachers in various institutions all over India. Another great musician and composer was Vishnu Digambar. He was the pupil of Balkrishna Buwa of Gwalior, a polished exponent of music. He also rescued music from the clutches of its vulgar caterers, educated the people in the right type of music, attracted educated men towards music and devised a simple system of musical notation. His tune of Raghupati Raghava Raja Rama has become famous. We had now a galaxy of musicians in India.

The present age is of strict individualism, lyricism and craftsmanship are dominant notes. Kheyal, Thumri and Ghazal hold the field. We have also the development of the Bengali music including Rabindra Sangit which is fluid, plastic, free and heterodox with emphasis on background music or orchestratian. There is also the hybrid film music which needs to be rescued from the hands of charlatans. The radio is also popularising music. Besides we have group music like the Kirtans and Loka-sangit. The modern age witnessed the revival of drama also but it declined in the thirties of the present century. Attempts were made, in particular, by the Indian

National Theatre of Bombay with its branches all over India and Prithvi Raj to revive this art. We have still a number of eminent musicians living amongst us and new talent is coming into the field.

The Hindustani music separated from the Southern music when the former became adulterated with the Mohammedan styles. The main differences between the two are (according to Bhatkhande) The Hindustani music mainly consists of three important groups of Ragas, viz., (1) Ragas taking Re and Dha Tira (sharp); (2) those taking Re and Dha Komal (soft); and (3) those taking Ga and Ni Komala. The Karnatic music is at variance with this arrangement. In the Southern music the Shuddha (pure) note is the lowest and the others are all sharp. In the North there are ten Primary 'Ragas' while in the South they are 72 with a large number of derivatives. Further, the two systems differ in their nomenclature, in their way of introducing the song and emphasis in the course of singing. Thus the graces, flourishes and embellishments of the two differ and so also the conception of musical composition. The northern system permits certain mixtures or flexibility not allowed in the rigid Southern system. Their 'Tala' systems also materially differ. But there are similarities also and emphasis should be laid upon them'.

The Indian music differs from the Western system also. The dominant factor here is melody; in the West it is harmony. In one case notes are related to a definite notes of a 'Raga' and in the other to varying chords, melody is produced by regulated succession of concordant notes while harmony arises from agreeable concord of various related notes. In one melody is one definite mood throughout while in the other mood is used to articulate the balance of the whole piece. In one salient notes have been fixed by traditions, in the other cluster of notes has a value while the individual notes can be varied. In one, there is attention to execution and accuracy while in the other there is greater emphasis upon tone and timbre. Western music is more secular while the Eastern is more religious. To quote Tagore, 'For us, music has above all a transcendental significance. It disengages the spiritual, from the happenings of life, it sings of the relationship of the human soul with the soul of things beyond'. But the differences are not so fundamental as it looks. According to Komain Rolland 'Western music should not be judged by that of the British and the American who are two of the least musical races on earth our comparison will be with the German, French, Russian and the Spanish music. Further, the profound universal essence in the Indian music cannot fail to set any musical soul quivering. Also there is no gulf between the musical art of Europe and that of Asia. It is the same Man whose soul, one and multitudinous like the tufted oak, seeks to embrace in its ramifications the illimitable and unseizable Life'.

Thus the great task before the Indian musicians is today to find a synthesis between the music of the North and the South and between the Indian and the Western music or at least to discover a common meeting ground.

Painting

We shall now take up the history of the development of modern Indian painting. The Indian art of painting had almost died down in the nineteenth century and people in Europe talked of the incapacity of the Indians to produce works of art. Ruskin had declared in 1858 that Indian art either forms its compositions out of meaningless fragments of colour and flowings of line; or if it represents any living creatures it represents that creature under some distorted or monstrous form. We had visits of the professional European artists (Tilly Kettle in 1769) who set the fashion of painting in the Western manner. Even today we have men like Beverely Nichols deploring the fact that he had not been able to find 'with one solitary exception, a single artist or art school of any major significance'. Even the Indians accepted their inferiority in this respect and men like Ravi Verma made Khidmatghars, (servants) pose for the heroes of the Mahabharata, Ayahs (maid-servants) for Radha or the lovely Sita, and the ugly cooli women for the Rakshasis—the dreaded demonesses of the primeval forest. We had no notion of being heir to a glorious artistic heritage. Everything that was best including the Taj had been designed by an European. Our eyes were first opened by an Englishman. Late E.B. Havell, the Head of the Calcutta School of Art together with his colleague and fellow-artist, Abanindranath Tagore began enthusiastically to preach the beauties of the Indian art. Their work was supplemented in America and Europe by Dr. Ananda Coomaraswamy so that the world began to recognise the significance and richness of our art and Tagore was by universal acclaim regarded as a creative artist who could reveal the soul of India to the world. Paris organised an exhibition of the Tagore School of paintings which captivated the heart of every French lover of art. Soon we had exhibitions in other places like London, New York, Japan, China, Korea, Java and Australia. What Europe appreciates today is admired by India tomorrow and so here also the walls of prejudice collapsed and patronage was extended both by the officials and private bodies. A society called 'The Indian Society of Oriental Art' was established and under its auspices classes were taken by Tagore; exhibitions were arranged and we also had the issue of a new journal of art called Rupam under the editorship of an artcritic O.C. Ganguli, The work of publicity and propaganda was also furthered by the tours of James H. Cousins who understood the significance of the Indian art to the fullest measure. Others who did this pioneer work for the Indian art were N.C. Mehta, Raval, Stella Kramrisch, Karl Khandalavala and G. Venkatachalam. We may add a few biographical details about Abanindranath Tagore the father of the new renaissance in painting. Born in 1871 he was at first taught by European teachers of art but he did not feel satisfied within himself. He came across Indian paintings; something stirred within his soul and he felt a call to go after the old Indian artistic styles. He took lessons from an expert Indian craftsman and painted his Radha Krishna series. The experience he had during this period has been clearly expressed in his own words. How can I express what I felt during all that period ? I was filled with pictures - that is how it was like. They dominated my entire being. I had only to close my eyes to get pictures come floating before my mind, form, line, colour, shade all complete, I would take up the brush and the pictures painted themselves as it were'. Afterwards he was inspired both by Havell and Tagore. He joined the Indian Society of Oriental Art and trained pupils who became famous namely, Avanindra Ganguli, Nandalal Bose, K. Venkatappa, Hakim Khan, Asit Kumar Haldar and Samarendranath Gupta.

These pupils were also taught the old Indian technique by Ishwari Prasad Varma a hereditary painter after the old Rajput style. Foreigners from different countries were also invited and an aesthetic co-operation was established between them and the artists of this country. All these pupils of Tagore became international figures.

Thus Abanindranath's work was a turning point in our artistic history. Tagore the great poet observed that 'he has saved the country from the sin of self-depreciation. He has raised her from the depths of humiliation and has regained for her the honoured position which was hers by right'. He used to live quietly in the peaceful and aesthetic atmosphere of Shantiniketan till his death in 1951. We shall now refer to some of the characteristics and works of art of the most important painters of modern times in India in the recent past.

In Abanindranath's works we can find a perfect blending of the Hindu motifs, Persian colouring and methods of Japanese painting. Thus he was not a doctrinaire either in his methods or in his appreciation. Freshness and vigour, individuality and synthesis are the qualities of his art. Some of his masterpieces are The passing of 'Shah-Jahan', 'The Queen of Asoka', 'Aurangzeb', 'Radha Krishna' and 'Buddha, the Mendicant'. He has laid under contribution the art of Ajanta for his 'Artistic anatomy' and 'psychological perspective'. But in essentials he was an individual genius with a flair for synthesis. He remained true to the basis of our culture, viz., creative spirituality, Gaganendranath Tagore was the elder brother of Abanindranath. His art collections were one of the best in India. His genius refused to be a prisoner of any school or theory of paintings. Caricatures, cartoons, landscapes and impressionistic or cubistic pictures came profusely and almost without an effort from his versatile hand. Some of his masterpieces are 'Rainy Landscape in the Himalayas', 'My Inner Garden', 'Flame of the Forest' and 'The First Gleam of Light'. He has also painted portraits of many public scenes like 'Poet Tagare addressing a Congress Crowd'. His early death was a great loss to India's artistic genius.

K. Venkatappa of Madras was another artistic genius of India. He reminded one of the asceticism of an 'Advaitvadi' with his reserved manners and forbidding exterior. If he had the hardness of a diamond he had also its brilliance. He was also a versatile genius and had painted portraits decorated with reliefs on the walls of Mysare palace, the Amba Vilas, and created other works of art like the landscape studies of 'Ooty', 'Bird study', and 'Ram and the Golden Deer'. As an artist he was a master of the art of colouring, his hand was perfectly trained to bring out a technically superb vignette and he knew how to bring out the 'Soul of things'.

Nandalal Bose enjoyed a popularity second to none, not only in the artistic world but also among the people of India. He was true to the ancient art of India and his decoration of the Congress 'Pandals ', gates and the pathway at Haripura and Faizpur show how vividly he brought out the import of our legends and religious stories. Some of his famous creations are 'Siva mourning over Parvati', 'Sati Uma's grief', 'Garuda' and 'Kaikeyi'. He had also illustrated poems of Tagore, Annuals of Times of India and had designed colourful decors and sets for Tagore's musical plays. As an artist his forte was the vigorous expression of his lines. He had re-created for us the masterpieces of Ajanta.

Asit Kumar Haldar living in Lucknow achieved fame as the Principal of the Luclnow School of Art. Belonging as he did to the Tagore School he remained true to our ancient traditions. He had also created a niche of his own in such types of art as lacquer painting on wood. He had also created memorable portraits of the Santhals, their manners, dress and living. His creative works are among others 'Akbar as a Builder', 'The

Flame of Music', 'Ras Leela', 'Krishna's Dance', and 'Moon and Lotus'. He was also a man of varied tastes and versatile genius and showed skill in architecture also.

Among other artists of fame we had Devi Prasad Choudhry, M.A. Rahman Chughtai, Sarda Charan Uikl, Mukul Chander Dey, D. Rama Ras, Sunayani Devi, Jamini Roy, Promode Kumar Chatterjee, Pulan Behari Dutt, Rabindranath Tagare and Amrita Sher Gil.

Recent trends are towards independence and there is to be no genuflexion to the Bengal School but in practice it means adoption of the Western art. Of such artists the best known have been A.F. Hussain, V.D. Chinchalkar, Abani Sen, Kamala Das Gupta, and Sailoz Mukerji of Delhi. They followed the latest styles of Europe-post impressionism to wit.

There are a number of art-centres or societies in India like Andhra Kalashala, Muslipatnam, Baroda Kala Bhawan, Art Schools in Calcutta, Patna, Lucknow, Bombay and Madras, Kala Bhavan, Shantiniketan and Ukil School of Art, Delhi besides the All India Fine Arts and Crafts Society of New Delhi. There are art Journals of which Marg today is the most famous. Many people and Societies posses valuable collections of art. Thus we find that India has registered a great progress in the art of painting. Some, however, opine that of late the art shows signs of flagging and inspiratian has disappeared. Originality has given place to caricature and playing of 'sedulous ape' to the Western art. Art-revival can come only when originality is combined with respect for tradition. It is also to be remembered that democracy in India demands popularising of the art to the masses. They should be taught to appreciate rhythm, balance and harmony which are the essentials of art. Universities and schools should become art-minded. Art galleries, museums, exhibitions and documentaries are some of the other devices to bring art at our doors. Then only art will no longer remain the Cinderelia as it is today. We shall end our description by a brief comparison of our art with that of the West.

Art in India was communal, deeply religious and followed traditions laid down in the Shilpashastras (treatises on arts). It was idealist in the sense that the real world was the inner world, from within to the outer was our motto. Hindu religion conceived of the universe as the creation of the desire kindled in the One of manifesting Himself in the Many. He gave in to the urge and joy of creation. Having created the Universe, the Supreme Being breathed His spirit into it. He entered it out of sheer excess of joy (Lila). He found joy in manifesting Himself in many forms and phases, in creating diversity out of oneness. This produced a corresponding reaction in the created. There sprang up, as a corollary to the creative process, in the universe of diversity, in the heart of the finite humanity, an inner urge to realise joy by the opposite process, by recapturing the original oneness out of the manyness, the lost unity out of multiplicity, the infinite out of its finitude. The religion of the Hindu art is based upon this philosophy. The artist must find the unity of one Godhead and this is possible only when he is endowed with form because human beings are limited and finite and can contemplate or mediate best before form rather than formlessness. Symbolism was developed to express the multiplicity of God. The idea of a Yogi inspired our art and further God unlike the method of the Greeks was portrayed in superhuman forms as he was not the image of man. When these things are understood, the bizarre forms of some of our statues will be intelligible as the attempt of the artist to convey the multiplicity and diverse qualities of God symbolised in the forms. Thus the Indian art is subjective in colour and for murals and miniatures, or of mannerisms, such as the slender waist, heavy busts, elongated eyes and tapering fingers, but in the ideals and functions of art and its relation to life, Indian art is linear, not massive and structural. The human form limits art and, therefore, models are discouraged. Indian painting, in its most realistic phases, is essentially a mental summary of visual perception rather than a faithful reproduction of an object or person from a certain point in space'. But these differences are the results of historical circumstances and when there is a more frequent intercourse between the peoples of the world they are bound to lose their sharpness or at least some common types may be evolved.

Thus the artistic developments of modern India are worthy of note and are of a piece with our ancient heritage.

Educational, Literary and Political Developments

State patronage has always been a conspicuous feature in our educational system and consequently with the dismemberment of the Mughal Empire and subsequent anarchy in the eighteenth century our educational system suffered a great set-back and it decayed in many parts of India. Till the East India Company squarely faced the situation after 1813 there was no systematic survey or thought in this field and even afterwards the remedies were hardly commensurate with the requirements of the situation. In fact as the history of education in modern India demonstrates the whole subject suffered from the blight of foreign occupation over India. There was no national outlook, no systematic planning, no enthusiasm in teaching, no worthwhile ideas and we had totally inadequate finances. All through the period we had conflict of ideas. This will be obvious from our brief survey of Indian educational developments.

The first controversy is between the Christian missionaries and the servants of the Company. The Charter of 1698 had directed the company to maintain ministers of religion and also schools in all their garrisons and bigger factories. The first school of the kind, St. Mary's Charity School was established in Madras in 1715. Other schools followed. Thus missionary work came to be associated with the educational enterprise aided by the Company. But the Company had developed a policy of neutrality towards religion and so we find conflicts between them and missionaries like Carey, Marshman and Ward who began their work in Serampore. Their friends began agitation in England and the Charter Act of 1813 forced the Company to set aside a sum of Rupees one lakh at least for 'the revival and improvement of literature and the encouragement of the learned natives of India and for the introduction and promotion of a knowledge of the sciences'. The Parliament also permitted the missionaries to go and reside in India. In other words they could attempt to enforce their ideas in India.

This controversy, however, soon merged into a bigger controversy between the Orientalists and the Anglicists. It may be pointed out that the early educational schemes of the Company had been carried out in the field of classics.

In 1781 Warren Hastings founded the Calcutta Madrassah for the cultivation of Arabic and Persian studies and in 1791, Jonathan Duncan the Resident at Banaras established a College there for the Sanskrit studies. It was hoped to conciliate the Muslims and the Hindus and also provide judges with native interpreters of Hindu and Muslim laws. So when the Company was allowed to spend one lakh of rupees a conflict arose between those who wanted the sum to be spent on classical education and those who favoured Western education through English. There was also a school favouring education through the Indian languages led by Elphinstone but it did not carry weight. The educational grant had been placed at the disposal of a 'General Committee of Public Instruction' constituted for the purpose but its members were divided about the question of Western education and in 1835 they submitted their disputes to the Governor-General in Council where Macaulay was the Law-Member. He gave his opinion in a minute of February, 1835 which is a great historical document. He favoured English as the medium and Western education–literature and sciences–as the proper subject for study believing that a 'single shelf of a good European library was worth the whole native literature of India and Arabia'.

His opinion was accepted by Bentinck on 7th March, 1835. Thus another conflict was resolved and since then English became the medium favoured in the schools aided by the Company.

We now meet another controversy centering round the question of elementary schools. It was believed that the upper classes should be educated and they would in their turn educate the masses, a theory known as the Downward Filtration Theory. Adams a missionary suggested a plan to be tried in select districts. A thorough educational survey was to be held in the districts concerned; a set of books in modern Indian languages was to be prepared for boys, an examiner was to be appointed as the Chief Executive Officer for the district and he was to meet teachers; conduct examinations, grant rewards and explain the books; normal schools for teachers should be established and endowments of lands to village schools should be granted in order to encourage teachers to settle down in villages and to educate the rural children. It was a plan which later on became the foundation of the Thomson scheme in the North-Western Province (U.P.). If Adam's plans had been adopted, mass education might have spread quickly in India but it was rejected by Auckland. In 1844 we had Government announcement that educated Indians will be given employment in Government services. But all through the period upto 1854 various controversies continued as for instance in Bombay there was conflict about education being imparted through indigenous languages or through English and the matter was only decided by a compromise retaining indigenous languages for non-collegiate schools. Further the company had not shed its commercial character completely and the work of political consolidation was yet to be completed, hence planning was partial and unmethodical. In this jungle of controversies came the Education Despatch of the Court of Directors dated 19th July, 1854 popularly known as Wood's Despatch as Sir Charles Wood was the President of the Board of Control. This despatch laid down the basis of an educational structure for the whole of India and our educational system right upto 1920 remained essentially what Wood had recommended. The despatch laid down an educational policy which was to encourage education for intellectual fitness and moral character so that the Indians might emulate us in the development of the vast resources of their country .... and, at the same time, secure to us a large and more certain supply of many articles necessary for our manufactures and extensively consumed by all classes of our population, as well as an almost inexhaustible demand for the produce of British labour'.

Thus the British policy in education was strictly utilitarian, to secure clerks and develop British commerce, other things only coming incidentally. The Despatch recommended European arts, sciences and literature as subjects of study and favoured both English and the Indian languages. For administration a Department of Public Instruction in each of the provinces was to be assisted by deputies and other inspecting officers and was to submit an annual report to the Government. Universities were to be established in Calcutta and Bombay on the model of London University with a Vice-Chancellor and Fellows as members of a Senate with the Governor as the Chancellor. All these were to be nominated and they were only to hold examinations and award degrees. There was to be no teaching work by the Universities. A graded system of educational structure was to be set up with universities and colleges at the top, High Schools and Middle Schools in the middle and primary schools at the bottom. Primary schools were to be given grants-in-aid by the administration but not run directly by the Government. Scholarships were to be given to poor, meritorious students to pursue higher studies. Teachers were to be trained in normal schools and plans were to be drawn up for vocational and female education. Thus the framework of our educational system was erected by this Despatch. But the history of education continues to be that of missed opportunities and even moderate recommendations of the Despatch were not carried out as for instance the Indian languages were not encouraged and private efforts did not receive sympathetic support. After having surveyed the history of the attempts to establish the foundations of an educational edifice for India we shall now indicate the main lines of advance in the subsequent period in the sphere of Primary, Secondary and University Education.

Primary Education remained the Cinderella of the system. In 1859 the Secretary of State for India, Stanley, asked the Government of India to establish Primary Schools under their direct control. But each province interpreted the order in its own way and thus primary education remained a matter mainly of private initiative. In the matter of finance local rates were to be raised for expenses but as there was no provision for a particular percentage of income from rates to be spent on education, the municipalities continued to neglect the matter. Further most of the schools came to be located in towns. The result was that from 75 to 92 per cent of children of school going age grew up in ignorance. The whole matter was thrashed out by the Hunter Commission appointed in 1882 presided over by Sir W.W. Hunter. The Commission recommended that primary education should be imparted in Vernacular, the state should devote greater attention to it, control over primary schools should be made over to local self governing bodies private indigenous schools should also be encouraged and grant-in-aid be given but only on the basis of results and finally while attempting to improve personnel or curricula, minimum of interference by the Government should be the rule. Practical subjects should be introduced, elasticity should be permitted regarding hours of the day and the seasons of the year, special fund should be created for primary education and the allotment for city and rural schools should be separate and the government should help by grants-in-aid. The recommendations of the Commission were the basis on which work now proceeded right upto the beginning of the twentieth century. They were hardly satisfactory and with the rise of political consciousness attempts were made to make primary education free and compulsory. For instance, we had Gokhale's Bill for this purpose in the Imperial Legislative Council in 1912. It was rejected. In the meanwhile we had pious declarations by the government for improvement of primary education as for example Lord Curzon in 1904 in his Resolution on Educational Policy laid down that governments should help primary education by liberal grant of money, grant-in-aid on the basis of results should be given up, teachers should be trained and better methods of teaching should be attempted. Expansion of education was also promised by the Government of India's Resolution of 1913. But in spite of all these resolutions the percentage of literacy in 1921 remained about 17 and only about 20 percent of the boys of school-going age received education. Between 1817 and 1922 acts were passed by the provincial governments making for compulsory and free education in the primary stage but as the whole matter was to be discretionary and by stages there was not much progress so that it may be said that by 1946 we had only about 11 per cent literacy in India. Reports, of course, continued to pour in as for instance the Hartog Committee Report stressing quality and not quantity in primary education. Abbot and Wood report, the Wardha Scheme and the Sargent report. We shall speak a few words about the Sargent report as it embodied features of the Wardha Scheme and has been adopted with some changes by the Indian provinces or states as they are now called. The report was issued in 1944 by the Central Advisory Board of Education reconstituted in 1935 and John Sargent, the Educational Commissioner with the Government of India was mainly responsible for it. According to the report :

(a) Pre-primary education for children between 3 and 6 years of age to be imparted;
(b) Universal, compulsory and free Primary or Basic Education for all children between the ages of 6 and 14 divided into the Junior Basic (6-11) and Senior Basic (11-14) be provided for;
(c) The liquidation of adult illiteracy and the development of a 'public libraries systems' should be further attempted;
(d) There was to be full provision for the proper training of teachers for the scheme;
(e) Compulsory physical education, medical inspection followed by treatment, provision of milk and midday meals;
(f) The education of the physically and mentally handicapped children was to be taken up; and
(g) Social and recreational activities on a fairly liberal scale were to be carried out.

'Learning through activity', the main principle of Wardha scheme was adopted though not the utilitarian aspect of it that education should be self sufficient. At the lower stages the activity will take many forms, leading gradually upto a basic craft or crafts suited to local conditions and round it the various subjects may be taught or correlated. With the dawn of freedom we have our state governments putting this scheme with suitable modifications into execution. But lack of finances is a great handicap and besides the ideals of education are not so well defined as to evoke enthusiasm for the work. Basic education was the fad of Mahatma Gandhi and many people did not believe in it but still it has been put into practice and we are still in an experimental stage. Thus from 1854 to 1951 in a course of about 100 years more than 85 out of every 100 persons in India remain yet essentially uneducated as compared with the cent per cent literacy achieved by Russia in 15 years. The same tale is unfolded in Secandary Education though in this sphere there was more of thought and expenditure by the Government than in the field of primary education.

Secondary Education

After Wood's despatch the first general survey of the progress of Secondary Education in India was made by the Hunter Commission of 1882. During this period English continued to hold the field ignoring the advice of Wood that the Indian languages also should be given a chance while no worthwhile arrangements were made for the training of teachers and private indigenous schools were neglected. We had increase in secondary institutions but the greater part of Government's finances was spent on schools directly conducted by the Government. During this period for the first time a greater proportion of the newly started secondary schools was the product of the Indian private enterprise though we had the beginning of Indian-managed institutions in 1816 when the nucleus of Hindu College came into being by the efforts of Raja Ram Mohun Roy. Thus by 1881-82 we had 1341 schools under Indian managers as compared with 757 schools under non-Indian managers.

All these schools also received grants-in-aid by the Government. But the defects in these schools remained. There was no vocational bias, over weightage to English language, absence of sufficient scholarships so that the masses did not benefit and divorce between home and school in the matter of curriculum continued. The Hunter Commission attempted to improve matters and recommended that schools directly managed by the government should not be increased and if possible they should be transferred to private management so that more grants-in-aid may be available to other schools, it also advocated least interference in private schools and greater support financially besides appointing officials who were sympathetic to private management. As for the missionary institutions the Commission allowed them to exist but laid greater emphasis on the need to encourage people's own efforts. Rules for grants-in-aid were to be liberalised. The Commission also recommended that a moral text-book based upon the fundamental principles of natural religion be prepared for Government and non-Government Colleges and the Principal or one of the Professors in colleges should deliver a series of lectures on the duties of man and citizen in every session. This recommendation remained a dead letter. The Commission recommended the introductian of vocational courses at the upper secondary stage so that people qualifying in these may leave after passing what was called the School Leaving Certificate Examinations. Training of teachers was also recommended. The question of medium of instruction was left to the managers of the schools. Thus the recommendations of the Commission were thorough and far reaching but sufficient heed was not paid to them and even in 1927 we have the lament that there is a great deal of wastage, that quality is sacrificed at the cost of quantity, that technical education is neglected, that female education has not been furthered and the students are crammers rather than self-reliant and capable of initiative. Of course, the demand for schools continued, they were an entrance to the university education which led to Government service. The Government attempted to meet the situation in a half hearted way and also expressed a wish to do better as for instance scientific, commercial and constructive (or art), and a student could take any ane of these groups. Institutions providing for these upto Intermediate standard are to be called Higher Secondary schools with the Head promoted into a Principal. But inspite of all these changes things have been no better and we have the University Commission of 1949 pointing out that 'University teachers almost unanimously complain of the low academic standard of the average university entrant'.

They further observe that 'Our schools and intermediate colleges are congested and understaffed; very few school'. teachers have a call for, or take pride in, their profession'. 'Our provincial governments are naturally keen on basic education' and are financing schemes for its wide extension, but unfortunately they do not seem to be equally keen on secondary education which is the real weak spot in our entire educational machinery'.

Various defects can be pointed out in our secondary education and we have pointed this above but the fundamental question is not so much the improvement in technique, methods of teaching as the improvement or reform of man. When we have surveyed the history of the University Education in India we shall discuss what orientation is needed so far as the human angle is concerned for we had had many ideal schemes of reform in the past but they have all failed because there has been no adequate recognition of the role of personality in the field of education and no attempt to find out how man can be transformed so that they may no longer be a creature of errors and a prisoner of stupidity.

University Education

We now look at the university education which began after the Wood's despatch of 1854 though even before we had the establishment of colleges as for instance the Hindu College founded by Raja Ram Mohun Roy in 1817. In 1834 was founded the Elphinstone College in Bombay, in 1836 one College was established in Hooghly, another in Dacca and Patna, about 1840 and at the same time we had the establishment of other colleges in Bombay, Madras, U.P. (North-West province) and Nagpur Wilson College, Madras Christian College, Agra College, St.

John's College at Agra, Bislop College (1818) at Nagpur, a College at Masulipatam founded by Robert Noble Wood's despatch allowed the establishment of universities as merely examining bodies and we had the establishment of Calcutta, Bombay and Madras Universities, all in the year 1857. there was no provision for a teaching university or inter-collegiate instruction. The first entrance examination was held at Calcutta in 1857, 244 candidates appearing of whom 162 passed and out of this batch 13 appeared for the first degree examinatian in 1858 and only two passed including Bankim Chandra Chatterjee, the famous novelist and author of the national song Bande Mataram. By 1882 we had further increase in Colleges so that in that year 7,429 candidates appeared and 2,778 passed. In 1882 an act was passed for the establishment of the Punjab University and it was allowed to encourage classical education and also appoint professors and lecturers to take up teaching work. The 1882 Commission was not specifically charged with the work of reviewing the University education but it made certain recommendations of which the novel one was the preparation of a moral text book already referred to. In 1886 we had the beginning of an annual report on University education. We find that only Punjab and Bombay Universities were receiving aid from the Government. In 1887 we had the establishment of Allahabad University in U.P. There were also increasing efforts by private bodies to establish Colleges, as for example, the Deccan Educational Society of Poona, Arya Samaj and National Council of Education in Calcutta. Persons like Ishwar Chandra Vidyasagar and Panchayappa Meduliar also contributed towards the growth of Collegiate education so that by 1901-02 we had 179 colleges in India; in 1902 Curzon appointed the University Commission which among other things recommended that the Universities should be made teaching bodies and their local limits should be defined more clearly, their senate, faculties and the syndicate should be reorganised; more strict rules for affiliation should be drawn up, a properly constituted governing body for each College should be set up; attention should be paid to the residence and discipline of students and the courses as well as methods of examinations should be changed according to the suggestions of this Commission. All these recommendations rellect the opinions of Curzon who believed that the university education had deteriorated in quality and needed to be drastically reformed. Indians did not like Curzon's ways and there were protests at the attempt to curtail facilities for University education. The Universities Act of 1904 was passed embodying these recommendations but the demand for such education was too wide and large to be baulked at and we had increasing enrolment of students in various colleges. In 1902 we had 20,000 students and in 1922 we had 50,000 students in the colleges. New political and economic consciousness born of nationalist sentiment and Japan's defeat of Russia led to the growth of the University education.

The resolution of 1913 also recommended the establishment of a large number of such universities at Banaras Hindu University (1916), Aligarh Muslim University (1917), Osmania University, Mysore University, and Lucknow University. Agra University was established in 1927 as an examining one taking up most of the work of Allahabad University which now became a local, teaching and unitary one. Today there are more than seventy Universities in India and the University Grants Commission of the Government of India takes care of the university education so far as provision of money for it is concerned. During this period we had the appointment of two University Commissions one in 1917 and another in 1948 famous as the Calcutta University Commission and University Education Commission under the chairmanship of Sadler and Radhakrishnan, respectively. In 1964, Education Commission under the chairmanship of Dr. D. S. Kothari with a team of sixteen other members was appointed.

All these commissions pointed to great defects which had crept in the university education. There was no planning, no clarity about aims, students joined the colleges regardless of their capacity for such work, there was too much of cramming, science and research were comparatively neglected, teachers were not sufficiently paid and had a tendency to become seekers after money through various devices and elections had become a personal affair, there was deterioration in discipline and teaching and there were too many holidays. In short both the aims and methods of education and university instruction had woefully failed. The Sadler Commission recommended that the Intermediate classes should be separated from the University and with the IX and X classes they should be joined to form intermediate Colleges for which a Board of Intermediate and High School Education should be set up; the duration of the Degree course should be three years. The Calcutta University should cease to have any special relationship with the Central Government; mofussil colleges should be recognised and the teaching work in Calcutta University should be strengthened, special attention should be paid to women's education and to vocational and professional training while the method of examinations needed radical improvement. The medium of instruction should be English in the universities and 'Vernacular' in High Schools. But inspite of these recommendations the education in our colleges did not improve much though we had greater emphasis on science and research so that the twentieth century in India might well be called an age of science. The Radhakrishnan Commission made many recommendations to improve our universities and redefined our cultural aims. According to it the aims of the University education were : organisation of civilisation and culture, so that they may be 'sanctuaries of the inner life of the nations intellectual adventure; an integrated way of life; wisdom and knowledge; right conception of social order and social harmony; education for development of individual personality in all aspects, spiritual, mental, aesthetics and physical; understanding of nature; (technology and science) unity of mind and inter-dependence of knowledge; proper adjustment in society; Securing Justice for all classes, need for social studies and research; training for leadership; liberal education; freedom of expression; cultural growth and synthesis; world-mindedness and eschewing of provincialism or caste-considerations. To sum up 'Utopias are sweet dreams', wrote Kant, 'but to strive relentlessly towards them is the duty of the citizen and of the statesman as well'. Universities must stand for these ideal causes which can never be lost so long as men seek wisdom and follow righteousness.

In the light of these aims the Commission recommended among other things the following :

(1) Teachers should be given better scales of salaries and they should be properly selected and for these purposes the Government should give greater financial aid and attention than hitherto.

(2) Admission should be made to the universities after the passing of the Intermediate and completing twelve years of study.

(3) A large number of occupational institutions should be started.

(4) Refresher courses should be organised by the universities for High School and Intermediate College teachers.

(5) Maximum number of students in Universities and colleges should be 3,000 and 1,500 respectively.

(6) There should be a minimum of 180 days' teaching work in a year.

(7) Lectures should be carefully planned and supplemented by tutorials, seminars, library work and written exercises.

(8) There should be no prescribed text-books for any courses of study.

(9) Laboratories should be improved.

(10) General education in arts and sciences should also be encouraged so that the student may have the best possible acquaintance with and master of the contents and methods of thinking and working in each field.

(11) Teaching universities should develop research training in as many branches of knowledge as they can.

(12) There should be a large number of Research Fellowships for those who have taken the Ph.D. degree and wish to pursue further studies.

(13) University teachers should give the community punctuality, efficiency and devotion to duty.

(14) Agricultural education should be recognised as a major national issue.

(15) A commerce student should be given opportunities for practical work also during his period of study.

(16) The training colleges for teachers should be remodelled.

(17) Existing engineering and technological institutions should be regarded as national assets and both these and other new institutions should be encouraged by the Government to improve further.

(18) Our law colleges should be thoroughly re-organised.

(19) The maximum number of admissions to a medical College should be 100 and there should be more facilities for medical research.

(20) All educational institutions should start with few minutes of silent meditation and there should be provision for a Progressive course consisting of studies of the work of great religious leaders, great scriptures and central problems of philosophy.

(21) A University degree should not be required for government administrative services; credit should be given for class work and passing in periodical examinations should be compulsory.

(22) Student welfare should be actively promoted by various means such as scholarships, medical care, establishment of national cadet corps, provision for social service, encouragement of politics free unions, sports and recreations and an advisory 'Board of Student Welfare' should be set up with an office of Dean of the Students.

(23) Women's education should be encouraged.

(24) University education should be placed on the concurrent list, better rules for control and constitution of the universities should be framed.

(25) Special attention should be paid to the development of higher education in rural areas

by setting up necessary bodies like a rural university.

Finally the Commission recommends greater financial aid as only in that way we shall have knowledge which is essential because 'there is no freedom without knowledge'.

We have now surveyed the whole history of educational developments in modern India. The conclusion to which one cannot help coming to is that while we have progressed quantitatively, there has not been much qualitative advancement. Recently we had the lament of the Union Public Service Commission that the standards of education were deteriorating. The problem is very acute because all nation-building activities depend upon proper education of man. Man is the central problem.

For this in the first place our conception of education has to be enlarged. Scientific, utilitarian and economic values must be supplemented by cultural values. Further the realisation must down that man is inwardly a soul and a conscious power of the Divine and that the evocation of this real man within is the right object of education and we have to develop a healthy body and a strong vitality to clarify his mind, created a field for aesthetic and emotional enjoyments, to found religious systems and further social and economic welfare but none of them have saved man from disillusionment, weariness and decay. Modern insistence on progress, social or economic, is a variation on the same theme which was there in the ancient intellectual cultures of Europe and in the pieties of Asia. But all this has not escaped from birth, growth, decay and death in the past and will not escape now unless not only individuals (as in the past) but the whole human society seizes on the discovery of the soul as a means for the discovery of the law of its own being or on a knowledge of the soul's true nature and need and its fulfilment as the right way of terrestrial perfection, even freedom to err because experience comes through many errors. Science and philosophy, Law and medicine, arts and morality will have a larger field and greater scope for in their attempt to reach the Infinite they will have to be infinite. The spiritual aim in education of man 'will reveal to man the divinity in himself as the Light, Strength, Beauty, Good, Delight,

Immortality that dwell within and build up in his outer life also the Kingdom of God which is first discovered within us'.

Education has so far failed to uplift and inspire us so that we become true exemplar of our spiritual culture. In order that our education becomes a means for our spiritual upliftment, it should be a five fold instruction, namely, physical education, vital education, mental education, psychic education and spiritual education. Such a broad-based education will ensure harmony, beauty and perfection together with universal love.

Physical education will ensure a healthy body; vital education will sublimate our passionate and desires-full nature, mental education will enable us to differentiate between truths and untruths, psychic education will bring out the soul in us to be our guide and spiritual education will position us to be a true link between God, nature and the Cosmos.

Literary and Scientific Developments

The growth and enrichment of modern Indian literatures is a recent phenomenon though the foundations were laid long ago. There were many common factors that inspired the literary renaissance of modern India. These were the impact of English literature, the revolt against old conventions, the necessity of a work-a-day prose, the vogue of the novel and the social drama, urge to experiment in literary forms and techniques including the revolution in mental patterns, the predominance of a secular outlook, the upsurge of national spirit and patriotic fervour, the example of Christian missionaries who cleared the path by printing works in modern Indian languages, progressive movements typified in translations and adaptations from English literature and the inspiration of Bengal. The fundamental features of this literary development were the growth of 'prose' and the secularisation of the themes treated in the modern literatures. 'But as regards quality, I am convinced that we have nothing to fear if we judge our literature by the standards laid down by critics in these foreign countries'. We have surveyed the development of modern Indian literatures and shall now take up the story of scientific developments in India.

Sciences in Modern India

India had developed scientific knowledge in her ancient past but the medieval age saw the discontinuance of progress in such a knowledge. The reasons were the loss of freedom by the majority, the absence of state patronage, invasions and internal disturbances, exhaustion of ancient vitality, development of the ideal of asceticism and a disinclination to worry about the material comforts which are increased by a knowledge of science, absorption into devotionalism as a defensive mechanism against foreign rule and consequent neglect of other interests, stoppage of foreign travels and so loss of contact with the scientific progress in the West and rise of feudal imperialism which sapped local initiative and vitality drawing all power and talents to the centre where power became the sole altar of worship.

But contact with the West awakened our curiosity and stimulated the renaissance of Indian scientific progress. Still in the nineteenth century scientific progress was not significant because of the lack of state patronage. But private initiative was not lacking and it has been demonstrated that India has a genius for science as well. The first great scientist Jagadish Chandra Bose startled the world in 1896 by his demonstration in short wave wireless and later on by his discovery that plants responded to stimuli like the animals and many of the effects of stimulation shown by living tissues were shown also by non-living tissues. His discoveries bare out the truth of the Vedas that all nature is one. Many institutions took up research work as for instance the Indian Institute of Science founded by Tata in Bangalare in 1911. Its chief activity was applied science. Its director in 1931 was Sir C.V. Raman, the first Asiatic and Indian to receive Nobel Prize for physics in 1930 in recognition of his researches into the behaviour of light. His versatility is astonishing. We have now a solid body of Indian scientists of international reputation.

Government have also been helping in this sphere and before 1947 we had a number of technical and scientific institutions like imperial Agricultural Research Institute, Forest Research Institute, All-India Institute of Hygiene and Public

Health, Pasteur Institute, Malaria Institute and Indian Research Fund Association. With the dawn of freedom we have better organisation, more progress and diversification of Sciences. The Government of India and of the states have organised a chain of laboratories all over India like National Physical Laboratory (Delhi), National Chemical Laboratory (Poona), National Metallurgical Laboratory (Jamshedpur), Fuel Research Institute (Jharia Coal-fields), Indian Institute of Technology, Hijli (Bengal), Madras Institute of Technology, Institute of Radio-Physics and Electronics (Calcutta), Central Glass and Ceramic Research Institute (Calcutta), Central Leather Research Institute (Madras), Central Food Technological Research Institute (Mysore), Central Drug Research Institute (Lucknow), Central Building Research Institute (Roorkee) and Central Potato Research Institute (Patna). Besides we have the hydro-electric schemes and River-Valley projects like the Damodar valley Project, Hirakund Dam, Tungabhadra Project, Rihand Dam, and Kosi River Project. As a result of all these projects and schemes we can say that the scientific advance of India has truly begun and may lead to the material welfare of her people.

Political Developments

Indian policy today is in doldrums. Reason for such a State of Affairs lies in our inability to evolve a state suited to our cultural genius. Our present constitution based on British Parliamentary System is not a natural growth. It is not an Indian State in the sense that its structure and ideological direction did not arise out of a political movement rooted in native Indian thought and traditions. The Modern Indian State was the invention of an intellectual elite whose understanding of Indian Society and its historical inheritance was based on an educational process designed in the Oceident. The emotional, psychological and spiritual bondings which have nurtured India over the millennia will have to be in the fore-front for any political organisation that wishes to take the nation out of the current quagmire. Hence our linking the political system to our spiritual inheritance is an absolute necessity for such a restructuring of our ancient polity that prevailed from the Vedic to the Gupta period can provide certain guiding principles or ideas. We observe that the King in ancient India was guided by the Dharma, the religious, ethical, social, political, judicial and customary law organically governing the life of the people. Thus the subjection of the sovereign power to the Dharma was a living reality. Taking this as our guide we should hedge our rulers by a council of sages hailing from an intellectual elite who are well-versed in our ethos and have no axe to grind.

Again according to Indian traditions our mission was to reconcile life and the spirit, to 'found the status and action of the collective being of man on the realisation of the deeper spiritual truth, the yet unrealised spiritual potentialities of our existence and so ensoul the life of our people as to make our life the Lila of the greater self in humanity, a conscious communal Soul and body of the Virat, the universal spirit'. (Sri Aurobindo).

All this led to the evolution of an Indian polity as a system of a very complex communal freedom and self determination, every group unit of the community (right from village Panchayats guilds) having its own natural existence and administering its own proper life and business, set off from the rest by a natural demarcation of its field and limits, but connected with the whole by well-understood relations, each a co-partner with the others in the powers and duties of the communal existence. The State was to be and must now be an instrument of co-ordination and of a general control and efficiency limited by the Law and by the will of the people as expressed in our Sabhas, Samities, Panchayats or Guilds.

The conclusion is obvious. Our present centralised structure must be toppled, the top heavy bureaucracy must be abolished and as Mahatma Gandhi said in the Round Table Conference in London we should have an indirect system of election with, full provincial autonomy, the Central Power be limited in its function only to defence, foreign policy, foreign trade, customs and currency. A system of financial devolution is to be evolved and the Central Government be provided with the necessary finances by the provinces. The party system in such an organisation will have no role to play. Each village and cluster of nearby villages will have their Panchayats whose members will be known to each other by their contiguity, character and personal work and will more or less be unanimously elected. The village Panchayats and the City Panchayats in various provinces will combine together to elect the general assembly for the provinces and the general assemblies will elect the members of the Central Assembly. All the members of the Panchayats and the assemblies will elect a President for the whole of India together with the Powers to nominate his Cabinet, the term of the President may be five or seven years.

To sum up the lifeless attempt of our generation to imitate and reproduce with a service fidelity the ideals and forms of the West has been no true indication of the political mind and genius of the Indian people. But again amid all the mist of confusion there is still the possibility of a new twilight, a morning Yuga sandhya. 'India of the ages is not dead nor has she spoken her last creative word; she lives and has still something to do for herself and the human peoples. And that which must seek now is not an anglicised oriental people, docile pupil of the West and doomed to repeat the cycle of the occident's success and failure, but still the ancient immemorable Shakti recovering her deepest self, lifting her head higher towards the Supreme source of light and strength and turning to discover the complete meaning and a vaster form of her Dharma'.

We have finished with our survey of Indian Renaissance in modern times. It only remains to draw up balance-sheet to see what progress has been achieved and where we are the weakest.

In religion we have arrested that atheism which was the immediate result of the contact of Hinduism with westernism, vividly symbolised in the slogans of the students of the Hindu College, 'Down with Hinduism, Down with orthodoxy!' Rama Krishna Paramhamsa, Vivekanand, Dayanand, Raman Maharshi and Sri Aurobindo brought out the inner core of our religion and the new generation in the beginning of the twentieth century was no longer decrying our faith and past. It is true that today we have again become a generation without faith but the malady is world-wide and we have also to remember that our masses remain wedded to their faiths and they will count in the long run. Further even the intellectuals will appreciate the true worth of religion when its crown, the integral spirituality will have gained a hearing from the world and in this task we have the prospective contribution of that International University which is being set up by Sri Aurobindo Ashram, Pondicherry which bids fair to be the spiritual lighthouse of the world.

In social sphere again various inequalities and types of discrimination are either fast disappearing or they are not invested with the same theoretical validity which they had in the ages gone by. Women are coming into their own; untouchables are vociferous and self assertive and the backward classes have gained a sympathetic audience. In the economic sphere feudalism crumbled and gave place to capitalism specially in the cities and in British India and with the dawn of freedom landlordism is on its last legs and the remnants of feudalism in India, states of yesterday are bound to be liquidated, our most serious problem, economic poverty has not yet been solved but here again freedom promises a better deal and we have also to remember that Indian capitalism bred certain evils not inherent in the situation. Just because of our inexperience and the unsympathetic attitude of the foreign government. Anyhow our acute consciousness of poverty is there to see that justice must be done. In the sphere of arts news channels have been opened and a just appreciation of our artistic heritage has been brought about by Havell, Abanindranath and Anand Coomaraswami. It remains a problem how to develop the aesthetic sense among the masses and how to bring about a balanced harmony between the East and the West. In literature, the era has seen an appreciable progress in all Indian literatures. Sometimes we have played the sedulous ape to the West but the best in the West is universal and there is no reason why we should not be affected by the currents of Western literature provided we are racy with our soil and do not become just pale imitators. In science again we have made an advance against heavy odds and proved that given money and opportunities India can be in the vanguard of scientific advancement.

But we have our failures also, our philosophy, architecture and drama have not developed in proportion to our achievements in other spheres. We may probably discover that behind these failures there is a comman cause. All these require a synthetic vision. Philosophy is the synthesis of all arts and of all sciences. Architecture is the matrix of civilisation and drama is a harmonisation of all arts specially music, painting and dancing. But ours is pre-eminently an age of analysis, an age of reason and science where theories are galore, hypotheses are legion, but unanimity, uniformity or harmony are conspicuous for their absence. We have, therefore, to develop a synthetic outlook. In philosophy, we have to become not merely doctrinaires or critical interpreters of the West but seers as our Rishis of old were. Indian philosophy developed in the past because our philosophers expressed what they had experienced or seen in their spiritual vision and so our philosophies were called Darshan (what had been seen). Philosophy is a quest for truth and truth must be lived before its validity can be assured and its permanence guaranteed.

Architecture again presupposes an integral understanding of all arts and a deep insight into the ethos of the race. We developed our architecture best in the ancient period because the race had lived fully and well and because the architect was primarily a yogi, a seer and believed in the impersonality of efforts. To quote Sri Aurobindo, 'Art has flowed in two separate streams in Europe and in Asia while the best European art satisfies the physical requirements of the aesthetic sense, the laws of formal beauty, the emotional demand of humanity, the portrayal of life and outward reality, the best Indian art reaches beyond them and expresses inner spiritual truth, the deeper not obvious reality of things, the joy of God in the world and its beauty and desirableness and the manifestation of divine force and energy in phenomenal creation'. Our architects have not yet found their feet and probably will not find so long as we remain without faith.

Again our drama had become moribund, effete and colourless. But Some efforts at regeneration are now being made. The films have hit it hard but here again the lost ground can be recaptured if we develop a synthetic vision. Romantic vision of the past or blind imitation of the West will not lead to its revival. Here we have some efforts in the right direction. Tagore's Shantiniketan, Indian National Theatre of Bombay and Prithvi Raj are attempting to be assimilative and not imitative in their arts. Eastern themes and Western techniques are being combined. Various Academies established by the Government of India are also encouraging new discoveries. Ballets and operas are being staged and short plays with a minimum of settings are being introduced. Those ballets which show the spirit of our culture have become a brilliant success for in them our artists are true to themselves. Thus the lesson of our modern Renaissance is that we must be true to our culture, to its basis, the integral spirituality.

To sum up - 'Greece developed to a high degree the intellectual reason and the sense of form and harmonious beauty, Rome founded firmly strength and power and patriotism and law and order, modern Europe has raised to enormous proportions practical reason, science and efficiency and economic capacity, India developed the spiritual mind working on the other powers of man and exceeding them, the intuitive reason, the philosophical harmony of the Dharma informed by the religious spirit, the sense of the eternal and the infinite'. It is the task and the duty of the new phase of Indian renaissance now beginning to go on to a greater and more comprehensive development of these things and to evolve fresh powers. In the new India(2001) the following message of the Mother to Srimati Indira Gandhi, the Prime Minister of India, is worth noticing : 'Let India work for the future and take the lead, Thus she will recover her true place in the world'. The greatness of a country does not depend on the victory of a party but on the union of all the parties'.

18

CONCLUSION

(Need of a Modern Synthesis)

INDIA IS FACING a great crisis of her destiny. There is a sense of deep frustration. There is talk of great corruption. All political parties are split in groups and factions. Genius seems to have stopped being born in any sphere of life whether arts, literature, society or politics. We talk of Indianisation, National integration and condemn communalism, provincialism and casteism. The younger generation as of old has no moornings in our traditions and is drifting headlong towards westernism. In economic life statism has been introduced with all its attendant evils. Centralisation and bureaucratism are other great evils according to many leaders of thought.

But all this is bound to happen in a society which is passing through a transition and we need not despair of India's destiny. India is bound to be one day one of the great leaders of the world and this can be facilitated if we have cultural synthesis on the basis of creative spirituality. What can be the main lines of a new cultural synthesis in our country?

Indian genius is called upon to accept the challenge of westernism and evolve solutions to her problems in her own way without resorting to cultural reactionarism. As Sri Aurobindo has said, 'Confronted with the huge rush of modern life and thought.....India can only survive by confronting this raw, new, aggressive, powerful world with fresh diviner creations of her own spirit, cast in the mould of her own spiritual ideals. In that connection I spoke of the acceptance and assimilation from the West of whatever in its knowledge, ideas, powers was assimilable, compatible with her spirit, reconcilable with her ideals, valuable for a new statement of life.'

As against this view there is a school of thought which indulges in dreams of revivalism, in Indianising Islam or resurrecting worn-out ideals. We are not to imitate European Civilisation and become what Bankim called 'Saheb-log'. Now there is no question of becoming a mere foster-child of western civilisation. 'But even then a certain amount of acceptance, of forms too, some imitation, if taking over of forms must be called imitation, is inevitable. We have, for instance, taken over in literature the form of the novel, the short story, the critical essay among a number of other adoptions, in science not only the discoveries and inventions, but the method and instrumentation of inductive research, in politics the press, the platform, the forms and habits of agitation, the public association. I do not suppose that anyone seriously thinks of renouncing or exiling these modern additions to our life....when I speak of acceptance and assimilation, I am thinking of certain influences, ideas, energies brought forward with a great living force by Europe....That was in fact what our own ancestors did, never losing originality, never effacing their uniqueness, because always vigorously creating from within, with whatever knowledge or artistic suggestion from outside they thought worthy of acceptance'. (Sri Aurobindo)

The main criterion of acceptance of foreign cultural elements – whether from Europe, from other parts of Asia and the world or from Christianity, Islam or other sects and religions should be, this'–that whatever helps me to find myself more intimately, nobly, with a greater and sounder possibility of self-expressive creation, is good; whatever carries me out of my orientation, whatever weakens and belittles my power, richness, breadth and height of self-being, is bad for me'. For instance we have to accept such ideals as political liberty, equality and democracy. But we have to re-interpret them in the light of our own ideals. 'What I mean by assimilation, is that we must not take it crudely in the European forms, but must go back to whatever corresponds to it, illumines its sense, justifies its highest purport in our own spiritual conception of life and existence, and in that light work out its extent, degree, form, relation to other ideas, application. To everything I would apply the same principle, to each its own kind, after its proper dharma, in its right mesasure of importance, its spiritual, intellectual, ethical, aesthetic, dynamic utility'. (Sri Aurobindo).

Thus the main law of cultural synthesis is in the words of Sri Aurobindo, 'assimilative appropriation'. That is 'a making the thing settle into oneself, and turn into characteristic form of our self-being'. Both self-development from within and acceptance of impacts from outside have to go on side by side. The external impacts stimulate in a healthy being the force for self-development. Indian culture declined in the past because it had shut its doors to the winds coming from outside. Alberuni the famous author, traveller and publicist who came to India in the eleventh century A.D. had remarked upon this isolation mentality of the Hindus. This lack of cultural adaptation led to our decline in all fields of life and was the most potent cause of our political slavery. Sri Aurobindo thus sums up this law of assimilative appropriation, 'The man who most finds and lives from the innerself, can most embrace the universal and become one with it; the Svarat, independent, self-possessed and self-ruler can most be the Samrat, possessor and shaper of the world in which he lives, can most too grow one with all in the Atman. That is the truth this developing existence teaches us, and it is one of the greatest secrets of the old Indian spiritual knowledge'.

Every country has its own characteristic way of looking at things, its own swadharma, its own ideal law of existence, its unique genius and its own characteristic method of operation. We have attempted to show in this history of Indian culture that this genius of India, its unique characteristic, lies in its pursuit of dynamic and integral spirituality, yet we are not to be untouchables. The windows of our cultural mansion must be open to all the influences coming from outside. It is for us to judge how these influences can be assimilated and re-invigorated in the light of our own genius. Thus secularism, industrialism, socialism, democracy, various facets of modernism in the fields of arts, fashions, literature, manners, social life etc., have to be accepted but only to the extent that they do not annihilate the characteristic inner Indian personality. Any attempt therefore of life in isolation and to ignore modern environment will be an exercise in futility.

Hence the law of adaptation and assimilation must hold and operate. 'Each capable Indian mind must think it out or, better, work it out in its own light and power and contribute some illumination or effectuation. The spirit of the Indian renaissance will take care of the rest, that power of the universal time-spirit which has begun to move in our midst for the creation of a new and greater India.'

However some aspects of our cultural life may be examined.

To take religion first because it has been a dominant influence in our life. In our modern life religion can have influence only if it is not dogmatic, universal in spirit, not wedded to any particular rite or ceremony and yet be able to appeal not only to the mind but also to the heart of man. Religion must be universalized, take into itself all that can be absorbed from outside and put into some valid relation with the truth of the supra-physical worlds and the truth of the Infinite; further it must take to each man where he stands and spiritualise him through what he can feel and not at once force on him something which he cannot yet grasp as a true and living power. It is because of this that Bhakti has a role to play in religion but it cannot be of any standard variety. Freedom in religion is a must provided it does not offend modern taste or decences of life. Here we must be very clear about Hinduism. Hinduism should not be interpreted in a very narrow manner. As Sri Aurobindo has observed about Hinduism, 'it gave itself no name, because it set itself no sectarian limits; it claimed no universal adhesion, asserted no sole infallible dogma, set up no single narrow path or gate of salvation; it was less a creed or cult than a continuous enlarging tradition of the Godward endeavour of the human spirit.

As the Vedas have put it 'Truth is one though sages call it by various names'. We have to be tolerant and assimilative in this sphere also. Above all the two conceptions of Maya and Asceticism must not be carried too far. This world is a fact of major importance. We have to accept its existence and develop the material basis of life otherwise spirituality will sink and shrivel into nothingness or disappear into Nirvana. Again asceticism should be an individual liking and not a universal phenomenon. Modern life has to be accepted with all its richness and variegated hues but of course with detachment, a sense of proportion and without loss of ethical values of life. Life is not an illusion but a divine play. It is a means by which the soul growing in nature through countless forms can approach, touch, feel and unite itself through love and knowledge and faith and adoration and a Godward will in works with the Transcendent Being and this Infinite existence. All life and thought are in the end a means of progress towards self-realisation and God-realisation. Thus viewed Hinduism will have no antagonism either with Christianity or Islam or any other religion. Indian religion never considered intellectual of theological conceptions about the supreme truth to be of central importance. To pursue that Truth (the Absolute) under whatsoever form, to attain to it by inner experience, to live it in consciousness, this is held to be the sole thing needful. Even the atheist was permitted to air his views. Stress was laid on inner development and not on conformity to externals of religion.

Again in the social field we have to abolish the caste system. It has lost its rationale. It is a hindrance in the development of an Indian personality. Patriotism cannot flourish on the basis of caste. We have to treat every Indian as an individual with a dignity and self-respect of his own. No idea of inferiority or superiority in terms of social life should be entertained. There should be no stress on particular food, dress or way of living. There cannot be stark uniformity in our social life. There should be no taboo on western dress or mode of living just because they have come from the West. The only inhibition should be on exhibitionism and epicureanism if they become offensive to decent taste of which the enlightened society should be the judge and not any rigorous law.

In the political sphere we tread on dangerous grounds. However, we must be assimilative but not totally imitative. Here also in the words of Sri Aurobindo we have to, 'reconcile life and the spirit, India's ancient mission, to found the status and action of the Collective being of man on the realisation of the deeper spiritual truth, the yet unrealised spiritual potentialities of our existence and so ensoul the life of her people as to make it the Lila of the greater self in humanity, a conscious communal soul and body of Virat, the universal spirit.'

Here the tendency to adopt western political models in toto must be depreciated. In Western political life we have had an exaggerated dependence on reason, on system and the institution, on legislation and administration and the deadly tendency to develop, in place of a living people, a mechanical state based on party-politics. It is this error of the scientific reason stifling the work of the vital and the spiritual intention under the dead weight of its mechanical method which is the weakness of Europe. In India we must aim at men in the collectivity beginning to live more deeply and to govern his collective life neither primarily by the needs, instincts, intuitions welling up out of the vital self, nor secondarily by the construction of the reasoning mind, but first, foremost and always by the power of unity, sympathy, spontaneous liberty, supple and living order of his discovered greater self and spirit in which the individual and the communal existence have their law of freedom, perfection and oneness. 'That is a rule that has not anywhere found its right conditions for even beginning its effort, for it can only come when man's attempt to reach and abide by the law of the spiritual existence is no longer an exceptional aim for individuals or else degraded in its more general aspiration to the form of a popular religion, but is recognised and followed out as the imperative need of his being and its true and right attainment, the necessity of the next step in the evolution of the race'. We have to guard against the so-called monstrous artificial organisation—the bureaucratic and industrial state. The British political model is not suited to our spiritual genius. It is for the best Indian minds to evolve a political system suited to our genius which is synthetic rather than analytic. We have to have a blend of the presidential, the aristocratic and the democratic elements in such a way that every individual has the freedom to develop to the full all his potentialities and at the same time subserve the collective ideals of the race. As Sri Aurobindo has put it, 'the one principle, permanent at the Base of construction throughout all the building and extension and rebuilding of the Indian polity was the principle of an organically self-determining not only in the mass and by means of the machinery of the vote and a representative body erected on the surface, representative only of the political mind of a part of the nation, which is all that the modern system has been able to manage, but in every pulse of its life and in each separate member of its existence'. A free synthetic communal order was its character. Thus Indian political life must guarantee freedom and self-development of every individual, of every group, social, regional, communal, functional, provincial, village or city-and at the same time foster inter-dependence, freedom, flexibility, progress and unity. This is not possible if we become mere servile imitators of the West.

There is also the Hindu-Muslim problem. The solution should be attempted along two lines. There should be developed a spiritual principle and formation which could reconcile both Hinduism and Islam. Both the Hindus and the Muslims should imbibe the true principles of their religion and remember that the rites and practices are a matter of private affair and should not prove to be apples of discords. Spirituality means freedom and variety of worship. The stress is on truth to be discovered by each one in his own way but not at the cost of the individuality of another person who may follow a different faith. Again we have to develop a patriotism surmounting the religious struggle and uniting the two communities. Politics of true and universal love and not hatred can alone solve the problem. But it requires patience, tact and understanding which only an appreciation of each other's culture can generate.

In the field of arts and literature also we have to develop

a new synthetic initiative but this we can do only if our appreciation of the 'motif' of our culture is genuine and in depth. It has been said that 'all Indian art is a throwing out of a certain profound self-vision formed by a going within to find out the secret significance of the giving of soul-form to that vision and a remoulding of the material and natural shape to express the psychic truth of it with the greatest possible purity and power of outline and the greatest possible concentrated rhythmic unity of significance in all the parts of an indivisible artistic whole'. Similarly in literature also we should aim at a creative literature flowering in all branches–mundance or religious-but at the same time being in conformity with the ideals of the race. The scene in these aspects of modern Indian life at present is rather chaotic and with certain exceptions devoid of worthwhile creations. We have to generate new enthusiasms and new motives but this requires hard work initiative and a true understanding of our spiritual culture and also a living of that culture.

Again in economic life we have had all sorts of experiments and the air is thick with slogans. Socialism has become the fashion. But here also the twin principles of Indian life must not be forgotton namely individuality and mutuality interpreted in the light of an integral spirituality. Socialism should not lead to statism or be the father of the ugly aspects of industrialism or bureaucratism. Welfare of the masses is a worthy aim but not at the cost of freedom. We have to discover our own way, away from capitalism or communism and the way must lead to a balanced development of not only the cities but also the villages. The end of communism in Europe is a pointer in this direction.

Socialism in India dangerously poised between socialistic regimentation and democratic liberty. In due course man discovers that there always occurs a discrepancy between the set ideas of the human thinker and the actual facts of human nature; for it ignores the complexity of man's being and all that that complexity means. And especially it ignores the soul of man. We may call democratic socialism as the ideal solution but in actual fact the government that operates is of a few individuals. History shows that these few individuals at the helm of affairs in course of time become selfish and grabbing. Individual interests begin to operate in the garb of collective interests. Further the state idea suffers from a tendency to mechanisation. Life is on the contrary mobile. It is also complex and involves interlocking of an immense number of things that are in conflict with each other. Hence the only true solution and also the Indian solution is when, 'the soul discovers itself in its highest and completest spiritual reality and effects a progressive upward transformation of its life-values into those of the spirit, for there they will all find their spiritual truth and in that truth their standing-ground of mutual recognition and reconciliation.

A synthetic civilisation can only develop if we have a right and proper education. National education is the need of the hour. But what is National education? National education is an education proper to the Indian soul and need and temperament and culture, not indeed something faithful merely 'to the past, but to the developing soul of India, to her future need, to the greatness of her coming self-creation, to her eternal spirit'. True education helps to bring out to the full advantage all that is in the individual man, helps him to enter into right relation with the life, mind and soul of his people and living, an accord with that great total life, mind and soul of humanity of which he himself is a unit and his people a separate and yet inseparable member. Each country has a different conception of man and his life. And naturally education in each country adapts itself to the values thus visualized. In India we have seen in man the individual a soul, a portion of the divinity enwrapped in mind and body. As Sri Aurobindo says, 'always she has distinguished and cultivated in him a mental, an intellectual, an ethical, dynamic and practical, an aesthetic and hedonistic, a vital and physical being, but all these have been seen as powers of a soul that manifests through them and grows with their growth. We have seen in the nation and in the humanity also a soul, National Purusha and Virat Purusha.

Thus our education, must be education that for the individual will make its one central object the growth of the soul and its powers and possibilities, for the nation will keep in view first, the preservation, strengthening and enrichment of the nation-soul and its dharma and raise both into powers of the life and ascending mind and soul of humanity. And at no time will it lose sight of man's highest object, the awakening and development of his spiritual being'. Thus viewed our education has to be fivefold, physical, vital, mental, psychic and spiritual. We have to develop a healthy and beautiful body, prepare an alert mind even on the look out for fresh initiatives and suppleness of thought, develop an outlook that knows how to direct or curb our desires, sentiments and emotions, further, through psychic and spiritual education the soul in us has to come out and become the leader of our march in life and in the world.

It is because we have not organised this type of national education that we are today suffering from all sorts of ills in all walks of life. Education too must be synthetic and global in its view. Here we must say that there should be no attempt to denigrate the English language. Hindi may become the link language but we must remember that English language is not the monopoly of England. It is par excellence the window on the world of today. It is the international language and its richness and universality are further developing. There is no harm in India being bilingual. The soul of India can be reflected in the English language also with the added benefit that experiments in Indian spirituality will be carried abroad through this language. If India is destined to lead the world, continued patronage of English language is a sine qua hon.

The need of the hour is cultural synthesis based on spirituality. As Sri Aurobindo so beautifully sums up, 'Out again amid all the mist of confusion there is still the possibility of a new twilight, not of an evening but a morning Yuga-sandhya. India of the ages is not dead nor has she spoken her last creative word; she lives and has still something to do for herself and the human peoples. And that which must seek now to awake is not an anglicised oriental people, docile part of the west and doomed to repeat the cycle of the occident's success and failure, but still the ancient immovable Shakti recoving her deepest self lifting her head higher towards the supreme source of light and strength and turning to discover the complete meaning and a vaster form of her Dharma'.

To conclude, Indian civilisation is neither morivund nor it is devoid of initiative, it is still on the march. The present crisis is only a precursor to a greater and more glorified future. The discrediting of party-politics and establishment of unity and stability are to be welcomed as they will lead to an agonizing re-appraisal and our constitutional social and economic structures will be rebased on true Indianism, on the basis of renovated idealism and spiritual realism.

APPENDIX–A

PROPHETS OF INDIAN NATIONALISM

INDIA'S CULTURAL AWAKENING found its great fruition in the birth of modern Indian nationalism which for the first time embraced with its fold all classes and creeds. The most visible symbol of nationalism in India was the Indian National Congress founded in 1885. At first confined to the moderates, gradually it was influenced by the radicals who became a factor to be reckoned with since 1905 when the partition of Bengal took place. It was, however, after 1918 that the Congress was finally captured by the extremists and Mahatama Gandhi assumed the leadership, bringing India to independence in 1947 through many trials and tribulations. Side by side a revolutionary movement for freedom together. Azad Hind Fauz of Netaji Subhash Chandra Bose was the climax of these attempts.

Indian National Congress has given us great and towering personalities like Hume, Surendranath Banerjee, Dadabhai Naoroji, Pherozeshah Mehta, M.G. Ranade, G.K. Gokhale, B.C. Pal, Sankaran Nair, C.R. Das, Motilal Nehru, Madan Mohan Malaviya, Lajpat Rai, Mrs. Annie Besant, B.G. Tilak, Sri Aurobindo, Mahatma Gandhi, Jawaharlal Nehru and Subhash Chandra Bose. Of these we select three, Tilak, Gandhi and Aurobindo, who in more recent times have been the cynosure of all eyes, for more detailed treatment. They are really the prophets of modern Indian nationalism. We shall mention here the abiding aspects of their thoughts and ideas.

Bal Gangadhar Tilak (1856-1920)

Bal Gangadhar Tilak became in the eyes of the Indians the symbol of the national endeavour, of the national aspiration, for freedom. His ringing slogan that 'Swaraj is our birth-right and we shall have it' went reverberating throughout the whispering galleries of the East and was the first nail driven into the coffin of British Imperialism. His advent on the stage of Indian politics dealt a knock-out blow at the policy of mendicancy which had become the fashion among the leading lights of the Congress. Tilak rose from the people, he had not been born with a silver spoon in his mouth. His terling character, his religious devotion and his profound patriotism gave him the first place in the hearts of the people. He was a great Sanskrit scholar, a powerful writer and a strong, subtle and lucid thinker. In the field of scholarship his three works *Orion, Arctic Home* and the *Gita Rahasya* occupy a most notable place. In *Orion* he has given proof positive of the antiquity of the Vedas, placing them 4,000 years before Christ and the discovery of Indus Valley civilisation may well bear out his claims. In *Arctic Home* he has attempted to show that the original home of the Aryans was in the Arctic. His work on the *Gita* is an original criticism and presentation of ethical truth, a monumental work, the first prose writing of the front rank and a classic in the Marathi language. His *Gita Rahasya* preaches the gospel of Karma, action without the thought of reward, disinterested performance of one's duty. He has discussed the western philosophy as expressed by the great thinkers of the West and tried to show that the great merit of the *Gita* is exhortation to the duty regardless of consequences. Its effect on the political life of India was profound; stirring the masses out of their torpor and activising the Indian leadership to do, dare and die for the cause of Indian freedom. Through his editorship of *Kesari* he carried on for decades a brilliant, vigorous and politically educative propaganda against the powers that be. He was associated with the educational movement of Poona that gave us the Fergusson College, a monument of co-operation in self-sacrifice. In the organisation of the Shivaji and the Ganapati festivals he attempted to reawaken the soul of the people.

Thus he linked up 'the new political spirit, the tradition and sentiment of the historic past and of both with the ineradicable religious temperament of the people of which these festivals were the symbol'. He indianised the political movement bringing into it the masses. Thus Tilak was a political genius who sensed the spirit of the times and showed the right direction for the political movement in India. His imprisonments, for the first time, awoke the people to the truth that freedom will come through suffering and sacrifice and not through arm-chair politics. He was a true representative of the Marathas, a rugged, strong, democratic, intelligent, practical pugnacious and shrewd race. All these qualities he possessed and in addition he displayed a genius, intensity of purpose, strength of will, single-mindedness in aims and a spiritual fervour which 'remind one of the brightness, sharpness and perfect temper of a fine sword hidden in a sober scabbard'. He gave practical shape to the slogans of Swaraj, Swadeshi, National Education and Boycott. In short, Tilak epitomised the genius of Hinduism at its best.

Mahatma Gahdhi (1869-1948)

Mahatma Gandhi made India in live issue in international politics. His forceful personality and zealous advocacy of freedom for India restored our self-respect and the West also began to revalue its notions of India's civilisation and culture. His prolific writings on social, political, religious, educational and economic subjects form a precious portion of modern Indian literature. His contribution in the field of politics was to re-introduce the spirit of religion which Tilak had expressed before and also to make the masses realize the value of freedom and struggle for it. As he says, 'To see the universal and all pervading spirit of Truth face to face one must be able to love the meanest of creation as oneself. And a man who aspires after that cannot afford to keep out of any field of life. That is why my devotion to Truth has drawn me into the field of politics; and I can say without the slightest hesitation and yet in all humility that those who say that religion has nothing to do with politics do not know what religion means'.

For him there is no other God than truth, and the only means for the realisation of truth is love or ahimsa (non-violence). For this realization purity of heart, purity of means or purity of motives are very necessary. Hence he emphasizes Brahmacharya (celibacy) in life, freedom from fear and attachments and a serene detachment coupled with humility. His love for truth was not merely theoretical like that of a seasoned politician. He practised what he preached. Though he was a great disciplinarian, he did not possess rigidity of temperament and had a keen sense of humour. He attempted to rid India of its divisions and disharmonies, teach the masses to stand on their own legs, raise woman to a status equal to that of man in all spheres, unite Hindus and Muslims and cleanse Hinduism of its social abomination of untouchability.

In the economic field he stood for decentralistation of industries, for village uplift and for economic betterment of the masses. According to him, 'the proper function of cities is to serve as clearing-houses for village products. His insistence on Khadi or home-spun cloth is a symbol of his desire for the economic betterment of the masses.

His insistence on non-violence led him to evolve the method of Satyagraha. Gandhiji asks us to leave fighting to the non-human species, behave like men and serve the right by quiet suffering. Love or self-suffering can overcome the enemy, not by destroying him but by changing him.

'Gandhi is the prophet of a liberated life wielding power over millions of human beings by virtue of his exceptional holiness and heroism. To be true, to be simple, to be pure and gentle of heart, to remain cheerful and contented in sorrow and danger, to love life and not to fear death, to serve the spirit and not to be haunted by the spirits of the dead, nothing better has ever been taught or lived since the world first began............Gandhi's death was a classical ending to his life. He died with the name of God on his lips and love in his heart. Even as he received the bullet wounds he greeted his murderer and wished him well.'

(S. Radhakrishnan).

Sri Aurobindo (1872-1950)

Sri Aurobindo is a name and a memory to the younger generation of today but to our fathers he was the poet of patriotism and the prophet of nationalism. Aurobindo Ghosh was born in Calcutta on August 15, 1872. At an early age, he went to England where he lived for 14 years leaving England in 1893. He read there in St. Paul's School in London and King's College in Cambridge University. He distinguished himself for his aptitude in literature, having attained great proficiency in foreign languages like English, French, Latin, Greek, German and Spanish. He also passed the open competition for the I.C.S. He met the Gaikwad of Baroda in London and obtained an appointment in the Baroda service. He passed thirteen years (1893-1906) there, first in the Settlement and Revenue Department and in Secretariat work for the Maharaja, afterwards as Professor of English and, finally Vice-Principal in the Baroda College. Here he made up for his deficiency in Indian culture and literature, learning Sanskrit, Marathi, Gujarati, Bengali and Hindi. He also worte dramas, essays and composed great poems during this period. His literary writings have been generally in the English language. From 1900 onwards he began secretly to work for a revolutionary violent movement to emancipate India from the bondage of foreigan rule.

With the partition of Bengal in 1905 he felt the call to come into the open field to fight the British. He left Baroda in 1906, joining the newly-founded Bengal National College in Calcutta as its Principal. His activities were threefold, secret revolutionary propaganda and organisation of which the central aim was the preparation of an armed insurrection; public propaganda intended to convert the whole nation to ideal of independence; organisaion of the people to carry on a public and united opposition and undermining of the foreign rule through an incressing non-co-operation and passive resistance. His speeches and writings stirred the Indian nation to its profound depth and the British government retaliated by imprisoning him in Alipore on charges connected with the revolutionary movement led by his brother. In the trial he was defended by C.R. Das whose advocacy convinced the judge of his innocence and he was acquitted. From 1908 to 1910 he remained in British India and then left for Pondicherry, founding there what is now known as Sri Aurobindo Ashram. He was joined there by a French lady in 1920, who is now known as 'The Mother' and has been responsible for the management of the Ashram since 1926 when Sri Aurobindo retired from direct contact with most of his sadhaks or disciples. The Mother has been a Yogin from her very childhood, has learnt Yoga from many countries like Japan and Egypt and her spiritual attainments are second to one in the present world. After his death the Mother has launched upon a project for an International University where Sri Aurobindo's teachings will form the basis of an education based on spirituality.

Sri Aurobindo's life be looked at from an evolutionary point of view. From 1879 to 1905 it is self-culture, from 1905 to 1910 it is service of country and from 1910 to 1950 it is service of God and through Him service of all. In a way all through this period he was proceeding towards his divine mission, the redemption of humanity by divinising it. His papers Bandemataram, Karmayogin and Dharma show how he was evolving from a mere human being towards divinity. Speaking of him C.R. Readdy, the Vice-Chancellor of Andhra University says 'I hail Sri Aurobindo as the sole-sufficing genius of the age. He is more than the hero of a nation. He is amongst the saviours of humanity, who belong to all ages and all nations, the Sanatanas who leaven our existence with their eternal presence, whether we are aware of it or not.'

Sri Aurobindo was the most versatile genius of his age and nothing compared to him has been born in the modern times. He has written extensively and creatively on politics, religion, philosophy, history, culture, poetry, arts, drama and even sports, Nothing that he touched, has he left unadorned. Our book is a proof positive of his versatile genius. His major works are *Life Divine, Essays on the Gita, Synthesis of Yoga, Ideal of Human Unity, Human Cycle* and *Savitri*. We shall conclude now by referring to some of his views on important topics.

Evolution

The mass of humanity evolves slowly, containing in itself all stages of the evolution from the material and the vital man to the mental man. A small minority has pushed beyond the barriers, opening the doors to occult and spiritual knowledge. We speak of the evolution of Life in Matter, the evolution of Mind in Matter; but evolution is a word which merely states the phenomenon without explaining it. For there seems to be no reason why Life should evolve out of material elements or Mind out of living forms, unless we accept the Vedantic solution that Life is already involved in Matter and Mind in Life because in essence matter is a form of veiled Life, Life a form of veiled consciousness, And then there seems to be little objection to a farther step in the series and the admission that mental consciousness may itself be only a form and a veil of higher states which are beyond Mind. In that case, the unconquerable impulse of man towards God, Light, Bliss, Freedom, Immortality presents itself in its right place in the chain as imply the imperative impulse by which nature is seeking to evolve beyond Mind and appears to be as natural, true and just as the impulse towards Life which she has planted in forms of Matter or the impulse towards Mind which she has planted in certain forms of Life. As there, so here, the impulse exists more or less obscurely in her different vessels with an ever-ascending series in the power of its will to be : as there, so here, it is gradually evolving and bound fully to evolve the necessary organs and faculties. The animal is a living laboratory in which Nature has, it is said, worked out man. Man himself may well be a thinking and living laboratory in whom and with whose conscious co-operation she wills to work out the superman, the God.

India's Mission in the World

Sri Aurobindo believes that the attaiment of political independence imposes upon the leaders of India a very deep responsibility. It is upto them to keep steadily before their minds the great mission of India as a world-force and as a unique power for peace, progress and harmony. There are certain things on which India has set the highest value and which have been the supreme endeavour of her greatest spirits. Without neglecting meterial interests, these things should occupy our primary attention. They are in his own words, 'the calm and compassion of Buddha victorious over suffering, the meditation of the thinker tranced in communion with the Eternal, passed above the seekings of thought into identify with the superme light of the Spirit, the rapture of the saint made one by love in the pure heart with the transcendent and universal love, the will of the Karma Yogin raised above egoistic desire and passion into the impersonality of the divine and universal will', 'India had the power to save mankind from the path of self-destruction and to lead human civilisation to a glorious self-fulfiment in the form of 'Divine out-flowering in Man.'*

The World Crisis Today—'At present mankind is undergoing an evolutionary crisis in which is concealed a choice of its destiny.....Man has created a system of civilisation which has become too big for him limited mental capacity......Science has put at his disposal many potencies of the Universal Force and has made the life of humanity materially one; but what uses this Universal Force is a little human individual or communal ego with nothing universal in its light of knowledge or its movement, on inner sense or power which would create in this physical drawing together of the human world a true life unity, a mental unity or a spiritual oneness. All that is there is a chaos of clashing mental ideas, urges of individual and collective, physical want and need, vital claims and desires, impulses of an ignorant lifepush, hungers and calls for life satisfaction of individuals, classes, nations, a rich fungus of political and social and economic nostrums and notions, a hustling medley of slogans and panaceas for which men are ready to oppress and be oppressed, to kill and he killed........

The evolution of human mind and life must necessarily lead towards an increasing universality; but on a basis of ego

* Haridas Chaudhury, *Sri Aurobindo : The Prophet of Life Divine,* p. 78.

and segmenting and dividing mind this opening to the universal can only create a vast pullulation of unaccorded ideas and impulses, a surge of enormous powers and desires, a chaotic mass of unassimilated and inter-mixed mental, vital and physical material of a larger existence which, because it is not taken up by a creative harmonising light of the spirit, must welter in a universalised confusion and discord out of which it is impossible to build a greater harmonic life......Even if this turns out to be a passing phase or appearance and a tolerable structural accommodation is found which will enable mankind to proceed less catastrophically on its uncertain journey, this can only be a respite. For the problem is fundamental and in putting it evolutionary Nature in man is confronting herself with a critical choice which must one day be solved in the true sense if the race is to arrive or even to survive. The evolutionary nisus is pushing towards a development of the cosmic force in terrestrial life which needs a larger mental and vital being to support it, a wider mind, a greater, wider, more conscious unanimised Life-Soul, Anima and that again needs an unveiling of the supporting Soul and spiritual Self within to maintain it......A total spiritual direction given to the whole life and the whole nature can alone lift humanity beyond itself.'*

---

* Sri Aurobindo, *The Life Divine* (America Edition), pp. 933-938

APPENDIX-B

TRIBAL AND FOLK CULTURE

IN INDIA WE have a great medley of races and tribes and it is very difficult to sort them out into some coherence. We have in the first chapter of the book described the races who inhabit our country. The tribal people or the aboriginals in India belong mainly to the Proto-Australoid, the Negrito and the Mongoloid elements.

All these three elements have in the course of centuries divided up into a large number of tribes all mutually exclusive, each marrying within the tribe, each again split up into sub-clans wherein members are forbidden to marry people of their own clan and most of them preserving their ancient names and customs to this day.

There are now over twenty-five million aboriginals and they are distributed throughout India. Among the interesting and picturesque tribes are the Nagas, Garo, Kachari, Khasi, Mikir and Lushai.

The chief tribe in Bihar is the Santhal whose total population is above the million mark. The Santhals are to be found in Orissa also as well as in some other parts of India. In the Chhota Nagpur plateau we have the habitation of the great Uraon tribe, the Mundas, the Hos, some Santhals, the Kharias and some smaller tribes including the very ancient Asur, iron-smelters, Orissa has also a high population of aboriginals. We may mention Bhuiyas and Bhumiji, the Khonds (once notorious for human sacrifice), the Sabaras, member of this tribe, it is said, gave good to Lord Ramachandra on his wanderings, and the Gadabas and Porojas who have got a fancy for ornaments and romantic dresses. To their south in the mountains are to be found the primitive Juangs, some of whom still dress themselves in leaves.

The Madhya Pradesh is occupied by over two million Gonds, once a royal tribe from whom the ancient name of the area 'Gondwana' was taken. Among their kinsmen we have the Pardhan minstrels who have an aptitude for romance and poetry. Then we have the Baigas living in wilder tracks, famous for their magic and their knowledge of the forest; in the Mahadeo Hills we have the Korkus.

Maharashtra, Gujarat, and Rajasthan contain the Bhils. Also in Western India we have some other tribes like the Dhodias, the Thakurs, the Varlis and the Katkaris.

Southern India contains one of the most primitive kinds of men that we could have in the world today. These tribes are to be found from the Cardamom Hills to the Nilgiris, through the forest of eastern Mysore and over the Nallamaja Hills and they are the Todas, Kurumber, Kanikar, Irular and Yanadi.

Their Culture

It is very difficult to speak of a common culture so far as the tribes are concerned. We find that they stand on various levels of cultural development. For the sake of convenience, we may distinguish four main cultural divisions. The first two classes comprise the small block of real primitives living in the hills. They are still characterised by adherence to their original customs and mode of living. In their religious life, in their tribal organisation, in their artistic achievements and tastes and in their mythology we find all the old fires still burning strong. These simple aboriginals may be divided into the most primitive and a bit less primitive. The most primitive have the following features. In the first place the communal life of these people is well-knit and strong. It is said that they build their houses all opening on to one another within a single enclosure. They all subscribe to a common club or a dormitory which plays an important part in their social life. Thus the lay-out of their villages emphasizes their communal living. Secondly, they still share with one another economically.

As a token of village solidarity we find in the tribal villages co-operative and corporate granaries, equality of taxes, common stores to meet the needs of the poorer members of the community, common property, distribution of land by the community and payment of taxes by the villages. In short we have a primitive communism among these tribes. As for the cultivation it is said that their life still revolves round agriculture in which they have evolved certain original forms of their own which is known as the axe-cultivation. Thus for example the Jhum cultivator of Assam first clears part of the forest, then after setting fire to the fallen trees and branches sows seeds in the ashes. We also find that there is no deep furrowing of the soil but only a scratching for planting, say, beans and pulses. The forest clearing for cultivation is used for two or three years and then deserted for a fresh patch of forest. This sort of cultivation has become part of their life and has been customary so long that it has become mythological. Most of their lives are spent around this business.

We find them behaving in an honest, upright, innocent and unostentations manner. They are not very 'fresh' with the strangers. Crime is rare and adultery negligible. An adulterer is not liked and is severely punished, e.g., he is tripped naked and paraded through the village. In their domestic life there are no excesses of any kind and they are faithful and loyal. They wear hardly any clothes including women. Such sorts of aboriginals can be found among the Hill-Marrias of Bastar, the Juangs of Keonjhar and some tribes of Orissa.

The second class of less primitive tribes are to be found in the remote parts of India and are also very conservative. We, however, find that in some respects they are changing as compared with the more primitive people mentioned above. For example, they are passing from the communal to the individualistic stage of society. Houses are no longer built round a common square or within a common fence. They no longer live in the common village dormitories. Economically they no longer believe in communism. A spirit of competition is now a mark of their life; distinctions have also appeared between rich and poor, properties becoming personal. Axe-cultivation is no longer a sacred part of tradition but only a habit. There is no longer any taboo on the use of the plough or on new fashions in cultivation. The cattle wealth has also been developed. Socially, shyness for the strangers is disappearing. Their contact with civilised life is becoming frequent. Clothes have come into fashion. There is less of simplicity and honesty. It is said that all these are the result of their coming into contact with the so-called civilised people of the cities.

We have the third class of aboriginals who are most numerous, probably numbering twenty million. They are shedding their primitive habits and are taking to the sophisticated ways of their civilised neighbours. On account of the development of communications in India they have been brought into contact both with the Government and with the merchant or the money-lender. Government, for example, in its attempt to develop the minerals or to clear the forest have had to encroach upon their lands, customs and habits. For instance, tribal customs regulating the ownership or transfer of land are being replaced by a code which in practice deprives the tribe of its property. The tribal people are also incurring debts. The criminal law of the Government is in many ways opposed to their customs and the result is that the villagers are confused by the new system of justice and such as they resort to dishonest practices to get over the law. As a result, their social solidarity and their habits of faithfulness and honesty are being nullified. Other social evils have also cropped up. Diesease has spread like venereal diseases, tuberculosis and epidemics. Social vices like prostitution are increasing. Foreign dress is being adopted but it takes away the beauty of their original ways of living. As they do not put off their dresses frequently, dirt is encouraged, chill spreads and other diseases due to their clothese remaining wet are also common. Their beauty of the landscape is being disfigured by ugly imported foreign houses. In place of the tribal life which is an integrated whole we now find a fragmented living, an individualistic life marred by servility, timidity and poverty. Contact with the civilised life is tearing up by the roots the old tribal life with its traditional dances, its healthy living, its natural background and its picturesque customs.

Finally, there is a fourth class of tribal people, the aristocrats. We have great Bhil and Naga chieftains, landlords, noblemen and even some 'Rajas'. They are for the most part well educated and cultured. We have, for example, one of them serving as a member of the Indian Parliament. He is very vocal in defence of the tribal interests. They have become Hinduised and some of them have adopted both the Hindu name and the modern ways of life. In some parts of their domain or houses, however, the old customs are still retained. For instance, the Gond Raja of Sarangarh has his home decorated with representations of his totem animal, the tortoise and in the heart of the palace is a small thatched hut where the cult of the old tribal Gods is maintained. Many of these tribal people have also become Christians. Some of them have joined Government service. It may be said that these people have over-come the old tribal shyness and unlike the tribes mentioned above they have won the battle of culture-contact, having become civilised without injury to their character.

Among their religious customs and institutions, we have the tribal hunt, the tendance of the dead, belief in witchcraft and other superstitions, cow-sacrifice, worship of the daemonic beings and ceremonial use of blood and liquor. We may say that their religious customs resemble a form of Shaivite sect among the Hindus.

So far as their amusements and social life are concerned, we find these people getting up early, drinking cold-gruel left from yesterday, washing with water from a gourd and then going for their work. The old people get busy on mats and baskets, men and women going for their cultivation work and children grazing the goats or hunting mice and little birds. Later on they play on their favourite instruments like the flute which with its sweet music is a call to the lovers. In the evening when the Sun is taking its final peep, we find the people refreshing themselves from the toddy palms; then comes the laughter of the children and if it is a festival day, we find boys and girls dressed with flowers and ornaments taking to merry-dances with the elders being busy at the more serious business of propitiating the heavens. Marriages are also a delightful picnic.

In open houses guests and others gather for feast and dance and other customary customs. We also find unmarried youths going on dancing expeditions in search of wives including even the girls who go out to seek husbands.

So far as their languages are concerned, they are many. The old languages have now, however, to struggle for survival. Among these the most important is Gondi cultivated by a million and a half people. It has several dialects and resembles the Dravidian and the Andhra tongues. Some of these dialects are Kurukh and Kandh. Another class is that of the Munda languages spoken in Chhota Nagpur and other adjoining places. They are divided into dialects according to the tribe that speaks it–Santhal for the Santhals. Then we have the special tongues of tribes like the Savaras and Gadabas. In Assam there are sixteen different languages apart from the dialects. Many of the tribesmen speak more than one language and are also fast forgetting their old dialects. This is not an advantageous thing. The old dialect contains the traditional memories and with the forgetting of the dialects a veil of oblivion is descending over their picturesque customs and traditions.

The demand for a cultural synthesis in India must naturally take these people also in its embrace. But so far 'the culturalisation', so to say, of these people has not been part of any considered and well-thought-out plan. The result has been that not only illness is increased or that foreign dress is spread or that the pleasure-loving temperament has given place to the cunning and intelligence of the men of the cities or the harmful amusements of the towns, the obscenities of Holi (Indian festival of March), gambling, prostitution, disappearane of old singing and dancing, but also the whole traditional environment and background have fast disappeared without their place being taken by any synthetic culture. Thus we have an awful monotony of village life in place of the old amusements. The need, therefore, is felt for a proper investigation and appreciation of these tribal ways of life. We must remember that 'The tribe that dances does not die'. There are many elements in their culture worth preserving as for example, their simple and natural existence, their magnificent dances, their songs with their haunting music, exciting and amusing games of the children, its colourful tribal festivals, traditions of communal living, sharing in the joys and sorrows of each by all, purity of taste and beauty of artistic creations in the decoration of the houses in the carving of the masks, combs and snuff-boxes; domestic fidelity and honour for women are other virtues, there is no early child-bearing or marriage, on restrictions of widow-hood or property. She shares with her husband in all the functions of life. Many tribes have common training and disciplining of young people. Of course, they have their evils like head-hunting, witchcraft, fear of the dark, superstitions and uncivilised religious customs. But many of them are disappearing and for the rest sympathy and a truer understanding will have disappeared. We must, therefore, be very alert in preventing the impending economic collapse, moral decadence and psychic despair that are fast enveloping these people. 'The aboriginals are the real swadeshi products of India, in whose presence every one is foreign. These are the ancient people with moral claims and rights, thousands of years old. They were here first; they should come first in our regard.' (Verrier Elwin)

Indian Flok Culture

Aboriginal culture is in many ways the basis of the folk-culture prevalent among the common people of India, the vast majority of whom are to be found in the villages. They are in more senses than one the inheriters of the old culture of India, having their roots in the old soil. For such persons there is no question of an intellectual discussion of the traditions of the country or need of a conscious effort to make contact with our past. To the villager the old culture is instinctive, a part of his being and a pattern of his life.

In Indian culture the basis is religious and so also the village life is fundamentally religious. Of course, there is much superstition about villages religion but the villagers are familiar with the great truths of India and in their own ways they express them in worship, in rituals, in songs, dance and drama.

The Indian villagers have their arts and we find a great

simplicity and at the same time much beauty in their life. They live in harmony with the fundamental processes of nature. They have none of the restlessness of the city-dweller; they have a serenity of life which provides them an instincitive opening for beauty, an instinctive grasp of beautiful forms and decorations.

The greatest of all Indian art is music. The air of the villages is filled with music; love songs, lullabies, laments, songs of ploughing, planting and reaping, rejoicings over births and weddings and aspirations towards God, rise from the villager's lips. Most of these songs spring from the soil or they belong to those composed by the great religious teachers of India. Music thus is transmitted through the ages. The great classics like the Ramayana and the Mahabharata have become part of their inheritance. Many of their songs enshrine profound mystical teachings. We also find varieties in dance connected either with religion or with festivals or with the events of village life like birth, wedding, planting and threshing. Many of these dances are performed in groups, some of them are accompanied by music with a leader and a chorus and whole stories are related in this way. Sometimes songs are improvised on the spur of the moment. Of these dances the harvest dance of the west-coast is a highly developed art. It is a round dance performed by young girls, arms and bodies swing with vigour while the feet trace a syncopated and rhythmic pattern. Among the crafts the Indian handicrafts are of great antiquity. Many craftsmen are to be found living from old times in a certain street or even in a separate village. The technique and the designs are traditional and some of them have a religious significance like the circle, the swastika and the lotus. The Indian textiles are proverbially famous. The work of embroidery is very fine. Certain types of clothes are the heritage from old times, e. g., the shawls of Kashmir or in the Punjab the embroidery of dark-red hand-spun cloth with the gayest of silk in flower or geometrical patterns or the 'Kanthas' of Bengal or the 'Chiken' of U.P. Another type of embroidery is to be found in Gujarat where a number of tiny round pieces of looking glass bound down with chain stitch at the centres of flowers or at bird's eye are fixed, giving a remarkably gay-effect. Articles of common use and toys are also beautifully made, for example, the earthen pots, water jars, wooden articles, enamelled beds, basket-work, carved doors and fresco-painting. In the house, women carve beautiful pictures of Gods, men, birds and animals on their walls illustrating traditional stories on the occasions of celebrating their festivals.

In religion, besides the worship of the great Gods we have also the worship of animals like the cow or the serpent or also the worship of the trees. In fact, all sorts of animals, things and elements of nature are deified and worship is offered to them. In all these features as also in their dances and songs the villagers resemble the tribal people about whom we have said above. The philosophical idea behind the worship of these is that they are all expressions of God and as such through worship of them the Supreme-being is offered worship and devotion.

The village life is by on means a very ideal life. These days economic troubles, moral degradation and the evils born of the present transitional stage of our culture have infected the villages also. With the competition of the machine-made goods the seeds of decay have entered in the folk-life. The villager likes to purchase the cheap machine-made articles and is losing whater unconscious appreciation of the beauty of his own culture he had. In his religion he has become very conservative and sometimes even reactionary. There is a great need of disengaging the more stable and perennial elements of the folk-culture from the impermanent and the superstitious aspects. In modern India we are witnessing a revival of interest in folk-culture and some of our great men have contributed much towards this, men like Tagore or Udai Shanker or Jemini Roy with their music, dances and pictures. They have taken many of their themes from these poeple. In many states the village songs are being edited and printed. The Radio also is doing its bit in the spread of the folk-culture.

Thus in modern India we are witnessing a serious attempt to conserve the best in the tribal and folk-culture.

APPENDIX-C

MATRI-SHAKTI
(The Mother as Power)

THE MOTHER AS Power or Shakti is the divine conscious force that dominates all existence, one and yet so many-sided that to follow her movement is impossible even for the quickest mind and for the freest and most vast intelligence. The Mother is the consciousness and force of the Supreme and for aboue all she creates. But something of her ways can be seen and felt through her embodiments. There are three ways of being of the Mother of which you can become aware when you enter into touch of oneness with the conscious force that upholds us and the universe. Transcendent, the original Supreme Shakti, she stands above the worlds and links the creation to the even unmanifest mystery of the Supreme.

Universal, the Cosmic Mahashakti, she creates all these beings and contains and enters, supports and conducts all these million processes and forces.

Individual, she embodies the power of these two vaster ways of her existence, makes them living and near to us and mediates between the human personality and the divine nature. The supreme is manifest in her for even as the everlasting Sachchidananda, manifested through her in the worlds as the one and dual consciousness of Ishwara-Shakti and the dual principle of Purusha-Prakriti, embodied by her in the Worlds and the Planes and the Gods and their Energies and figured because of her as all that is in the known worlds and in unknown others. All is her play with the supreme, all is her manifestation of the mysteries of the Eternal, the miracles of the Infinite. All is she, for all are parcel and portion of the divine conscious force. Nothing can be here or elsewhere but what she decides and the Supreme sanctions; nothing can take shape except what she moved by the Supreme perceives and forms after casting it into seed in her creating Ananda.

Surrender of oneself and all one is and has and every plane of the consciousness and every movement to the Divine and Shakti is imperative for a disciple (Sadhaka) of the Mother. In proportion as the Surrender and self-conservation progress the Sadhaka becomes conscious of the Divine Shakti doing the Sadhna, pouring intó him more and more of herself, founding in him the freedom and perfection of the Divine nature.

Let every one conscious of his or her divine mission try to see the Mother in All, All in the Mother and become conscious that all are the Mother.

(With qvatitude from the
Mother by Sri Aurobindo)

BIBLIOGRAPHY

Ain-i-Akbari, Vol. III.

Alberuni's India, Vol. I.

Altekar, A.S. (ed.) *A New History of the Indian People*, Vol. VI.

Archaeology in India, Government of India Publication.

Ashraf, K.M. , *Life and Condition of the People of Hindustan.*

Bhandarkar, *Vaisnavism, Shaivism, and minor religious systems.*

Capra T., *'The New Vision of Reality,'* Bhartiya Vidya Bhavan, Bombay.

Chaudhury, Haridas. *Sri Aurobindo : The Prophet of Life Divine.*

Coomarasvami A.K. : *The Art and Crafts of India and Ceylon.*

Cultural Heritage of India, Vol. I.

Edwards and Garret, *Moghul Rule in India.*

Habib, M. *Indian Culture and Social life at the time of the Turkish Invasion.*

Jain, Hiralal. *Cultural Heritage of India*, vol. I.

Kabir, Humayun. *Our Heritage.*

Law, N.N. *Promotion of Learning in India.*

Lucien Febvre, *A Geographical Introduction to History.*

Majumdar, R.C. et.al, *An Advanced History of India.*

Mitra, S.K. *The Vision of India.*

Mookerji, Radha Kumud. *Fundamental Unit of India.*

Mookerji, Radha Kumud. *Hindu Civilization.*

Nasadiya Sukta of the *Rig-Veda.*

Oursel, P.M. et.al., *Ancient India and Indian Civilization.*

Percy Brown, *Indian Architecture.*

Rajendra Prasad, *India Divided.*

Roy Choudhury, *The Din-i-Ilahi.*

Roy, Dilip Kumar, *Among the Great.*

Sakti and Sakta.

Sarkar, Jadunath. *India through the Ages.*

Shri Aurobindo, *Life Divine,* Vol. 1.

Shri Aurobindo, *The Human Cycle.*

Sri Aurobindo *'The Renaissance in India'.*

Sri Aurobindo, 'Defence of Indian Culture', *The Arya,* Vol. VI, Chapter VII.

Sri Aurobindo, *Human Cycle.*

Sri Aurobindo, *The Life Divine* (America Edition).

Sri Aurobindo. (translated) *Gita.*

Sri Aurobindo. (translated) *Swetaswatara Upanishad.*

Sri Aurobindo. (translated) *Vamadeva - Rig Veda.*

Sri Aurobindo. (translated) *Vishnu Purana.*

Tarachand, *Influence of Islam on Indian Culture.*

The Arya, Vol. VI.

The Gazetteer of India, Vol. II.

The Pageant of India's History.

The Vision of India.

Whitney, *Language and its study.*

INDEX

BANGLADESH WAR